BATHROOM DESIGN, INSTALLATION, AND REMODELING

Pamela Korejwo

McGraw-Hill

New York   San Francisco   Washington, D.C.   Auckland   Bogotá
Caracas   Lisbon   London   Madrid   Mexico City   Milan
Montreal   New Delhi   San Juan   Singapore
Sydney   Tokyo   Toronto

McGraw-Hill

A Division of The McGraw·Hill Companies

1 2 3 4 5 6 7 8 9 0   AGM/AGM   9 0 4 3 2 1 0 9

ISBN 0-07-058069-3

The sponsoring editor for this book was Zoe G. Foundotos, the editing supervisor was Caroline R. Levine, and the production supervisor was Sherri Souffrance. It was set in Melior per the CMS design by Deirdre Sheean of McGraw-Hill's Professional Book Group composition unit, Hightstown, N.J.

Printed and bound by Quebecor, Inc..

 This book is printed on recycled, acid-free paper containing a minimum of 50% recycled de-inked fiber.

McGraw-Hill books are available at special quantity discounts to use as premiums and sales promotions, or for use in corporate training programs. For more information, please write to the Director of Special Sales, McGraw-Hill, 11 West 19th Street, New York, NY 10011. Or contact your local bookstore.

BATHROOM DESIGN, INSTALLATION, AND REMODELING

Other Books in McGraw-Hill's Complete Construction Series

Bianchina ∎ *Room Additions*
Carrow ∎ *Energy Systems*
Gerhart ∎ *Home Automation and Wiring*
Powers ∎ *Heating Handbook*
Vizi ∎ *Forced Hot Air Furnaces: Troubleshooting and Repair*
Woodson ∎ *Radiant Floor Heating*
Gleason ∎ *Paint Contractor's Handbook*
Korejwo ∎ *Kitchen Design, Installation, and Remodeling*
Beall ∎ *Masonry & Concrete*

Dodge Cost Guides ++ Series

All from McGraw-Hill and Marshall & Swift

Unit Cost Book
Repair & Remodel Cost Book
Electrical Cost Book

This book is dedicated to the memory of Robert Scharff, who is so dearly missed. Bob instilled within us an unending fascination and an abiding love for this work and we are truly honored to have had the opportunity to work by his side to discover the path to writing. We thank him for the years of knowledge, guidance, faith, and wisdom, which he passed on to us to make this book as well as every book hereafter possible, to continue his dreams. Although we are left with the absence of this wonderful man from our lives, it strengthens us to know that he has been with us every step of the way. He is in our memories daily, and will continue with us on every journey through life.

All of our love and gratitude
p.l.k. & l.e.k.

CONTENTS

PREFACE

There has been significant growth in the residential bathroom industry, in both remodeling and new construction. This growth has created the need for knowledgeable and skilled bathroom installers. The complexity of bathroom remodeling projects has increased along with the need for professionalism in installation. Few consumers have the time to be do-it-yourselfers; instead they look for professionals who can handle the entire project for them. Today's customers want accountability, speed, choice, and convenience— as well as quality.

This book was written for the professional bathroom installer/remodeler with knowledge of basic construction skills. It concentrates on skills and techniques (directing attention to major tasks) rather than on extremely detailed step-by-step processes. Basic business concepts needed for the successful installation of bathrooms are presented as well. The demand for service and quality and, consequently, the need for installers who are personable, well-trained, technically adept, and professional in every way, is greater than ever. A professional installer must have the skills and knowledge to meet the high standards that today's consumers demand.

Installers must be able to competently manage a project from start to finish. In addition to specific and detailed knowledge of the bathroom fixtures and fixture installation work, they need to have a thorough understanding of cabinet and countertop installation and carpentry work, and a basic knowledge of the mechanical systems (electrical, plumbing, and HVAC), drywall, painting, wallpapering work, and other associated items, as permitted by local laws and codes. A successful professional installer needs to master the principles of design to make decisions in the field and communicate with the designer, have a clear understanding of safety rules and procedures, and know how to deal effectively with clients.

Bathroom Design, Installation, and Remodeling shows anyone from a nonprofessional craftsman with basic construction knowledge to a home construction contractor the different skills needed and how to expand into a full business home construction contractor. In addition to the self-employed installer (who needs to know every aspect of the installation business), this book can help someone who has strengths only in one area (such as cabinet installation) to recognize where their weaknesses may be, and therefore educate themselves or successfully subcontract to others.

For already established bathroom installers, *Bathroom Design, Installation, and Remodeling* gives a good overview of all aspects of the business, possibly from a different point of view, so that installers may improve their knowledge and skills, as well as address issues of which they may not have been aware.

Written in a clear, easy-to-understand format, this book describes an installation project as it physically progresses and unfolds in a logical process from initial customer contact, to concept development fabrication, all the way through the installation to the job completion. This approach allows the reader to decide what aspects require increased effort, subcontracting, hiring, or training, to arrive at the level today's customer demands.

This book includes more than 300 fully detailed illustrations, all thoroughly and graphically oriented, to help you visualize the functions necessary for a successful bathroom installation. The book's wealth of photographs and illustrations, while enhancing the text, make it easy for the reader to grasp the principles and materials presented. Checklists, charts, and tables offer quick, instantly usable data.

To accomplish the above tasks, the necessary subject matter was broken down into 10 chapters as follows:

Chapter 1, "The Bathroom Installation Business," covers the basics of what the business is all about. It includes dealing with the client, customer communication, contracts, proposals, codes and permits, employees, code of ethics, working relations, job safety, and more.

Chapter 2, "Sizing Up the Job and the Customer," discusses the foundation of your business: meeting with the customer to size up the job, scheduling for the job, and obtaining the equipment necessary to prepare for the installation project.

Chapter 3, "Basic Principles of Bathroom Design," gives an overview of the basics for bathroom design. For the bathroom to be functional, the designer must take into consideration its location within the home, its size and shape, and the arrangement of its fixtures and equipment. Whether or not the bathroom installer is involved with the design process, it is important to master the principles of design so the installer can make decisions in the field and communicate effectively with the designer. Not all bathroom installers will be responsible for preparing bathroom plans. However, all will need to be able to read and understand them. This chapter also gives detailed steps for measuring the bathroom and familiarizes the installer with the different types of construction drawing sets.

Chapter 4, "Bathroom Extras," is for the installer who may need to assist a client in choosing bathroom extras. This chapter provides many unique ideas that today's customers are seeking.

Chapter 5, "Bathroom Fixtures," provides a thorough understanding of all of the fixtures and equipment typically installed in bathrooms. The installer should be knowledgeable in fixture sales, customer education, and the maintenance of fixtures.

Chapter 6, "Bathroom Cabinets, Storage, and Countertops," provides the knowledge necessary for assisting the client when choosing cabinets and countertops. Cabinets can be a permanent part of any bathroom and therefore should be chosen with care for their quality and lasting value.

Chapter 7, "Getting the Bathroom Ready," covers the steps necessary to prepare the bathroom for the final installation. The bathroom remodeler must be on the lookout for design and structural traps. For example, work put in by amateurs is often overengineered (and hard to remove) and often ignores codes (which makes it harder to get the job accepted) and standard practices (so studs, pipes, and wires may not be where one would expect them). These steps include the proper removal of fixtures, old cabinets, countertops, and flooring. The structural system is explained, including the removal of existing walls or partitions, doors, or windows, as well as preparing for new walls, doors, windows, and flooring.

Chapter 8, "Bathroom Installation Procedures," provides specific and detailed knowledge of cabinet and countertop construction and installation, as well as installation instructions for major bathroom fixtures. The installer needs to be an expert at all of the related skills that pertain to the installation trade.

In many situations, the installer will hire licensed subcontractors for mechanical systems, but the installer needs to have a clear understanding of electrical, plumbing, HVAC, etc., to accurately plan, coordinate, and install a bathroom. Chapter 9, "Mechanical Systems," provides that knowledge.

Chapter 10, "Finishing the Project," covers the basics on finishing products for floors, walls, ceilings, and lighting. If the installer subcontracts the finishing work or has excluded it from the contract altogether, the ultimate responsibility for the client's satisfaction lies with the installer. Being knowledgeable in these areas is important to an installer. The installer needs to supply and coordinate the installation of a wide variety of floor, wall, and ceiling finishes and understand the installation techniques for each of these materials. In addition, this chapter covers the final cleanup, as well as a post-completion meeting to review the completed installation.

ACKNOWLEDGMENTS

To organize a book of this size requires the assistance of many people, corporations, and associations. I would like to thank the following for their help in providing technical data, photographs, forms, and various other materials used to complete this book:

American Home Lighting Institute
American Lighting Association
American Standard, Inc.: Fred A. Allardyce, Bob Srenaski, Lisa Glover, and Lisa Lajka
Absolute by American Standard, Sally Benson
Andersen Windows, Inc., John Gillstrom, Stacy Einck
Armstrong World Industries, Jody Harnish
Belvedere Communications/Anaglypta-Crown Decorative Products, Darwen, England; Annie McDonald
Brandywine Tile & Flooring, Jim McCormick
Fantec, Glenn Thompson
Saunatec, Inc., two divisions: Finnleo Sauna & Steam, Helo Sauna & Steam, Keith Raisanen
Finlandia Sauna, Tanja Tarkiainen
Florida Tile Industries, Inc., Shannon Mitchell
Home Tech Information Systems, Inc., Walter W. Stoeppelworth
Juno Lighting, Inc.
Kitchen & Bath Design News
Kitchen Cabinet Manufacturers Association (KCMA), Janet Titus
Kohler Company, Jill Cavil
Leon E. Korejwo, Illustrator
KraftMaid Cabinetry, Inc., Kimberly Craig
David G. Leitheiser, Master Electrician
Merillat Industries, Inc., Wendy Knox

Ted Mountz, Plumber
National Kitchen Cabinet Association
National Kitchen & Bath Association
Phillips Communications, Frances Phillips
Planit—Autograph, Kira Thaler
QuakerMaid Kitchen of Reading, Inc., Juan Guillama, Designer
Thomas Lighting, Chandra Cantrell
Weck Glass Block/Glashaus, Inc., Bjorn Kunz
Weixler, Peterson, & Luzi Interior Designers, Philadelphia, PA
Wellborn Cabinet, Inc., Susan McGill

In addition, many thanks to:

- A special thank you to Fred A. Allardyce, SVP, Medical Systems of American Standard, Inc., Piscataway, NJ, for his guidance and support.

- Bob Srenaski, Lisa Glover, and Lisa Lajka of American Standard, Inc., Piscataway, NJ, for always being available to answer questions and provide technical illustrations and photographs.

- Bill Yatron of Adelphi Kitchens, Robesonia, Pennsylvania, for continuous assistance and advice.

- Juan Guillama of QuakerMaid Kitchens of Reading, Inc., for the fabulous bathroom designs and plans.

- Zoe Foundotos, acquisitions editor, as well as the entire staff of McGraw-Hill for their continuous encouragement and support.

- To my family (yes, mother!) who are always there when it matters, for all the big things, and the little.

- To all who knew I had always truly mastered every aspect of the water closet, with pure class and style, of course!

- One final and special thank you to my illustrator and my father, Leon E. Korejwo, for all the support, guidance, and knowledge he provided me throughout the completion of this book. Without him, this book simply could not have been possible.

BATHROOM DESIGN, INSTALLATION, AND REMODELING

The Bathroom Installation Business

Today's bathroom is the most frequently remodeled room in the house. It also can be one of the most complex and challenging parts of a house to design and remodel. An adequate number of eye-catching, fully functioning bathrooms is among one of the first things people look for when shopping for a house; homeowners usually want more bathrooms, as well as more amenities (Fig. 1.1). To a customer, knowledge of what can be accomplished with a bathroom may not be easily visualized, and therefore may be overlooked. What a creative and experienced bathroom professional quickly envisions can turn the potential client into a satisfied buyer. The role of a professional bathroom installer may be the factor that turns a questionable or out-of-date bathroom into the homeowner's dream. This chapter discusses the place of the bathroom builder in a rapidly expanding business.

What the Bathroom Installation Business Is All About

The kitchen and bathroom installation business is large. According to a leading trade periodical in the kitchen and bath industry, nearly 5 million bathrooms were remodeled in 1994, over 2.8 million were installed in new homes. These figures may double by the end of 1999.

FIGURE 1.1

Today's bathrooms offer so many attractive, stylish, and graceful possibilities. *(American Standard.)*

The functions of other rooms in a house are defined by the room's furnishings, and those furnishings can be easily changed or moved around (e.g., a bedroom can be changed to a home office at any time simply by moving the furnishings). The bathroom, on the other hand, must be designed and installed with permanent wiring and plumbing.

Bathroom installations require much more than just the ability to physically install plumbing fixtures and storage cabinets. Bathroom builders must combine many skills and trades to merge the needs and budget of their clients with the products available and the physical limitations of the space available. Professional installers are, in many cases, running a business. They must also be able to competently manage a project from start to finish. To ensure that they can run an efficient and profitable business, installers must be equipped with the skills necessary to realistically estimate and price projects, produce professional proposals and documents, and keep accurate records. They must also have the skills to plan and closely supervise an installation schedule. According to industry projections, the demand for skilled installers is growing at a much greater rate than is the number of new installers entering the bathroom industry.

Today's consumers are looking for the most efficient way to handle their bathroom projects. Few consumers have the time to be do-it-yourselfers; they look for professionals who can handle the entire project for them. They want speed, choice, convenience, high-quality materials, and excellent service and accountability at all stages of the project. A professional installer must have the skills and knowledge to meet the high standards that today's consumers demand.

Installers not only work with homeowners but also provide installation services to bathroom retailers, dealers, designers, contractors, home centers, and lumberyards.

The Bathroom Marketplace

According to the National Kitchen and Bath Association (NKBA), bathrooms and kitchens are sold in three major marketplaces: replacement, remodeling, and new-home construction.

Replacement

In the replacement market, homeowners or builders buy new fixtures or vanities to replace what has grown old or worn out. It is a good way to get a new look in a bathroom, although it might preserve an inadequate design. Price is usually the main consideration. While design is seldom involved, good sales ability is important to the bathroom builder who is involved in the replacement business.

Remodeling

Over the years, the complexity of bathroom remodeling projects has increased and, therefore, has created the need for competent professional installers. Traditional bathroom remodeling, typically fixture replacement along with other minor cosmetic changes, has given way to more sophisticated and extensive remodeling projects. In the past, most bathroom remodeling projects were done within the existing bathroom. Now many major projects involve dramatic expansions beyond the existing space (Fig. 1.2).

According to Home Tech Information Systems, residential remodeling is now being recognized as a major segment of the construction industry. In 1997, over 80 percent of all residential remodeling was professionally installed, and 20 percent was performed by do-it-yourselfers. All the growth in the 1990s is expected to be in the professionally installed segment. It is expected to grow at a rate of 5 to 10 percent per year. At this rate, total residential remodeling annual volume should reach $160 billion by the year 2000.

Homeowners, interior designers, and contractors who want professional design and planning for a new bathroom can go to the showroom of a kitchen and/or bathroom specialist, preferably one who is an NKBA member. High-end remodeling normally is done by professionals at a kitchen/bathroom specialist's dealership. This is where most kitchen and bathroom remodeling jobs are sold.

FIGURE 1.2

Expanding a bathroom may include an outside addition. *(Leon E. Korejwo, Illustrations.)*

Professional design and planning services are also available from independent designers and architects, if they qualify as bathroom specialists. The independent bathroom designer is a growing factor in design and product specification. Such designers do not have showrooms, but might take clients around to visit showrooms of other specialists. Professionalism in this specialized field requires detailed knowledge of bathroom products, materials, and techniques. Some architectural or design firms set up separate bathroom departments in which a level of advanced training is maintained.

Clients look to the company from which they are buying the product or service to be accountable and to service what they sell. They have a right to expect the most for their investment. As a result, bathroom specialists find it necessary to handle the entire job from inception to installation—that means the total remodeling job if the bathroom is part of a larger project. This way all aspects of the project can be controlled for quality.

As reported by Walter Stoeppelwerth, of Home Tech Information Systems, building industries are going through total quality management and changing the way they do business. One of the most significant changes is from top–down to a bottom–up approach to management. The old way was to have each worker handle one small part of the process, with supervisors for every 10 or 15 people to make sure that the quality was maintained. The new trend is to build quality teams of workers who are responsible for many different jobs. They also have the responsibility for building quality the first time.

A current trend in the remodeling bathroom business is the introduction of lead carpenters or lead installers. This lead worker is assigned the responsibilities for the job from start to finish and is given help on an as-needed basis. Basically, bathroom projects require one, or, at most, two people to work effectively.

If the industry is to gain maximum efficiency from installation personnel, these workers must not only be able to do all the cabinet and countertop installation and carpentry work but also the electrical, plumbing, mechanical, drywall, painting, wallpapering work, and other associated items as permitted by local laws and codes. Codes in some areas may limit the areas of work that an installer may perform; the building codes always prevail. In these instances, subcontractors will need to be hired.

New-home construction

In most cases, new-home construction is served by kitchen and bathroom distributors that keep several lines of stock and semicustom cabinets in their warehouses for builders. Bathroom distributors often serve as independent factory representatives for custom-cabinet producers and act as liaison between a custom manufacturer and both home builders and bathroom specialists in the area. Bathroom dealers also serve specialists in the construction industry who focus on featuring custom cabinetry in their upscale homes. Both bathroom dealers and distributors set up showrooms and offer a professional design service to which the builder may bring a client for visual support in the early planning stages.

Changes in new-home construction have also contributed to the growth of the bathroom industry. In the past 10 to 15 years, new home builders have begun to realize that bathrooms (as well as kitchens) are no longer basic utilitarian spaces; they have become prime selling features of homes. The more than one million new homes being constructed each year represents a substantial portion of the bathroom market. Those involved in new-home construction have started to pay more attention not only to the design of bathrooms but also to the quality of the products that are installed, thereby making these new homes more attractive to potential buyers. With the tremendous increase in the variety and styles of fixtures, cabinets, and countertops, there is an increasing need for sophistication and technical expertise in bathroom installations.

The NKBA has stated that a significant trend gaining momentum in the new-home segment of the industry is that builders, especially tract-home builders and developers, are requiring that suppliers of building materials such as roofing, siding, doors, windows, fireplaces, and closet accessories provide the materials on an installed basis. This fact is especially true for bathroom cabinets. This trend will lead directly to an increasing demand for trained bathroom installers in the new home market over the next 10 years.

Builders who use their carpenters to install specialty products (such as bathroom cabinets) have found that, while they may save a small amount initially on labor costs, the additional costs of service or adjustments due to the lack of knowledge of certain features of these products makes the use of a specialized bathroom installer more cost-effective. As discussed later in this chapter, the warranty offered by the installer is also an attractive feature for residential contractors.

Today, the buyer of a bathroom can also be a middleperson—a developer or a home builder—rather than the homeowner, with the homeowner as the ultimate purchaser, or end user. Therefore, the dynamics of dealing with the client are somewhat different.

A number of key competencies have been identified by the NKBA as important to bathroom installations. Depending on your experience or the number of installation projects you have completed, your familiarity with these key competencies will vary. It is incumbent to your professional success to master and use these key competencies.

1. *A basic knowledge of bathroom design.* While you may not be required to do the complete design, you need to master the principles of design so that you can make decisions in the field and communicate effectively with the designer.

2. *A clear understanding of installation and construction terms used in the industry.* The complex nature of this profession requires you to be familiar with a wide array of terms used by installers and the other related trades who work with you.

3. *A thorough understanding of carpentry skills.* Your base of knowledge and experience in carpentry needs to include everything related to the construction of a shell, including the construction of a stud wall and other framing; door and window installation and the construction of openings for these doors and windows; blocking required for cabinet and fixture installation; and general finish trim requirements.

4. *Specific and detailed knowledge of cabinet and countertop construction and installation.* You need to be an expert at all of the related skills that pertain to the installation trade, including everything from field measurement and survey work to actual layout and installation of cabinetry and equipment.

5. *Familiarity with finish materials.* You are required to supply and coordinate the installation of a wide variety of floor, wall, and ceiling finishes, including vinyl tile and sheet goods, wood, ceramic tile, paint, and wallpaper. You will need to understand the installation techniques for each of these materials and their impact on the cabinet and fixture installation.

6. *A thorough understanding of all of the fixtures and equipment items that are typically installed in bathrooms.* You need to understand standard installation and mounting techniques for these items, as well as their electrical, plumbing, and ventilation requirements.

7. *A basic knowledge of mechanical systems.* Familiarity with all the various mechanical systems and their impact on your project is valuable. These systems include electrical, plumbing, heating, ventilation, and air-conditioning. The goal here is not to eliminate the need for electricians, plumbers, and other tradespeople, nor circumvent code requirements, but to have the ability to perform some basic mechanical tasks, including the removal of electrical and plumbing fixtures to permit tear-out of existing bathrooms and the installation of fixtures and equipment such as bathtubs, lavatories, toilets, or lighting fixtures where the electrical or plumbing rough-ins have already been completed. A good, basic knowledge of all of these mechanical systems equips you to plan and sequence

efficiently the work of the various mechanical trades with your installation work.

8. *Techniques for ceiling construction.* You should know how to install ceiling joists and frame soffits in preparation for drywall, plaster, or other finishes as necessary. Your ability to do this work well significantly enhances your installation work.

9. *A good general mechanical ability and a clear understanding of how to maintain tools and equipment.* You need to possess a good general mechanical ability that allows you to deal with all of the side issues that arise in conjunction with installations. This mechanical ability also includes understanding and using all of the state-of-the-art tools and equipment available to the profession and maintaining this equipment in good working condition.

10. *An understanding of the importance of preinstallation conferences.* The consistent scheduling of preinstallation conferences is important to your success as an installer. You must understand what items require discussion at these meetings and who the key players are.

11. *Strongly developed people skills.* To deal effectively with clients and successfully sell your services, it is vital to be able to get along with people, including establishing comfortable relationships with clients and working well with others involved in your installation projects.

12. *The practice of good job site management.* An understanding and adherence to effective staging and sequencing of an installation job is extremely important to ensure that the job is completed in a timely and efficient manner. A thorough knowledge of staging and sequencing enables you to provide the client with a realistic schedule for your work.

13. *Adherence to job site and safety recommendations.* To protect yourself, your client, and the client's home and possessions, you must have a clear understanding of established safety rules and procedures and the most effective way to carry out these recommendations.

14. *Familiarity with the legal issues facing the profession.* You are running a business and therefore are subject to the laws that regulate and affect your work. In the eyes of the law, ignorance is no excuse. You must be aware of your liability and understand the best ways to protect yourself from litigation.

Ethics

Professional installers must maintain the highest standards of honesty, integrity, and responsibility while conducting business within the profession. Always strive to uphold these ethical standards in your work, with your fellow professional colleagues, and when dealing with the public. By operating in an ethical manner, you will quickly gain a reputation for honesty and integrity. This code of ethics earns high regard from your clients as well as continued work from dealers or designers. A satisfied client is truly the best form of advertising.

The code of ethics, quoted here from the NKBA, applies to all your professional activities, whenever or wherever they occur. They do not supersede or alter in any way the local or federal regulations that control this profession or the general provision of services to the consumer. Your ethical obligations include the following:

1. Uphold all laws and regulations while conducting your professional activities, and report to the proper authorities those who are knowingly violating established laws.

2. In all of your dealings with the public, represent the profession in a positive light and continually attempt to advance the stature of the profession in the public eye.

3. Always strive to improve your knowledge and skills in the profession and offer to your clients the best possible service available.

4. Serve your clients in a timely and competent manner. Promptly acknowledge and respond to all customer complaints and seek mutually agreeable solutions.

5. Uphold the human rights of all of the individuals with whom you deal without regard for race, religion, gender, national origin, age, disability, or sexual orientation.

6. Offer only those warranties or guarantees for products or services that you can actually fulfill.

7. Always provide contracted products and services to the best of your ability, and honor all contractual obligations (unless they are altered or dissolved by the mutual consent of all parties).

8. Always respect your clients' privacy, and keep confidential any sensitive information concerning your dealings with clients and their homes.

9. Only use the terms *insured, licensed,* or *bonded* in your advertising if you can provide proof of these to the client.

10. Always be clear in your description of the products and services you are including, as well as those that are specifically excluded or are available at additional charge.

11. Always honestly represent your experience in the profession and the product or service that you are offering to your client.

12. Never attempt to reuse a design prepared for one client for another client.

13. Compensation paid to you by the client for services performed by subcontractors under your supervision should be paid to the subcontractors without delay.

14. Accept additional or side work from a client for whom you are working under contract from a dealer/designer only with permission of that dealer/designer.

15. Free competition among members of the profession is encouraged, but honesty and fairness in the pricing of products and services are your professional responsibility.

Client Relationships

In this industry, there are many different types of relationships between the installer and the customer. These include the turnkey installer working for a bathroom-kitchen specialist, the installer working as subcontractor to a contractor, installer working for the buy-it-yourself (BIY) homeowner, and the installer working for a home center or lumberyard.

The Turnkey Installer

Many bathroom specialists are not in the contracting business, but they provide construction management services for the homeowner when requested. In this role, the designer assists the homeowner in finding a "turnkey" installer who can handle the ordering of all materials and payment of the subcontractors, coordinate the subcontractors, and basically run the job.

In this case, the installer really has two masters. While you are working directly for the client, and are likely to be paid by that client directly, you may also be working under the supervision of the dealer or designer.

Before the job begins, be sure to thoroughly review the plans and investigate the job. If you discover any problems, notify the dealer or designer directly. It is important to work together to come up with a solution, as well as to convey to all involved parties any revisions.

The Installer as Subcontractor

The installer as subcontractor to a remodeling contractor or to a contractor who is building a new home represents another type of relationship between installers and clients. You may be working as an independent contractor or on an hourly basis. In either case, the general contractor takes responsibility for the total job. However, this does not mean that you are not working for the client. Most importantly, while you are being paid by the contractor, you are working for the client.

Using the bottom—up management approach, as recommended by Home Tech Information Systems, you take over the job at the preconstruction conference. The chain of command is then passed from salesperson to installer, and from then on you are responsible for dealing with the homeowner or client, meeting the conditions of the contract, writing change orders, completing the job to the client's satisfaction, and collecting payments.

The Buy-It-Yourself Homeowner

Many people purchase their own fixtures and cabinets, and then hire an installer to handle the installation. These homeowners are basically do-it-yourselfers who do not want to actually undertake the bathroom installation project. However, they are willing to purchase the fixtures, cabinets, and other components themselves; contract directly with the plumber, electrician, flooring contractor, and heating—air-conditioning mechanic; then hire an installer or remodeling contractor to do the installation. The installer, in this case, is working directly for the homeowner, probably on an hourly or a fixed-price basis. The homeowner may pay the installer a small percentage above actual labor costs to coordinate the efforts of the other subcontractors.

Today, this relationship between the client and installer is popular. Many home centers offer bathroom design services and then sell materials to their customers at competitive prices, roughly equal to what a contractor might pay.

Home-Center or Lumberyard Installations

Finally, there is the installer who works for a home center or lumberyard. In this instance, the home center or lumberyard sells the materials to the homeowner and may offer installation service only or all the subcontractor trades. Although the installer is paid by the home center or lumberyard, the responsibility to satisfy the end user or client still exists.

As described above, there are many possible relationships in the bathroom business. Ultimately, however, you are working for the end user, and you must always strive to meet the highest standards of quality to successfully complete the job and therefore receive payment. While the chain of command may vary, the steps to complete a quality installation differ very little.

Dealing with the Client

There is much more to this business than just providing a quality installation. You must possess the necessary people skills to deal with the clients, whether they are developers, home builders, or homeowners. If you are dealing with homeowners, the installation of a bathroom may be one of the largest construction projects they have ever undertaken. As a result, they may have many questions and fears concerning the installation work. The more you can do to develop solutions to these problems and fears, the better off you are.

Maintaining a professional image with clients is of the utmost importance at the beginning of an installation. The clients are counting on you to build a bathroom or transform an existing bathroom into the room of their dreams.

Soon after a job begins, your positive image with the client may begin to drop. Remodeling a bathroom is tough for everyone involved. Keep in mind that in many cases you are putting the client's bathroom completely out of commission for quite some time. Obviously, especially if there is only one bathroom in the house, this can be very inconvenient. It becomes worse if the project runs longer than originally anticipated. Every time the job is delayed a day or two waiting for materials or for the plumbing or electrical inspector, the client's anger increases. Obviously, these instances detract from your image.

You must be aware of when you need to meet with the client to help remedy any problems. You may need to clear the air, explain the problems, and give the client a revised schedule for completion. If you are organized and efficient, by the time the installation is complete, your relationship with the client will be strong.

It is important to establish a realistic assessment of the time required to complete the installation project. A preconstruction conference is usually required, involving the client, the designer, and the installer. At this meeting, the client is advised as to what to expect during the installation, and questions concerning the installation are answered. If delays do occur that will affect the project schedule, inform the client as soon as possible. Clearly explain the situation and the anticipated length of the delay. The most common complaint by clients is unexplained delays. It is also important to make the clients feel that they are involved with and are an important part of the whole installation process. When questions arise during the installation, you should respond to them immediately and courteously.

Client Communication

Establishing Good Communication

The primary reason for failure of relationships between installers and their clients is lack of communication between parties. It is imperative to establish an open line of communication with the client at the preconstruction conference, and it is just as important to continue it throughout the project. Keep the client informed at all times.

Your client has, up to this point, most likely been dealing with a retailer, dealer, or designer who has spent much time listening to that person's needs and desires for a new bathroom. Now the responsibility for the client and maintaining the established line of communication is shifted to the installer. Provide the client with the same level of open communication as in the design and sales stages of the bathroom project. It is important that retailer, dealer, or designer clarify to the customer that responsibility is being passed to the installer. It is also important for the initial contact person to express confidence in the installer's abilities. If this transition does not occur, the customer will continue to call the dealer or designer with questions and concerns. This situation is neither efficient nor practical since the dealer or designer does not have firsthand experience of what is occurring during the actual installation process. If two or more customers are involved, installers must first determine which one is the designated customer to communicate with.

Because installers are seldom involved in the design and sales of bathroom projects and are not introduced to customers until later, they must make a great effort to gain their trust so that the line of communication can be established. The preconstruction conference is the time to do this (see Chap. 2). Encourage the customer to view the relationship with the installer as a partnership. The more customers are made to feel a part of the process, the more comfortable they are in handling project communication—both positive and negative.

Many clients may not be at home during the day when work is being completed, so phone communication has become the standard for answering questions. The telephone works fine for passing small bits of information (e.g., changes in the job schedule); however, explaining large problems and their potential solutions by phone can be difficult. It is much better to meet with the client in person to answer questions or solve problems. Set up an appointment as soon as possible to review or repair any problems or defects. This way, there is much less room for misunderstanding.

An excellent way to communicate between the installer and client is with a memo or on-site communication form (Fig. 1.3a). Let the client know that this form can be used for transmitting questions and concerns. Establish a convenient place to keep the forms during the installation (Fig. 1.3b). When the customers have a question or concern, they can simply write it down and leave it for the installer to reply. This procedure also provides written verification of unplanned changes or uncalculated cost overruns. It is advisable to evaluate the client's general demeanor to determine whether that person is likely to become overly inquisitive or indecisive, causing expensive delays or changes. The person in the field then must be diplomatic while proceeding with the work.

Keep in mind that installers must be sensitive to the wide range of languages spoken, and, if necessary, provide installers who can communicate with non-English-speaking clients.

If no one will be at the project site for a day or two, or if the project is delayed, make sure that the client knows this and clearly understands the reason for this delay. Otherwise, the client may assume that this project is being pushed aside in favor of someone else's project. Be

ON-SITE JOB COMMUNICATION FORM

MESSAGE	**REPLY**
Date:	Date:
To:	To:
From:	From:
By: **Signature of Addressor**	By: **Signature of Addressee**

1. **Addressor:** Write message and leave on pad without removing copy.

2. **Addressor:** After receiving reply, detach pink copy for records.

1. **Addressee:** Write reply and detach yellow copy for records.

FIGURE 1.3a

Always keep an on-site job communication form in a central location to keep good communication with the client. *(Leon E. Korejwo, Illustrations.)*

honest with your client. Getting caught deceiving the client results in loss of trust and creates a negative reputation.

Patiently and thoroughly answer every question that a client asks, despite how ridiculous it may seem. Remember, installers have been through possibly hundreds of bathroom installations. But for the clients, this may be their first, and because everything is new to them, will have many questions.

Communication with clients is not necessarily limited to the homeowner. On larger projects, installers may also need to communicate with an architect or designer who may be supervising the overall construction of a project. Contract installers also must deal with retailers, dealers, and designers as clients. The same basic rules apply to all project communications. Be honest, answer their questions thoroughly, and keep them informed.

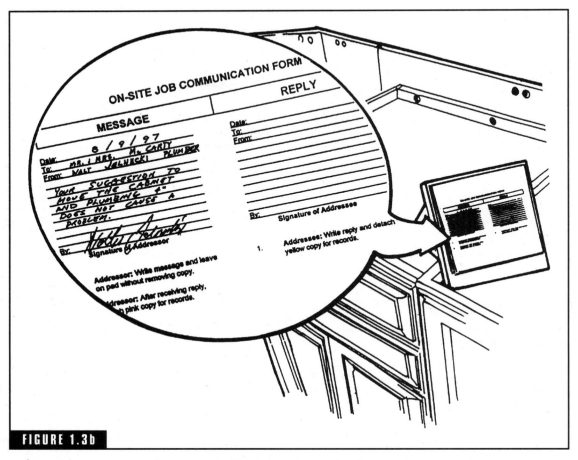

FIGURE 1.3b

Close-up view of an on-site job communication form. *(Home Tech Information Systems, Inc.)*

It is important to realize that there is a real cost involved in taking the time to effectively communicate with clients. This time must be planned for as a part of the whole installation project.

Dealing with Other Professionals

Besides dealing with the homeowner who, in most instances, is your primary client, you will also be dealing with tradespeople who will contribute to the success of the installation project. The scope of the project will help you decide which kind of professional to consult. For example, small jobs, such as replacing bathroom fixtures, do not require an architect's skills. If your renovation involves remodeling a cramped or complicated space, however, an architect may be able to advise you better than anyone else can.

Subcontractors

Because almost all bathroom projects include plumbing and electrical work, and many also require heating, ventilation, and air-conditioning (HVAC) work, subcontractors who specialize in these trades are crucial to the installation. Even if installers could do some of this work themselves, many building codes require licensed professionals to handle these specialty tasks. Hiring a plumber, electrician, or other contractor who is licensed guarantees that the provider has satisfied the state's requirements to perform a certain service; however, this license does not necessarily guarantee quality of the service. Installers must build a team of subcontractors who can work together to deliver a project in a quality and timely fashion. When choosing, do not be tempted to make price your only criterion for selection; reliability, quality of work, and on-time performance are also important.

The installer is looking for professional subcontractors who work to meet the schedule, keep the job site clean and organized, handle problems, provide prompt warranty service, and overall, do a top-quality job. Installers want their subcontractors to provide the same level of quality that they provide. Remember that your clients will not distinguish between subcontractors and your company. In their eyes, everyone is working for the same company.

It is valuable to spend time recruiting and managing subcontractors. The subcontractor's overall appearance and skill in communication should be evaluated. Installers should also check out references with other installers, retailers, dealers, designers, and so forth on similar projects. Ask for proof of liability insurance; also check bank and credit references to determine their financial responsibility. This step is especially important when determining plumbers' and electricians' level of experience with similar projects.

Installers should set up monthly meetings with their subcontractors to review the job progress, as well as to go over the subcontractor's performance on these jobs. Their comments and suggestions may lead to more efficient ways of integrating subcontractors into the installer's project. These meetings help keep communication open as well as build team spirit between installers and subcontractors.

Bathroom Dealers and Designers

Your first contact is with the dealer and designer (who may or may not be the same person). Your relationship with this individual will vary somewhat depending on whether you are an installer working as an employee of a bathroom retailer or have been contracted by a dealer or designer to do the installation. Field problems and design interpretations are referred to the dealer or designer for resolution. The client will probably contact the dealer or designer if a problem arises during the installation. As a result, many of these issues are relayed to you from the dealer or designer.

Dealers or designers should be well informed about the latest trends in fixtures and furnishings; they can both design and build the project. However, they may have neither the structural knowledge of the architect (which may be required by code) nor the artistic skills of a good interior designer. Their experience and expertise may be required in special design. They prepare sketches—via a computer simulation or the traditional (hardcopy) way—as to what things will look like, draw plans for the contractor, and even supervise the work. Since the designer is the source of most of your installation work, a strong relationship will ensure that this designer will consider you for future bathroom installations.

If you are working with a bathroom designer, look for a member of the National Kitchen and Bath Association (NKBA) or a certified bathroom designer. The NKBA will provide a list of names of certified bathroom designers in your area. The *certified bathroom designer* (CBD) will have completed and mastered rigorous instruction, including certified training programs in room layout, storage planning, cabinet installation, plumbing, and lighting. Each association has a continuing program to inform members about the latest building materials and techniques.

Architect

In some cases, you need to coordinate with an architect. This is most often the case when the bathroom job is part of a larger remodeling effort. Architects are state-licensed professionals with degrees in architecture; can oversee engineering and design, including a building's structural, electrical, plumbing, HVAC, and mechanical systems. They will provide drawings (drawing plans which are acceptable to building department officials) from which the contractor can work: floor plans, elevations (front views), "sections" (side views), and plan details. They are trained to create designs that are structurally sound, functional, and artistically pleasing. They may be required by code in some areas. Architects also know construction materials, can negotiate bids from contractors, and can supervise the actual work. If stress calculations must be made, architects can make them; other professionals need state-licensed engineers to design the structure and sign the working drawings. If the project involves major structural changes, an architect should be consulted. The architect should visit the project regularly, and may, at times, want to adjust or make changes to the design in the field. Most states do not require designers to be licensed, but architects must be.

If you are an employee of or under contract with a dealer or designer, these requests for changes should be referred to the dealer or designer with whom the client has a contract. The architect may ask whether a change being considered is feasible or what problems might be encountered if a change were made, and you should provide this information so that an informed decision can be made.

Interior Designers

Interior designers specialize in the furnishing and decorating of rooms. Although you may be working with a bathroom designer or an architect, for finishing touches, your client might need the assistance of an interior designer who specializes in kitchens and baths. Interior designers can advise (and offer quite unique ideas) with the choice of materials and layout. They can't help with engineering details, but their assistance is extremely valuable in determining how the bath will look and function.

Contractor or Lead Carpenter

If the scope of work for the bathroom installation project includes structural modifications or expansion of existing space, a contractor or lead carpenter is part of the project team. The role of the contractor would be to coordinate the efforts of the subcontractors, and, in some cases, to handle some of the construction work. Often, the contractor plays the role of lead carpenter and actually does most of the construction work.

Plumbers, Electricians, and HVAC Technicians

Plumbing, electrical, and HVAC work generally is done by licensed subcontractors (Fig. 1.4). Because these specialists provide the services that make the bathroom that you are installing actually function, you need to coordinate closely with them to ensure that the total project runs smoothly and efficiently. Establish, as early as possible, the place in the schedule for your part of the project relative to these other tradespeople. You may be unable to perform your job before they have done theirs, and, as a result, you may be the one who appears to be behind schedule.

Miscellaneous Specialty Subcontractors

Specialty subcontractors, such as painters, tile setters, flooring installers, and installers of solid-surface materials, may be needed to finish the bathroom.

FIGURE 1.4

A subcontractor who specializes in plumbing is critical to the whole bathroom installation. *(Leon E. Korejwo, Illustrations.)*

Code-Enforcement Officials

Finally, you are required to have portions of your work inspected by local code-enforcement officials. Often, the contractor (or lead carpenter) arranges for these inspections, so you need to coordinate scheduling and completion of inspections to ensure that your work is not delayed. Code-enforcement officials have the authority to delay an unsatisfactory or noncomplying job. If a permit is required and has not been applied for, the official may stop the job or subject a fine. Establish who is responsible for the permit application: the homeowner, the contractor, or you. Electrical, plumbing, and disposal may require permits. If enlarging a home is in the plan, local codes may require a zoning change. The municipal zoning officer or building inspector should be consulted if a question arises.

When going into a new area with an unfamiliar inspector, it is a good idea to call this inspector before completing the work. Ask if there are any requirements that warrant special attention. Ascertaining these details in advance can save a lot of time down the road. Make any inspector who comes on the job the center of your attention. Be courteous, respectful, thoughtful, and friendly. Good working relationships can be developed with certain inspectors which will eventually give them a level of confidence in your work. Keep in mind that certain inspectors will be much more strict with an unknown contractor; however, if you exhibit the right ability and attitude, they will become much more cooperative.

Informative Research

Installers must keep themselves informed of new products, applications, jobs out for bidding, available clients, and so on. Excellent aids in gathering this information are subcontractors and material suppliers, via a good working relationship. Never underestimate the value of a subcontractor's information. These specialists can keep you abreast of new job developments in the area. They know much more than you may realize. However, you should be careful to respect their need to protect their other clients' interests just as you would want them to protect your interests.

Most material suppliers are in constant contact with manufacturer's representatives, new products, and product literature that keep them in touch with the ever-changing construction industry. Because of the constant change and advancement in technology, not every supplier is able to keep up with all the available products. In fact, some are and will continue to be useless in regard to what is going on in the world around them. Therefore, make contacts and establish credit accounts with a variety of suppliers. If you have to purchase a specialized product for a particular job and one supplier does not have it or can't get it, then it is a good idea to have credit with a variety of suppliers. The difference between the installer who was awarded the contract and one who wasn't is sometimes the knowledge of materials, practices, and application procedures of new products and technology. New methods appear on the market every day. It is your job to be informed as much as possible about each one, and suppliers can provide the closest contact with these new products.

Working Relations

Professional Appearance

Always keep in mind that personal appearance can say a lot about the way you do your work, as well as the quality of the finished project. A neat and professional appearance suggests to the client that your work will be done neatly and professionally. Torn or soiled clothing and a sloppy appearance may suggest a poor finished product. While this may not actually be the case, a client's first impression is hard to change. Remember, you and the members of your staff are walking advertisements for your company.

Today, in most cases, it is not unusual for both adults in a household to be working outside the home. Therefore, in many cases, you may be left alone to work in your client's home. To the client, you are a stranger. As irrelevant as it may seem, a good personal appearance will go a long way to ease your client's fears about leaving home. It is advisable to wear work shirts, or uniforms, with the name of your company. This presents a neat, organized team look and easily identifies you and your staff. Although it may seem like common sense, you should be clean and well groomed at all times. However, clients tend to be a bit more forgiving by the end of a long day of work.

In addition, the service vehicle brought to the job site should be clean and in good condition and, if possible, should bear the name of your company. Also, equipment and tools brought into the home should be organized and well maintained. This not only increases the efficiency of your work but also contributes to the client's first impression of you.

Another important item to keep in mind is that smoking inside the home greatly increases your liability for the installation project. Do not do it under any circumstances. Alcohol or drugs should never be used before or during work. Finally, the use of profanity in the presence of the client or other residents of the home detracts from your professionalism. Never use it on the job site.

Designer Awareness

Today's clients can go to any bookstore or newsstand to find magazines full of design ideas and, as a result, are more sophisticated and better informed than ever before. This increased awareness of design options has everyone interested in good design, regardless of the project budget. Interest in personalized design has led to a trend toward highly individualized bathrooms. Today's designers are being challenged to create much more than merely a functional environment.

For you as an installer, this trend means that there is an increasing level of complexity to the installation of these nontraditional designs. While the designer has the responsibility to follow accepted design principles and good common sense, you will often be asked to create new installation techniques to respond to the designer's intent.

Each installation must be approached as a team effort between the installer, designer, manufacturer, and other tradespeople. You will need to be considerate of all parties involved. Be certain to maintain an open line of communication between these parties to ensure the success of the project. It is your skill that makes the design a reality. No matter how carefully a project site has been verified and surveyed, there will, in most cases, be minor adjustments required to transform the design into the finished product. You must assess what changes are needed from the original design intent and work with the designer to develop the correct measures.

When problems and conflicts arise between the design and the actual field conditions, you should always be supportive of the design and the products being installed. Explain in a positive manner what measures can be taken to produce, as closely as possible, the original design intent.

Maintaining a Professional Attitude

Never degrade the design, the designer, the manufacturer, or other persons working on the project in front of the client, no matter how frustrated you might be. Just as importantly, never blame problems that you may be experiencing with the installation on any of the other members of the team. The client's confidence in the project will be lost. A healthy mutual respect for the skills and limitations of all team players is the key to any successful bathroom remodeling or installation effort.

Job Safety for Workers

Anything that you can do to promote safety on the job will be of great benefit to you; accidents are very costly to your business. Frequent accidents will increase your workers' compensation rates, and you do not want to have to raise your prices to cover these higher rates. Injuries on the job also result in loss of time for the injured person and delays in your project.

You can prevent most accidents fairly easily if you recognize the high-risk situations that cause most injuries. Most of the key situations you encounter on the job include

1. Failure to use safety equipment such as face masks, goggles, or hard-soled shoes

2. Improper handling of large or heavy machinery or equipment

3. Careless or improper use of machinery or equipment

4. The collapse of ladders or other temporary platforms

5. Failure to leave safety guards on portable saws

The wedging of safety guards has injured more workers than almost any other single factor. Take the time to anticipate safety risks, and plan to avoid accidents. The few minutes that it takes to avoid an accident can save hours or days of project time.

Since you cannot be on the job 24 hours a day, ensure that dangerous equipment and tools are not left out. Daily cleanup of the job site also eliminates many of the tripping and stumbling hazards common to construction projects. It is a good idea to post safety signs.

Perform routine inspections of your equipment to ensure that it is in proper working condition. If you are working alone, do not assume that because you are the sole user of the equipment you are aware of its condition. Make it a habit to inspect your equipment before you begin work. If you are inspecting equipment for use by others, check to make sure that safety features have not been overridden and that electrical cords are not damaged.

Make certain that all workers are familiar with the locations and telephone numbers of nearby hospitals, ambulance services, and physicians. A professional-quality, well-stocked first-aid kit should be kept on the job site at all times, and a second kit should be kept in your truck or car.

Clients may want to walk through the job site to view the progress. Discourage them from doing so unless you are available to accompany them. When clients are on the job site, they should also wear protective clothing. Children should not be allowed in the work area at any time. Again, post safety signs after you have left the job site.

OSHA Regulations

Make sure that you are aware of all the Occupational Safety and Health Administration (OSHA) regulations that apply to your work, and be diligent in your compliance with these regulations. While OSHA regulations can seem unreasonable in some cases, they have been established for your safety and to reduce the injuries that lead to workers' compensation claims.

As a result of increased injuries in residential construction, OSHA has increased inspections and imposed fines for violations such as lack of hard hats or failure to maintain a safe construction site.

Insurance

Business insurance is mandatory for today's small business. No one can afford to run a business without adequate coverage. Virtually all services that an installer offers are performed inside a client's home; therefore, the installer must be protected should anything happen to the home or to the client personally as a result of work being performed. One claim could ruin the entire business.

The most important source of coverage is general liability insurance, which protects against claims attributed to negligence or installer performance. This type of coverage would usually include uninsured or underinsured subcontractors. It is often available on a project-by-project basis. Some companies offer this coverage, and, if there are gaps between jobs, it may help lower insurance costs. Installers who choose this type of insurance should verify that the insurance provisions remain active after a project is complete and the policy is canceled. Other types of insurance that may be needed by installers include automobile insurance for company vehicles, property insurance to cover tools and equipment, and health, life, and disability policies.

Installers must also ensure that subcontractors who work for them have sufficient coverage. Always ask for a certificate of insurance when a contract for services is executed. If subcontractors are uninsured, a claim against the installer's insurance can be placed for subcontractor negligence. Often installers can be listed as an additional name insured on the subcontractors' policies. Installers would then be notified if the subcontractor's insurance was no longer in force.

Selecting the correct insurance for an installation business is important. But even more important is working to ensure that claims against the company do not occur. Installers should review insurance requirements with an attorney or insurance agent knowledgeable in these areas. Nothing can drive the cost of business up more quickly than increasing insurance rates due to claims.

Employee Benefits

Employee benefits are a significant part of any compensation package and can account for nearly 40 percent of total payroll expenses. Employees are seeking health insurance coverage, vacation leave, sick or personal leave, paid holidays, and profit-sharing, pension plans, or retirement plans. As an employer, you must provide workers' compensation and Social Security benefits.

Health Insurance

If you have only a few employees or are a self-employed installer, you may find it difficult to offer or obtain affordable health insurance coverage. Some companies pay the full insurance premium for an employee. However, it is becoming more common for the employee to be responsible for a portion of the premium.

Workers' Compensation

According to recent industry surveys, the major business concern for installers/remodelers is the high cost of workers' compensation. The cost of this mandatory benefit has tripled in just the past 10 years. You are required to provide and pay for workers' compensation for all (full-time or part-time) workers. Your rates are based on your record of safety on the job, so your attention to safety procedures is very important in controlling this cost.

Of course it is advisable to attract excellent installers to your company, and it is even more important to keep them. Offering good compensation and benefit packages builds a strong sense of job security. However, the costs for these fringe benefits must be included in your direct costs, and you need to add up the numbers to determine what you can realistically offer while still remaining competitive.

Codes and Permits

The best plans may go to waste if you are not familiar with the multitude of legal restrictions that control the building of new baths and bath additions. Building, plumbing, mechanical, and electrical codes, in addition to zoning ordinances and easements, may all play a part in determining what you can and can't do. Most construction work today is governed by a set of rules, standards, and regulations known as building codes. A *building code* is a legal document used by state and local building inspection departments as a means of controlling and inspecting the construction process. The use of building codes is the government's way of protecting public health and safety. Regulations and stipulations, and the way in which they are enforced, vary greatly from area to area.

As reported by the NKBA, three model codes are widely used in the United States today for general construction purposes. The *Building Officials and Code Administrators International* (BOCA) code is used predominantly in the Northeast and the Midwest. Along the Gulf Coast, and in the majority of the South, builders follow the *Southern Building Code Congress International* (SBCCI). In the West, the *Uniform Building Code* (UBC), published by the *International Conference of Building Officials* (ICBO), is widely used.

All three of these model codes must be adopted by states, cities, or counties before they can be enforced. In many cases, cities adopt different versions of the code. To make the matter even more complicated, local governments frequently amend model codes to include extras that they feel contribute to the health and safety of city residents. In addition to having a copy of the published code book, you need a list of the local amendments to the code. Local codes may change frequently, so be sure that you have the latest amendments.

If your bathroom installation work is going to occur in one- or two-family residential dwellings, your code requirements will come from yet another model code, known as the *Council of American Building Officials* (CABO) *One and Two Family Dwelling Code.* All three of the recognized model codes have agreed on this model code for residential use only. In most communities, the designer can choose either the model code adopted by the community or the *CABO One and Two Family Dwelling Code.*

In addition to the uniform codes, national codes, and standard codes, other codes have been widely used and accepted by most cities and states. The *National Electrical Code* (NEC), in particular, is accepted in most areas as the electrical standard.

Remember that building codes and regulations are minimum standards. They are designed to protect and enhance the life, health, and safety of occupants. By *building to code,* you are building to a minimum standard. Remember that as a professional bathroom installer, you should also be concerned about quality. Quality, in most cases, requires going beyond the minimum requirements of codes.

Most localities require a permit if the installer plans to take out a bearing wall or work on an exterior wall. A few codes also regulate less complicated tasks, such as constructing or removing nonbearing partitions. In addition, nearly every community requires that ventilation—through either a window or an exhaust fan—be provided for in a new bathroom. Plumbing codes are varied in what they do and do not allow. Adjacent towns in the same area, for example, may have codes that differ. Plumbing codes determine not only who can do the job but also what materials you can use and how you can use them. Mechanical and electrical codes govern those systems in your house and may affect how you put up a new bath. Check each carefully.

Obtaining Permits

To begin work, you are required to obtain building permits from the local code-enforcement officials. A *permit* is essentially a license that gives you permission to do the work, while an *inspection* ensures that you did the work in accordance to the codes. The main stipulation of a building permit is conformity to local building codes. They set minimum acceptability standards for structural integrity and sanitation and system design. They cover issues such as adequate ventilation, natural light, and electrical details. The requirements for filing for and obtaining these permits vary. In some cases, you may be required to file for the permit; in other cases, the dealer, designer, or architect submits the required drawings for the permit. Some jurisdictions require the seal of a registered architect or engineer on the drawings to obtain a permit; however, this requirement is generally for larger projects. The fee for the permit is set by the locality and varies widely by the established rate and the value of the project. If the contract requires you to file for and pay for permits, make sure that you have included this amount in your estimate.

For minor repairs or remodeling work, you don't need a permit, but you may need one if you add or resupport walls, extend the water supply and drain-waste-vent system, or add an electrical circuit. You probably will not need a building permit for simple jobs, such as replacing a window with one of the same size, installing a vanity, or changing floor or wall coverings. You will nearly always need one if the new bathroom is in a new addition to the house.

In some jurisdictions, interior work that does not involve extending the house does not require a building permit. Thus many bathroom projects are done without a building permit, and many projects do not even pull an electrical or plumbing permit. It can be dangerous to do work that is not inspected for safety and code requirements. You should always follow the requirements of your local jurisdiction and obtain all required permits.

In addition, separate permits are required for mechanical trades, such as electrical or plumbing. In most instances, these permits can be filed for and obtained only by licensed plumbers and electricians. However, this requirement can also vary by jurisdiction.

Inspections

Once your project has been cleared for construction, you must post the required permits at the job site at all times. When you have completed certain portions of work, request an inspection by the building inspector. If this portion of the work is found acceptable, the building inspector issues a certificate to this effect, and you are allowed to proceed to the next level of completion. It is important that you be fully aware of the required sequence of inspections and that you notify the building official when you are ready for a certain inspection. If you proceed beyond a required inspection, such as putting up the drywall without first obtaining a *close-in* inspection, the inspector can place a *stop-work order* on your project and require you to take off all the drywall. This can cost you time, materials, and money.

When you have passed all the required inspections, the building inspector issues a certificate of occupance for your project, giving your client permission to reinhabit the area of the home in which you were working. Working with codes and permits can be very confusing. The most important thing is to make sure that you know which codes you are to follow and that you understand your responsibilities under the codes in force in your jurisdiction.

Licensing Requirements

Because licensing requirements vary from state to state, and from locality to locality, licensing is discussed here in the most general terms. Installers must become familiar with the licensing regulations for their particular area. At minimum, most localities require all businesses to obtain a business license. There is an initial fee for the license and usually annual renewal fees.

In most major metropolitan areas, installers without a plumber's license are barred from handling any plumbing disconnects, rough-ins, or connections. The same is often true for electrical work in bathroom installation projects.

If installers are required to obtain building permits for bathroom installation projects, the building permit office requires proof of licensure for the regulated trades. Installers who do not have a plumber's or electrician's license must contract with subcontractors to accomplish this work. The subcontractors are responsible for pulling permits for their portion of the work. Once obtained, building permits need to be on display at all times (Fig. 1.5)

Contracts and Proposals

Two agreements involve a bathroom specialist:

1. A *contract,* which is a written and signed agreement between two parties (e.g., the installer and a dealer, designer, customer, or contractor) that describes in detail what work is to be accomplished, how and when it will be accomplished, what services are to be provided, and how much this will cost.

2. A *proposal* is a bid presented to the prospective customer to obtain work. Like a contract, the proposal spells out what services are to be provided for the proposed price. Although it may not be necessary to detail all the specifications of the project, installers should be careful to qualify a proposal so that it is clear what is being provided. The customer may seek competitive proposals, and your most professional approach may be necessary to have the job awarded to you.

Contracts

It is very important to have a detailed, written contract with whomever you hire to do the job. Aside from its merit as a written instrument to be used in case of problems, a contract prevents misunderstanding. Without a written contract or proposal, the client can easily misunderstand or assume that a much larger scope of work is included in the price; what an installer may think is perfectly clear may

FIGURE 1.5

A building permit is one of the first steps needed for a major bathroom addition. *(Leon E. Korejwo, Illustrations.)*

be perceived quite differently by the customer. Simply put, the agreement is down in black and white. When contracts are executed (or signed) by both parties, they become binding agreements both parties must observe. A party that does not live up to contractual obligations is considered to be in *breach of contract.*

Quite a bit of work, especially in the construction industry, is done with only a verbal agreement. This has certainly worked from time to time, but the risks are extremely high. No matter what kind of relationship you have with the client, always have the agreement in writing signed and dated by both parties. Installers should never work without a contract. Doing so leaves them open to loss of money and a variety of misunderstandings, with no legal means of redress or setting things straight.

Installers running their own business should have standard written contract forms. The contract needs to be reviewed by an attorney who is familiar with construction law, to ensure that the contract covers all business interests, while also checking it against federal and local laws and regulations to ensure compliance.

A good contract should contain at least the following elements:

- Name, date, address, and phone number of the parties entering the contract.

- Legal description of the property where installation services are to be provided.

- Scope of work or description of the project. This portion is a list of work and actions to be performed on the job.

- Any subcontractor's name, address, phone number, license number, proof of liability, and worker's compensation insurance.

- Reference to the design drawings (the easiest and clearest way to describe the project, and limits the installer's responsibilities of the installation of the fixtures, cabinets, and equipment shown on the drawings).

- A schedule for completion of the project (with clauses so that the installer cannot be penalized if the project is not totally finished by the stipulated date, e.g., for delays in material deliveries, delays by subcontractors, weather-related delays, delays resulting from earthquakes or other natural disasters, or if the customer fails to make scheduled payments).

- Contract amount and terms of payment. All financial terms need to be clearly spelled out, including when payments are due and any penalties for late payments. Many contracts stipulate that draws be scheduled for the completion of a certain portion of work, such as installation of cabinets or countertops; however, it is wiser to schedule draws for the beginning rather than completion of a portion of work. Installers must take the time to become familiar with state, provincial, or local regulations that govern payments and deposits received from customers. Ignorance of such regulations results in fines that penalize the contractor, therefore adding costs which were not figured into the original budget.

- Right of rescission. This provision gives the client the right to back out of the contract within 3 days of signing. It is required under federal law. It says that any time within 3 days from the signing of the contract, they are entitled to cancel.

- A clause guaranteeing an installer's work and that of their subcontractors. It is customary to provide a one-year warranty on workmanship, but the warranty should specifically exclude any materials or equipment supplied by the customer or by others. These warranties are typically provided by the manufacturers. At an additional cost, some installers offer extended warranties that cover materials, equipment, and workmanship for a longer period of time. For the additional fee, the installer fixes basically anything that goes wrong over the life of the warranty.

- Certificate of insurance. This section guarantees that the contractor has appropriate insurance and names the insurance agent.

- Fees and permits. Depending on the job, permits will be required from the local authority. This clause should state that all required permits have been obtained, and they should be attached to the contract. In addition, it should contain information about who is responsible for obtaining any necessary permits and inspections and who will pay for them.

- Change-order procedures. If prepayment is required, or if there is an administrative fee for processing a change order, this must be stated.

At the time of signing, the installer should review the contract with the customer and ensure that all contract provisions are understood to avoid disputes caused by misunderstandings. In the United States, the 1974 Truth in Lending Act and Federal Trade Commission rules give customers the right to cancel a transaction. This right affects all agreements made in the customer's home or in any location other than the installer's place of business. The U.S. government guarantees a 3-day right of cancellation or rescission, whether a job is paid in cash or financed.

When working directly for the homeowners, you are required by law to notify them of this right, usually stated in a contract clause. If you fail to notify the customer, that customer has the right to cancel the contract at any time during the project and get a full refund. Change orders under the original contract are not subject to this regulation. This forces the return of money for work that has already been completed should a customer invoke the right to rescind the contract.

Proposals

A *proposal* is simply a document that conveys a scope of work and a proposed price for installation of a project. The prospective dealer, designer, or customer may solicit and review several proposals from several installers before deciding to enter into a contract.

Proposals are usually based on drawings and specifications that have been prepared by a dealer or designer for a customer. These drawings establish the services on which the contracted party is bidding. Like a contract, the proposal should include the date, the name of the customer, a description of the project location, and the proposed price.

The proposal should be hand-delivered to the prospective dealer, designer, or customer, and, if possible, should be reviewed with this person at the time of delivery. Proposals that are simply dropped in the mail generally are not received as favorably. It should stipulate how long the prospective customer has to review and sign the document. Generally, proposals are good for 30 to 60 days. Beyond this point, the proposal may need to be revised to reflect current pricing and workload considerations. If left open-ended, the prospective customer could sign the proposal a year later and expect the installation at last year's proposed cost.

If a proposal has qualifications, installers should state them. Perhaps the drawings and specifications call for painting and wallpapering work but an installer may not handle this work. The proposal should simply state that the price does not include these services.

There should be a line at the end of the proposal requesting the contracting party or customer's signature to accept the proposal, as well as the signing date. This is an expedient way for the customer to accept the proposal, indicating a readiness to enter into a contract for the installation project.

Sizing Up the Job and the Customer

As discussed in Chap. 1, keep in mind that while the client of the bathroom installer is often the home builder, the primary customer for the bathroom remodeler is the homeowner. In a project development, for instance, the installer works for the contractor or home builder. A builder's demands are usually different from those of an individual homeowner. When working for a contractor on a new custom house, you may have to work with the prospective owner as well as with the contractor, which may require considerable tact. The new prospective homeowner and contractor are both your clients. It is vital to know from whom you take instructions.

When a homeowner wants a new bathroom, the professional bathroom remodeler's job may be to listen to the customer's complaints about the present bathroom and their desires for a new bathroom, and to make a personal inspection of the present bathroom (Fig. 2.1). After completing this procedure, a remodeler can make informed suggestions for the renovation of the space. In some instances, the bathroom installer will not have to help "sell" the bathroom; in most cases, that is the designer's or salesperson's job. But in the case where an installer's responsibilities may include assisting a client with the initial stages (interview, inspections, etc.), the installer must take time to work with the homeowner to identify and propose solutions to existing bathroom problems.

What Makes a Good Bathroom

The bathroom in a home should be custom-planned to provide for the needs and personal preferences of the individual family. Of course, how the family lives is most important in designing the bathroom. It is a good idea to have the customer make a list of the family's likes and dislikes about the current bathroom. Good bathrooms do not just happen; they start with careful planning. The number of other bathrooms, the number and their ages of the family members, and even the physi-

FIGURE 2.1

Help your client choose what is best for their bathroom. *(Leon E. Korejwo, Illustrations.)*

cal characteristics of the principal users of the room, all have a bearing on planning a bathroom that is right for the individual family. Have your customer list the things that must be in the bathroom and the things that would be nice to have if the budget permitted. It is a good idea to submit plans for approval before the work is done. It may be expensive to change things if the finished job does not pass inspection. The bathroom must reflect the individual needs and lifestyle of the family, not those of anyone else.

Wearing a Designer's Hat

The project builder designs bathroom plans around an average family and a typical life pattern. Builders, designers, and architects should keep up to date on all trends in bathroom styles and fixtures. Although trend-setting surveys are good indicators as to what goes into home-buying decisions, the best advice to follow is to use a good bathroom plan. A bad bathroom costs just as much money as a good one.

The remodeling of an existing bathroom does present problems. For instance, the physical limitations of the space available for a bathroom is perhaps one of the first considerations. A completely free plan usually occurs only in the planning stages of a house and very seldom in remodeling work. The bathroom remodeler is limited by the space already allotted for the bathroom. Even then, cost, limitations of size, and the amount of space in proportion to the rest of the house frequently restrain the designer from complete freedom of design. Therefore, the size—the number of square feet within the space for the bathroom—is important.

Often, simple square footage does not permit the designer an ample layout of the necessary fixtures, cabinetry, storage, and bathroom extras. Just what is the basic plan? These considerations are a vital part in determining the bathroom installation. The location of the bathroom with reference to other rooms is often a determining factor in the design. Despite many physical limitations of an existing bathroom, you have a much greater chance of coming up with the perfect plan if you ask your customers a series of pertinent questions. It is then easier to design the bathroom around their lifestyles.

The answers to these and similar questions will go a long way toward providing a solid basis as to what your customers' exact needs and desires are. Satisfactory design cannot be formulated without a thorough investigation of their needs, wants, and living habits. To ensure individuality, satisfy the functional requirements, and obtain the preferred appearance of a bathroom, you must be aware of the variables and work within the limitations. You should be able to guide the homeowner through the many decisions involved in bathroom remodeling, blending their tastes and desires into a practical, functioning room. You need to ask the homeowners questions to help them to evaluate their needs.

After the client has shown interest in a new bathroom, the installer should visit the home to identify the needs and measure the space. At this point you can interview the customers and have them complete a survey form (Table 2.1). You should begin by measuring the space and examining the area for special conditions in the floors, walls, and so on—anything that may affect the installation project. There is no way to know if the new bathroom design will work until the clients have decided why the old design doesn't work. The questionnaire helps your clients do just that. Have them write down things about their existing bathroom that bother them.

Once you have assessed the room's current condition and developed the remodeling goals, it will be easier to uncover the room's potential for more convenience, improved appearance, and greater comfort.

Project Management

Professional project management is an absolute must in today's bathroom installation market. You need to understand how to successfully market, schedule, estimate, and construct bathroom installation projects. A well-managed project starts with an open line of communication with the client, accurate field measurements, a detailed set of plans and specifications, a realistic cost estimate, and a closely supervised installation schedule. The management of the job requires you to handle specific project conditions as they arise.

As a bathroom installer, you need to understand your responsibilities, as well as the responsibilities of the other professionals involved. In some cases, the dealer or designer may sell the job, make the major decisions, order the materials, and then look to you for the installation.

Table 2.1 Before You Begin: A Bathroom Questionnaire

Name:
Residence Address:
Jobsite Address
Phone:
Work:
Date:

YOUR FAMILY

1. How many people are in your family? _____

   List adults, children, and their ages? _____
   _____

2. How long do you plan to stay in this house? _____

3. Are you planning on enlarging your family while living in this
   house? _____

4. How many other bathrooms are in the house? _____

5. Will more than one person be using the bathroom at one time?_____
   If yes, how many? _____

6. Are users left-handed? Right-handed?_____
   How tall is each user? _____

7. Do any of the users have physical limitations? _____
   Is the individual confined to a wheelchair? _____

8. Is the bathroom just for kids? _____ If so, is it child-safe? _____

9. If this is the main family bathroom or a children's bath, is it close to the
   bedrooms? _____

KITCHEN LOCATION

10. Are the present bathrooms located conveniently?_____

11. On what floor in the home is your bathroom located? _____

12. Are you planning any structural changes, i.e. room addition to existing
    house, windows, skylight, door, walls, floors, ceiling, other ? _____
    _____

13. Is it possible to move doors, windows and/or plumbing? _____

14. Is there a basement, crawl space, concrete slab or finished ceiling
    below it? _____

15. What is above your bathroom? An attic, roof, or open ceiling? The
    second floor? _____

16. Do you want an open or vaulted ceiling? _____

Once you have decided who will be using the bathroom and what part of
the house the bathroom will best serve , ask yourself what type of
bathroom you are planning. To help guide you with your answers, consider
your present bathroom.

YOUR PRESENT BATHROOM

Take detailed stock of your existing bathroom. Determine what works and
which elements need to be changed. Consider everything from surface
materials to issues, such as layout and location. What do you like and
want to keep about your present bathroom? _____
_____
_____
_____
_____

17. Why do you want to change your bathroom?
    _____Inefficient layout
    _____It looks dated

_____Needs more storage space
_____It is too crowded
_____Too small/needs more space
_____Other_____
_____

18. Are there any elements that exist in your present bath-cabinets, for
    example-that can be retained and attractively updated rather than
    replaced? _____

Fixtures:

19. Are fixtures - lavatory, tub, shower, toilet - in good condition? Do any
    fixtures leak? Is the overall appearance pleasing? _____

20. What features do you like and dislike about your current equipment
    (sizes, shapes, and materials) and fixtures (i.e. are faucets easy to turn
    on/off)?_____

21. Do members of your household prefer to wash in a tub, shower, or
    both? Do the present fixtures accommodate these preferences?
    _____

22. Is the bathtub or shower large enough? _____

23. Is the shower head at a comfortable height for all users? _____

24. Is the shower safe (grab bars, non-slip floor, temperature
    controlled faucet, bench seat)? _____

25. Is the bathtub safe (non-slip bottom, faucets within reach, grab bars,
    easy to get into)?_____

26. Is the sink of adequate size? Or, would two sinks be better?_____

27. Is the lavatory (sink) at a comfortable height (34" - 36" high)?
    _____

28. Is the room primarily a shower/bath/toilet area, or is it also a place to
    shave or apply makeup? _____

Layout:

Consider the following questions in relation to your bathroom's layout.

29. Are the size and layout efficient and comfortable for bathing and
    grooming? _____

30. Can two people use the bathroom comfortably and conveniently at
    the same time? _____

31. Is there enough counter space? _____

32. Are there frequent traffic jams in or near the bathroom? Is there a
    door that swings into the traffic path? _____

33. When open, do cabinet or vanity doors and drawers block the door ?
    _____

Mechanical elements:

34. Are all the mechanical elements - plumbing, lighting, ventilation-
    adequate and in good working order? _____

35. Examine the surfaces in your present bathroom for cracks, bubbles,
    mold, mildew, etc.. Have any subsurfaces been damaged by excess
    moisture, i.e., mildew on tiles, curled floor tiles, or loose paint or
    wallcovering? _____

36. Do you have an efficient ventilation system to remove odors and
    moisture? Would you prefer natural or mechanical ventilation?
    _____

Table 2.1 Before You Begin: A Bathroom Questionnaire (*Continued*)

37. What type of heating system do you have? Do you have any problems with heating? Does any ducting run through a bathroom wall? _____

38. Are all the electrical outlets protected with ground-fault circuit interrupters (GFCI) to prevent electric shock? Are there enough electrical outlets (i.e., near the sink and mirror)? Are the switches and outlets conveniently placed? _____

39. What is right and wrong with your bathroom lighting? Is there adequate lighting in the right places for your bathroom activities (applying make-up, shaving, etc.) ? _____

40. Do you have ample artificial lighting and general lighting? Would you like to add task lighting? Consider natural light sources by adding a skylight, enlarging an existing window or creating a new window. _____

Privacy:

41. Does the door or window of your bathroom open to a public area? _____

42. Is the toilet in a good location or is it visible through an open door? _____

43. Would you like to consider relocating the opening to increase privacy? _____

YOUR DREAM BATHROOM

44. What elements/activity areas do you already know you want to incorporate into your new bathroom design?

Double sinks	_____	Sauna	_____
Separate tub & shower	_____	Spas	_____
Separate dressing area/room	_____	Whirlpool tub	_____
Garden bath	_____	Exercise facilities	_____
Steam compartment	_____	Laundry facilities	_____
Well-lit makeup vanity	_____	Open shelving	_____
Storage shelves	_____	Telephone	_____
Entertainment center/T.V.	_____		
Space for a coffee maker	_____		

Space to lounge or relax (by incorporating furniture)_____
Other _____

45. What new fixtures are you planning?

Bathtub	_____
Shower	_____
Tub/shower combination	_____
Vanity	_____
Sink	_____
Toilet	_____
Bidet	_____

46. Are stored items within easy reach? What storage requirements are desired? Is there allotted space for

Medicine cabinet	_____	Linen closet	_____
Drawers	_____	Rollout baskets	_____
Cabinets (wall)	_____	Tilt-out bins	_____
Towels	_____	Cleaning supplies	_____
Laundry hamper/chute	_____	Plunger	_____
Personal hygiene items	_____	Linens	_____
Bathroom scale	_____	Bathrobes	_____
Toilet brush	_____		

Floor-to-ceiling unit complete with shelves & bins _____
Other _____

47. What else will you be replacing?

Wall coverings	_____	Ceiling treatment	_____
Countertops	_____	Plumbing	_____
Electrical	_____	Lighting	_____
Flooring	_____	Windows	_____
Sink(s)	_____		
Other	_____		

YOUR PERSONAL TASTE

48. What type of style would you like your new bathroom space to have?

Traditional	_____	Family retreat	_____
Sleek/Contemporary	_____	Formal	_____
Country	_____	Open and airy	_____
Strictly functional	_____	European	_____
Personal design statement	_____	Southwestern	_____
Other	_____		

49. Would the bathroom's style be improved if you changed the

Walls	_____	Floor	_____
Ceiling	_____	Countertops	_____
Cabinetry	_____		

50. What color schemes do you like?

Earth tones	_____	Black and white	_____
Neutrals	_____	Pastels	_____
Bright colors	_____	Current fashion colors	_____
Other			

51. What type/color cabinets would you like?

Whitewashed	_____	Light wood	_____
White laminates	_____	Medium wood	_____
Colored laminates	_____	Dark wood	_____
Other	_____		

52. Do you prefer framed or frameless cabinets?_____

53. What type of cabinet accessories interest you? _____

54. Do you have ample counter space in your bathroom? If not, where would you like more room for storage or display? Would you prefer a different type of countertop material than you presently have?_____
_____

55. What countertop materials do you prefer?

Laminate	_____	Ceramic tile	_____
Solid-surface	_____	Wood	_____
Stone	_____		
Other	_____		

56. What type of flooring would you like in the new bathroom?

Wood	_____	Stone	_____
Vinyl	_____	Carpet	_____
Ceramic tile	_____		
Other	_____		

THE TASK AHEAD

57. What portion of the project, if any, will be your responsibility? _____
_____

58. Who will perform the following tasks if needed?

Obtain permits_____
Remove walls and other structural changes_____
Remove old floor_____
Replace plumbing and electrical_____
Paint or wallpaper_____
Install tiling or floor_____
Install new cabinets_____
Install new Countertops_____
Add trim, moldings, etc. _____
Purchase fixtures _____
Other_____

59. Realistically, by what date would you like to have your new bathroom?_____

60. What is your preliminary budget? _____

61. What is your maximum budget? _____

62. Is financing a possibility? _____

You (as the lead installer) take full responsibility for the installation job from start to finish. The lead installer is on the job every day, all day, managing the project and doing the bulk of the carpentry work. Your project management responsibilities include coordinating all subcontractors, ordering materials when there are shortages, writing change orders, performing quality control, completing precompletion punch lists, and sometimes collecting payments. Your management procedures will continuously change as you evaluate what is most effective for your projects. The bathroom installation profession can be a continuing learning process for you.

Many bathroom installers are in business for themselves because they want to be independent; however, this independence does come with a price. A successful project installation requires someone to make the tough decisions and direct the course of the project. You must be able to manage yourself as well as others.

Scheduling the Job

The most common questions asked by clients is when you can begin the installation and how long it will take. This information is just as important to you, too. To properly estimate the job start and end, you need an accurate schedule to organize the project. A schedule is extremely important to make the best use of workers and subcontractors and to avoid problems. If you do not prepare a realistic schedule, and the project takes longer than expected, you will have a very unhappy client.

You need to prepare a schedule that identifies the major categories of work to be done and the time required to accomplish the work. Depending on how many other bathrooms there are in the home, you may be disrupting your client's daily routine significantly. No client has ever been unhappy because a remodeling project was completed ahead of schedule. So, plan ahead and factor in extra time for delays, and other obstacles, which, unfortunately, are inevitable.

You must consider many factors when you prepare a construction schedule. The more experience you have and the more projects you have completed, the easier it is to identify all these factors and assign them a completion date. Reviewing your cost estimate for the project is a good place to begin in preparing a schedule. Every item identified as a cost takes a certain amount of time to perform. Consider the time requirements for the delivery of materials and fixtures, and plan accordingly. It is important not to begin until everything is in local stock.

Subcontractors must be scheduled so that they do not delay the project. Finding subcontractors who meet schedules and are disciplined is one of the hardest things in construction. Arriving on time is one of the most important qualities to look for in a subcontractor. Therefore, you must be sure to have the job ready for those subcontractors on schedule so that they can do their work efficiently. If a delay is unavoidable, inform any subcontractors, and, as soon as possible, provide a revised schedule reflecting this delay.

When preparing the schedule, keep in mind that inspections are required by local code officials. Failure to schedule these inspections will cause a major interruption while you wait for the inspector to approve completed work and give you permission to continue.

Types of Schedules

Various visual aids can be used as schedules. The first type is the bar-graph schedule. The *bar-graph* or *bar-chart schedule* lists the categories of work in a column on the left side and dates for the duration of the project in a row across the top of the schedule. The projected start and completion of each category of work are plotted on the schedule.

To decide the best time for a task to begin, you need to know what categories of work must be completed. If your schedule shows overlaps for different categories of work, make sure that these tasks can physically occur within the bathroom space at the same time. A bar graph can be produced rather quickly with a computer; therefore, revisions can be made easily when changes occur.

A *critical path method* (CPM) schedule is useful for planning and management of all types of projects. It is a schematic diagram or network that shows the sequence and interrelation of all the categories of work for the project. It provides a more precise approach than do conventional bar graphs. It clearly shows the difference between activities that are critical and those that are not.

Another method of scheduling is with a *flowchart,* which is simply a written, week-by-week list of the critical tasks to be done on a job. A flowchart is not as easy to quickly review as a CPM or bar graph; however, it is a good place to start. You may find that it will be a sufficient scheduling method. The more experience you acquire with installation projects, the better you will be at polishing your management and scheduling techniques.

A good way to keep everyone involved with the project up to date is to post the project schedule at the project site. Remember to update it as often as possible. Keep in mind that if your client visibly sees the schedule on a daily basis, you must be prepared to keep to the schedule. A well-scheduled project with little or no wasted time can be very profitable for you.

Pricing, Estimating, and Quotations

The installer with the lowest price does not always get the job. Sales and marketing are at least as important as, if not more important than, the price. An installer with a reputation for reliability, quality work, and effective people skills gets more business than one with a low bid.

Throughout the installation, many hours may be spent dealing with unforeseen problems on the job, meeting with clients, and coordinating with the architect or dealer or designer. These projects often have small budgets, which means that you may have several small projects running at the same time. A large amount of your time is spent traveling between jobs. To be profitable, your estimating must take into account all these inefficiencies.

Certain unexpected conditions need to be figured into the job estimate. It is difficult to put a reasonable cost on these problems. For example, in some homes, a large whirlpool may be difficult to move through narrow hallways and doorways. Bathroom remodeling jobs in condominiums or other large buildings may present problems, such as parking fees if free parking is unavailable for your service vehicle.

Figure in added costs for additional help if the project is not easily accessible. If the project is in an apartment building, for example, be certain to verify that the elevators are large enough to handle all the materials and equipment needed. If you don't plan ahead for this potential problem, you will lose valuable time and money.

A few factors should be figured into all projected costs, including, as mentioned earlier, unusual job conditions such as difficult access; difficult customers, such as a couple who can't agree on anything;

unusual project requirements, such as matching of existing materials; and company capability—do you have the workers and experience for the project?

The additional costs that come with any of the situations vary from project to project. Your ability to accurately identify the situations and figure in the costs can make the difference between making money and losing money on a project. Estimate one job at a time so that you do not confuse one job with another. The longer you wait to prepare the estimate, the harder it is to evaluate any of these mentioned situations.

Every element of the job must be included in the estimate. Leaving anything out seriously affects your net profit. If all the items are included, the overall effect of misfiguring a minor item is insignificant compared to leaving something out.

To evaluate the actual cost of the job versus the estimated cost, keep a time sheet for each individual job. A comparison of these figures may help point out mistakes or shortcomings in the estimate. Even if you are installing highly specialized, custom bathrooms, most of the job involves standard items and tasks. It is most efficient to use a computer for estimating. Add custom designs and finishes into the estimating database, and they then become standard items. When you are doing something for the first time, keep cost records so that you can develop accurate unit costs for the next time that option is used.

Preconstruction Conference

A *preconstruction conference* should be held after the client's 3-day right of rescission (or cancellation) has passed, and before any work begins (Table 2.2). The contractor or production manager, dealer or designer, architect, installer, and homeowners are all generally included at this meeting. However, this may vary according to the size and type of project.

This meeting passes the chain of command from the dealer and designer to the installer, which must be made clear to the customers. They must understand that they will now be working with the installer rather than the salesperson. The installer will not be able to take full control of the project or gain the respect of the customers if the customers continue to call the dealer or designer during the course of the project.

Table 2.2 Pre-construction Conference Form

PRE-CONSTRUCTION
CONFERENCE FORM

Date _____ 19 ____

Job No. _____

Owner _____

Address _____

Job Location
_____
_____

1. The contract and specifications have been reviewed and are completely understood:

_____   _____
Contractor's Representative   Owner

_____   _____
Contractor   Owner

2. The plans have been reviewed and are approved in present form:

_____   _____
Contractor's Representative   Owner

_____   _____
Contractor   Owner

3. The original contract and specifications include allowances on the following items and a decision has been made or will be made prior to start of work on any addition or deductions:				4. Customer decisions on model numbers, color or pattern selection, etc., have been made or will be made prior to start of work on the following items:	
Item	Amount Allowed	Amount of Customer Selection	Addition or Deduction to Contract	Item	Description (Model Number, Color, etc.)

5. The payment schedule is as follows:

TOTAL AMOUNT $ _____   The balance of payments to be made as follows:

DEPOSIT $ _____   _____

BALANCE $ _____   _____

6. Scheduled Starting Date _____ 19 _____   7. Estimated Completion Date _____ 19 _____

8. Other subjects discussed and agreed to at the pre-construction conference:

_____

_____

_____

HOME-TECH FORM 335

45

Table 2.2 Pre-construction Conference Form (*Continued*)

9. The company policy on Change Orders has been explained and it is understood that any changes not required by unforeseen conditions or beyond the control of the customer will be priced according to the contractor's normal pricing policy and will also include an administrative charge of $50 to compensate the company for time lost, scheduling changes and other administrative costs.

10. All Change Orders must be completed in writing with signatures of both customer and contractor's representative. All Change Orders will be priced prior to start of work and payment is to be made in full immediately on completion. For changes costing over $500, a partial payment will be required in advance with balance on completion of the work called for in the Change Order.

11. While an estimated completion date has been given, we understand that this date is subject to change due to delays in material availability and delivery, Change Orders, inclement weather and other unforeseen circumstances.

12. It is understood that the workmen on the job will use the customer's bathroom and telephone. Any toll calls will be paid by the company upon submission of the bill.

13. It is understood that work normally starts at 8 A.M. and that the areas in which work is to be performed will be accessible at that time.

14. It is understood that the company will place a site sign on the premises to help delivery trucks and crews to locate the job site as well as for company advertising.

15. It is understood that at the completion of the project, a company representative and all parties to the contract will compile "Quality Control Pre-Completion Punch List." When all the items on the list have been satisfactorily completed, the final payment will be made. All other items will be covered under the one year warranty.

The foregoing terms and specifications and the conditions listed on this pre-construction conference form are satisfactory and are hereby accepted and agreed to.

Contractor's Representative	Owner
Contractor	Contractor

The installer often presents the details of the project at the preconstruction conference, explaining the specifications in a way that is often more thorough than the dealer or designer may have done. While a good salesperson may mention some of the limits of a bathroom project, the sales emphasis is on exciting the customer to buy. The installer must point out potential misunderstandings in detail. Every time an installer undertakes an installation, this education process must take place.

Good communication skills are very important to the success of the project. The line of communication between installer and customer is established at the preconstruction conference. The more clearly an installer explains the limits of work and what the customer can expect, the happier the customer will be.

When there is more than one customer, one individual should be designated as key decision-maker and liaison with the installer. This person should also be responsible for handling payments so that the installer is not expected to communicate with both parties, or agree to a change order with one but try to collect from the other.

As reported by Walter W. Stoeppelwerth in his NKBA *Kitchen and Bathroom Installation Manual,* some of the most important issues to be covered at a preconstruction conference, which can last from 1 to 2 hours, include

- *Every specification in the contract is reviewed and explained.* This explanation is vital so that you know what is expected of you and the homeowners know what will be done to their house. For example, if an existing floor is not level, or if an existing wall has a bow in it, explain to the owner the impact on your work. Make certain that the client understands that these existing conditions will remain once the new work is completed, and that you will do your best to minimize any problems that may result from these conditions.

   Another common problem is the matching of new materials to existing materials. For example, if the client is not willing to repaint an entire room during the installation project, explain that you will do your best to match the color. They must understand that paint colors age over time, especially in bathrooms, and repainting with the same paint color used previously does not guarantee a match.

   Clearly explain to the client what is and is not included in the project so that they have a good understanding of what the finished project will be like. Do not assume that they can read the blueprints or specifications, even if they continuously nod their heads and say that they understand. Always operate under the assumption that the client has a very limited knowledge of construction.

   Throughout the preconstruction conference, attempt to determine if the project that the client has contracted for is the project they believe they are getting. If they have unreal expectations for the project, this is the time to bring them back to reality. It is better to do this at the preconstruction conference than to deal with this later when all the materials and equipment have been ordered or installed.

■ *Areas of the home affected by the work.* The homeowners must clearly understand which areas of the home will be affected, as well as what furniture and equipment must be moved or stored to permit the work to occur. They must be aware of the possible damage that can occur if they are not removed. Bathroom cabinets which are to be completely removed, will, obviously, have to be totally emptied.

■ *Areas of the house off limits to workers.* If the client is going to allow workers to use a particular bathroom in the house, for example, it should be designated by the owner at the meeting.

■ *Who will be at the job site on a regular basis and at what time.* Many people in the construction trades like to begin early in the morning, so everyone needs to be out of bed and out of the way by a mutually agreed-upon time. You may have to start a little later than you would like. Once the start time is set, you should have workers at the job site promptly.

■ *The construction schedule.* The construction schedule should be presented at the conference. Review the basic steps that occur throughout the project. If the client must leave the home for an extended period of time, such as when the plumbing, heating, or electrical utilities will be shut down, schedule these times now.

■ *Basic safety precautions.* Inform the client of all of the safety procedures that need to be followed during the remodeling process. If possible, the homeowners and the inhabitants of the house should stay out of the construction area. Explain to the client the possible dangers of walking around the construction area. The client should not attempt to turn on light switches or use outlets in the designated area until the project is complete.

■ *Existing materials to be removed or salvaged.* A list of items to be salvaged should be completed by the client, along with your assistance. Items that look worthless to you, could be very important to the client. If items such as cabinets or plumbing fixtures are to be saved, the client needs to provide an area where these items can be stored. Also, decide who is responsible for the removal of salvaged items. Explain that if the client wants you to remove these items and put them in the basement or garage, you will have to charge for this service. If the client decides they want to be responsible for removal of such items, give them a date by which the items must be removed. Inform the client that, while you will take every precaution to safely remove and store the items that are your responsibility to remove, you cannot be responsible for any damage that might occur during the removal or relocation process. In addition, if the plans call for the reuse of some or all of the existing appliances, you want to make sure that the client understands that you cannot ensure the working condition of the appliances at the end of the job. Obviously, you must see that the existing appliances are safeguarded during construction.

■ *Verification that every important decision has to be made before work starts.* Decisions such as paint color, tile selections, light fixtures, and so on should all be decided upon before work is started. Customers should have already made these decisions as well as been given samples to study, so they have not made decisions under pressure. Many contractors and bathroom specialists have showroom selection centers where customers can go to make all these choices at one time, which allows decisions to be made more quickly and efficiently. A customer can often select from pre-designed ensembles that coordinate fixture selections with wall paper, paint, and tile. If any decisions are not finalized at this time, a deadline should be set with the stipulation that the job will not start until the decisions are made.

■ *Change orders.* Most installers do not like change orders because they seldom make any money on them. Inform customers that change orders can delay a project, as well as be quite expensive for both you and them. This conference is an important time to ask whether they have any additions to the project. If any such additions are brought up at this time, they can be priced according to normal policy and a change order written (see example of change-order form in Table 2.3). If any changes come up later, the price might include an administrative charge (amount to be decided upon by the company) added to the price of the work. This fee is charged to help pay for the cost of workers standing around while change orders are contemplated and figured, as well as cover the administrative costs of notifying subcontractors or suppliers of the change in plans.

■ *Procedure for payment.* If you will be collecting payment from the homeowner, now is the time to discuss the procedures for doing so. If you are working for a lumberyard or home center or are a subcontractor, your arrangements for payments should be part of your contract with that company. In these cases, details of your payment

Table 2.3 Change-Order Form

CHANGE ORDER

Page _____ of _____

Date _____ 19 _____

We agree to make change(s) or perform additional work at the request and order of:

NAME, ADDRESS, CITY, STATE & ZIP CODE		Job No.		Job Address	
		Date of Existing Contract			
		Home Phone	Office Phone	Job Phone	

hereinafter referred to as Owner, for work performed at premises set forth above. It is proposed to make change(s) or perform additional work as follows:

_____

_____

_____

_____

_____

_____

_____

_____

_____

_____

_____

_____

_____

_____

_____

_____

_____

_____

_____

_____

_____

Additional work specified above becomes part of and is to be performed under the same conditions as the existing contract between Contractor and Owner unless otherwise stipulated.

ADDITIONAL PRICE FOR ABOVE WORK IS $ _____	DEDUCTION IN PRICE TO OWNER IS $ _____	Previous Contract Total Amount	$	
Payment to be made as follows: _____	Deduction to be made as follows: _____	Revised Contract Total Amount	$	

CONTRACTOR'S ACCEPTANCE	OWNER'S ACCEPTANCE
Additional work to be started on or before _____ 19____.	The foregoing terms, specifications and conditions are satisfactory and are hereby agreed to. You are authorized to perform the work as specified.
and substantially completed on or before _____ 19____.	
Company Representative _____	Owner _____
	Owner _____
Accepted by Contractor _____ Lic.No.	Date of Acceptance _____ 19____.

FORM NO. 320 HOME-TECH, WASHINGTON, D.C. 20014

schedule and contract should not be disclosed to the homeowner. You should not discuss the amount of money that the homeowner is being charged by the lumberyard, home center, or contractor.

Payment procedures differ greatly throughout different parts of the country. The most common procedure is to collect 30 percent of the payment at the start of the job, another 30 percent midway, and 30 percent at substantial completion. The final 10 percent is due upon completion of the punch list. Some companies wait until the end of the job and collect all of the money at that time.

If there is to be a down payment, explain when it is due (customarily at the time the contract is signed). Be familiar with the limits set by your locality or state as to the amount of down payment you can legally charge. If you will be collecting payments at milestones during the progress of the project, it is better to tie the payment to the start rather than completion of a certain part of the work. For example, if one-third of the payment is due upon completion of cabinet installation and one cabinet is delivered damaged, you may have to wait to collect your money until the replacement cabinet arrives and is installed. If payment is due at the start of cabinet installation, this incident is not a problem.

Final payment should be based on substantial completion. If there are punch list items to be corrected, a mutually agreed-upon amount can be withheld from the final payment. On a larger job, a percentage of your payment may be held in retainage (customarily 10 percent) until the punch list items are completed. Collect your money in person; going to the project site to collect money allows you to check on the quality of the job. If something has gone wrong and the client wants to hold up payment, the sooner you find out and solve the problem, the better.

■ *Items to be removed from the project area.* Working with the client to determine what furnishings, equipment, and personal belongings must be removed from the project area prior to the start of work is an important part of the preconstruction conference. Be realistic about how much of the home will be affected by the project, and make sure the client is aware of what will be affected. Rooms adjacent to the bathroom will also be affected; these spaces need to be cleared of furnishings and possessions as well to allow you enough room to work. When you need to have items moved, give the clients a couple days' notice. It is also important that they know you will not be responsible if damage occurs because the items were not previously moved.

If items must remain in the project work area, you need to protect them as much as possible. If there is a risk of damage, make sure that the client understands this from the beginning of the project. Drop cloths or polyethylene may be sufficient protection for most items, but larger items may need greater protection from accidental impact.

Before You Start

Delivery and Storage

For kitchen and bathroom remodeling, many installers feel that storing materials in a warehouse is not cost-effective. This kind of storage is a waste of money when you take into account the cost for space, delivery time, and inventory. However, large kitchen or bathroom companies might use a warehouse as a staging area. When cabinets are delivered, they are stored in the warehouse until all related items such as fixtures, light fixtures, and tile, are ready and are then transported to the job.

Bathroom installers have begun to form closer alliances with single-source suppliers. The suppliers provide storage and staging areas in their larger warehouses where all the required materials and equipment for a project can be held. An initial delivery is made to the project at the beginning of the installation, and a second delivery is scheduled midway through the project. This trend toward the supplier-provided staging area is expected to continue to grow.

Scheduling Delivery

If you do not use a warehouse or staging area, you need to schedule delivery of materials so they are on the job when you need them. You will not want to store or work around materials and equipment that you are not ready to install. Some dealers and designers maintain a small storage area as a part of their showroom or at a separate location. If this is the case, cabinets and large fixtures should be delivered and held at this location until you are ready to install them. If your client has garage space available, it can sometimes be used.

Do not attempt to stock materials that you use for bathroom installation projects. Purchase what you need for each job when you need it. Even if you have materials left over at the end of the project, it is probably more cost-effective to offer them to the client than to take them with you and attempt to store them for later use. The cost of your labor to haul these materials quickly exceeds their value.

Protecting the Area

Flooring finishes that are not being replaced must be protected, including any area that will be a path for workers. In most cases, drop cloths or polyethylene are sufficient to protect these surfaces, but in areas where you will be rolling or dragging heavy equipment, consider a more substantial material, such as plywood. Refinishing damaged hardwood flooring or replacing stained or torn carpet in a home can be very expensive and time-consuming. Take time to ensure that all is protected.

In addition, rooms that will not be affected by the work should be separated from the work area by polyethylene or plywood barriers to reduce the passage of dust and dirt. The type of barrier selected depends on whether access is needed to the area closed off. Determine your required paths of travel through the home, as well as the client's, before making this decision.

You may sometimes need to suggest that some items be placed in an off-site storage facility for the duration of the project. This situation is most likely when the home has little or no storage space or if a project will leave the home in an unsecured condition that would put the client's possessions at risk of theft. If you do not feel that you can adequately protect the contents of the house, you must press the client to exercise this option.

Recording Existing Conditions

Some companies have instituted a policy of videotaping the area prior to the start of work so that they have a permanent record of the existing conditions. This may not be necessary in all cases, but it does underline the necessity of making at least a written inventory of the existing materials and equipment and their condition before beginning your installation work.

Sequencing of New-Material Delivery

Once the contract is signed and the clients have made themselves ready for their bathroom remodeling project, they want to see work begin immediately. However, you should not begin the tear-out or other preparation work until the new fixtures, cabinets, and materials are in local stock. If you begin the tear-out process too soon, the client will be left with deadtime between tear-out and installation. Because the clients cannot use the bathroom, this deadtime can be very inconvenient.

Most installers have found it good practice to wait for everything to be in local stock. While this guarantees that the client will not experience deadtime, the time between contract signing and the start of work can seem extremely long for the clients. Help them to understand that you are looking out for their best interests by compressing the time that their lives are disrupted by the project.

Prestart Checklist

For planning purposes, you will want to maintain a prestart checklist that allows you to keep track of items on order and their anticipated arrival date. An example of a typical prestart checklist is shown in Table 2.4. Obviously, the requirements of each individual job will dictate the contents of the prestart checklist. If you intend to delay the start of the installation until crucial materials for the project have arrived, track them on this checklist. Generally, special-order or custom items fall into the crucial category. This information allows you to gauge with some accuracy when to tell the client that the tear-out will begin.

Ordering Materials

Before a job can begin, the installer must determine what materials are needed to construct the project and when they will be needed on the project site to keep the job running on schedule. If an insufficient quantity of materials is ordered, the job could be delayed while waiting for another delivery. On the other hand, if installers order too much, the materials are wasted and the profit on the project is reduced. Leftover materials are rarely usable on another job, and the cost of moving and storing them negates any savings.

In most cases, installers working directly for dealers will not order cabinets or fixtures or other major items, such as doors and windows. The order for these materials is placed by the salesperson once the design is accepted by the customer and the contract for the project is

Table 2.4 Bathroom Installation Prestart Checklist

Name of Client:_____
Home Address:_____
_____
Telephone (Home):_____
(Work):_____
(Job Site):_____
Job Site Address:_____

BUILDING PERMITS:

☐   Obtained and posted all required permits, including general building permit, plumbing permit, electrical permit, etc.

Material/Equipment Items	Recv'd in Local Stock	Date Ordered	Estimated Delivery
Cabinets	☐		
Shower	☐		
Bathtub	☐		
Whirlpool	☐		
Toilet	☐		
Bidet	☐		
Sauna	☐		
Steam Bath	☐		
Spa/Hot Tub	☐		
Lavatory	☐		
Lavatory Faucet(s)	☐		
Bath/Shower Fittings	☐		
Lighting Fixtures	☐		
Flooring	☐		
Windows	☐		
Doors	☐		
HVAC Vents and Accessories	☐		
Wall Finishes (Ceramic Tile, etc.)	☐		
Framing Lumber	☐		
Wallboard and Accessories	☐		
Medicine Cabinet(s)	☐		
Mirror(s)	☐		
Accessories	☐		
	☐		
	☐		
	☐		

SUBCONTRACTORS:

☐   Scheduled electrician   Name:_____ Start Date:_____
☐   Scheduled flooring
    installer   Name:_____ Start Date:_____
☐   Scheduled plumber   Name:_____ Start Date:_____
☐   Scheduled wallpaperer   Name:_____ Start Date:_____
☐   Scheduled painter   Name:_____ Start Date:_____
☐   Scheduled counter top
    fabricator   Name:_____ Start Date:_____
☐   Others   Name:_____ Start Date:_____
    Name:_____ Start Date:_____

COLOR & MATERIAL SELECTIONS:

☐   Client has made all color and material selections, and they have been checked against the specifications for the project.

MISCELLANEOUS:

☐   The project site has been inspected. All field conditions have been confirmed.
☐   If necessary, contact has been made with the local utility companies to arrange for utility changes or connections.

signed. Dealer-employed installers order from other building materials for the project, such as framing lumber, drywall, and trim. Contract installers, on the other hand, when not working through a dealer or designer, order all materials required on a project.

Part of the process of turning over a project to the installer should be to establish what materials have already been ordered, and what items are left for the installer to handle. Installers need to carefully review the paperwork for materials that have been ordered in advance so that they are clear as to what is and is not included in these orders. If they detect discrepancies or omissions in the orders, installers should notify the dealer or designer at once so that the problem can be corrected. Many of the materials used in bathroom projects are special-order products, which have substantial lead times for delivery. The timing of orders for these materials and their anticipated delivery is extremely important to a project schedule. Special-order items should be ordered as soon as possible after contract signing and should be in local stock before a job is started. If precise measurements are required, they should be checked and double-checked.

Even when materials ordering is handled by others, installers have an important role to play. There should be an established line of communication between installers and those placing material orders. If installers have experienced problems with a certain product or supplier or know of products that may perform better for a given task, this information should be conveyed to the material orderer.

It is helpful for dealers or designers and installers to establish relationships with one or more suppliers that stock, or have available for special order, materials that are typically needed for bathroom projects. An established, ongoing relationship with a supplier that provides installers with priority service, quick turnaround on orders, and reliable delivery of material is an important factor in the on-time completion of a project. Installers who have established relationships with material suppliers know that they can count on having their materials delivered when promised and that the deliveries will be complete and accurate.

Installers should carefully inspect all deliveries to the job site, especially special-order materials. Defects and deficiencies should be noted on the delivery ticket, and damaged items should be refused. Manufacturers are reluctant to accept responsibility for damage that is not noted at the time of delivery. While it does take time away from production for installers to do a complete and adequate check of a delivery of bathroom cabinets, for example, it relieves installers of responsibility for damages that occurred before the cabinets arrived at the site. Damage that is missed during this inspection can be very costly to the installer later in the project and can lead to a delay in completion.

Tools and Equipment

Bathroom installations require a wide assortment of tools and equipment. It is important for you to understand the intended use of each tool you will be using, and to use and maintain them as they were designed to be. If you are working for an installation company, some of the equipment may be provided for your use. In many cases, however, you need to provide your own tool box with a basic assortment of screw drivers, pliers, wrenches, hammers, tape measures, and other tools (Figs. 2.2 through 2.11). Having the right tools readily available makes your job go much more smoothly and therefore leads to a higher-quality installation.

Today, basic power tools can increase the speed and precision of your project. Many power tools are made in cordless versions. Cordless is fast becoming a good choice as more powerful, reliable cordless tools are available. They can be used anywhere and are not restricted by electrical power connections. When purchasing power tools, read specifications to compare features. More horsepower, faster motor speeds, and higher amperage ratings indicate a well-engineered tool. Better-quality tools also have roller or ball bearings instead of sleeve bearings. A good recommendation is to utilize or standardize the tools of one manufacturer so that you will be able to interchange rechargeable batteries. If you have several batteries on hand, you can keep one in the charger while operating another.

Table 2.5 is a good base to get started for a bathroom installation. You won't need all these tools for every project. These tools are considered your main basic tools, not a complete list. As you gain experience, you will find many more tools useful. Build on this list. Plan ahead so that you will know which tools will be required for a project and have them on hand when you need them.

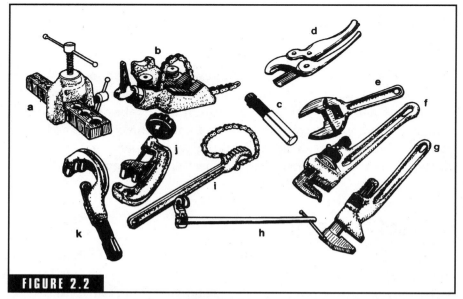

FIGURE 2.2

Plumbing equipment includes a flaring tool (*a*), pipe vise (*b*), inside pipe wrench (*c*), plastic pipe cutter (*d*), spud wrench (*e*), pipe wrench (*f*), monkey wrench (*g*), basin wrench (*h*), chain wrench (*i*), pipe cutter (*j*), and tubing cutter (*k*). *(Leon E. Korejwo, Illustrations.)*

FIGURE 2.3

Safety equipment includes a paper dust mask (*a*), a single-filter dust-paint mask filter (*b*), safety goggles (*c*), ear protectors (*d*), a face shield (*e*), a fire extinguisher (*f*), and a double-filter spray paint mask (*g*). *(Leon E. Korejwo, Illustrations.)*

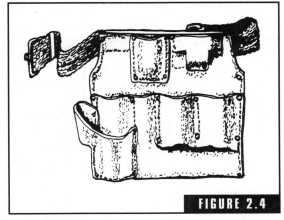

Tool belt. *(Leon E. Korejwo, Illustrations.)*

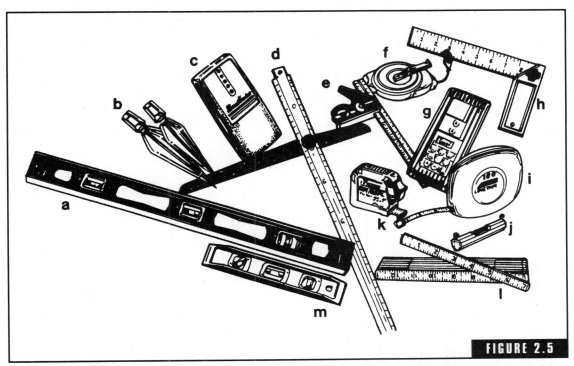

Measuring tools include a carpenter's level (*a*), plumb bobs (*b*), a stud finder (*c*), a drywall T-square (*d*), a combination square (*e*), a chalk line (*f*), a laser-measuring device (*g*), a tri-square (*h*), a 100-foot retractable tape measure (*i*), a string level (*j*), an 8-m (26-foot) tape measure (*k*), a folding ruler (*l*), and a torpedo level (*m*). *(Leon E. Korejwo, Illustrations.)*

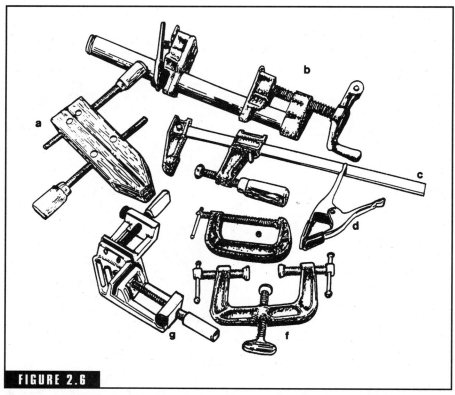

FIGURE 2.6

Various types of clamps: hand-screw clamp (*a*); dual-action pipe clamp (*b*); bar clamp (*c*); spring clamp (*d*); C-clamp (*e*); three-way clamp (*f*); and miter or right-angle clamp (*g*). *(Leon E. Korejwo, Illustrations.)*

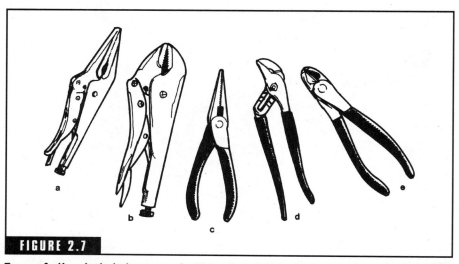

FIGURE 2.7

Types of pliers include long-nose locking pliers (*a*), locking-jaw pliers (*b*), long-reach needlenose pliers (*c*), channel-lock (arc-lock) pliers (*d*), and diagonal cutting pliers (*e*). *(Leon E. Korejwo, Illustrations.)*

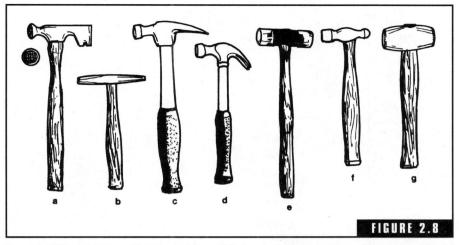

Several different types of hammers: drywall hammer (*a*), magnetic tack hammer (*b*), rip hammer (*c*), claw hammer (*d*), soft-tip (plastic) hammer (*e*), ball-peen hammer (*f*), mallet (*g*). *(Leon E. Korejwo, Illustrations.)*

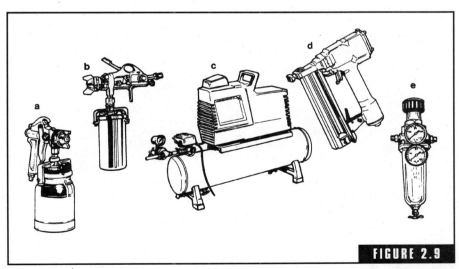

Various air tools useful to the kitchen installer include an external-mix, siphon-feed spray gun (*a*), a touchup spray guy (*b*), an air compressor (*c*), a 16-gauge finishing nailer (*d*), and an air transformer that combines a pressure regulator and a filter (*e*). *(Leon E. Korejwo, Illustrations.)*

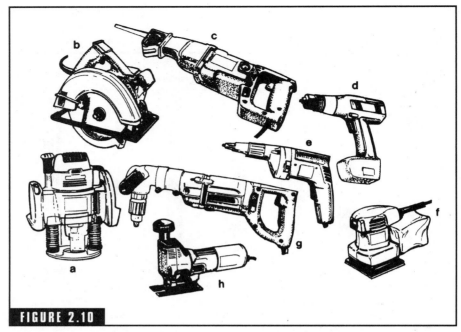

FIGURE 2.10

Various electric hand tools: plunge router (*a*), 2¼-horsepower circular saw (*b*), reciprocating saw (*c*), ⅜-inch cordless drill driver (*d*), ½-horsepower drywall screw gun (*e*), ¼-sheet finishing sander with dust collector (*f*), angle drill (*g*), and variable-speed jigsaw (*h*). *(Leon E. Korejwo, Illustrations.)*

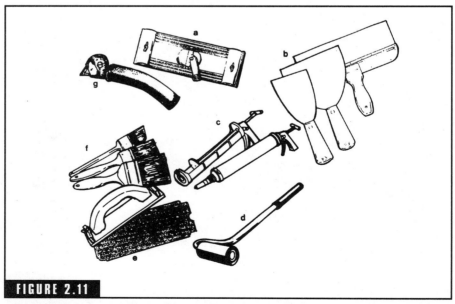

FIGURE 2.11

A pole sander (*a*); scraper, putty knife, and spreader (*b*); caulking and adhesive guns (*c*); J-roller (*d*); sanding block with precut drywall sanding screen (*e*); various shapes of brushes (*f*); and Douglas-type craft knife (*g*). *(Leon E. Korejwo, Illustrations.)*

Table 2.5 Bathroom Installation Tools and Equipment

Safety equipment

Disposable latex or vinyl gloves
Face masks
Filter masks
Fire extinguisher
First-aid kit
Hard hat
Heavy-duty safety gloves
Knee pads
Lifting harness or back brace
Proper ear protection (ear plugs or muffs)
Safety glasses with side shields or wraparound safety goggles
Safety guards on portable saws
Safety signs
Steel tipped with nonslip shoes

Measuring equipment

Squares
    12″ combination square
    4′ drywall T-square
    Framers or carpenter's steel square
    T-square
    Tri-square
    Triangle
Levels
    2′ and 4′ carpenter's levels (6′ occasionally useful)
    Line level
    Torpedo level
Measuring aids
    Adjustable T-bevel
    Chalk line
    Contour gauge
    Folding rule
    Foot ruler
    Laser alignment tool or laser measuring tool
    Marking gauge
    Metric tape measure
    Plumb bobs

Table 2.5 Bathroom Installation Tools and Equipment (*Continued*)

Retractable steel measuring tape (25', 30', 50')
Scribing compass
Straight-edge
Stud finder

Cutting tools

Chisels
  Masonry chisels
  Wood chisels
*Drills**
  $1/2$" drill
  $3/8$" variable-speed reversible (corded and/or cordless)
  Right-angle (90°) drill (occasionally useful)
  Drill driver
  Hammer drill (occasionally useful)
Drill bits
  Auger bits
  Carbide masonry bits
  Combination bits (used for hardwood floors)
  Complete assortment of standard twist bits
  Countersinks or counterbore
  Forstner bits (used for hardwood floors)
  Hole saw bits ($3/4$–$2^1/2$")
  Spade bits
Knives
  4–6" finishing knife
  Drywall knife (taping)
  Hook-bill knife (linoleum knife)
  Utility knife (matte knife)
Planes
  Block plane (end grains)
  Jack plane (trimming)
  Power planer
  Smooth bench plane (general-purpose)
Routers
  Laminate trimmer with offset base
  Standard router
Router bits
  Bevel-cut

Table 2.5 Bathroom Installation Tools and Equipment (*Continued*)

Cove bits
  Dado bits
  Flush-cut
  Rounded-corner
  Variety of other profiles (carbide preferred)
Power saws
  $7^1/4''$ circular saw
  Bench-size table saw (10" preferred)
  Jigsaw
  Power-band saw
  Power-miter saw
  Reciprocating saw
Hand saws
  Back saw with miter box
  Circle cutter
  Coping saw
  Cross-cut
  Drywall saw
  Hack saw
  Keyhole saw
  Rip saw
Saw blades
  40-tooth carbide circular saw blade
  Abrasive masonry-cutting blade
  Fine-tooth (80-tooth) miter box blade
  Jigsaw, reciprocating saw blade assortment
  Metal-cutting blades
Miscellaneous
  Craft knife
  Floor scraper
  Metal snips (for straight or curved cut)
  Various files and rasps

Attaching tools

Clamps
  Three-way clamp
  Bar type clamp
  C-clamps
  Hand-screw clamps

Table 2.5 Bathroom Installation Tools and Equipment (*Continued*)

Miter or right angle clamps
Pads (to protect finished surfaces)
Pipe clamp
Spring clamps
Strap clamp
Wood clamps (6″, 8″, 10″)
Electric screwdrivers (corded or cordless)
Electric screwdriver tips
Cabinet blades
Extension ($\leq 12″$)
Flat
Jeweler's screw drivers
Magnetic head
Nut drivers
Offset
Phillips head 1, 2, and 3 screwdrivers
Ratchet driver
Robertson (square drive)
Screw-holder-equipped driver
Square heads, various lengths
Torx bit set
Staple gun
Stud driver (powder-driven)
Wrenches
Adjustable wrenches
Allen wrench set (standard and metric)
Box wrenches (standard and metric)
Open-end wrenches (standard and metric)
Ratchet-and-socket set: $3/8″$ and $1/2″$ drives (standard and metric)
Various extensions

Various hand tools†

Hammers
13-oz. claw hammer
16-oz. claw hammer
20-oz. claw hammer
Ball-peen hammer
Drywall hammer
Heavy sledge
Mallet

Table 2.5 Bathroom Installation Tools and Equipment (*Continued*)

Mason's hammer
Soft-faced hammer
Tack hammer
Pliers
   Channel lock pliers (arc lock)
   Diagonal cutters
   Duckbill
   Line maintainer's
   Locking pliers (vice grip)
   Needlenose
   Nippers
   Various sizes of standard pliers
Other
   Cat's claw
   Crow bars
   Flat pry bar
   Nail puller

Air tools

Items required for basic air-supply system
   Air compressor
   Air filter (in-line)
   Air hose
   Air regulator (in-line)
   Air-tool lubricant
   Quick-disconnect couplings
Tools
   Blow gun
   Finishing nailer
   Spray gun (production or finish)
   Stapler
   Touchup spray gun
Optional
   Caulker
   Orbital sander

Additional equipment

Brooms
Brushes
Doweling jig

Table 2.5 Bathroom Installation Tools and Equipment (*Continued*)

Drop light
Dust Pans
Extension cords (proper gauge for length and tools)
Flashlight (rechargeable)
Folding trestle
Hand truck
Heat gun
Hot-melt glue gun
Ladders
Mechanical taper
Portable midget scaffold
Putty knives
Saw guides (edge guides)
Sawhorses
Soldering gun
Tool pouch or holder
Vacuum cleaner(s)

Optional but useful equipment

Automatic screw remover
Cabinet installation jack(s)
Flooring nailer (hardwood floors)
Hardware drilling jigs

Electrical

Circuit tester
GFCI tester
Line maintainer's pliers
Sniffer
Wire nuts
Wire stripper

Plumbing tools

For drain cleaning
Closet (toilet) auger
Drain-and-trap auger
Expansion nozzle

Table 2.5 Bathroom Installation Tools and Equipment (*Continued*)

Motorized drain auger
Power auger
Sink plunger
Toilet plunger
Pipe cutters
    Cast-iron cutters
        Snap-style soil pipe cutter
        Ratchet-style soil pipe cutter
    Copper tubing cutter
    Internal pipe cutter
    Pipe vise
    Plastic tubing cutter
    Steel pipe cutter
Wrenches
    Basin wrench
    Chain wrench
    Internal pipe wrench
    Monkey wrench
    Offset hexagonal wrench
    Pipe wrenches (12–18″)
    Seat wrench
    Shanknut wrench
    Spud wrench
    Strap wrench
    Valve-seat wrench
Other
    Faucet-handle puller
    Flaring tool (copper tube)
    Grade level
    Mechanical fingers
    Propane torch with soldering tip (and various other tips) and striker
    Reamer
    Small hand pump
    Soldering iron
    Tap-and-die set
    Torch
    Tube bender
    Valve-seat dresser
    Valve-seat reamer

Table 2.5 Bathroom Installation Tools and Equipment (*Continued*)

Drywall tools
Abrasive mesh cloth
Adhesive spreader
Drywall dolly
Drywall panel lifter
Joint compound and tape
Mechanical cradle lifter
T-brace

Tools for laying tile flooring or tile countertops
Caulking gun
Float
Glass cutter
Grout float
Jointer
Notched trowels
Tile-nipper pliers
Tile-setting block (2 × 4″) covered with towel or carpet
Tile spacers (plastic and wood)
Tile trimmer

Countertop tools (laminate)
Three-way clamps
Bevel-cut bit (router)
Cove bit (router)
Flush-cut bit (router)
J-roller
Nail sets
Nail spotters
Rounding corner bit (router)
Router
Scribing compass
Straight bit (router)
Thin wood strip for laminate spacers

Paint
Supplies
Angled-trim brushes
Brushes (various sizes and types)

Table 2.5 Bathroom Installation Tools and Equipment (*Continued*)

Cheesecloth
Corner finishing pads
Corner rollers
Edge guides
Paint mixers
Paint scraper
Putty knives
Rollers
Roller trays with disposable inserts
Strainer cups
Tack cloths
Tape creasers
Tape and dispensers
Various grits of sand paper
Sanders
Belt sander with various paper grits
Detail sander
Drywall block handheld sander
Electric hand sander (with dust collector)
Long-handled pole sander
Orbital sander
Universal angle sander

Additional supplies

Carpenter's glue
Caulk
Cleaning solvents
Compass
Construction adhesive
Contact cement
Degreasing agent
Drop cloths (preferably canvas)
Drywall screws
Duct tape
Electrical tape
Foam pipe insulation
Hanger wires
Head mounted flashlight
Lacquer thinner

Table 2.5 Bathroom Installation Tools and Equipment (*Continued*)

Masking tape
Mild nonabrasive cleaning products
Mineral spirits
Molly bolts and toggle bolts
Nails and brads
Penetrating oil
Pipe-thread tape
Plumber's putty
Plumber's tape (steel strapping with holes)
Polish and wax for wood finishes
Polyethylene sheets
Rags
Set of taps and dies
Silicone grease
Small wire brush
Solder and flux (lead-free wire solder)
Steel wool
String
Touchup paint and stain (from the cabinet and countertop manufacturer)
Vapor barriers
Wax for screws
Wood filler putty (various colors)
Wood screws
Wood shims

*Drills with keyless chucks are time savers.
†Most hand tools available in electric models are also available in air-tool models.
‡Ground-fault insulation.

Equipment and tools brought into the home should be organized and well maintained. No matter how carefully you use and maintain your tools, they will eventually wear out. Invest in top-grade tools made by reputable manufacturers. A quality tool always carries a full warranty. Be sure to check for this feature when you purchase them.

Basic Principles of Bathroom Design

"Form follows function," our great designers tell us. Certainly nothing could be more true than when planning a new or remodeled bathroom. While everyone wishes for a bathroom to be beautiful, they also want it to be efficient. No matter how beautiful it is, if it is not functional, it is not good. When a bathroom looks great and functions smoothly, you can be sure that hours of planning went into its realization (Fig. 3.1). Behind those shiny new fixtures and tiles are codes and clearances, critical dimensions, and effective design principles that when effectively used will not be given a second thought by its user.

To be functional, the bathroom plan for either a new or a remodeled house must take into consideration the location within the home, size and shape, and arrangement of the equipment and fixtures of the bathroom. The bathroom installer, who seldom is directly involved in the design process, will become aware of the importance of thoroughly thought-out design, by the lack of problems. Be prepared because the design phase of a successful bathroom remodel has been known to take at least as long as the construction phase. This chapter gives the installer an overview of the basics for bathroom design.

Bathroom remodeling can be as simple as replacing an old-style lavatory with a new vanity unit or as complex as an addition with a

FIGURE 3.1

Old-fashioned elegance and modern amenities make this a beautiful and functional bathroom design. *(American Standard.)*

garden bath or a full health center with sauna, whirlpool, and exercise gear. Regardless of how ambitious the project, remember not to let the current bath inhibit the planning; bathrooms are no longer the minimal, utilitarian, limited spaces they once were. True, a bathroom's function is much the same today as it was more than half a century ago, and the basic equipment has not changed a great deal (Figs. 3.2 and

Fig. 3.3). What has happened is that the bathroom has now become an aesthetically pleasing room as well as a functional one.

A bathroom reflects good bathroom design insofar as it fills the needs and desires of the people who live in it (Fig. 3.4). The bathroom arrangement must be right for the house, which, in turn, must be right for the family who lives there. Thus, have your client begin overall planning by considering all the ways the bath area will be used. The family bathroom, in particular, deserves careful study. The changing lifestyles of today's families call for new approaches to bathroom design (Fig. 3.5). Many bathrooms may need to accommodate an increase in usage (e.g., two adults) during the morning. These new demands mean new design approaches, for example, separate tubs and showers, double lavatories, whirlpools,

FIGURE 3.2

Bathroom designs of the past, with an ode to the Roman debauchery, with pillars and statues, lilypads, and psychedelic art. *(American Standard.)*

steam compartments, and separate dressing rooms. The answers to the questionnaire in Chap. 2 (Table 2.1) will help to determine the size, location, and arrangement of the bathroom—apply the customer's likes and dislikes to an appropriate design. In addition, have them dream up exactly what they would do if they could do anything to the bathroom, with cost as no object. This way, at the beginning, you can get an accurate idea of what they absolutely love and then scale it down later. The

more thorough and specific your client can be from the beginning, the more satisfying the final results will be. A sudden increase in household population can't exactly be dealt with by using one of those portable toilet rentals you see on construction sites.

Basic Bathroom Layouts

Of course, a new home affords full opportunity for planning the selection and arrangement of plumbing fixtures to meet

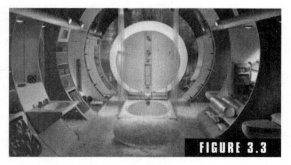

FIGURE 3.3

Who knows what trends will return to our bathrooms—as seen here, a sci-fi spaceship-to-Venus look. *(American Standard.)*

FIGURE 3.4

A modern approach to a bathroom that obviously fits the needs of the people who live there. *(American Standard.)*

individual requirements. Usually it is just a question of placing the fixtures in the most convenient arrangement in the space available. The remodeling of a bathroom, however, brings up the question of how to first utilize existing plumbing without many costly changes. A floor plan should be selected that will make use of the present soil pipes, vent stack, and water-supply lines, if possible. In any case, the planning of a bathroom should take into consideration the availability of the plumbing connections and the requirements of all local building codes. If you are adding on to the house, try to locate the new bathroom near an existing bathroom or the kitchen. Zoning codes also restrict position on a lot such as distance to property lines, and some developments may also have certain restrictions that may affect design.

Although it is possible to have an almost infinite number of arrangements and combinations of fixtures for bathrooms, the most commonly used and generally the most efficient types of bathrooms are discussed here. The arrangement used depends on the size and shape of the area allocated for the bathroom; the location of windows, doors, and services (plumbing, electricity, etc.); and the proximity of the bathroom to the home's other rooms.

When remodeling an old bathroom, there is usually a limit to work within the existing area, although it is sometimes possible to expand the room by moving a wall or rearranging the existing space to obtain a more workable plan.

There are, of course, many variations to these basic bathroom and fixture arrangements. By fixture count, the three basic bath options are half baths (powder rooms), three-quarter baths, and full baths. Help your homeowners decide which layout describes the bathroom best for them in their bathroom design.

The Half Bath or Powder Room

A *half bath,* also often referred to as a *powder room* or *guest bath,* is typically a two-fixture room containing a lavatory and toilet, along with some limited storage space (Fig. 3.6*a*). A half bath can fit into a

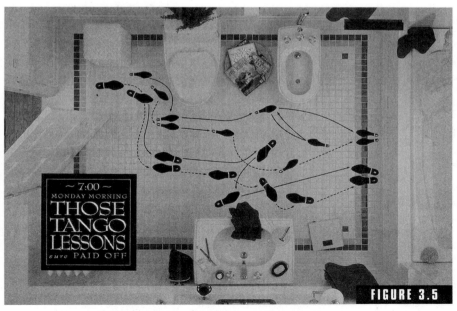

A fabulous approach to bathroom design. *(American Standard.)*

very small space and serve as an efficient addition, especially if the homeowner is unable to find room for a full bath. Typically, a half bath is located on the home's main level, close to the main living areas (often located off the foyer), so it can also serve as a facility for guests. A powder room can be placed almost anywhere in a new home, with consideration given to privacy; for example, it may be wedged under stairs, in the attic, placed in an entry hall (open off a hallway—not directly into a living, family, or dining room), a bedroom hall, or a utility area. The most important point to remember is to place a half bath in the most accessible, most functional spot for the homeowner. The half bath can provide backup for the main bath while providing a solution to morning arguments over who gets to wash up first. Keep the entry door in mind; its placement should allow some privacy.

Half baths require a minimum of 18 sq ft; however, common half-bath dimensions for them vary: 4 × 5 feet or 3 × 7 feet are the more common dimensions, but a half bath can be installed in even smaller spaces, for instance, as small as 3 × 3, 3 × 6, or 4^{1}/2 × 4^{1}/2 feet and still work effectively. Fixtures can be placed side by side, on adjacent or on opposite walls, depending, of course, on the shape of the room.

If planning a half bath in a very small area, consider using fixtures that are adapted for use in small spaces. Very small lavatories are available for tight spaces. Toilets are also available in small sizes; however, installation of a full-sized toilet is still recommended.

Because half baths have less humidity than other bathrooms, just about any finish flooring is appropriate, including wood, tile, vinyl, carpet, terra cotta, and stone. The half bath also provides a good place to take advantage of more decorative but perhaps less durable finishes, such as a copper basin. This is an excellent room for taking a unique independent style and approach.

Three-Quarter Bath

A three-quarter bath is equipped with a shower stall instead of a tub (Fig. 3.6*b*). If the family prefers showering to bathing, this style of bathroom will be a benefit. A

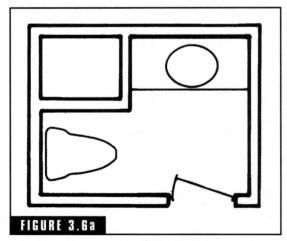

FIGURE 3.6a

Typical half bath design. *(Leon E. Korejwo, Illustrations.)*

three-quarter bath requires 30 sq ft minimum. Overall, this type of bath can be an excellent second bathroom and backup to the main family bath; it will help to minimize morning traffic jams.

Full Bath

A full bathroom is typically equipped with three fixtures: a lavatory, toilet, and a bathtub or shower or combination tub-shower (Fig.3.6c). The most common sizes for a full bathroom are a 5 × 7-foot or 5 × 8 space; 5 × 7 feet is the minimum size needed to accommodate this number of fixtures. The fixture arrangement varies, depending on the size and shape of the room. In most cases, the full bath is located close to the bedrooms; it shouldn't be located directly at the head of the stairs on the second floor, where it may be easily visible from the lower front entrance hall or living room. For more privacy, move the door a few feet away. The family bath is one of the most frequently used rooms in the house. Therefore, assisting your client in choosing durable, easy-to-clean fixtures and finishes is where experience counts.

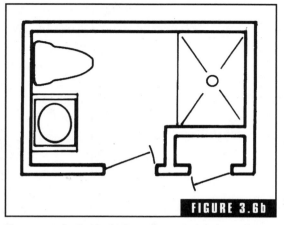

Three-quarter-bath design. *(Leon E. Korejwo, Illustrations.)*

COMPARTMENTALIZING

Compartmented baths are popular—the addition of one or two fixtures, and the multiple use of others, adds convenience and flexibility. In remodeling, a compartmented bath often makes the best use of space, particularly if a large area is being converted into a bathroom. That is, compartmenting can go a long way toward easing the bathroom traffic; it enables several family members to use the bathroom at the same time. The basic idea is to separate functional areas so that one person does not enter the bathroom, close the door, and tie up everything.

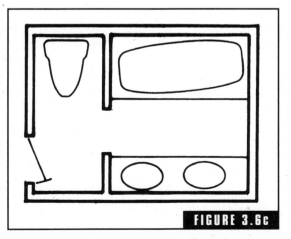

Full-bath design. *(Leon E. Korejwo, Illustrations.)*

A compartmented bathroom allows others to use the facilities not being used by the person who got there first. Minimal compartmenting, almost a must in a one-bathroom house, amounts to separating the toilet from the bath and grooming area. Various kinds of practical and attractive dividers, from opaque glass to louvered doors, can be used for this purpose. Enclosing the tub area with a sliding glass door, for example, can double the function of a bathroom without taking up an inch of extra space.

Additional types of bathrooms for your client to consider are master baths, luxury baths, barrier-free baths, and bathrooms for children. For more on these types of bathrooms, see Chap. 4. Keep in mind that many different floor plans are possible and these layouts can be combined, adapted, and expanded depending on the homeowner's particular wants, needs, and budget.

Location of Bath

One of the most important considerations for the new bath is the location (Fig. 3.7). Legal restrictions, as well as budget, can affect how and where a new bathroom is located, but the house itself is, in most cases, the largest determining factor. Most families wish they had two things: more and bigger bathrooms. There are space-saving tricks for both purposes. Therefore, once you and your client decide on the kind and number of bath areas needed, the next step is to consider the best possible location for each ideally. The new bathroom can be located almost anywhere in the house, but keep in mind that drainpipe runs and privacy are primary considerations.

1. *In the basement.* The bathroom can be anywhere in the basement as long as the main house drain is lower than the basement floor, or the headroom of the basement is sufficient to permit the bathroom floor to be at a level above the house drain. In new construction, drains can be run before concrete floor is poured. With remodels, the floor may need to be jack hammered open.

2. *First-floor level.* The bathroom may be located anywhere on the first floor, as long as the bathroom drains can be sloped downward to the main drain. Drains may run under joists, but headroom or codes may be factors.

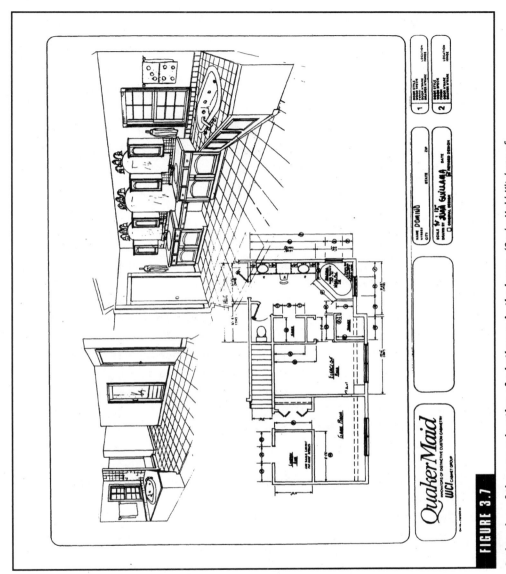

FIGURE 3.7

A plan view of the proper location of a bathroom in the home. *(QuakerMaid Kitchens of Reading, Inc.)*

3. *Upper or attic floors.* The only restriction here is that the planned bathroom's soil pipe should not run across joists to reach the main drain. Typically, there is no existing plumbing in the attic. For an attic expansion, place the new bath above existing plumbing (the new wall to contain plumbing should be directly above the existing plumbing wall).

When the location of a new bathroom is planned, it is important to keep it as close to other plumbing facilities in the home as possible. In this way, a great deal of pipe and labor can be saved. Thus, when locating the new bathroom, keep in mind the following money saving tips:

1. Locate the new bathroom next to an existing bathroom, kitchen, or laundry area. In fact, if at all possible, the fixtures should be located back to back with those on the other side of the wall. Doing this will mean that only very short lengths of pipe are necessary to connect into the old drain and supply lines. A new bath that is far from any existing plumbing may require considerable cutting and patching of the walls, and costly work on stack and supply pipes (especially if your client's home rests on a concrete slab foundation).

2. Arrange the new bathroom over or under the existing bath, laundry room, or kitchen with its plumbing. In cases where the new fixtures cannot be located with connections directly into simple extensions of old pipes, any over or under setup will reduce piping costs and work.

3. Do not rule out the possibility of using a bathroom within the building and not adjacent to an outside wall. Most building codes no longer require a window as long as the bathroom has a ventilating fan. Therefore, if carpentry and piping costs are reduced substantially by locating the new bathroom in the center of the home, it may be a wise choice to do so. It is never a wise decision to install the bathroom in an area where extensive remodeling is required. The expense of tearing out and putting up walls, changing windows and doors, plus other alterations, is usually higher than the cost of running pipes to an area not served by pipe.

Plumbing Layouts

The more facts you have available, the easier it will be to work with your layouts. As stated earlier, you will keep costs down if you select a layout that uses the existing water supply, drain lines, and vent stack. It is also more economical to arrange fixtures against one or two walls, eliminating the need for additional plumbing lines. Generally, you can locate side-by-side fixtures closer together than fixtures positioned opposite each other.

You and your client will probably experiment with several layouts before determining the best overall plan. Most likely, compromises will need to be made somewhere. If all priorities are identified clearly, it should be easy to choose the best solution.

One-Wall Layout

This may be a one-wall or a one–"wet wall" layout. A bathroom with all the plumbing located in a row, arranged along a single wall, is the simplest bathroom design for a limited space (Fig. 3.8a). This design requires the least amount of changes to the house structure and uses the fewest plumbing fittings. Although the one-wall layout is efficient in many ways, keep in mind that floor space is not always used the most efficiently and the design possibilities are limited.

FIGURE 3.8a

A one-wall bathroom layout. *(American Standard.)*

FIGURE 3.8b

A two-wall bathroom layout. *(American Standard.)*

Two-Wall Layout

A bathroom with all the plumbing located within two adjoining walls provides more floor and storage space around the lavatory than a one-wall bathroom layout (Fig. 3.8b). This design requires slightly more complicated plumbing work, generally requiring more cutting of studs and joists to accommodate the pipes, than the one-wall design. Run the horizontal parallel to joists rather than through the walls to minimize cutting vertical wall studs or penetration of joists.

Three-Wall Layout

A bathroom with all the plumbing located along three walls offers the greatest design flexibility and provides the largest wall and counter spaces of all the three basic bathroom plans. This bathroom design is more expensive because it requires room area and more complex plumbing systems. The room must be at least $5\frac{1}{2}$ feet × 7 feet 2 inches to accommodate the minimum clearances required between fixtures; therefore, three-wall bathrooms are usually set up in larger rooms—at least 7 feet 8 inches × 6 feet.

With these location limitation factors in mind, once again review the user's living pattern (see Table 2.1). Determine the preferred location for the bath from the standpoint of use; then decide where it can be installed most easily.

Guidelines for Bathroom Planning

Knowing what fixture clearances to use is extremely important when planning the bathroom. Every bathroom fixture needs free space around it to allow adequate room for use, cleaning, and repair. At the same time, the layout of the bathroom is influenced by the location of existing plumbing or the routes of new pipes. Being able to plan and position the fixtures to meet both requirements calls for some experience. Minimum required clearances around fixtures are mandated by most community building codes. Be sure to check your area's code if adding or moving fixtures or building a new bathroom. If not, let comfort be your guide, and place fixtures so that you can easily move and clean around them, always remembering, of course, that their layout will be influenced by the location of existing plumbing or new plumbing runs.

To summarize the important points of design, the National Kitchen and Bath Association has developed standards based on extensive research conducted, known as the "41 Guidelines for Bathroom Planning." Our society is growing more diverse, and this requires the guidelines to constantly be revised. It requires also that they remain constantly under scrutiny for further changes in our population and the living habits of the various population segments. These revisions more fully incorporate universal design as clarified by the *Uniform Federal Accessibility Standards* (UFAS) and the *American National Standard for Accessible and Usable Buildings and Facilities* (ANSI A117.1-1992). The dimensions included in these NKBA guidelines are based in ANSI and UFAS, but they are not intended to replace them.

If a particular project is subject to local, state, or national laws or codes, the designer must comply with those requirements. These guidelines are intended to be useful design standards, supplemental to the applicable codes—not hard-and-fast rules, but guidelines, that will help in planning bathrooms that are functional and flexible, or universal, to better meet the needs of today's varied lifestyles. Keep in mind that minimum clearances may mean minimal comfort, exceed the figures if at all possible.

NKBA's "41 Guidelines for Bathroom Planning" are as follows:

Clear Floor Spaces & Door Openings

1. (a) The clear space at doorways should be at least 32" (81 cm) wide and not more than 24" (61 cm) deep in the direction of travel.
   (b) The clear space at a doorway must be measured at the narrowest point.
   (c) Walkways (passages between vertical objects greater than 24" (61 cm) deep in the direction of travel) should be a minimum of 36" (91 cm) wide.

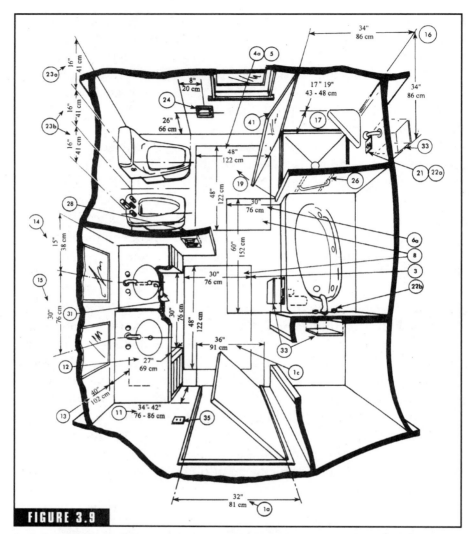

FIGURE 3.9

Encircled numbers represent the suggested NKBA bathroom planning guidelines as have been applied to areas of this particular bathroom design. (This drawing is an artistic interpretation and is not meant to be an exact rendition.) *(Leon E. Korejwo, Illustrations.)*

2. A clear floor space at least the width of the door on the push side and a larger clear floor space on the pull side should be planned at doors for maneuvering to open, close, and pass through the doorway. The exact amount needed will depend on the type of door and the approach.

3. A minimum clear floor space of 30″ × 48″ (76 cm × 122 cm) either parallel or perpendicular should be provided at the lavatory.

4. (a) A minimum clear floor space of 48″ × 48″ (122 cm × 122 cm) should be provided in front of the toilet. A minimum of 16″ (41 cm) of that clear floor space must extend to each side of the centerline of the fixture.

   (b) Up to 12″ (30 cm) of the 48″ × 48″ (122 cm × 122 cm) clear floor space can extend under the lavatory when total access to a knee space is provided.

5. A minimum clear floor space of 48″ × 48″ (122 cm × 122 cm) from the front of the bidet should be provided.

6. (a) The minimum clear floor space at a bathtub is 60″ (152 cm) wide by 30″ (76 cm) deep for a parallel approach, even with the length of the tub.

   (b) The minimum clear floor space at a bath tub is 60″ (152 cm) wide × 48″ (122 cm) deep for a perpendicular approach.

7. The minimum clear floor space at showers less than 60″ (152 cm) wide should be 36″ (91 cm) deep by the width of the shower plus 12″ (30 cm). The 12″ (30 cm) should extend beyond the seat wall. At a shower that is 60″ (152 cm) wide or greater, clear floor space should be 36″ (91 cm) deep by the width of the shower.

8. Clear floor spaces required at each fixture may overlap.

9. Space for turning (mobility aids) 180° should be planned in the bathroom. A minimum diameter of 60″ (152 cm) for 360° turns and/or a minimum T-turn space of 36″ (91 cm) × 36″ (91 cm) × 60″ (152 cm).

10. A minimum clear floor space of 30″ × 48″ (76 cm–122 cm) is required beyond the door swing in a bathroom.

Lavatories

11. When more than one vanity is included, one may be 30″–34″ (76 cm–86 cm) high and another at 34″–42″ (86 cm–107 cm) high. Vanity height should fit the user(s).

12. Kneespace (which may be open or adaptable) should be provided at a lavatory. The kneespace should be a minimum of 27″ (69 cm) above the floor at the front edge, decreasing progressively

as the depth increases, and the recommended width is a minimum of 30″ (76 cm) wide.

13. The bottom edge of the mirror over the lavatory should be a maximum of 40″ (102 cm) above the floor or a maximum of 48″ (122 cm) above the floor if it is tilted.

14. The minimum clearance from the centerline of the lavatory to any side wall is 15″ (38 cm).

15. The minimum clearance between two bowls in the lavatory center is 30″ (76 cm), centerline to centerline.

Showers and Bathtubs

16. In an enclosed shower, the minimum usable interior dimensions are 34″ (86 cm) × 34″ (86 cm). These dimensions are measured from wall to wall. Grab bars, controls, movable and folding seats do not diminish the measurement.

17. Showers should include a bench or seat that is 17–19″ (43 cm–48 cm) above the floor and a minimum of 15″ (38 cm) deep.

18. The width of the door opening must take into consideration the interior space in the shower for entry and maneuvering. When the shower is 60″ (152 cm) deep, a person can enter straight into the shower and turn after entry, therefore 32″ (81 cm) is adequate. If the shower is 42″ (107 cm) deep, the entry must be increased to 36″ (91 cm) in order to allow for turning space.

19. Shower doors must open into the bathroom.

20. Steps should not be planned at the tub or shower area. Safety rails should be installed to facilitate transfer to and from the fixture.

21. All showerheads should be equipped with pressure balance/temperature regulator or temperature limiting device.

22. (a) Shower controls should be accessible from inside and outside the fixture. Shower controls should be located between 38″–48″ (96 cm–122 cm) above the floor (placed above the grab bar) and offset toward the room.

    (b) Tub controls should be accessible from inside and outside the fixture. Controls should be located between the rim of the tub and 33″ (84 cm) above the floor, placed below the grab bar and offset toward the room.

Toilets and Bidets

23. (a) A minimum 16″ (41 cm) clearance should be allowed from the centerline of the toilet or bidet to any obstruction, fixture, or equipment (except grab bars) on either side.

(b) When the toilet and bidet are planned adjacent to one another, the 16″ minimum (41 cm) centerline clearance to all obstructions should be maintained.

24. The toilet paper holder should be installed within reach of a person seated on the toilet. Ideal location is slightly in front of the edge of the toilet bowl, centered at 26″ (66 cm) above the floor.

25. Compartmental toilet areas should be a minimum 36″ (91 cm) × 66″ (168 cm) with a swing-out door or a pocket door.

Grab Bars, Storage, and Flooring

26. Walls should be prepared (reinforced) to receive grab bars at the time of construction. Grab bars should also be installed in the bath tub, shower, and toilet areas at the time of construction.

27. Storage for toiletries, linens, grooming, and general bathroom supplies should be provided within 15″–48″ (38 cm–122 cm) above the floor.

28. Storage for soap, towels, and other personal hygiene items should be installed within reach of a person seated on the bidet or toilet and within 15″–48″ (38 cm–122 cm) above the floor. Storage areas should not interfere with the use of the fixture.

29. In the tub/shower area, storage for soap and other personal hygiene items should be provided within the 15″–48″ (38 cm–122 cm) above the floor within the universal reach range.

30. All flooring should be slip resistant.

Controls and Mechanical Systems

31. Exposed pipes and mechanicals should be covered by a protective panel or shroud. When using a console table, care must be given to keep plumbing attractive and out of contact with a seated user.

32. Controls, dispensers, outlets, and operating mechanisms should be 15″–48″ (38 cm–122 cm) above the floor and should be operable with a closed fist.

33. All mechanical, electrical, and plumbing systems should have access panels.

34. Mechanical ventilation systems to the outside should be included in the plan to vent the entire room. The minimum size of the system can be calculated [where L = length, W = width, H = height] as follows:

$$\frac{\text{Cubic space } (L \times W \times H) \times 8 \text{ (changes of air per hour)}}{60 \text{ minutes}} =$$

minimum cubic feet per minute (CFM)

35. Ground fault circuit interrupters must be specified on all receptacles, lights, and switches in the bathroom. All light fixtures above the bathtub/shower units must be moisture-proof special-purpose fixtures.

36. In addition to a primary heat source, auxiliary heating may be planned in the bathroom.

37. Every functional area in the bathroom should be well illuminated by appropriate task lighting, night lights, and/or general lighting. No lighting fixture, including hanging fixtures, should be within reach of a person seated or standing in the tub/shower area.

38. When possible, bathroom lighting should include a window/sky-light area equal to a minimum of 10% of the square footage of the bathroom.

39. Controls, handles, and door/drawer pulls should be operable with one hand, require only a minimal amount of strength for operation, and should not require tight grasping, pinching, or twisting of the wrist. (Includes handles knobs/pulls on entry and exit doors, cabinets, drawers, and plumbing fixtures, as well as light and thermostat controls/switches, intercoms, and other room controls.)

40. Use clipped or radius corners for open countertops; countertop edges should be eased to eliminate sharp edges.

41. Any glass used as a tub/shower enclosure, partition, or other glass application within 18″ (46 cm) of the floor should be one of the three kinds of safety glazing; laminated glass with a plastic interlayer, tempered glass, or approved plastics such as those found in the model safety glazing code.

Fixture Arrangements

The bathroom, like the kitchen, is a room in which the furniture is permanently installed, so considerable attention should be given as to what fixtures are placed in the room's natural focal points and in sight lines from adjoining rooms. The fixtures are what makes bathrooms different from other rooms in the house, so your planning should revolve around them. By now, you probably have a pretty good idea of what fixtures are wanted. To serve the desired goals effectively, the fixtures will have to be located efficiently with respect to one another and with enough space in and around them to make them convenient to use. But the fixtures themselves are only part of the picture. The part you don't see is the network of hot- and cold-water-supply piping and waste piping. Unless you are ready to gut the entire room and completely rework the piping (sometimes the best tack), keep a few guidelines in mind for economical fixture locations. Keep as many fixtures as possible on the original wall. When placing fixtures in the bathroom layout, think about the order in which they are used and the manner of that usage. For example, in the morning, which fixture is first to be used?

To begin preparation for the layout, position the largest unit, the bathtub or shower, within the floor plan, allowing space for convenient access, for plumbing repair, cleaning, and so on. The best position is along a wall or in a corner because the floor joists ordinarily need extra support to handle the weight. Examine the support walls on the floor below. Position the foot of the tub against a wall that can be opened from the other side for when plumbing repairs are necessary.

The lavatory can be placed next. Because it is the most frequently used fixture in the bathroom, it should be placed out of the traffic pattern and away from the tub and toilet, making sure that there is enough space around it for storage. Be sure to allow ample room in front for reaching below the lavatory, and give plenty of elbow room at the sides. A good location for the lavatory is positioned closest to the door, because it is the last stop in most bathroom routines. A lavatory is the easiest and least costly fixture to move. It can be moved a few inches from its present position with only minor plumbing changes. Existing supply and drain lines can usually support a second lavatory, and existing supply and drain lines can be extended if the distance from the vent is less than the maximum distance allowed by local codes. If not, a secondary vent will need to be installed, which can be quite a job.

The toilet is the most expensive of all fixtures to be located, because of its large waste pipe, and it requires the most drain work. In a room with an existing soil stack or one in which a new stack must be located in a particular area, position the toilet first—it must be near the stack. Locate the toilet and bidet (usually positioned next to each other) away from the door. The toilet is often located next to the tub or shower. Keep in mind the swing radius for windows and doors. For convenience, also try to position it next to a wall; otherwise, its drain must drop beneath the ceiling below. When expense is an issue (of which it usually is), install the new toilet in the old location. Consider enclosing the toilet, away from other fixtures, in a separate compartment for greater privacy.

When planning and locating a bathroom you should have the client determine the mood or feeling to be created in the bathroom. Do they prefer a setting that is traditional or contemporary, formal or informal, French provincial or Mediterranean? It does not really matter what they choose. What is important is that they be consistent. Nothing could be prettier, for instance, than a warm French provincial bathroom in a French provincial home, on the other hand, an extremely contemporary bathroom in an authentically styled and decorated colonial house is something of a jolt.

There are so many variations in bathroom categories and styles that it is impossible to cover all the possibilities in this book. When you consider that a bathroom can be luxurious or economical, elegant or utilitarian, masculine or feminine, colorful or subtle, conservative or modern, it becomes apparent that only the cost, the homeowner's personal preferences, the number of individuals in the family, and the use planned for the bath facility affect the final design of the bathroom. Actually, the word *bathroom* may be a misnomer; the homeowner may really be planning a cosmetic center, a mud room, an exercise and health center, a utility room to serve a family swimming pool, a master bathroom, a facility for several youngsters, or a guest powder room; the list is endless. No bathroom can be all these things, so the first thing to do when planning the bath is to consider its prime purpose and the people who will be using it. Next, consider how to decorate it and put more living room into it for them.

Developing a Design from Concept to Plans

The final step in planning a bathroom is making the plan or blueprint. First make a rough sketch of the room, usually on a grid or graph paper. Not all bathroom builders are responsible for preparing bathroom plans. However, all need to be able to read and understand them. If you are not responsible for the initial field measurements, be certain to verify any dimensions given to you before starting the project. Even if the original house plans for a remodeling project are still available, it is best for you to physically take measurements and check the room conditions. Changes in floor and wall levels may have taken place, and there may have been revisions that were not recorded on the plans. The verification of existing measurements and conditions in the bathroom is crucial to the success of the installation project. For an excellent visual record of a bathroom layout, use a videocamera.

Measuring the Bathroom

To take a room's rough dimensions, a folding wood carpenter's rule is more accurate and easier to handle than a retractable tape measure. A tape requires someone to hold one end to keep it taut. It is, however, handier for taking full-length room dimensions. A clipboard with an 8 × 10-inch (20 × 25) quadrille pad, pencil with an eraser end, a red pencil for special notations, and a 6-inch (15-cm) architect's ruler are needed for recording the plan and dimensions. Also, a carpenter's level and a large steel square may be needed. If your budget allows, look into a laser device used to measure rooms.

The first step in making the rough sketch is to measure the room. Start at any corner above the counters at a comfortable height, measure the room, and mark all dimensions in a rough sketch. Take the overall width and length dimensions of the room, and draw its outline on the quadrille pad, using the blue lines as a guide. It is not necessary to do the drawing in scale at this time. Just approximate the location of doors and windows. If the dimensions are going to be turned over to a drafter, redraw the sketch at the office, if there is any doubt that it is understandable. For accuracy, measure and show on your drawing all dimensions in inches or fractions of inches, never a mixture of feet and inches. Remember that accuracy and correct information helps you, the manufacturer, and the client save time and money. When using a calculator, the fractions must be converted to decimals of an inch. A conversion chart is handy.

After placing the room outline on the paper, take detailed measurements. Place the rule against the wall at a height of about 36 inches (91 cm). Begin at one corner and measure to the nearest door or window. Measure to the edge of the trim. Mark off this distance on the outline and also note the exact inches and fractions between arrow points as in the sketch. Also measure and note width of the trim and check the possibility, if needed, for cutting down the trim.

Next, measure the width of the door or window, including casing or trim. Mark off this distance on the outline, and note the distance between arrow points. Note on the sketch the swing of each door, and label them to show where they lead—such as to the hall, another bathroom, or outdoors. Proceed in this way around the room. Note all critical measurements and irregularities: chimneys, closets, radiators, or any other similar structures. When finished, add the detailed dimensions of each wall. Then take overall wall-to-wall dimensions. Make sure that these figures are equal.

Measure from floor to bottom of the window stool (the underside of the inside window sill). This measurement is essential to show if units can go beneath windows and also to determine the height of the backsplash. If there is not sufficient clearance under the stool, check and note the possibility of cutting it down, if necessary. If this is impossible, use a window notch in the backsplash. Also measure from bottom of the stool to the top of the window trim. Show these measurements in the space for the window.

Measure the height of the room from floor to ceiling. Enter this figure in a space below or to one side of the sketch. It is a good idea to take this measurement at two diagonally opposite points to see what allowance may have to be made for a floor that is out of level. This method won't indicate that the floor is out of level if the ceiling also slopes at the same angle. Therefore, as an added precaution, check that the floor is level.

Check also for any inequalities in the walls that must be considered in building the lavatory top or counter and in planning proper use of fillers. Check corners with a square and walls with a level. Measure in several spots in case the floor is uneven. Be sure to measure from the floor to the bottom of the window sill and from the top of the window trim to the ceiling. If there are discrepancies, be sure to record them for consideration when planning built-in cabinetry and counters.

It seldom happens this way, but in new construction the walls should be finished before you measure (sometimes this is referred to as *clear dimensions*). If you must measure before the interior is finished, measure the actual frame dimensions and add what the window and wall materials will be. Allow for the thickness, then add a little extra.

Show the size and location of heat, air-conditioning, and ventilating outlets, electrical and plumbing outlets, pipes, chimneys, or any other obstructions that cannot be changed and may affect the plan. If you are familiar with architectural symbols, use them. Otherwise, make careful notations and add the symbols when redrawing the plan at the office.

When taking the measurements, try to determine what is inside the walls—gas, electric, or water pipes; ductwork; plumbing stacks; and chimneys—by reference to blueprints, if available, or by careful examination of the area all around the bathroom. Thus, on remodeling jobs, it is necessary to check and take notes on the following:

1. Present drain location and distance from the plumbing stack or drain vent pipe

2. Air ducts concealed in walls, soil pipes, vent pipes, and water pipes

3. Exterior walls for construction type

4. Heating and location of ducts, radiators, pipes, and other components

5. Electrical system and size and type of service, condition of wires, and general condition

6. Any unusual situations

7. Which walls are bearing or nonbearing

8. Size and style of doors and windows to be used

On new construction, when finished dimensions are established, the bathroom planner is generally limited to the existing conditions, since any changes at this point would prove quite costly. In the case of a complete remodeling job, considerable latitude is usually allowed, and, consequently, more specific, detailed information is required. Remember, as stated numerous times throughout this book, that it is less expensive to plan around plumbing and heating systems and other obstructions than to relocate them.

Construction Drawing Sets

You may be working from a prepared set of plans, or you may be preparing them yourself. In either case, a clear knowledge of how to read and understand the bathroom plan or blueprints is vital to the installation project. The building industry has an established set of symbols and material indications that are used consistently on building plans. You need to become familiar with the symbols and standards in order to successfully use the building plans. Usually a list of the symbols and material indications, as well as any abbreviations (different kinds of switches, lights, appliances, etc.) used on the plans, can be found on the title page (first sheet of the building plan). Before trying to read a set of plans or before beginning any work, be sure that you understand the symbols being used on the drawings. Take the time to become fully acquainted with the work on the plans. Use a separate blank copy of the floor plan for each discipline, such as one for plumbing, one for electric, and one for HVAC, since each has its own symbols and contractor.

Few people are familiar with reading blueprints or plans; therefore, fully explain layouts, and other items to your clients, even if they are unable to read the plans. In almost all instances, your clients will ask you about the drawings, and therefore, you must be able to answer them. In addition, it is extremely important that everyone involved with the project be given a set of drawings to review before starting work. Have them review the entire set against the work they will be performing for any possible conflicts, for instance.

In many cases, plans of the project are required by the local building inspector or zoning officer before a permit is issued. A set of plans may be reviewed by the municipality to check for code compliance before issuing a building permit. The responsible party may be a zoning officer. If so, you must submit clear and complete drawings (in the instance of a remodeling project) of the existing floor plan as well as the new one. You may need to show areas adjacent to the bathroom to enable inspecting municipal officials to determine how the project will affect the rest of the house.

Drawing sets for bathroom projects with more limited scopes of work do not necessarily contain all these items. However, if your project requires a building permit, many of these sheets are required regardless of project size.

Residential building projects ranging from new-home construction to simple remodeling of an existing room are universally organized with drawings. The extent of a drawing or blueprint set is determined by municipal code compliance as well as the size and complexity of the job. A bathroom project for new-building construction is only one part of the full construction drawing set. The designer of a bathroom will need certain drawings before starting the design or proposal. The best way to demonstrate these drawings would be to discuss the largest project situation a builder must address. The reader may then decide what is needed for individual jobs as they occur. A well-developed set of plans provides you with all the information required to complete your installation work. It should generally include the following.

A building drawing set for complete new home construction includes

1. Title page
2. Site plan (prepared by surveyor or engineer)
3. Foundation plan (prepared by an architect, builder, or designer)
4. Floor plan (prepared by an architect, builder, or designer)
5. Elevations, interior and exterior (prepared by an architect, builder, or designer)
6. Structural framing plan (prepared by an architect or builder) (Fig.3.10)
7. Construction details and sections (prepared by an architect or builder; the bathroom drawing set is included here)
8. Mechanical plans (prepared by a subcontractor)
   a. Electrical (prepared by electrician or mechanical contractor)
   b. Plumbing (prepared by plumber or mechanical contractor)
   c. HVAC (prepared by an HVAC engineer or mechanical contractor)
9. Reflected ceiling plan (prepared by an architect, builder, or designer)

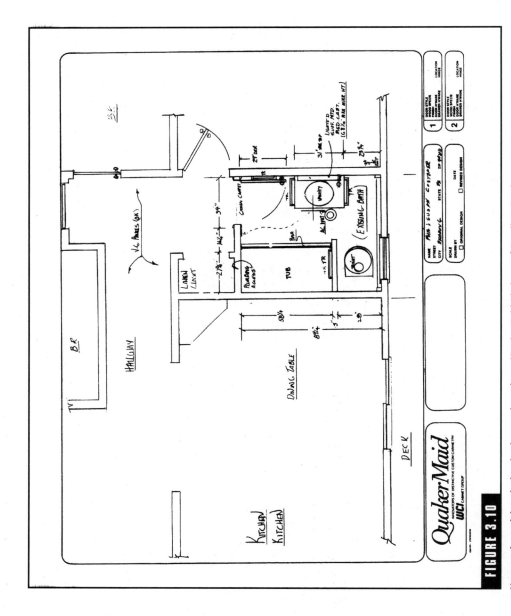

FIGURE 3.10

House plan with existing bathroom location. *(QuakerMaid Kitchens of Reading, Inc.)*

10. Specifications (prepared by an architect, builder, or designer)

A bathroom drawing set includes:

1. Title page with specifications (optional)

2. Bathroom floor plan (Fig. 3.11)

3. Bathroom soffit plan (include this drawing only if highly detailed soffit work is required)

4. Bathroom elevation drawings

5. Bathroom perspective drawings (Fig. 3.12)

6. Bathroom countertop plan

7. Bathroom mechanical drawings (locations of electrical outlets, switches, lighting, location, and size of fixtures, plumbing, location of drain and pipe connection, low voltage, intercom, video, and security system, etc.)

A bathroom drawing set can be prepared by the designer, supplier, or another specialist. The drawings listed above are an all-inclusive set for the full construction of a new residence. Remodeling may also require a demolition drawing, showing any walls, structure, or mechanical equipment to be removed before proceeding with new construction.

The bathroom designer's responsibilities may vary as to what information they provide. For each contract, as little as a floor plan may be adequate. But in some cases, a full set of design drawings may be agreed on, including bathroom floor plan, a bathroom mechanical plan (showing desired fixtures, lighting, receptacle and switch locations, with a legend for symbols and power requirements, and location of water and drainage plumbing), a bathroom soffit plan, and bathroom elevation drawings.

As reported by NKBA, by standardizing floor plans and presentation drawings, the remodeler

- Limits errors caused by misinterpreting the floor plans

- Avoids misreading dimensions, which can result in costly errors

- Prevents cluttering floor plans and drawings with secondary information, which often make the documents difficult to interpret

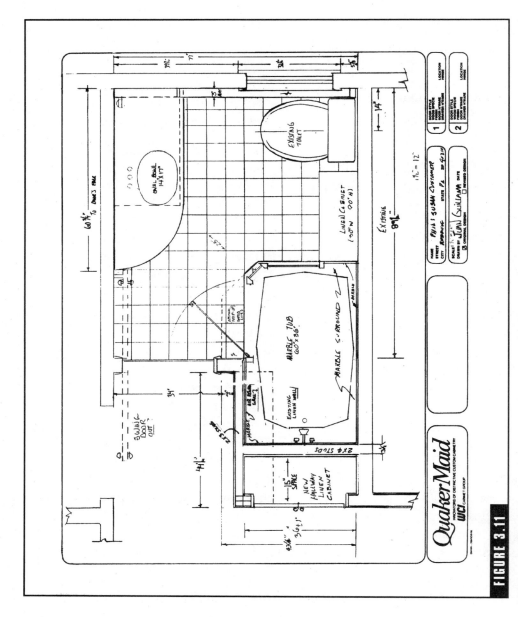

FIGURE 3.11

Bathroom floor plan. (QuakerMaid Kitchens of Reading, Inc.)

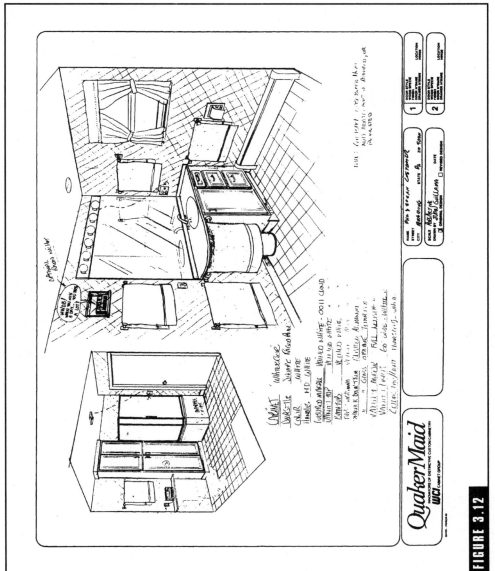

FIGURE 3.12

Bathroom perspective. *(QuakerMaid Kitchens of Reading, Inc.)*

- Creates a clear understanding of the scope of the project for all persons involved in the job
- Presents a professional image to the client
- Permits faster processing of orders
- Simplifies estimating and specification preparation
- Helps in the standardization of uniform nomenclature and symbols

TITLE PAGE

The first page in a building plan set is the *title page.* It may include some or all of the following: the client's name; the location of the project; the name of the building or project; names of consulting engineers, designers, architects, and other specialists; a key to the symbols for materials, appliances, and cabinet information; a list of abbreviations and acronyms; an index of the drawings contained in the whole building plan set; the number of sets distributed and to whom; a space for municipal approvals, one for each body responsible for review of plans; and local, planning commission, building inspector, county, or city stamps and signatures. The title page is optional, and, therefore, all this information may be included on the floor plan.

SITE PLAN (OR PLOT PLAN)

The *site plan* is an overhead view of the entire property around a building showing lot lines and layout of the land prior to construction. To the bathroom builder, one of the most important aspects of the site plan is the location of electric, water, sewer, gas services, and excavations. They are located by a surveyor with plotted points or dimensions and are subject to municipal approval if it is a new building or remodeling addition.

FOUNDATION PLAN

The *foundation plan* shows the extent of the building footings and foundations and generally describes how the building structure is attached to the foundation wall.

FLOOR PLAN

There are many types of floor plans, ranging from very simple sketches to completely dimensioned, detailed working drawings. A *floor plan* is drawn as if viewed from overhead, showing the outline and walls and partitions of a building as you would see them if the top of the house were cut off horizontally about 4 feet (121.9 cm) above the floor line. Most people can envision the home as if they were looking down into the rooms and walking through them.

Prepare the floor-plan layout of the bathroom to scale: either $3/8$ inch to the foot ($3/8$ inch = 1 foot 0 inches) or $1/2$ inch to the foot ($1/2$ inch = 1 foot 0 inches). Metric dimensions for floor plans should be drawn to a scale of 1 to 20 (i.e., 1 cm = 20 cm) to the foot. This plan is the central reference point for all the other construction drawings, and it is here that indications for details, sections, and schedules are referenced. The floor plan is usually the simplest of the drawings to read and understand. The rooms should be divided by "break lines" and should show all major structural elements (walls, door swings, door openings, windows, archways, stairs, equipment, partitions, etc.) with adjoining areas indicated and labeled. It is also helpful to note the direction of joists, mark any bearing walls, and sketch in other features that might affect the remodeling plans, although these structural details may be shown on a separate plan to avoid crowding too much on the floor plan. When possible, it should depict the entire room. When the entire room cannot be depicted, it must show the area where fixtures and cabinets are permanently installed. Indicate all measurements, obstructions, and peculiarities.

When the bathroom is designed, all fixtures, cabinets, and other equipment are drawn in place and labeled with proper nomenclature on the floor plan. Use a ruler or T-square to draw horizontal lines, a triangle to draw vertical lines and right angles to horizontal lines, and a compass for drawing the doors' directions of swing. Complete the floor plan using your sketch as a model. Drawing to scale will reveal many problems on the board, saving many hours on the site later. When scaled figures do not agree, recheck the field sketch for errors.

Review all original survey notes and the householder's desires. Lightly lay in the major fixture areas as per the basic layout. Lay in a dashed line (- - -) along the walls of the bathroom, 24 inches (61 cm) from the wall (remember that an unsquare room may lead to problems). This line indicates the base cabinet line, while countertops are depicted using a solid line. If the bathroom has wall cabinets, lightly lay a line 12 inches (30 cm) from the walls; this line indicates the area for the wall cabinets.

Lay out the perimeter of the bathroom from the measurements made on the rough sketch. Be sure to transfer measurements accurately, and include all the details noted while measuring the room. Try several room arrangements by drawing on tracing paper or by making cutouts from templates (when cutting out templates, include both the fixture and its required front and side clearances) and moving them around (Fig. 3.13a–d). A template is simply a pattern that's used as a guide to the arrangement of elements in a room; paper templates of fixtures and cabinets are an easy way to experiment with different layouts. As you experiment, keep in mind clearance requirements and what each scheme would entail in plumbing work. Figures 3.14, 3.15 and 3.16 show sample templates of fixtures and cabinets. With the use of a photocopy machine, they may be increased or reduced to match a specific scale. As noted, these are only generic. The dimensions of these fixture templates—3/8 inch-to-1-foot scale—are typical. Be sure for the final drawing, however, to consult specifications in the manufacturer's literature for cutout dimensions, required clearances, and exact size of fixtures and cabinets, with their indicated door swing, that will be used. Any fixtures that are presently in the bathroom and are going to be used in the new one should be measured accurately

Cabinet type, shape, and size are identified by the manufacturer code or nomenclature (see Chap. 6), for instance, W 24 36, which is written within that cabinet's drawn outline on the bathroom plan. Any molding, trim, or finishing pieces are called out adjacent to the cabinet on which they are to be attached; an arrow points to their location.

If the plan is elaborate, the clearest method is to designate an encircled number to each item and locate that number on the floor plan and elevation. The information would then be listed in a table located on the same drawing sheet or on another sheet entirely. The table would organize size, style, and pertinent information without cluttering the floor plan. This method also aids in gathering the ordering data for purchasing.

A floor plan does not show customers how the room really looks or how it would actually appear to them as they stand in it. For this effect, we add interpretive drawings that include elevations and perspective drawings. A *perspective drawing* shows a section or entire bathroom in perspective, from a viewpoint at eye level. You also might add sketches or other types of drawings to help the customer visualize

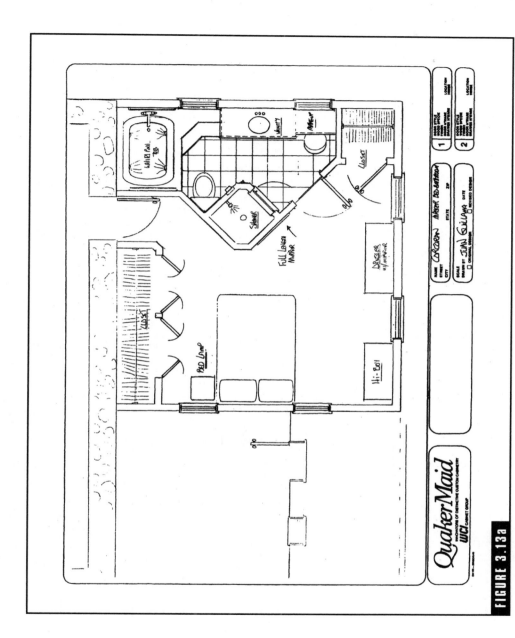

QuakerMaid
INNOVATORS OF DISTINCTIVE CUSTOM CABINETRY
WCI CABINET GROUP

FIGURE 3.13a

Rough sketch of the basic floor plan of a bathroom: four different ways of laying out a bathroom in basically the same area: **Plan 1.** *(QuakerMaid Kitchens of Reading, Inc.)*

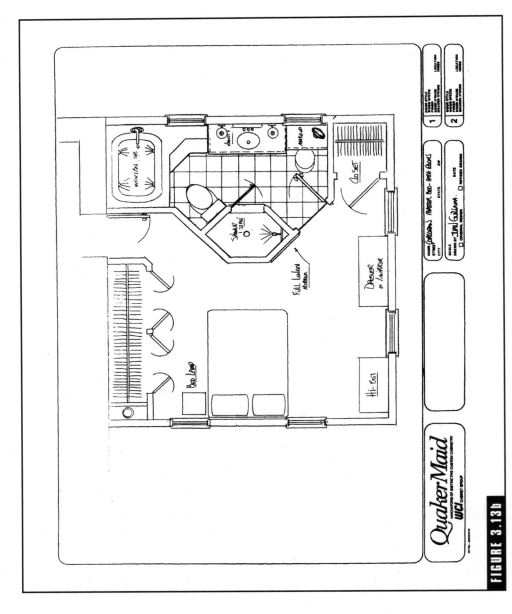

FIGURE 3.13b

Rough sketch of the basic floor plan of a bathroom: four different ways of laying out a bathroom in basically the same area: Plan 2. *(QuakerMaid Kitchens of Reading, Inc.)*

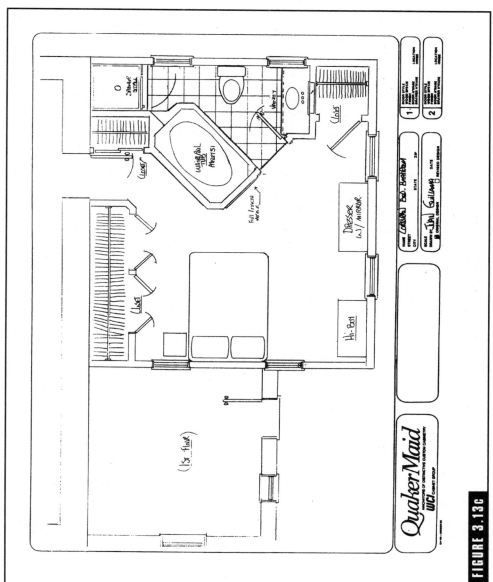

Rough sketch of the basic floor plan of a bathroom: four different ways of laying out a bathroom in basically the same area: Plan 3. (*QuakerMaid Kitchens of Reading, Inc.*)

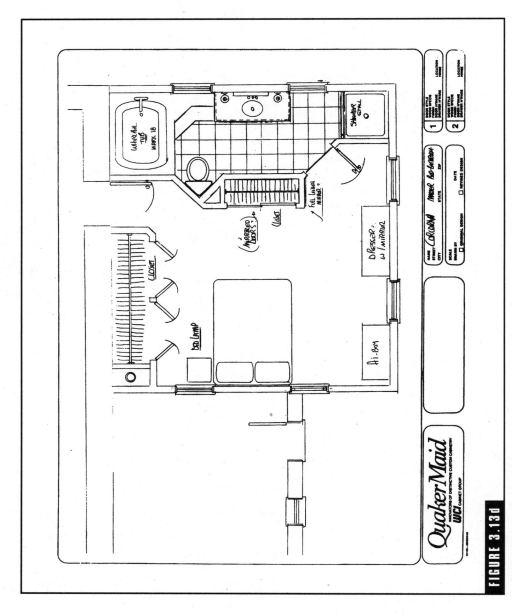

FIGURE 3.13d

Rough sketch of the basic floor plan of a bathroom: four different ways of laying out a bathroom in basically the same area: Plan 4. *(QuakerMaid Kitchens of Reading, Inc.)*

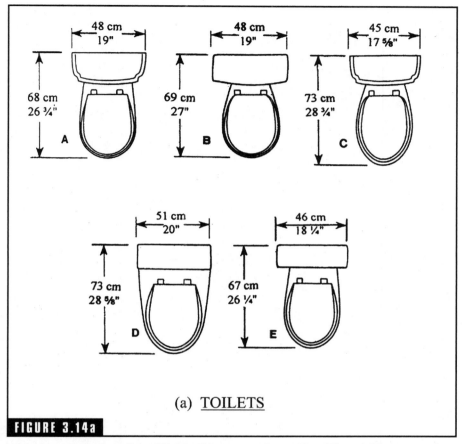

(a) TOILETS

FIGURE 3.14a

Typical templates for toilets: **(A)** round front two-piece toilet; **(B)** round front one-piece toilet; **(C)** elongated two-piece toilet; **(D)** elongated one-piece toilet; and **(E)** elongated space-saving, one-piece toilet.

the bathroom. Always draw to a consistent scale, and clearly include the dimensions of any feature and its location. Do not omit dimensions for others to guess or estimate. Someone else's interpretation may differ from yours. Prints or computer printouts are not always accurate enough to measure with a scale. If you have designed correctly, it saves others from wasting time recalculating.

SOFFIT PLAN

A soffit plan is not used very much today. However, if highly detailed soffit work is required, include this drawing. If soffits must be

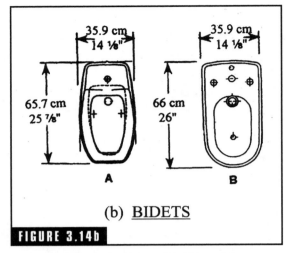

(b) BIDETS

FIGURE 3.14b

Typical templates for bidets: **(A)** bidet with an over-the-rim fitting with less flushing rim and spray, single hole; **(B)** bidet with deck-mounted fitting with flushing rim and vertical cleansing spray.

built before hanging wall cabinets, show side views and dimensions of cabinets at the walls. Interpretative or perspectives may also include this. Keep in mind any lights that are to be installed in the soffit.

CONSTRUCTION PLANS FOR REMODELING

When building remodeling projects, the floor plan or construction may encompass only the area of a home that is to be remodeled and those affected by the remodeling. The purpose of the construction plan is to show the relationship of the existing space with that of the new design. The construction plan is detailed separately so that is does not clutter the floor plan. However, if construction changes are minimal, it is acceptable to combine the construction plan with either the floor plan or the mechanical plan. Existing walls are shown with solid lines or hollowed-out lines at their full thickness. Wall sections to be removed are shown with an outline of broken lines. New walls show the material symbols applicable to the type of construction or use a symbol that is identified in the legend in order to distinguish the new walls from existing partitions.

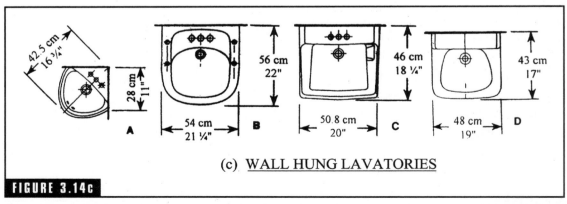

(c) WALL HUNG LAVATORIES

FIGURE 3.14c

Typical templates for wall-hung lavatories: **(A)** vitreous china wall-hung corner lavatory; **(B)** vitreous china wall-hung lavatory with recessed self-draining deck, which has a shroud knee contact guard and concealed arm support; **(C)** vitreous china wall-hung lavatory; **(D)** enamel cast-iron wall-hung lavatory.

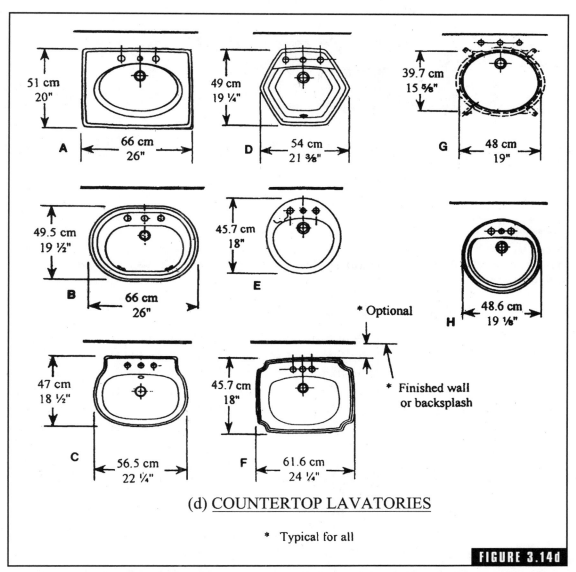

(d) COUNTERTOP LAVATORIES

* Typical for all

FIGURE 3.14d

Typical templates for countertop lavatories: **(A)** vitreous china self-rimming countertop lavatory; **(B)** vitreous china self-rimming countertop lavatory; **(C)** vitreous china self-rimming countertop lavatory; **(D)** vitreous china self-rimming hexagon-shaped countertop lavatory; **(E)** enamel cast-iron metal mounting frame countertop lavatory; **(F)** vitreous china self-rimming countertop lavatory; **(G)** vitreous china undercounter lavatory; **(H)** self-rimming linear round countertop lavatory.

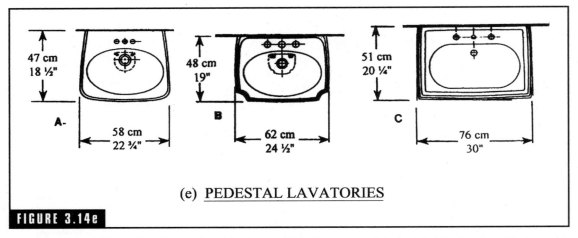

(e) <u>PEDESTAL LAVATORIES</u>

FIGURE 3.14e

Typical templates for pedestal lavatories: **(A)** vitreous china lavatory and pedestal; **(B)** vitreous china turn-of-the-century detailed lavatory and pedestal; **(C)** vitreous china lavatory with pedestal. *(American Standard/Leon E. Korejwo, Illustrations.)*

INTERPRETIVE DRAWINGS

Drawings (orthographic projection) and perspective renderings are considered *interpretive drawings.* They are used as an explanatory means of understanding the floor plans. The interpretive drawings should never be used as a substitute for floor plans. In case of dispute, the floor plans are the legally binding documents. Because perspective drawings are not drawn to scale, many bathroom specialists include a disclaimer on their rendering such as this:

This drawing is an artistic interpretation of the general appearance of the floor plan. It is not meant to be an exact rendition.

ELEVATION DRAWINGS

Elevation drawings help with the installation, making it easier to visualize what the finished bathroom will look like. These drawings can take the form of a front view of all wall areas receiving fixtures and cabinets as shown on the floor plan. Drawn to scale, these drawings also provide the designer with a problem-solving tool. Elevations should be designated on the floor plans with arrows in alphabetical order, leading from left to right. The elevation should then be drawn in the same order. According to NKBA, an elevation drawing should illustrate a front view of all cabinets, showing fixtures and equipment.

The following features are most effectively shown on elevations:

- Cabinets with toekick and finished height.

- A portion of the cabinet doors and drawer fronts indicating style and, when applicable, placement of handles or pulls.

- Countertops indicating thickness and showing backsplash. Also, note heights of the light fixtures, window trim, and any valances.

- All doors, windows, or other openings in walls that will receive equipment. The window/door casing or trim will be listed within the overall opening dimensions.

- All permanent fixtures, such as radiators.

- All main structural elements and protrusions, such as chimneys and partitions.

- Centerlines for all mechanical equipment.

PERSPECTIVE DRAWINGS

Designers have the option of preparing a one-point or two-point perspective, with or without the use of a grid (refer back to Fig. 3.12). The minimum requirements for perspectives shall be the reasonably correct representation of the longest cabinet or fixture run or the most important area in terms of usage. They need not show the entire bathroom. Separate sectional views of significant areas are acceptable.

Anyone can learn to draw reasonable perspective views even without previous art training. Systems have been worked out that are entirely mechanical. Only two requisites are needed: patience and practice. While one learns to draw floor plans and elevations, visualization (spatial thinking) should be practiced. In other words, while drawing layouts, constantly practice visualizing how the bathroom area and furnishing would look in three dimensions. This is called "seeing in the round." Perspectives are *not* drawn to scale, but proportion is the key to successful drawings.

PERSPECTIVE CHARTS

Two mechanical methods for drawing perspective views are available. Printed charts (often called *grids* or *screens*) are available at drafting supply houses or art stores. Practicing with a grid sheet helps.

The grid is divided for you, and the squares decrease proportionally as they get farther away from the viewer.

PROJECTION METHOD

One point perspective view is simpler than *two-point,* but if a room is long and narrow, the view tapers too much. The advantage of this method is that three walls can be shown. With *two-point* perspective, two or three views may be required, but the result is more photographic. With these methods, many variations are possible, just as if a camera were held high, low, or at one or the other end of the room.

MECHANICAL PLAN

The mechanical plan, usually found at the back of the plan set, consists of the electrical/lighting, plumbing, and HVAC systems. If any minor wall or door construction changes are part of the plan, they should also be detailed on the mechanical plan. Indicate where plumbing, gas, and electric lines enter the room and how they will reach the appliances. Also, mark the tentative locations of electrical outlets, switches, and lighting fixtures.

The various mechanical drawings can be difficult to understand. Each trade has its own subset of symbols, and these symbols are usually included as a part of the mechanical drawings. The mechanical legend should be prepared on the plan. This legend will be used to describe the meaning of each symbol for special-purpose outlets, fixtures, or equipment.

The mechanical plan should show an outline of the fixtures, cabinets, and countertops without cabinet nomenclature. It should include only the information and appropriate symbols for that item. The location of equipment should be noted. The overall room dimensions should be listed. Be sure to note the location of all lavatory plumbing (where they are and where you plan to relocate them). You must have a clear understanding of all mechanical work that affects your installation. You need to read features (e.g., heating supply vent located in the toespace of a base cabinet) on these drawings and coordinate for their installation, such as providing openings.

Centerline dimensions must be given for all equipment in two directions when possible. Mechanicals requiring centerlines include lavatories, fan units, light fixtures, heating and air-conditioning ducts, and radiators. Centerline dimensions should be pulled from return walls or from the face of cabinets or equipment opposite the mechanical element. Any differences from the plan that are discovered as a result of your installation work should be reported to the appropriate mechanical trade promptly for resolution. If a room is very irregular in shape, or walls are uneven, it is possible to locate the known centerline of the room and dimension from it.

REFLECTED CEILING PLANS

This plan indicates the location of all ceiling features, including skylights, mechanical vents, light fixtures, soffits, and steps in the ceiling construction. If the ceiling is a suspended acoustical tile ceiling, the reflected ceiling plan will indicate the size and layout of the tile grid. This plan is extremely important for you to be sure that equipment and cabinetry extending up to the ceiling will not interfere with soffits or any other ceiling features. If soffits are to be constructed above the cabinets, the depth of the soffits needs to be carefully coordinated with the cabinet depth. A reflected ceiling plan may not be provided in some projects. Separate plans for the mechanical, construction, and other aspects may help clearly identify such work without cluttering the bathroom floor plan.

Specifications

Specifications are written instructions describing the basic requirements for the construction of a building. They should clearly describe sizes, types, and quality of all building materials and work affected by the job (either directly or indirectly). The methods of construction, fabrication, or installation and the expected quality of work to be produced are also spelled out explicitly. They define the area of responsibility between you and the purchaser. They must clearly indicate which individual has the ultimate responsibility for all or part of the work. In addition, information that cannot be conveniently included in the drawings, such as the legal responsibilities, methods of purchasing materials, and insurance requirements, is included in the specifications. If there is a difference between the drawings and the specifications, the information contained in the specifications is to be followed, unless there is a note in the drawings or specifications.

If you are hiring a subcontractor, specifications tell that person: "These are the materials you must use, this is how you must use them, and these are the conditions under which you undertake this job." In other words, specifications help guarantee that the contractor delivers the job as specified. They also help ensure that the project will be done according to the standards that the building laws require. Specifications may be listed on a separate form, may be part of the working drawings, or may be a combination of both. In all cases, the owner and the owner's agent must receive a completed copy of the project documents prior to the commencement of any work.

One of the most useful ways to increase productivity in the bathroom installation business is through the use of standard master specifications. If specifications must be drawn up from scratch for each project, especially when unfamiliar products are being used, a great deal of time will be required to complete this task. While it is true that no two jobs are the same, a large percentage of the work for bathroom installations can be standardized.

There is no question that the project of developing standard specifications is a time-consuming project, and many builders are not willing to commit the time necessary to undertake the task. Still, the benefits are tremendous. Using standard specifications saves a lot of time and research for the builder or the retailer or dealer or designer who is writing the specifications. These standard specifications can be carefully written to eliminate vagueness or gray areas that are often found in hastily written specifications. Standard specifications such as those designed by NKBA also allow for fine-tuning of the estimating system for increased accuracy. As an operation is repeated time and time again, using the same method and products, closer attention can be given to labor and material costs for that particular item, and the unit price can be adjusted accordingly.

Standard specifications are easily adaptable to a computer system. A project specification can be quickly and accurately assembled from the specifications stored on the computer. New specifications can continually be added so that they can be reused in future projects. Standard specifications that call out the use of the same products on a regular basis mean that builders learn the individual characteristics of each product and increase their efficiency at installation of the product. This familiarity leads to a reduction in mistakes and an increase in productivity. And finally, it is much easier to keep abreast of price changes when the standard specifications are written around a limited number of standard products.

To set up standard specifications, the builder should review projects over the past year and try to identify operations that were repeated more than five times. One way to classify the elements of a job is to use a 16-category system standard developed by Construction Specifications Institute (CSI). It presents the material specifications in an order very close to that in which the products will be installed. Or the builder can organize specifications in the categories of work established by a unit-cost estimating manual. In some cases, standard specifications need to give the customer some selection in style or color. In the case of flooring, for example, the usual method is to select a brand name with a low-, medium-, or high-priced selection, which is almost always enough choice for a customer. On rare occasions, a customer may want a particular color that is available only from another manufacturer. When it is necessary to have more style choices, say, for floor tile, it is still best to stay with one manufacturer or supplier.

When selections have been made, standard specifications can be customized for a specific job by including specific model numbers. This should routinely be done at least for plumbing fittings, windows, skylights, and flooring. For items that are subcontracted, meet with subcontractors to develop standard specifications. For example, the electrician and the builder can decide that a 200-ampere circuit breaker box by a particular manufacturer, with 24 circuits and a master cutoff, will be used on all jobs. That will be the standard specification, and the electrician will always know that this box is expected.

Builders can also agree on certain minimum requirements with their subcontractors, such as using only copper romex cable for branch wiring. With this sort of arrangement, builders and their subcontractors always know what to expect, and customers can be assured of the quality and safety that they expect.

When builders have developed master specifications and put them into a book or on the computer, the time required during estimating to write up specifications can be enormously reduced. Master specifications can even be referred to by number, which helps identify them easily in the computer. Of course, after master specifications are developed, builders must continue the same ongoing process of review that was used to create the original specifications. Projects must be reviewed periodically to see if new procedures or techniques are being adopted that can be added to the master specifications. In this way, the master specifications can continue to grow with the company.

Specifications are generally written by an architect or by a specifications writer. You, as well as any of your subcontractors, should review the drawings and specifications to verify that all codes and project expectations have been met.

Building plans and specifications are actually legal documents that are a part of your installation contract. By accepting the terms and conditions of your contract, you are agreeing to provide the materials and labor necessary to produce all work indicated on the drawings, unless otherwise stated. In the event that the designer or architect fails to include some portion of work that might be necessary to complete the project, be sure to report the possible omission and request a change order to complete this additional work.

Computer-Generated Drawings

With proper software, bathroom specialists can produce suitable reproduction drawings of bathroom designs and layouts. Some computer program product drawings completely eliminate manual boardwork. They can help you and your clients turn ideas into working plans accurate enough to be used in construction. In addition to computer-drawn floor plans and perspectives, many of these programs provide a "bill of materials." However, the program cannot replace a skilled designer's knowledge or experience.

Several software programs for computer-generated drawings are available. Each operates slightly differently, but each can save you time in presenting a visual bathroom plan. As with manual drawings, practice hones the skills. Verification of figures and dimensions is often seen as a waste of time, but a minor oversight can result in a fixture or cabinet misfit that may require a work stoppage and costly materials reorder.

Once the final blueprint drawings are made, the bathroom is no longer in the planning stage, but the room is now ready for the construction phase.

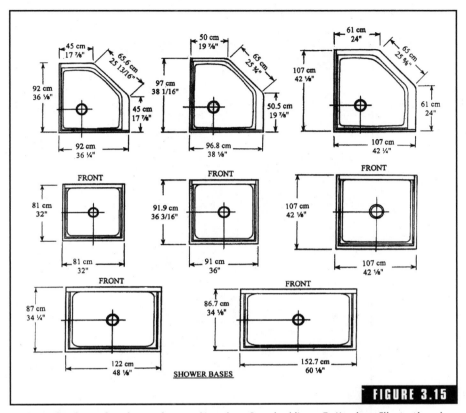

SHOWER BASES

FIGURE 3.15

Typical templates for shower bases. *(American Standard/Leon E. Korejwo, Illustrations.)*

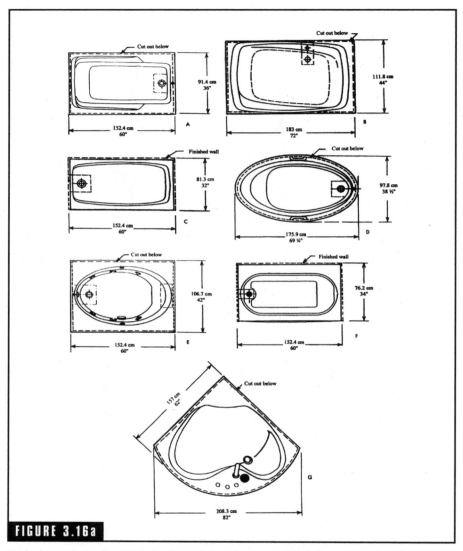

FIGURE 3.16a

Typical templates for (A) 5-foot acrylic bathing pool; (B) 6-foot acrylic bathing pool to be installed as pier, island, or peninsula; (C) 5-foot bath; (D) acrylic oval bathing pool to be installed above or below floor line as pier, island, or peninsula; (E) acrylic whirlpool, which may be installed as pier, island, or peninsula; (F) recessed bath with luxury ledge; (G) acrylic corner bathing pool to be installed above or below floor line as pier, island, or peninsula. *(American Standard/Leon E. Korejwo, Illustrations.)*

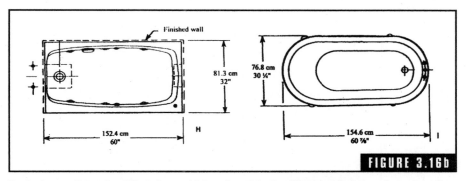

Finished wall

81.3 cm
32"

152.4 cm
60"

H

76.8 cm
30 ¼"

154.6 cm
60 ⅞"

I

FIGURE 3.16b

Typical templates for (H) 5-foot whirlpool and bath; (I) enameled cast-iron claw-foot tub. *(American Standard/Leon E. Korejwo, Illustrations.)*

Bathroom Extras

In the past, bathrooms were functional yet spartan: simple, small, cold, and not much more than a basic utilitarian room—a room in the house where comfort was either kept to a bare minimum or was simply not an option. With all of today's luxurious fixtures, specialized equipment, and unique design possibilities, this no longer has to be the case. Bathrooms have become more than a necessity; people are making them more of a focal point of the home. They are now larger and geared for escape and relaxation as well as efficiency; in short, homeowners look to the bathroom to provide a luxurious yet personalized retreat.

The bathroom's role of today has expanded to that of a multifunctioning room where homeowners can and should customize the bath to suit their needs and interests. Some extras which may be of interest to homeowners are barrier-free bathrooms with accessible facilities (if not for this stage of their lives, they may plan a structure that can handle these fixtures in the future), master suites with amenities such as whirlpool tubs, saunas, steam units, and areas for exercise, laundry, separate dressing, grooming, and entertainment.

Because you are responsible mainly for the installation, in many cases your client will not require you to assist in choosing bathroom extras. However, it is a good idea to be aware of the different options that are available. For those who may need to handle this part of the business, this chapter provides many unique ideas that you or your client may have never thought about installing in the bathroom.

A bathroom should always be designed to give some "extras." The size and layout of homes have changed dramatically over the years. Small bathrooms have been replaced with rooms double the size, with more fixtures and specialized equipment. However, it may be necessary to do a great deal of planning to obtain the necessary space in which to put these extras. With homeowners' personalized desires, interest, and activities, the trend has moved toward highly individualized bathroom designs. Designers are being challenged to produce much more than the functional bathroom of the past. This means that for you, as the installer, there is an increasing level of complexity with the installation of these designs. Although the designer has the real responsibility to follow accepted design principles, you will often be asked to perform new installation techniques in response to the designer's intent.

Remind the homeowner that the bathroom should match the period or architectural character of the rest of the home. For instance, there have been cases where a bath or kitchen is too modern for a colonial-styled development, which, as a result, devalues the property.

Handicapped-Accessible and Barrier-Free Bathrooms

In today's world, the aging population, as well as a wide range of physical and mental abilities and impairments, need to be recognized. *Barrier-free* is a principle of design which utilizes standard appliances, materials, and construction techniques for designs flexible enough for people of all ages and physical abilities (Fig. 4.1). Aside from wheelchair confinement, other impairments that require specialized bathrooms may include vision impairment or blindness, or limited ability to move the arms or hands, for those who must use crutches or a walker, and for the elderly and children. Those people who are considerably shorter than average may also require special configurations to meet their needs. People with physical impairments that do not confine them to a wheelchair may be able to use a more standard bathroom. For example, vision-impaired people will need larger numbers and letters on fixture controls, but the layout of the bathroom may not need to change. For those who are blind, special braille controls are available. For the elderly who may have decreased mobility and be unable to reach or grasp various items, a somewhat modified standard bathroom may be appropriate. Some users desire a bathroom that would be functional for both disabled and for those who are not, while others want a bathroom that is designed and completely arranged for only a wheelchair-bound user. Bathrooms can be created that will be appealing and functional for everyone. The desire for this type of bathroom is getting attention as older couples are renovating their homes with the idea of aging in their current residence, or as young families renovate, they may anticipate taking care of an aging parent.

Planning a barrier-free arrangement depends, to some extent, on the desires and abilities of the persons involved. Most of the bathrooms that you install will have been designed with a specific user in mind and to their particular needs; as a result, for you, the personalized nature of these installations will require attention to detail and much

FIGURE 4.1

An oversize, doorless shower stall with pull-down chair and handheld shower, a low sink, and grab bars next to the toilet help to make this bathroom accessible to a wheelchair user. *(American Standard.)*

patience, as well as knowledgeable planning and considerable departure from basic standards (many standards will not be applicable or will need to be substantially modified).

While you may not be required to design a bathroom for the physically impaired, as the installer, you need to be aware of the fundamental principles in these specialized designs to ensure a successful installation. This type of specialized work requires a strong working relationship between the installer, the designer, and the client. Be open to the chance that, quite often, minor adjustments will be required through the course of the project as the client observes the work in process.

The first step is choosing where in the home to locate this bathroom, which, obviously, is extremely important. There will be more flexibility in new-home construction versus remodeling an existing bath. For the bathroom to be easily accessible to people of all abilities, it is best when located on the ground floor.

The planning process should start with an inventory of the intended user's skills, focusing on their capabilities, preferences, and tastes. They are best qualified to determine what is essential for comfort and convenience. The first priority in bathrooms intended for people who use wheelchairs is plenty of room for access and maneuvering. Barrier-free bathrooms are usually larger than average. When planning the bathroom, remember that a barrier-free bath does not need to look institutional; it can be practical as well as beautiful.

In most homes, bathrooms contain annoying barriers for anyone in a wheelchair (e.g., wall cabinets may be out of reach, countertops may be too high, and base cabinets or vanities may block access to them). A number of relatively simple modifications can make life much better for those confined to a wheelchair. The following guidelines can be followed in order to make the bath safe and accessible for people of varying physical abilities (Fig. 4.2).

1. Doors leading to the bathroom must have clear openings of 34″ (86.36 cm) to provide clearance for the wheelchair. The bathroom door must swing outward rather than inward (to allow easy movement in and out of the room and so as to not trap someone who had fallen inside), and should be fitted with a lever-type handle, not a knob; a pocket door is a possible solution if the user's impairment allows them to operate one.

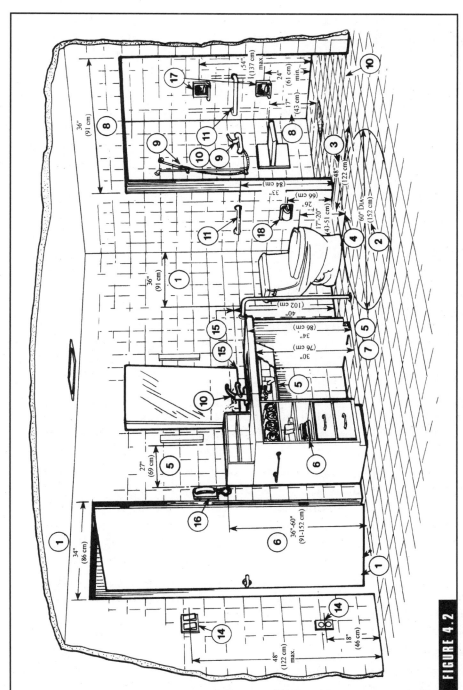

FIGURE 4.2

Suggested standards for a handicapped-accessible bathroom. *(Leon E. Korejwo, Illustrations.)*

2. When planning, be sure to check the turning diameter of the particular wheelchair, motorized cart, or other vehicle. An open area within the bathroom that is at least 60″ (152.40 cm) in diameter is needed to allow the wheelchair user room to rotate the chair and move freely to each fixture.

3. Provide 48 × 48″ (121.91 × 121.91 cm) of clear space in front of each fixture. A space should be provided 48″ (121.91 cm) wide between the lavatory and the toilet, if both fixtures share the same wall. This is to accommodate the full length or width of the wheelchair between them. These spaces also will allow room for a care giver, if needed. Normally, fixtures should be placed within a 36″ (91.44-cm)-wide area, and no closer than 18″ (45.72 cm) from its centerline to any vertical surface.

4. Provide a toilet seat 17 to 20″ (43.18 to 50.80 cm) off the floor; standard seats are 14 to 16″ (35.56 to 40.64 cm).

5. The lavatory should be no higher than 34″ (86.36 cm) off the floor and should extend 27″ (68.58 cm) from the wall. Water supply and drain pipes should be relocated inside the wall to free knee space beneath the lavatory. Any exposed hot-water plumbing should be insulated. Hydraulic, height-adjustable lavatories can be smoothly raised (making it easier for a tall person to use) or lowered (for a seated user). Vanities can be purchased specifically designed for use from a wheelchair. The seated person should be able to reach the faucets.

6. Conventional floor- or wall-mounted bathroom storage cabinet or vanity arrangements are not suitable for most wheelchair users since, for the most part, they are located out of a seated person's reach. Varying the height of the cabinets and vanities makes their contents more accessible to a wide range of people. Open shelves and racks aid the user's reach (rather than deep storage behind doors); locate them 36 to 60″ (91.44 to 152.4 cm) above the floor.

7. For wheelchair accessibility, countertops can be raised a few inches above the standard 30″ (76.20 cm) in bathrooms, with clear knee space below so the chair can pull in close. In order to provide unobstructed access to the lavatory and counters, base cabinets and vanities should be eliminated below these areas. Some bathroom designers prefer long sections of counters without base cabinets so that the wheelchair can slide under at any point along the counter. However, eliminating all base cabinets, which typically provide support for the countertop, makes the countertop installation a challenge. Removable base cabinets that can be pulled or rolled out to allow for wheelchair access, and replaced when access is not required, are popular. In a master bath with two vanities, consider making one higher or lower than the other to accommodate users of different heights.

8. Plumbing fixture manufacturers provide accessible shower stalls and bathtubs; walk-in shower stalls are the most commonly used means for bathing. While a large shower stall can accommodate an individual in a wheelchair, it is more typical for a smaller shower to be provided with grab bars and a transfer seat [a pull-down or permanent seat 17″ (43.18 cm) above the floor]. Hydraulic lifts that use water pressure to lower and raise a seat into and out of the tub can be added. The stall should measure at least 48″ square (121.92 × 121.92 cm), and its opening should be at least 36″ (91.44 cm) wide. The shower stall entrance should have no threshold that would impede the entrance and exit of a wheelchair.

9. Control valves and showerheads should be installed at two different heights or include a handheld nozzle that can be used from a seated position. There should also be a height-adjustable showerhead attached to a hose at least 5′ long for those of short stature, young or old. Shower controls must be located within the reach of the user while seated, but never higher than 48″ (121.92 cm). For those who might lack grasping power, install a single-lever shower control with a built-in antiscald mechanism. The control can be positioned inside the shower enclosure for easy access; it does not have to be on the same wall as the showerhead. Install easy-to-manipulate single-lever faucets at the lavatory, shower, and tub.

10. Choose fittings for the water supply to the tub or shower that have a pressure-balancing antiscald control valve or temperature-limiting plumbing fitting, which is essential to keep the water temperature from turning hot or cold without warning.

11. Accessibility to fixtures is of great importance, with safety as a major consideration. One of the most common modifications in the bathroom is the installation of grab bars with nonslip textures at strategic locations to assist a wheelchair-bound user in and out of the wheelchair. Individual requirements should guide decisions about the number and placement of grab bars. Typically, grab bars are necessary in the bath or shower area (installed on the wall not far above the top of the tub for support during transfer and bathing), and next to the toilet. The bars should be located so that their central handhold is 33″ (83.82 cm) off the floor. Because the grab bars must support a substantial amount of weight (install those designed to support at least 300 pounds), they must be secured firmly to the wall studs so they will not come loose when grasped. Typically, wood blocking is placed between wall studs for this purpose. Before the drywall is installed, check to make sure that sufficient blocking has been installed for this purpose.

12. Bathtubs, particularly built-in jetted tubs, should have wide ledges that allow a user to sit to enter while holding on to a nearby grab bar. For safety, there should be no steps around a bathtub.

13. In the bathrooms, slipping hazards represent one of the biggest problems. Fixtures and surfaces to be walked or stood on should have nonslip finishes.

14. There should be plenty of ground-fault electrical outlets and switches that are adjusted for easier access for those confined to a wheelchair. Switches are generally lowered to approximately 48″ (121.92 cm) above the floor and outlets are raised to 15 to 18″ (38.1 to 45.72 cm) above the floor. Change toggle switches to larger rocker switches. There are to be no switches within 60″ (152.4 cm) of a water source.

15. Mirrors should be mounted at a maximum of 40″ (101.6 cm) above the floor. They can be angled toward the viewer or be adjustable for greater flexibility when viewing from the wheelchair.

16. For an extra sense of security, add a telephone, an intercom, a panic button, or a child monitor.

17. For a seated user, soap dishes should be located at a height of approximately 24″ (60.96 cm) high. For those who stand when showering, or for those who are assisting someone seated, an additional soap dish can be installed 54″ (137.16 cm) from the floor.

18. For easy accessibility, the toilet paper holder should be installed in front of the seat, approximately 26″ (66.04 cm) above the floor.

With careful design and attention to detail, bathrooms need not be off limits to any person with physical limitations. In planning and pricing your installation work, however, you will need to remember the custom nature of this work and the involvement of the designer and the client. Designers may look up to you for innovative ways to install countertops and counters, and the success of these projects may well depend on your ability to understand the needs of the client and develop a good working relationship with the designer.

Additional suggestions in a bath for the disabled include using shatterproof materials and fixtures with rounded corners to prevent injury.

Master Suites

The successful master suite—an integration of bedroom, bath, and auxiliary spaces—links multiple elements in a single efficient, private retreat. In the past, master bathrooms were considered a luxury. However, today, for many homeowners, master baths are thought of as a necessity; a place to escape from the everyday world and a place to rejuvenate the body. The master bath has definitely become more than just a place to grab a quick shower.

Every homeowner's master suite desires are a little different; therefore, the master suite should reflect the specific needs, interests, and personality of its users, while offering some savvy strategies (Fig. 4.3). For some, the key ingredients are privacy and seclusion. For others, it is a certain degree of luxury and pampering. With master suites gaining popularity in new and remodeled homes, homeowners are more sure than ever about what they want from these rooms.

The most luxurious master baths are divided into zones consisting of a large shower, a whirlpool tub, two lavatories, and plenty of storage space. Another zone typically contains the toilet, which is isolated for privacy. Luxury, privacy, and amenities are high priorities.

Designers, architects, and homeowners are focusing on designing attractive and efficient spaces that two people can share and enjoy at the same time; master suites with his-and-her bathroom arrangements. What sets a his-and-her suite apart from the more familiar master bath is the amount of privacy and personal space for each individual. Basic fixtures are physically separated from each other by walls and doors. For example, toilets, lavatories (extralong vanities or separate lavatory stations with two bowls to enable two to get ready comfortably at the same time), and cabinets are divided into two distinct areas, one for him and one for her, while having only one whirlpool tub and one shower. The separate areas allow each user to have privacy, while the common areas can bring them together again.

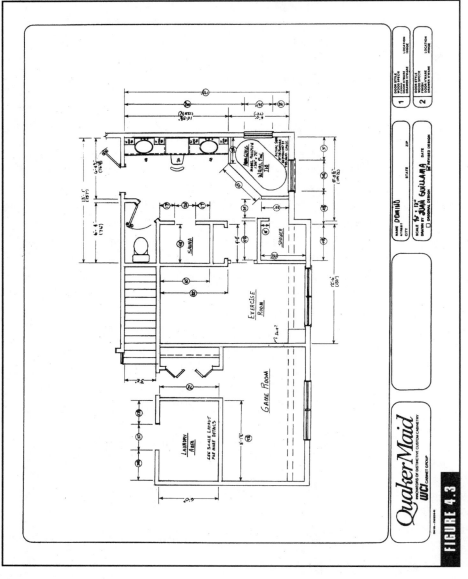

FIGURE 4.3

An elaborate master bathroom plan. *(QuakerMaid Kitchens of Reading, Inc./Juan Guillama, designer.)*

Note: It is extremely important to remember that the gallon-per-minute (gpm) delivery of an added large shower may necessitate increasing the size of the supply lines, or even adding a larger water heater. Make sure the hot water supply system can maintain required amounts for multiple hot showers.

Aside from the separated toilet and bathing fixtures, additional amenities often include

- Separate grooming area. The woman's side can be designed with extra storage for makeup and toiletries and may include a dressing table (or vanity) with extra lighting.

- Bathroom spa. A spa typically includes a sauna, steam bath, hot tub, and even some exercise equipment. It is best to locate a spa with convenience and privacy in mind; adjacency to the master bedroom and bath provides for a good location.

- Large walk-in closets. These can also be designed to function as a separate dressing area. Built-ins in the closet area provide for great storage. If the closet doubles as a passageway, the homeowner will get a lot more out of the space if the storage is built in. Pull-out shoe racks, stacking clothes racks, shelves for towels, and slide-out bins all can be added to existing closets.

- Separate dressing area. A separate dressing area that forms a transition zone between the bedroom and the bath. Create a dressing area by cutting a doorway into an adjacent bedroom, or annex the necessary space from an adjacent closet or hallway or the master bedroom.

- A sitting or reading area. If there is enough space to just lounge or relax, incorporate a comfortable piece of upholstered furniture. This area does not necessarily require a lot of extra room and may be created by simply rearranging the existing area furniture creatively.

- An aesthetically pleasing fireplace.

- Include a wet-bar area or a complete kitchenette with sink, refrigerator, and microwave oven. While this feature can make life very enjoyable for the homeowners, installing them can be very difficult for the installer. Designers may fail to take into account the difficulty of providing plumbing and electrical requirements for these fixtures and equipment.

■ An entertainment center with television, telephone, video, and stereo equipment. Consider the function of such devices, they should be capable of survival in a humid environment. Location is a safety consideration; a radio would not be welcome if it fell in a tub.

Any of the extras mentioned can make an ordinary room extraordinary and provide for a private retreat. These suites often have elegant finishing materials, such as marble and handmade ceramic tile; however, remind the homeowners that although the baths can be quite luxurious, they should keep maintenance in mind when choosing the materials.

Whirlpools

Once considered a fixture that defined luxury in the bathroom, whirlpool tubs have now become standard equipment—even in modest installations. These hydromassage units—simply put, bathtubs with air jets—have become a focal point for many designs (Fig. 4.4). Unlike an outdoor spa, the whirlpool uses a standard hot-water connection; once the soak is over, the water is drained. A whirlpool is operated by motor, pump, and jets. Jet designs vary, generally, high volume and low pressure (a few strong jets) or low pressure and high volume (lots of softer jets). Typically, the more jets there are, the easier it is to pinpoint an aching body part.

FIGURE 4.4

A whirlpool tub can be configured to fit any bathroom scheme; this tub fits perfectly into the corner of the bathroom. *(American Standard.)*

Like other fixtures, whirlpools are available in a variety of materials. Cast iron coated with enamel is considered the best material. With care, it will retain a high-gloss finish indefinitely. Cast acrylic models, which maintain water temperature better and are lighter than cast iron, are gaining in popularity because they can be molded in a variety of shapes. Cultured marble is plastic manufactured to look like marble.

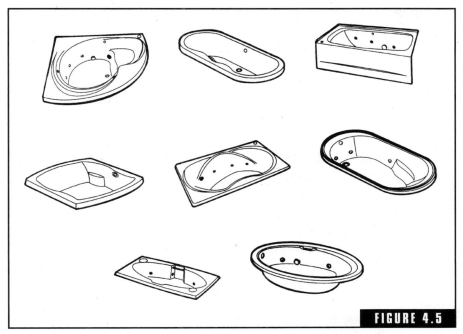

Various sizes and shapes of whirlpool tubs. *(American Standard.)*

Whirlpools are available in a variety of shapes and sizes and will fit in most homes (Fig. 4.5). Most whirlpool manufacturers offer units 60 inches (152.4 cm) long by 32 inches (81.28 cm) wide that can be used in spaces that standard tubs previously occupied. Some models are as small as 48 inches (121.92 cm) long, and some are shaped to fit into corners. Larger models are available 66 or 72 inches (167.64 or 182.88 cm) long and 36, 42, or 48 inches (91.44, 106.68, or 121.92 cm) wide, and larger. Because of their extra weight, the bathroom floor may need to be reinforced prior to installation. It could be disastrous if you forget to think about, and plan for, the amount of stress a floor will have to bear once the user adds the water to a 700-pound tub.

The best hydrojet systems are fully adjustable. These systems allow the user to change the direction of the water flow and the air:water ratio. A higher proportion of air to water means a stronger massage, while more water than air is gentler. Make sure that there are a sufficient number of jets to reach all the major muscle groups.

The capacity of the home's water heater is another consideration; whirlpools may require an extra capacity main water heater or separate in-line heater. Larger whirlpool and soaking tubs hold up to 90 gallons of water. If the water heater can't handle the load—or if the community faces water shortages—perhaps they should choose a smaller tub. Some tubs have heaters built in, eliminating the need for a larger heater.

The following are among the most desired luxury features in demand when researching a whirlpool: in-line heaters, adjustable jets and multiple jet locations, an integral heater to maintain the desired water temperature throughout the length of a soak, timers, sound-reducing features to minimize noise, contoured backrests, cushioned headrests, neck and back massage, convenient hand grips, handheld showers, storage compartments, and cascading faucets. The addition of low-voltage lights to accent the whirlpool creates a luxurious mood.

Along with being a luxurious amenity, installing a whirlpool offers many health benefits. Whirlpools activate blood circulation and improve cell oxygenation and facilitates drainage of lymphatic ducts. While delivering a localized massage, they provide a relaxing full-body massage that relieves stress, invigorates the body, and relieves tension and strain, which is great for the lower back and neck. They also provide toning effects.

If helping the homeowners decide on a whirlpool, discuss with them how often they plan on using it and for what purpose. After owning one, many couples find they don't take the time to soak together. Have them keep this in mind when choosing the size; often the room required for a double-size tub is wasted. Also, remind them that large whirlpools take a long time to fill with water and are difficult and time-consuming to clean. On the other hand, many people are spending more time inside their homes or offices, and have less time to get away from it all. For an increasing number of people, the whirlpool is an excellent source for the release of tension and stress.

Soaking Tubs

Although the homeowners may not have the time to indulge themselves daily, a tub is a prerequisite to relaxation in any bathroom. Although whirlpools have become practically standard in today's master suites, soaking tubs are now gaining in popularity. Unlike a whirlpool, a soaking tub, excellent for relaxing, does not have jets (although they can be added). These circular tubs, usually 29 to 32 inches (73.66 to 81.28 cm) high, do not require an integral heater and take less time to fill than a whirlpool. They have deep interiors and are ideal for use in small spaces. Soaking tubs are available in platform, recessed, and corner models, with rectangular or round interiors of fiberglass or acrylic. These tubs can be installed above floor level, partially below it, or completely below it. In any case, be sure to reinforce the joists.

Note: An important point you may want to look into is whether the addition of any of these fixtures will overload an on-site septic system.

Saunas

Saunas and steam baths, luxurious features once found mainly in gyms and health clubs, are an excellent extra for the residential bathroom and should be planned for ultimate enjoyment and relaxation (Fig. 4.6). A *sauna* is a dry heat bath taken in a well-insulated room lined with untreated, kiln-dried, soft wood (walls, ceiling, and slatted benches inside the sauna are generally constructed of a water-resistant softwood such as redwood or cedar) and heated by igneous rocks. The sauna is the only bath in the world in which both dry air and damp air are present at the same time. The heat causes the body to perspire extensively, cleansing the skin and its pores. The high heat (160 to 220°F) and the low humidity [10 to 30% relative humidity (RH)] create an environment which promotes overall perspiration and the deep cleansing of pores. Impurities as well as lactic acid buildup from physical exertion are removed from the body. With the special heat and humidity and by raising the body temperature and increasing blood circulation, tired muscles are soothed and pain and stress can be relieved.

An added benefit of a sauna is that it is a very inexpensive bathroom extra to operate. It is "on" only when being used, and there is a short heatup time; air is being heated rather than water such as in a hot tub. There is no major upkeep, there are no harmful chemicals being absorbed into the body, and there are no moisture problems for other areas of the house. The sauna is a self-contained unit. Besides insulated walls, a solid-core door, and double-paned glass (if any), an electric or gas sauna heater will also be needed.

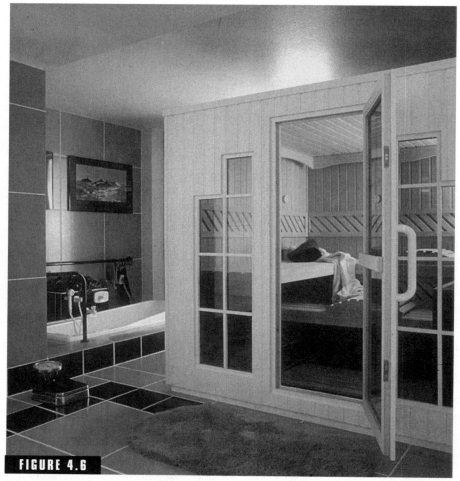

FIGURE 4.6

A dramatic, geometrically patterned front window wall sauna. *(Finnleo Sauna and Steam.)*

The size of a sauna depends on how many people will use it at one time. Small saunas that fit one or two people can easily be built into a large closet. The minimum size for a sauna is about 65 cu ft/person. If possible, the space should be large enough for adequate seating and reclining. Minimum suggested standards (Fig. 4.7*a*), according to Finlandia Sauna, are as follows:

1. The sauna door should be only 24″ (61 cm) wide and swing outward, with no lock. At this width, the door minimizes heat loss. If

anticipating use by a nonambulatory user, a wider door will be needed. Do not put a handicapped door on a sauna unless the room is large enough to accommodate the movement of a wheelchair, with proper ramp and grab bar. Wheelchair users need to be advised that the metal of a wheelchair will become extremely hot to handle in a sauna. Consider an expanded design only when the user is assured of another person to assist them during their use.

2. Plan 1 or 2 levels of benches long enough for an adult to stretch out. As a guide, allow 24″ (61 cm) of bench space per person, for sitting purposes; it is necessary to have a 72″ (182.88 cm) long bench to accommodate a reclining bather. Bench widths should be 20″ (50.80 cm) for an upper bench, and about 16″ (40.64 cm) for a lower bench. Bench heights of 19″ (48 cm) and 38″ (97 cm) above the floor are convenient. Two levels of benches are very important in a good sauna; the upper bench is necessary to make use of the heat (which rises to the ceiling level). The lower bench can be used as a step up to the upper bench or as a sitting bench at the lower temperature level [Fig. 4.7*b*].

3. Ceiling height is critical. A normal 8′-0″ (96″/244 cm) ceiling height will waste heat by taking longer to bring the area up to temperature. The heat rises to the ceiling, so if lowered to approximately 7′-0″ (84″/213 cm), the temperature will be contained in a more usable space.

4. To allow the heater to supply the sauna properly, fresh air inlets and exhaust vents should be sized and placed according to the manufacturer's recommendations.

One of the benefits of a sauna is to cleanse the body by opening pores and flushing out the body's impurities. Years of practice has demonstrated that a cooling shower (with soap to rinse off this waste) is part of the whole process. The rinse cleans, closes the pores, and invigorates. For this reason, a small dressing room and shower should be located conveniently close to the sauna.

Steam Baths

Another healthy way to relax at home is to take a steam bath. It is good for sinus conditions, allergies, and asthma; helps loosen tight muscles; and also increases the flow of blood and supply of oxygen to the body's tissues. A steam bath is a refuge where the homeowner can

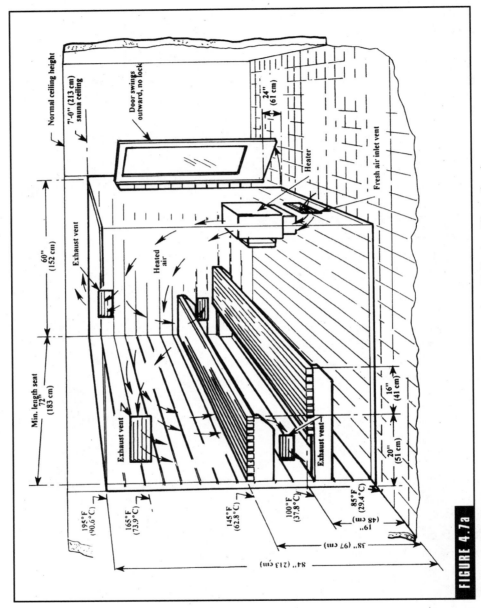

Normal ceiling height

7'-0" (213 cm) sauna ceiling

Door swings outward, no lock

24" (61 cm)

Heater

Fresh air inlet vent

Exhaust vent

60" (152 cm)

Heated air

Min. length seat 72" (183 cm)

Exhaust vent

Exhaust vent

16" (41 cm)

20" (51 cm)

195°F (90.6°C)

165°F (73.9°C)

145°F (62.8°C)

100°F (37.8°C)

85°F (29.4°C)

19" (48 cm)

38" (97 cm)

84" (213 cm)

FIGURE 4.7a

Minimum suggested standards for the interior of a sauna. (*Leon E. Korejwo, Illustrations.*)

escape and unwind. People feel a sensation of complete relaxation when they take a steam bath; the warmth and high humidity massages the skin, increases blood circulation, and eases tense muscles. A luxurious steam bath adds a touch of elegance to all types of bathing and recreation facilities, and is the perfect complement to a sauna (Fig. 4.8).

Any shower or tub can double as a steam bath with the addition of a steam generator, vaporproof doors, and a comfortable seat. However,

FIGURE 4.7b

A sauna interior. (*Finnleo Sauna and Steam.*)

FIGURE 4.8

An elaborate steam suite (left) with sauna (right) and in-home fitness center. *(Finnleo Sauna and Steam.)*

if space allows, a separate steam room can be installed. Steam rooms and baths are available in a variety of designs and finishes, in sizes suitable for anything from one person up to large groups; space-saving layouts are great for the bathroom. The steam bath can be assembled as a freestanding unit or integrated discreetly into a bathroom.

Whether adding a steam bath to an existing shower or bath or installing a separate steam room, it is necessary to dedicate an area for the generator, which boils water with an electric element to produce the steam. The size of the generator will vary depending on the cubic footage of the enclosure. Some manufacturers offer generators that allow steam to be piped in from as far away as 50 feet (for greater flexibility). This space must be constructed with materials that resist water and high temperatures. When installing the unit, consider the manufacturer recommendations for insulation, ventilation, and maintenance.

Prefabricated steam rooms are generally made from molded acrylic panels; custom units can be built of granite or ceramic tile or glass block (Fig. 4.9). Extra features to consider include timers and temperature controls. Several manufacturers produce units that allow the homeowner to enjoy steam and an overhead elongated showerhead that releases water in a gentle cascade. Units can also feature sculpted seats, tempered glass doors, programmable jets, handheld showerheads, and compact-disk (CD) players. External paneling can be finished with ceramic tiles, wood paneling, vinyl wallcovering, wallpaper, or paint. Many steam rooms are supplied in prefabricated wall and ceiling sections with integrated seating, and come complete with air vents, insulation, and exclusive doors in tempered safety glass with aluminum frames, handles, and catch.

Garden Baths

Plants are a vital part of many people's lifestyle. They are found not only outdoors but in almost every room of many houses. Because of the high moisture and humidity level, plants often thrive in a bathroom. It is an ideal place to bring a touch of nature into the house. Keep in mind when planning a garden bath that lighting is equally important to plants in the bathroom.

In new construction, this area can be figured in the bathroom layout. The remodeling of a bathroom usually involves bumping out either a wall or a window. The latter simply involves extending the window out from the wall into a bay-window-type frame. There are also prefab(ricated) three-sided window greenhouses manufactured that will fit most window-size openings; a greenhouse window brings in lots of natural daylight.

A dramatic master bath can be opened up, linking the indoors with a private sunny garden outside. These garden baths create a natural place for a whirlpool tub,

FIGURE 4.9

A custom steam bath with steam doors, windows, and glass block convert a shower into a luxurious private health spa. *(Finnleo Sauna and Steam.)*

spa, or sunbathing deck. Decorative windowpanes can be installed to focus attention on trees and to screen bathers from outside view. French doors, matching overhead transoms, tub-side double-hung windows, and skylights all help to create a functional and atmospheric garden bath.

Luxury Showers

With the bathroom becoming a major focal point of the home—as an escape for relaxation and luxury—there has been a growing trend in all-inclusive luxury showers. While many people bathe for relaxation and therapy, many people shower as a part of the daily grooming process. Showering takes less time than bathing; therefore, a luxuriously designed shower with high-tech features allows the users to take a few minutes to relax while they groom. Because it is being used every day, the luxury shower may be a better investment than some other bathroom extras.

Today's demand is for larger, more comfortable shower spaces, including two-person showers. Basically, the luxury shower system has become what the bathtub is now, not only a place to wash, but a place of relaxation. With the continuing popularity of the whirlpool bath, many homeowners want a separate tub and shower. Whether the whirlpool tub is elsewhere in the bathroom (or adjoining area) or nonexistent because of a lack of space, the shower can become the room's focal point, both functionally and aesthetically. For those who are including a luxury shower only, with the advances in shower technology, the user can experience many of the same pleasures of a whirlpool tub in only a fraction of the space.

For the installer, preplanning is important when creating a luxury bath. Starting with the original plans, a plumber should be consulted to determine the amount of work involved and whether the home's water pressure is sufficient to accommodate the desired water features. Certain needs must be accounted for, and will have an impact on the bathroom's plumbing; be sure that it all coordinates and fits with the fixtures.

Showers can be custom-designed and built on site or prefabricated. With custom enclosures, the possibilities are endless. Custom showers are framed like walls and finished with a variety of materials. With ceramic tile, glass block, stone tiles, or marble, the size and shape of the shower space are completely up to the designer and installer (Fig. 4.10). Prefabricated units, which are often less expensive than custom-made showers, are generally fabricated of molded plastics such as acrylic or fiberglass. Acrylic incorporates designs for pre-molded accessories (shelves, soap dishes, etc.), all things that can't be included as easily with a custom-made tile shower. They are available in a wide range of colors.

Many manufacturers have one-piece and sectional versions of showers applicable to any building or renovation requirement. A one-piece model should not be chosen without first making sure it will fit through the house. The widths of doorways, hallways, and any points to turn corners or stairs should first be measured. Even if working with a small existing bathroom space, a lot of exciting and useful things can still be incorporated into the luxury shower.

These popular luxury shower systems, whether custom-made or pre-fabricated, offer many amenities. Some of the desired features include systems with the traditional shower plus body sprays, fully program-mable showers (electronic versus manual controls) with adjustable mul-tiple-massaging showerheads (provides health benefits, too—a massage that tones and revives, and stimulates blood circula-tion), showerheads in different positions (on the ceiling, shower spray bars, rainbars, etc.), adjustable handheld sprayers (also great for cleaning the tub), and cascading waterfalls. Full-bodied steam units can also be incorporated into the shower.

To completely personalize the shower experience, faucets can be preprogrammed for water-temperature and water-volume control, which brings up the issue of pres-sure balance versus thermostatic valves. Thermostatically controlled valves are important because they actually allow users to personalize the shower by setting it to a specific temperature; it is integral to getting the best effect from the shower

FIGURE 4.10

This luxury shower illustrates customization and how glass block can be used to create a unique shower enclosure shape. *(Weck Glass Block/Glashaus, Inc.)*

experience. The pressure balance valve only prevents against scalding; it doesn't hold the temperature. The thermostatic valve has a much better flow and provides enough water to handle several body sprays, rainbars, and so on. Volume of flow, along with safety and control, are what make thermostatic valves an important part of the luxury shower. Locating the controls near the shower entry allows the user to adjust water flow and temperature before entering.

Homeowners are also interested in items that will make their shower spaces well organized and comfortable. People like fog-free shaving mirrors, built-in shelving, hooks, decorative grab bars, a seat or bench (one that folds down to save space), armrest rails, soap dishes, and overhead lighting and fan systems. Built-in shower stereo sound systems with radio and CD players are also very popular. In many instances, these individual extras and components can be ordered separately, to create a completely customized space, or they can be purchased in upscale luxury shower packages.

Safety issues are also an important part in the design of a luxury shower. As mentioned earlier in this chapter, it is easier to achieve safe entry and exit in the shower than in a tub; therefore, the luxury shower may be the answer for the aging population, for people with varying physical abilities, and for those planning ahead for accessibility in their later years. For safety, all showers should include grab bars, seating, handheld sprays, slip-resistant flooring, and faucets that have scald protection. Luxury showers can be manufactured to conform with universal design standards, and with a less institutional look. Safety features are always important with the luxury shower, and universal design will be a concern at some point in almost everyone's life.

Many homeowners prefer the choice of creating their own personal environment. Overall, the design possibilities for a luxury shower are limitless.

Exercise Bath—Fitness Center

Dedicated exercise areas incorporated into the bathroom design, or just adjacent to, are often requested by homeowners. Depending on the amount of space available, an exercise room can be as simple as one treadmill to as elaborate as a fully equipped in-house gym, with weight machines, a steam room, and bathing facilities (Fig. 4.11).

When planning the exercise bath/fitness center, it should be located and constructed so that sound will not be transmitted through the rest of the house. An exercise area, depending on what it consists of, can add considerable stress to the static load that the floors and walls must support. Walking on a treadmill, jumping, or dancing can shake the structure, and as a result excessive flexing of the floor can cause walls or ceilings to crack. Be certain to analyze the existing structure and specify any necessary modifications to handle the load.

If incorporating a fitness area, plan for and discuss the following points with the homeowner:

FIGURE 4.11

An open and airy exercise area, along with a whirlpool and place to relax, is becoming a popular extra to incorporate into, or adjacent to, the master bathroom. *(Andersen Windows, Inc.)*

- Plan enough space for the user to perform exercises if desired.

- Install easy-to-clean, durable surfaces. Make sure that the surfaces are compatible with the exercises the user will perform.

- The user should be able to adjust the temperature of the exercise area independently from the rest of the house. An exhaust fan or some other mechanical ventilation device would be useful here.

- Be certain that all equipment is properly installed.

Some extras to incorporate into an exercise area are mirrored walls, a separate shower stall, whirlpool tub, walk-in steam shower, or sauna. Include a stereo, radio, or television with VCR; this is excellent for exercise videos and a great diversion during tedious exercises.

Grooming-Cosmetic Center

A well-lit area for grooming and storage is an asset to almost any bathroom. An area with adequate light and space to apply makeup and perform other grooming tasks (e.g., styling hair or shaving), is an easy extra to incorporate (Fig. 4.12). The cosmetic center should be placed out of high-traffic areas so the homeowner is not jostled as they apply makeup.

When planning, be certain to include enough electrical outlets. On a daily basis, if the user needs two curling irons and a hair dryer, more than one outlet should be planned. Another nifty extra is to light this center to duplicate the lighting in the place where the user spends most of the time in the bathroom. Thus, if the user applies makeup in a setting with fluorescent lighting, the makeup center should have fluorescent lighting. Although quite expensive, the best makeup centers allow the user to switch from one type of light to another. Drawer organizers for cosmetics and hooks for hanging curling irons and hair dryers can be included in the cosmetic center.

Laundry Center

Another suggestion for a bathroom extra is a laundry center. If the current laundry facilities are located in the basement, save the homeowner time and trouble by installing a washer and dryer in or near the bath and master bedroom or walk-in closet. There should, however, be some type of separation from the bathroom. When planning, place laundry equipment in an area that permits the dryer to exhaust to the outside. Locating the laundry center in or near the bathroom is wise because it allows easy access to plumbing supply lines and drain. The laundry facilities should be easy to conceal, perhaps behind bifold doors, sliding doors, or in a walk-in closet to provide a quick access and visual barrier.

A laundry area must be planned logically. Activity centers in the laundry include (1) soiled clothes storage, (2) sorting-and-preparation area, (3) washing-drying centers, and (4) ironing center and clean-clothes storage. Each center should contain the appliances, storage space, and

FIGURE 4.12

This grooming center provides varying counter levels, as well as mirrors on three sides. *(Thomas Lighting.)*

work surfaces needed for that task. Organize laundry activity centers into a work triangle. Even if space for the laundry center is extremely limited, there are certain basics necessary for even a minimum installation: appliances (washer and dryer); storage for soiled clothes (preferably at least three bins); counter space for sorting, pretreating (nearby water supply necessary), and folding; and storage for laundry aids.

An optimum laundry center would include the following:

1. Laundry equipment consisting of an automatic washer and dryer. Because of floor space or preference, a combination washer-dryer may be chosen. Remind the homeowner to inquire about load capacities of the appliance selected. Frequently, in the case of a large family, a large-capacity washer and dryer will save time and money. Washers and dryers in these rooms need special features, however. Look for extra insulation and heavy-duty stabilizing springs, which reduce vibration and subsequent noise.

2. Space to presort and store soiled clothes. Providing storage for each category into which the laundry is sorted makes it easy to know when a washer load of each has accumulated. A minimum of three storage units is required for adequate presorting by laundry procedure. Types of storage containers can vary. Tilt bins or large roll-out drawers built in under a counter are convenient (Fig. 4.13). The bins or drawers can be labeled for placement in the proper bin as it is soiled.

3. Storage for laundry aids and stain removal supplies. Adequate space must be provided near the washer for all detergents, bleaches, fabric softeners, and other laundry aids used. To eliminate stooping, and to keep these items out of reach of pets or small children, overhead storage is best.

4. Sink for pretreating and other laundering needs. This sink should be located between the sorting bins and the

FIGURE 4.13

Built-in tilt bins provide convenience for the laundry center. *(Leon E. Korejwo, Illustrations.)*

washer; however, if a lavatory bowl is located nearby, it can be used instead.

5. Space to fold clothes and store those that require ironing. A counter is most desirable for folding, but if the space is inadequate, the tops of the appliances can be used. A shelf over the appliances is useful for the temporary storage of folded items. However, if the washer is the top-loading type, the shelf should be high enough to allow the top to open without interference. A drop-down or pull-out table, or ironing board, can provide this utility.

6. Place to hang permanent press items. A full-length hanging closet next to the dryer is especially desirable for hanging items as they are removed from the dryer. A clothes rack can also be used for this purpose, or, if no room is available, a wall hook can be installed. Retracting clothes line reels may be used in unique situations.

7. If the laundry room is located on the lower level, a laundry chute can be a great way to remove soiled clothing from the bathroom area and eliminate carrying the laundry load.

Laundry-Center Space Requirements

The space required for the laundry center will vary with the type of appliances selected and the other activities planned for the area. A washer and dryer, typically, require a space from 54 inches (137 cm) up to 63 inches (160 cm) wide, and 30 inches (76 cm) deep, depending on the widths of the appliances chosen (Fig. 4.14a). The amount of space needed for a washer and dryer depends on whether the dryer is wall-hung, or equipped with casters and rolled out of storage only when needed. If the dryer is wall-hung over a narrow sorting counter next to the washer, for example, only 42 inches (107 cm) would be required. But adequate work space should either be provided or be accessible nearby.

A University of Illinois study of home laundry operations shows that the amount of work space needed for most people is relatively constant. The following recommendations are the minimum to permit freedom of action. These measurements are in addition to space for the appliances.

Washer and dryer. At least 66″ (168 cm) wide × 42″ (107 cm) deep in front of the appliance's floor space.

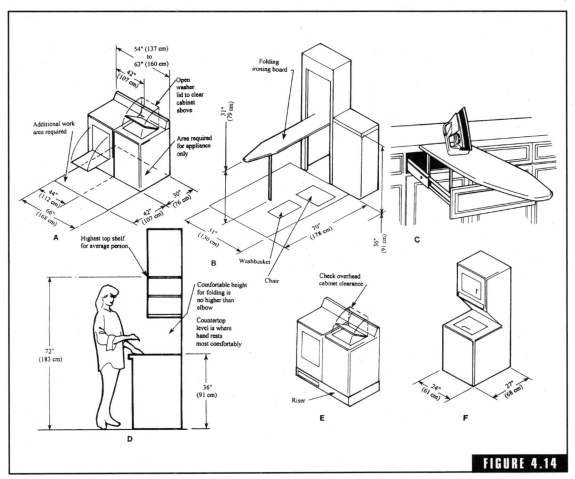

FIGURE 4.14

(*a*) Dimensions for storing a typical washer and dryer; (*b*) required dimensions for a typical ironing board, laundry cart/basket, and chair; (*c*) an ironing board can be easily stored away; (*d*) working surfaces should be at a comfortable level; (*e*) a typical dryer placed on a riser; (*f*) dimensions for a typical washer and dryer stack-on unit. (*Leon E. Korejwo, Illustrations.*)

Washer or dryer alone. At least 44″ (112 cm) wide × 42″ (107 cm) deep in front of the appliance. If the appliances are located in a traffic area, or if the washer and dryer are opposite each other, the work space should be increased to at least 48″ (122 cm) deep.

Ironing. A space at least 70″ (178 cm) wide × 51″ (130 cm) deep will be required for an ironing board, a chair, and a laundry cart or basket

(Fig. 4.14b). If a clothes rack is used, 28" (71 cm) of working space should be allowed in addition to the rack measurements. Figure 4.14c illustrates a pull-out ironing board that may solve a space problem, for a quick morning touchup.

In order to justify locating a laundry center in a master bathroom, consider additional uses for the space. Many of the facilities required for the laundry can be used for other purposes, depending on the location in the home and the amount of space available, such as ironing and sewing.

Planning a Laundry Center

When planning the laundry-center arrangement, consider the homemaker's height and build. Working surfaces should be at a comfortable level. A counter is at the correct work height when the homemakers can stand and rest their hands on the counter with arms comfortably relaxed from the shoulder. Hands should not have to be raised above the level of the elbows while folding clothes. People of average height maintain good posture and avoid fatigue when working at a counter 36 inches (91 cm) above the floor (Fig. 4.14d). The depth of the counter depends on the length of the homemaker's arms, overall build, and physical agility.

Wall cabinets should be low enough so that the homemaker can easily reach the top shelf. For the average person, this is about 72 inches (183 cm) from the floor; shelves should be adjustable. When a wall cabinet is to be directly above the washer, allow for clearance of the washer lid when open. Hamper-type cabinets are very popular in a laundry center, especially when located near the washer.

Placing the dryer on a riser to prevent stooping is often convenient (Fig. 4.14e), especially for the older homemaker. The riser can be a solid base, or it can contain a drawer.

For the washer and dryer, the use of stack-on units is ideal. By using stack-on units a floor space of only 27 × 24 inches (69 × 61 cm) is required, depending on the model selected. The two stack-on units (washer on the bottom, dryer on top) (Fig. 4.14f) also have the advantage that a standard wall cabinet can be placed over them to serve as a storage area.

Because one purpose of a laundry center is to ease the homemaker's workload, it should also be easy to keep clean. Wall cabinets built to the ceiling, and flush drawers and doors without paneling, prevent dust from accumulating. Wall coverings or paint should be washable. Durable, stain-resistant countertops make cleaning simpler.

Locating a laundry center in a bath area is something that can be decided on with several factors in mind. The convenience of having laundry facilities close to the place where the homeowner dresses and relaxes after a full day are desirable. Mornings can be well organized, running the wash while doing the morning preparations. In the evening, the finished laundry is ready to iron and fold or hang. Unfortunately, this convenience can be offset by the sounds generated by the machines, especially at times when quiet may be important to those sleeping.

If a large family is using the laundry area in an area of privacy, such as the bathroom, unwanted intrusions can become annoying. If the laundry area is in question, locate the primary laundry station elsewhere, and add only a small unit to the bathroom area. A compact washer-dryer over-under unit can be used if the laundry area is a secondary one; supplies would not require a lot of space. If the homeowner is fond of hanging the laundry on an outside wash line, the lugging of baskets over a long distance may be inconvenient. Another idea can be to locate a laundry station near a back entry and include a shower with handheld spray to double as drip-dry and utility shower area for people, pets, plants, or equipment.

Children's Bath

Children want a bathroom that is fun. Parents want a bathroom that is safe with nonslip surfaces, scaldproof fittings, and want a space that is easy to keep clean. With children, two points hold great importance: safety and ease of maintenance.

More accidents occur in the bathroom than in any other part of the house, and these dangers are especially great for children because of their inexperience. The many hazards include slippery surfaces, sharp or pointed objects, scalding water, dangerous medicines, and cleaning substances. These dangers can be greatly reduced with sensible design, furnishings, and equipment in the room. Some ideas to incorporate into a children's bathroom are as follows:

1. Single-lever controls are preferable; separate faucets for hot and cold water are not a good idea. Water controls for the bath or

shower should be equipped with a pressure-balanced antiscald valve, even if not required by local code.

2. In a children's bath, it is not necessary to have a separate shower and bathtub. To bathe a child, a tub is needed; for greater versatility, choose a tub-shower combo.

3. A medicine cabinet should not be located in the children's bathroom, unless it has a childproof lock.

4. When choosing a lavatory, consider a pedestal sink which has no storage room for children to explore. If using a vanity, never store cleaning products where they can be reached.

5. When deciding on hardware and furnishings, choose objects that are soft or with rounded corners.

6. The required and code-compliant ground-fault single outlet near the lavatory is probably all that is needed in the children's bathroom. This receptacle must have childproof protection. Electric hair dryers, shavers, curler, and so on can fall into little hands and become quite hazardous.

If the homeowner decides to incorporate a children's bath, be certain to make it easily convertible for when the children grow up. For example, fixtures should be installed at normal heights now; otherwise, low fixtures will be a hindrance to the children in their later years. For example, while still young, children can't reach sinks set at standard heights. A unique, temporary resolution to this problem is to have pull-out, built-in steps in the bottom drawer of the vanity.

A Wet Bar

If the homeowner likes to entertain, especially on the executive level, a wet bar near a relaxing whirlpool or spa area is almost an essential component of convincing prospective clients of the successful host. In many cases, an out-of-town executive and spouse will occupy a suite which includes these extras. To create a wet bar, consider any or all of these options:

Sink. A plumbing hookup and counter space is needed to accommodate a sink (for preparing drinks or cleaning up glassware).

Hospitality sinks range in size from 15″ (38 cm) square to 15 × 25″ (38 × 64 cm).

Refrigerator. A refrigerator is a convenient addition to the wet bar. It will require a power outlet and a space 17 to 18$^1/_2$″ (43 to 47 cm) wide. Some compact refrigerators are square and can be built into a base vanity or cabinet unit; others are countertop height with laminated tops that give a built-in look.

Storage. Consider the items used with the bar, and plan space to house them. For example, glasses may be stored on shelves, in cabinets, or hung from racks. Racks to store stemmed glasses can be built or purchased and installed on the underside of shelves or wall cabinets. Beverage storage will require a closed-door cabinet. Bar accessories such as the blender; ice crusher; mixing, stirring, and muddling tools; an ice bucket; and any other miscellany will require storage in drawers or cabinets.

The convenience of a small coffeepot and perhaps a toaster or microwave can ease the homeowner into their morning routine.

Bathroom Automation

Consider the impact of current and rapidly expanding technologies within the use and design of bathroom space. The bathroom, while not as obviously impacted as the kitchen or study (where most household information is channeled), is often where the homeowner may deal with personal health and fitness issues. This is a great place to keep medication records and reminders. Home automation allows the homeowner to control such elements as lighting, the opening and closing of windows and skylights (as well as shades or blinds), and music and video throughout the house. And with this, all electronics can be controlled by the flick of a remote control. However, keep in mind that handheld remote-control units, which many of us seem to misplace, can be ruined if dropped in water.

Many people are spending more time in their bathrooms; therefore, a television provides for a nice bathroom extra. There are many TV/VCR combinations (13-inch sets) that fit perfectly between most bathroom cabinets or that can be hung from the ceiling. Televisions that pop up at the touch of a button add a convenient extra to the bathroom; this is great for exercise videos in the exercise room, or for those who like to watch television while soaking in the tub.

Speakers for the television or stereo can be wired throughout the room (and the rest of the house); for instance, speakers may be placed at ear level when one is relaxing in the tub. The speakers can be wired with a relay across the pump, so that when the pump comes on, the sound can increase and vice versa. This center in the bathroom can also be used for an intercom system—once again, with speakers wired throughout. A security system employing remote cameras can locate a monitoring screen in the bathroom, which is ideal for monitoring the front door or a child's room. Motion-detection sensors to turn lights on or off help make someone located elsewhere in the home aware that a child or handicapped person is in the bathroom. Mini caller identification screens (which identify the telephone caller) usually have several message centers, and can be located in the bathroom. At the rate that computers and technology are progressing, in the near future, more computer conveniences will be integrated into the bathroom such as voice-activated telephones, intercoms, and lighting.

Additional Bathroom Extras

A few additional inspired touches to consider that will help to give any bathroom that extra feeling are as follows:

- A separate exit from the bathroom is convenient so that an early-morning bather does not have to go back through the bedroom to leave the master suite, so as not to wake those still sleeping.

- A temperature-controlled "safe" area for jewelry and other valuables.

- Consider including an area incorporating a bath, laundry, and mudroom into one (or utility bath). This room can be located so that family members who come in from outside can remove their dirty clothing, throw them into the washer, and shower themselves off. It is a great place for washing pets, too.

- Customized vanity drawers are great for storing grooming supplies.

■ When stepping out of the shower, bath, whirlpool, or similar, it is quite a luxury to have a towel warmer or overhead heat lamp to keep the bather warm (Fig. 4.15).

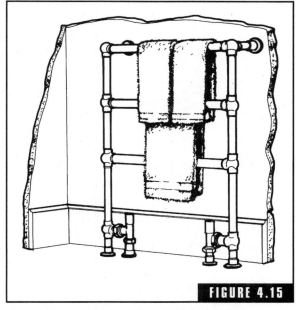

FIGURE 4.15

A heated towel rack is an excellent bathroom extra.
(Leon E. Korejwo, Illustrations.)

Fixtures

Since plumbing fixtures are the permanent furniture of the bathroom, they should be among the first items chosen. Most manufacturers offer fixtures in white and in a wide range of colors that are easy to work into any decorative scheme. It is a good idea to plan the decorating scheme for the bath areas early, before ordering bathroom fixtures, especially when using colored fixtures. Bathroom fixtures are expensive; therefore, these permanent furnishings should be as pleasing in 5, 10, or even 20 years as they are now. Be certain to have the homeowners take plenty of time and shop widely before they make their final selections. When choosing fixtures, consider both function and style (Fig. 5.1). A few extra dollars spent initially may be saved down the road in reductions in maintenance and replacement.

Toilets

It has been said by many that, over 100 years ago, England's Sir Thomas Crapper invented the "valveless water-waste preventer." At the London Health Exhibition in 1884, Mr. Crapper showed off his water closet. He tugged the pull chain, and down went three wads of paper. On the other hand, many say that Mr. Crapper was, in fact, a competent and successful plumber, but he was not the inventor. He's

FIGURE 5.1

This beautiful console vanitytop provides the look of vintage along with lasting quality construction. *(American Standard.)*

either the inventor of the valveless water-waste preventer or it's an amusing hoax, depending on whom you believe. There are vast differences between today's toilets and the original water closet of Sir Thomas Crapper; however, a toilet's basic flushing principle, all that is in the tank and bowl, has not changed much since it was invented.

How a Toilet Works

Essentially, all toilets work the same way. The toilet is the one plumbing fixture that must automatically perform a full cycle of functions. When the toilet lever is pushed (or flushed), a certain volume of water passes out of the tank and into the toilet, removing the existing water from the bowl. As the tank empties, a float ball inside goes down. The ball is attached to a rod, which is attached to a valve on a ballcock mechanism, allowing new water to flow in. As the water rises, the ballcock mechanism is gradually turned off to stop the flow. An overflow tube shunts water into the bowl itself, filling it.

The trap is a crucial element of toilet design. This is a section of the toilet that has an S-shaped trap in the drainpipe and is formed like a pipe that curves down, then up, and finally enters the drain in floor. A certain volume of water is "trapped" in the bottom of the bowl and trap after the flushing action is complete. This water acts as a seal against gases and vermin passing through the toilet and into the house.

Three different flushing actions are commonly used for residential construction; these different actions result from bowl design. The traditional method or traditional flush can be referred to as *gravity-fed.* All the water stored up in the tank rushes down (the customary way), using the force of gravity to flush everything out through a built-in pipe called the *trap.* The water in the tank is released, creating a siphon in the bowl. On gravity-fed models, the bowl is narrowed and the trapway area reduced to create more force. This type of toilet has been improved to reduce the volume of water required for flushing. Taller and narrower tanks, steeper bowls, and smaller water spots (the water surface in the bowl) account for most of the improved design. Although many users report general satisfaction with new 1.6 gallon/ flush models, 1-gallon/flush models sometimes require more than a single flush to clear the bowl. Gravity-fed toilets are a little quieter than others; however, the sound lasts longer.

The alternative to gravity-fed are *pressure-assisted* models. American Standard refers to their pressure-assisted models as a tank within a tank; the tank holding trapped, compressed air (Fig. 5.2). It acts like a spring to shoot the water forward. Incoming water compresses the air. When released, it creates a pushing action, using a strong air pressure to power a quick, intensive flush. The compressed air then works with a small amount of water to empty the bowl. Pressure-assisted toilets are the most effective at disposing waste, but the flushing sound is sharp and a bit louder than in other low-flush toilets, but diminishes in 4 or 5 seconds; a second flush is never needed. There's also no condensation or sweating on the outer tank. These models tend to be more expensive; they can cost up to two to three times more than the standard gravity-operated toilet.

The third variety of flushing actions is a *washdown toilet,* which is no longer accepted by many code authorities; however, you may see them in remodeling projects. The washdown is used in other countries but no longer in the United States. This type drains through the front

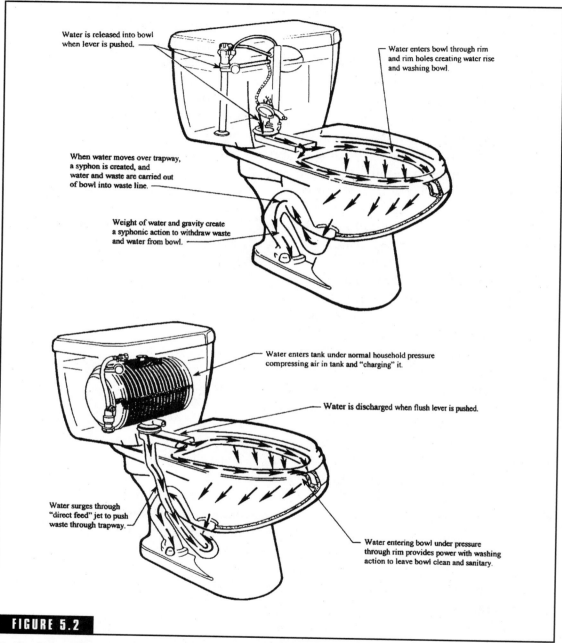

Water is released into bowl when lever is pushed.

Water enters bowl through rim and rim holes creating water rise and washing bowl.

When water moves over trapway, a syphon is created, and water and waste are carried out of bowl into waste line.

Weight of water and gravity create a syphonic action to withdraw waste and water from bowl.

Water enters tank under normal household pressure compressing air in tank and "charging" it.

Water is discharged when flush lever is pushed.

Water surges through "direct feed" jet to push waste through trapway.

Water entering bowl under pressure through rim provides power with washing action to leave bowl clean and sanitary.

FIGURE 5.2

Gravity-fed versus pressure-assisted toilets. *(American Standard.)*

of the bowl, is the most noisy of the various models, the least expensive, and least efficient. It has the smallest water surface and the smallest trap opening and is subject to fouling because of the design of the front area of the bowl, and the small trap opening tends to clog. The bowl can become stained and contaminated very easily. If working on an older home with washdown toilets, have the homeowners replace them with one of the other types mentioned.

Water Conservation

A major factor to consider when deciding on a toilet is water conservation. For many years, older standard toilets required at least 5 to 7 gallons/flush, making them the largest single user of household water. In 1983, codes were changed to require $3^1/_2$-gallon/flush (gpf) toilets for new construction. However, with water conservation rising as a top concern in many parts of the United States, many states started to mandate that all new residential construction install toilets that use no more than 1.6 gpf. As a result, the federal government enacted a national standard limiting the water use by residential toilets; in compliance with the Energy Policy Act of 1992, toilets manufactured in the United States after January 1, 1994, must use no more than 1.6 gallons of water per flush.

Water-conserving toilets presently cost more than the older 3.5- or 5-gpf models, but the savings on water and sewer bills will eventually make up for the difference. A homeowner who depends on a well for water and a septic system to handle waste will see other advantages; less water per flush means a smaller load on the septic system, and less demand on the electric well pump.

Although conserving water is a real concern today, some homeowners complained that earlier ultra-low-flush toilets did not really save water because they didn't always remove the waste in one flush, sometimes requiring several flushings to clear the bowl, thereby defeating the purpose of saving water. To keep up with these demands, manufacturers have developed, as discussed earlier in this chapter, improved versions of standard gravity-fed toilets with better flow and trap design to increase velocity, and the pressure-assisted design, which uses a strong air pressure to power a quick, intensive flush. Today's units are much more reliable than the early water-saving models.

Selecting toilets (or "water closets," as they are formally called) can be quite a confusing task. Today's toilets now come in a great variety of sizes, shapes, colors, and styles. Almost all toilets are made of porcelain–vitreous china, a durable, stain-resistant material. This is a hard, brittle material coated with a nonporous glaze. There are variations among these; better-quality toilets will have smoother glazing and no pinholes in the glaze.

Like other fixtures, toilets are available in a wide variety of colors—from classic white to shiny black, with soft pastels and varying shades of blues, greens, and other colors in between—basically a color available for every bathroom style or theme. Some manufacturers, with a sample (i.e., fabric swatch, tile, or paint sample), can custom-glaze the fixture in almost any color possible. Although all of these colors are available, the majority of people do use white. Choosing a toilet with color costs more; a client who chooses white can save up to 25 percent.

Regardless of the toilet's color or style, the homeowner wants one that will function dependably and quietly. Most manufacturers offer collections of similarly styled toilets, bidets, lavatories, and bathtubs, with styles ranging from contemporary, art deco, to traditional, Victorian styling. Because the fixtures are offered in collections, the bathroom's design can be unified. Generally, high style is synonymous with high price; however, some functional differences do exist between styles. Toilets are available in varying widths, heights, and bowl shapes, some of which the user might find more comfortable than others.

Toilet Sizes

When choosing a toilet, calculate the amount of room available between the wall and the center of the floor flange. Typically, the distance will be 12 inches (30.5 cm), but in some baths, it may be only 10 inches (25.4 cm). Whatever the measurement, the new toilet must match precisely.

When selecting a toilet for a bathroom, it will help to know basic toilet sizes. Tank widths vary from 20 to 24 inches (50.8 to 60.9 cm). Toilets with the tank mounted high on the wall are approximately 15 inches (38 cm) wide. Toilets project out from the wall (the depth) 26 to 30 inches (66 to 76 cm), requiring a minimum room depth of 44 and 48 inches (111.7 and 121.9 cm), respectively. Some newer toilets are 16 or

17 inches (40.6 to 43 cm) high at the seat level (as opposed to the conventional 14-inch-tall (35.5-cm) models and are designed for taller people and those with back problems. Before installing a new toilet in an older house, check the *offset*—the distance between the back wall stud and the center of the drain hub (measure to the hold-down nuts). The newer models are designed for a 12-inch (30.5-cm) offset.

Toilet-Bowl Shapes

Toilets usually have round or elongated bowls. Elongated toilets have bowls that extend about 2 inches (5 cm) farther in front than those in standard models and are available in both one- and two-piece versions. They are generally considered to be more comfortable to sit on and are easier to keep clean because of the increased water surface.

Toilet Designs

Toilets are available in two basic designs: (1) one-piece, where the tank is part of the bowl design, tank, and base are in a single molded unit; and (2) two-piece, where the water tank is a separate unit coupled or bolted to the bowl. In the most common type the tank is directly behind the base.

One-piece toilets combine the tank and bowl into a single unit, molded together (Fig. 5.3*a–f*). They are designed for floor and wall mounting. One-piece toilets are characterized by their low profile, usually 19 to 26 inches (48.3 to 66 cm) high. They take up the same floor space as standard toilets but are less intrusive visually; low-profile models may offer more wall space or potential for storage, such as when built into a wall unit or as an extension of a vanity. Ordinarily their flushing sound is quieter than in other styles. One-piece models are generally easier to clean than others. These toilets cost more than most two-piece models; however, their design, efficiency, and easy installation make them a popular choice. Lower toilets have less water height, which decreases the force of flushing velocity.

Two-piece toilets are available in many models and can be mounted on the floor or hung on the wall (Fig. 5.4*a–e*). With wall-hung toilets, the weight is supported from the wall frame; therefore it must be reinforced. If the bathroom doesn't already have a wall-hung toilet, then major alterations to the wall framing and the floor will be necessary for installation. Floor-mounted traditional two-piece styles have a

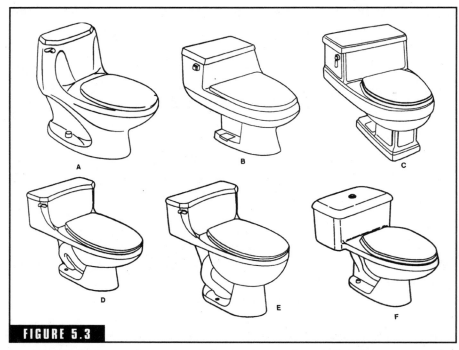

FIGURE 5.3

Several different types of one-piece toilets: a clean, contemporary-designed one-piece toilet with round front and concealed trapway (a); a sleek, low-profile design which uses gravity-fed flushing action (b); low-profile toilet with traditional styling and elongated seat and cover (c); exclusive space-saving low-profile toilet with gravity-fed flushing action (d); an elongated bowl that fits into the same space as most round bowls with extra height; meets ADA requirements (e); a one-piece design which uses pressure-assisted flushing action and a chrome-plated top button actuator (f). *(American Standard.)*

separate water tank that fits on top of a commode base, or bowl. They are less expensive than other models; however, they are a little more difficult to install. When remodeling, it is less expensive to replace a two-piece toilet with a two-piece rather than a one-piece toilet because the water supply line won't have to be lowered.

A third design features a tank raised high on the wall. This design is used to provide a Victorian motif (Fig. 5.4f).

Additional factors to consider when selecting a toilet are to look for styles with accessible bases, for easy cleaning. For the least amount of scrubbing, consider a wall-mounted model or buy the toilet with the largest horizontal water surface in the bowl. Some toilet tanks have optional liners to reduce tank sweating. Others are available with odor-eliminating features; some work by creating a vacuum in the bowl; others require fans, complete with their own outlets. For people with special needs, consider special toilet designs. The rim of a higher-seat safety toilet is 18 inches (45.7 cm) above the floor, compared to the 14-inch (35.5 cm) height of a conventional bowl (see Chap. 4).

According to American Standard, the future of toilets sees better uses of small spaces. They predict a clean-running half-gallon toilet. And space savers such as on a train, where the lavatory flips up to reveal the toilet.

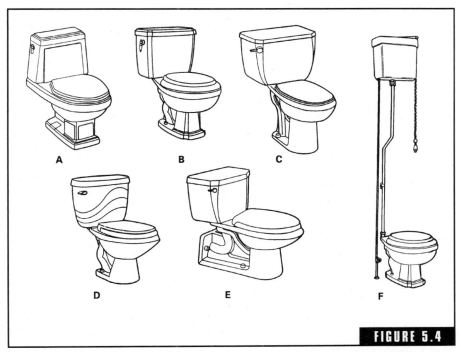

FIGURE 5.4

Several different types of two-piece toilets: a traditional styled two-piece toilet which uses gravity-fed flushing (*a*) turn-of-the-century detailing with 1.6-gallon low consumption (*b*); this toilet provides extra height (17 inches) for comfort and accessibility while meeting ADA requirements (*c*); a beautifully sculpted tank (*d*); floor-mounted wall outlet toilet with pressure-assisted flushing action and 1.6-gallon low consumption (*e*); the old-fashioned look of a raised tank lends authenticity to a Victorian-style bathroom (*f*). *(American Standard/Leon E. Korejwo, Illustrations.)*

Bidets

The bidet was first introduced in France circa 1710. After riding horses all day, soldiers used to bathe their pelvic areas by sitting on a small carpenter's bench—called a *bidet* in French ("small pony"). The bidet, which helped to prevent irritations, was considered much better than toilet paper, and was, in simple terms, very convenient. The use of the bidet spread quickly throughout Europe; eventually, entire families were using them. Widely used for decades in Europe, bidets are now—although it has taken time for the United States to catch on—gaining popularity and becoming more common in American bathrooms. Today, the bidet has become a bathroom basic for many.

A companion to the toilet, the bidet is a fixture that is used for cleaning the perineal area of the body after using the toilet. Basically, it looks like a toilet without the tank or lid. Male or female, the user sits astride the bowl of the bidet either facing the faucet handles, which regulate water volume and temperature, or away from the wall. A gentle spray allows the user to cleanse the pelvic area more conveniently than by using other methods.

Although bidets are used primarily for personal hygiene, there are several medical benefits to their use; when employed as an aspect of daily personal care, bidet use has been reported to reduce the frequency of many ailments common to the perineal area. Many physicians believe that this washing practice prevents skin infections and irritations in the genitourinary area. The thermal effect and soothing action created by water under pressure striking the body are also advantageous in the hygienic care of postoperative patients, the physically challenged, or elderly people. Bidets can be a therapeutic aid when dealing with chronic urinary-tract infections, yeast infections, the inflammatory symptoms of hemorrhoids, incontinence, constipation, and postpartum complications. Their use can reduce the recurrence of cystitis and vaginitis, as well as the soreness associated with diarrhea. Always fresh, the nonirritating water wash provides a natural and soothing cleansing not achieved with dry paper; hygiene is improved and comfort is increased. Regular users of the bidet consider it far superior to using only toilet paper.

Bidets, like toilets, are made almost exclusively of vitreous china. They are made by all major fixture manufacturers in the same range of colors and styles (contemporary design to traditional styling) as other fixtures, and are offered in a number of designs and finishes to match toilets and other fixtures (Fig. 5.5). Some are even available with designs by architectural detailings (Fig. 5.6).

Available with wall- or deck-mounted water controls, bidets come with the traditional rim-and-spray combination, with upward spurt located in the center of the bowl (vertical cleansing spray), or the simpler over-the-rim spray, where the user can fill the bowl or wash in the spray (Fig. 5.7). Either type will leave the bidet user with a feeling of freshness and cleanliness. Some models have rim jets for rinsing to help maintain bowl cleanliness. Most models also have a mechanical pop-up stopper that permits water to accumulate in the bowl when desired. This also allows the unit to double as a foot bath, laundry basin, or a place to soak plants and flowers.

The optimum location for a bidet is alongside the toilet. When planning the bathroom, locate the bidet conveniently and not wedged into a space that makes it inaccessible or unpleasant to use. Especially when planning a compartmented bathroom, do not place the bidet in one compartment and the toilet in another. Ensure that there is enough space for the unit and that access is available for underfloor plumbing. Drain plumbing is set up the same as for toilets; however, a bidet's fresh water supply requires both hot- and cold-water-supply lines, in

FIGURE 5.5

Bidets, like toilets, are now available in many shapes and styles. *(American Standard.)*

FIGURE 5.6

Beautiful artistic edition of toilet and bidet can set the style of any bathroom. *(Kohler Company.)*

FIGURE 5.7

This contemporary-designed bidet provides the option of vertical cleansing spray or over-the-rim spray. *(American Standard.)*

addition to a drainpipe. Water, at the desired temperature, is supplied by a spray mounted on the back wall or bottom of the bowl.

Designed for through-the-floor or above-the-floor installations, the bidet unit usually requires a space approximately 30 inches (76 cm) of clear width and plan for the fixture to project out from the wall 25 to 27 inches (63.5 to 68.58 cm). The bowl of the fixture should be long enough [an interior dimension of 20 inches (50.8 cm) is recommended] so that one can reach both the front and back of one's body without shifting. Since most models require at least 3 sq ft (91 cm) of floor space; this fixture must be carefully factored into the floor plan. Remember that storage for towels, soaps, and accessories should be within reach when one is seated.

As in all choices of fixtures and design, have the homeowners examine their personal habits and ask them if they really will use a bidet—bidets have been known to be converted to planters. Handheld-shower manufacturers offer bidet attachments with quick-disconnect features that allow the user to change from a handheld showerhead to a handheld bidet fitting in seconds. Advise an unsure homeowner to try one of these before deciding on the floor-mounted model. Along with the continuing growth of bidet use is use of the *personal hygiene seats* which is a modified bidet that is either added to a standard water closet (toilet) or purchased as part of an integrated water-closet system. It gives not only the water advantage of a bidet but usually has a warm-air drying system as part of the package.

Lavatories

Sinks, called *lavatories* by the fixture industry, with standard fittings, accommodate shaving, washing, and tooth brushing. The lavatory is the bathroom's most frequently used element; therefore, locating it in the best possible location with all the necessities close at hand (towels, soaps, shaving cream, makeup, etc.) is vital to the whole bathroom plan. The sink area should be an important and carefully designed area; it is no longer just a mirror and a basin. Unless a large tub, whirlpool, or luxury shower will be the focal point of the bathroom, the vanity and lavatory (especially a lavatory bowl with a dramatic design) are likely to be the most influential features in the room, with the greatest run of horizontal surface.

When deciding to replace an existing lavatory, make sure that it is with one that is appropriate. Before making any decision, have the homeowner consider all the options available, and how they will work in the space that is available. If the sink is too shallow, a shampooed head won't fit. If it is too deep, the user may as well use the bathtub. If it is too wide and square, there will not be enough room to arrange makeup on the side. If it's too narrow and ovular, it won't accommodate four or five reaching hands.

Today, bathroom lavatories are available in a range of sizes, styles, materials, and mounting methods. Elegant shapes from beautiful materials, rich colors, and decorative finishes can transform the bathroom lavatory into a work of art. Some manufacturers have even commissioned well-known artists to create numbered and signed designs. Along with sizes, styles, and varying depths and shapes, one can choose from many different colors and finishes.

Materials

Inform the homeowner that before choosing a bathroom lavatory, it is important to consider how the material will influence its appearance as well as its durability and level of maintenance. Lavatories, like all bathroom fixtures, are constantly being upgraded as the search for new materials allows more creative styles. Although most lavatories are made of vitreous china, many other materials are available, such as enameled (porcelainized) steel, cast polymer, enameled (porcelainized) cast iron, and solid-surface materials. Today, sinks constructed of plastic compounds, custom-glazed china, wood, or metals such as steel, copper, or even brass and fiberglass-reinforced plastic, are available. Marble and other stones and stainless steel offer top performance and high style. Lavatories are available in the following different materials, each with its own characteristics:

1. *Porcelain-enameled cast-iron* lavatories, typically the most popular choice for bathtubs for its durability and comfort, is an excellent choice for lavatory basins. Cast iron is considered one of the best lavatory materials. These sinks are manufactured with a heavy wall thickness of iron with a baked-on enamel applied to all exposed surfaces. The enamel-on-cast-iron sink is four times thicker than other types of sinks, which provides much greater resistance to cracking, chipping, and marring. Porcelain-enameled cast-iron lavatories are extremely durable, smooth, attractive, and easy to maintain. They are available in a variety of colors, and are competitively priced. However, because it is the heaviest fixture material, which can cause problems in installation, these lavatories need a sturdy support system.

At one time, enameled cast iron was used extensively for pedestal and wall-hung lavatories. Today, however, cast-iron lavatories are used almost exclusively for cabinet installation. All things considered, of all fixture materials, cast iron offers the best value for the money. Some manufacturers have created their own cast-iron formula. For example, American Standard states that their products are developed through a patented process bonding a high-quality porcelain enamel surface with an enameling grade metal and a structural composite backing. Their exclusive bonding process yields a product that is tougher than ordinary cast iron, weighs less, and outperforms ordinary cast iron in dependability and durability. It consistently resists chips, nicks, and cracks better than do the porcelain surfaces of traditional cast-iron lavatories.

2. *Vitreous china* is probably the most common material available for lavatories. Vitreous (impervious to water) china is crafted from a special clay-water mixture fired at intense heat to produce a durable, high-gloss finish. Vitreous china has proved impervious to water, mold, and mildew and is resistant to damage (scratches and abrasion). This material has definitely earned a reputation for durability, easy cleaning, and reasonable cost. The smooth, glazed surface will not rust, corrode, fade, or discolor; however, it is subject to chipping and cracking if struck with a heavy object. Vitreous china lavatories are available in many original styles with colorful patterns and textured surfaces. Quality varies among these lavatories, depending on the quality of the clay used to manufacture the unit and the way it is fired. The sign of a good-quality vitreous china lavatory is a smooth surface, free of bubbles, pinholes, or discoloration. Painted china lavatories, which have a delicate, ornamental quality, have become quite popular recently (Fig. 5.8).

3. *Fireclay,* much like vitreous china, is another elegant option. Fired at high intense heat, this durable ceramic has a hard (30 percent thicker than vitreous china), glossy finish. Their one-of-a-kind color and patterns make these bowls irresistible. Take caution when installing the waste and faucet with these pieces of art, because, in some instances, these bowls may be too irregular for standard-sized mounting rings and will need to be custom-mounted to the counter-top. Some of the larger-sized lavatory designs are so elaborate that they almost resemble furniture.

4. *Synthetic composites* have been combined to form very popular, durable lavatories. Many different manufacturers have produced their own varieties and blends of natural mineral fillers (such as quartz) and resins to create an exceptionally strong and resilient solid surfaced material. The actual contents vary between the different products on

FIGURE 5.8

A classic nursery rhyme adds a touch of style to a child's bathroom. *(American Standard.)*

today's market, as well as between different manufacturers. The very strong, nonporous materials are easy to clean and highly resistant to tough stains (including dyes, coffee, and other household products), scratches, chips, and burns. They are available in various colors and patterns, and some are formed like a fine stone, providing the elegant look and feel of natural granites and marbles (lavatories are also available in real marble, but they are extremely expensive). They are heat- and fade-resistant, although some have been known to show fine cracks around the drains after years of use. If minor cuts and scratches were to occur, they could be easily removed by sanding gently with fine-grade sandpaper. This type of sink can be finished to a matte or polished surface, with unlimited design possibilities. It is solid with the color and pattern all the way through. Today's solid-surface countertops can be coupled with a molded integral sink for a sleek, sculpted look. The sink color can either match the countertop exactly or complement it.

5. *Porcelain enameled-on-steel* is formed of sheet steel in one piece and sprayed and fired to produce a glasslike finish, much like the surface found on cast-iron sinks. However, because of the unique physical characteristics of the material used, the finish on porcelain enameled-on-steel sinks is only one-fourth as heavy as that on cast-iron sinks. These porcelain sinks are available in white and in colors. The advantages are its low cost and light weight, which make it especially good for remodeling. Unfortunately, enameled-on-steel sinks do not wear as well as others, and if something is dropped on it, it can chip with no way to hide the blemishes. In addition, water against this lavatory can be noisy. The overflow passageway is an additional handicap for the enameled-on-steel lavatory basins. The *overflow* is the sealed channel that is supposed to catch any excess water in the bowl and deliver it to the sink waste (below the stopper) before the water can flood the basin. On enameled-on-steel sinks it is a separate, stamped piece of steel that has been spot-welded to the bowl to form the passage, prior to enameling. The junction between the two invariably rusts out and starts to leak, and the bowl has to be replaced. On cultured-marble, acrylic, and cast-iron sinks, this passage is molded or cast as an integral part of the bowl.

6. *Metal sinks* are beautiful accents; however, they require a great deal of maintenance and are best when installed in low-use areas (powder rooms, guest baths, etc.). Beautiful, hand-crafted metal basins can be made from brass, bronze, copper, and aluminum. Before purchasing one of these, consider the following potential drawbacks. For one, they are often incompatible with standard mounting practices. In addition, they seldom have an overflow, which may be mandatory depending on the project's location, and their drain holes also may not be a standard size. Before deciding to purchase a metal sink, it is important to check with the local authority regarding the installation.

7. *Stainless-steel sinks* are rarely used in lavatory basins, in part for aesthetic reasons, but also because of the need to add an overflow channel. They have, however, been used in unique bathroom plans. Stainless steel is light, durable, and unaffected by household chemicals. The surfaces are easy to keep clean and stain-resistant, and will not fade, chip, crack, or rust. The steel, however, does tend to collect spots from hard water and soap residue. They will provide a lifetime of service. Since stainless steel is the finish, this type of sink is not available in colors. But the natural finish blends well with most color schemes.

Lavatories are no longer limited to one shape and one size. They are available in an almost limitless number of sizes, shapes, and styles—from sleek sculptured-shell-patterned pedestal units to designs with special features for shampooing. The hottest trends in bath sinks and faucets right now combine new finishes and manufacturing techniques with classic, retro designs and elegant, rounded shapes. When it comes to bath sinks and faucets, classic styles that evoke past eras are gaining in popularity, particularly in transitional, updated incarnations. Smooth, rounded lines for sinks and a new, more durable coating for faucets are hot trends, as well, according to manufacturers. There are many contemporary hexagons and triangles, along with the more traditional squares, rectangles, circles, and ovals.

Styles

Just as lavatories vary in shapes, sizes, and materials, they are mounted in a number of different ways (Fig. 5.9*a–c*). The most commonly available styles of sinks, each with its advantages and disadvantages, basically fall into the following categories:

1. *Pedestal lavatories.* This one-piece, freestanding, lavatory consists of the lavatory or basin mounted on a pedestal base, typically positioned at a comfortable standing height (Fig. 5.9*a*). Pedestal lavatories—which are based on a design that dates back to the turn of the century—are making a big comeback today, in a wide range of traditional, classic, and contemporary designs; they add a classic elegance to any bathroom (Fig. 5.10). Typically made of vitreous china, these elegant sinks are easy to install and clean around. With most designs, the pedestal usually hides the plumbing. Drainpipes are hidden from view inside the pedestal and only the water-supply valves are visible. Pedestal lavatories are secured to walls with screws as well as supported by their pedestal. The major disadvantage of a pedestal sink is that there is no counter space; therefore, it is basically for use in bathrooms that already have plenty of other counter space. This can, however, be resolved by installing a larger pedestal sink. In addition, there is not any storage space under the basin. A pedestal sink not only gives a bathroom distinctive charm but can also make a small bathroom look

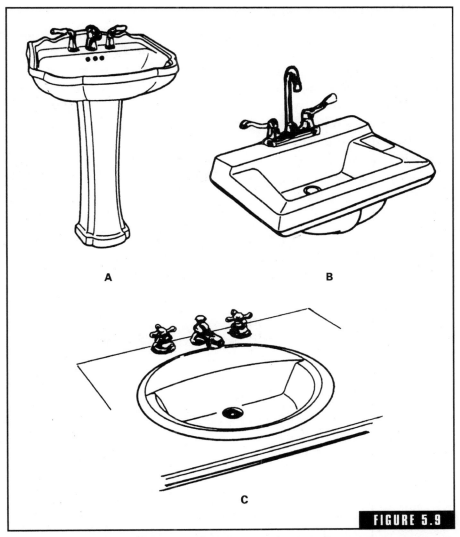

A   B

C

FIGURE 5.9

Lavatories can be mounted in three different ways: pedestal or freestanding (*a*); wall-mounted (*b*); or countertop- or deck-mounted (*c*). *(American Standard.)*

larger because of the lack of wide counter (around the sink) and storage below. Pedestal sinks are ideal for small bathrooms because they require a minimum of space. They take up little floor space so they can be placed in unusual spots. A pedestal sink can be installed into a space as narrow as 22″ (56 cm), although it will look better with a generous open space on each side. In a larger bathroom, they can be installed side by side to provide separate wash areas for two people. Unfortunately, pedestal sinks are typically among the highest-priced basins. Things to look for in a pedestal sink are the quality of the material, how well the bowl mates to the pedestal, and how well the finished product maintains a trueness of shape. Many models are offered with a large deck area with backsplash rim and ledge area for soap, cloth, or sponge. They have either flat tops or raised backsplashes where they meet the wall.

2. *Wall-mounted lavatories.* This type of lavatory features a basin that is hung from the wall, at a desired, comfortable, functional height (Fig.

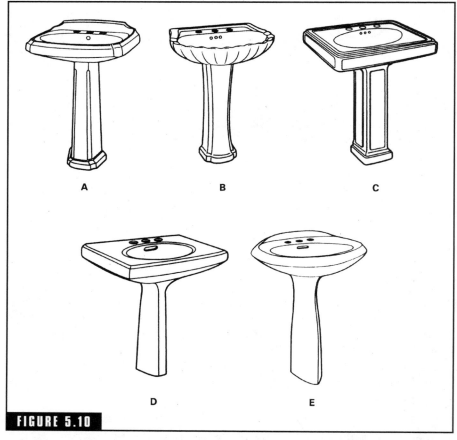

FIGURE 5.10

Pedestal sinks add a classic elegance to any bathroom with turn-of-the-century styling (*a*), sculptured shell patterned bowls (*b*), traditional styling (*c*), clean-lined styling (*d*), and graceful designs (*e*). *(American Standard.)*

5.9*b*). They are mounted on the wall by means of hangers or angle brackets for support that are secured to the studs. Like pedestals, wall-hung sinks are enjoying a contemporary revival. Most wall-mounted lavatories include a matching shroud for placement beneath the basin to conceal the piping. They have the advantage of fitting into tight spaces (e.g., a small unique corner installation). However, wall-hung sinks have no storage below and may not always conceal the plumbing below. This style of sink is great in bathrooms designed for people with disabilities because the sink can be installed at any height and have a clear space underneath that allows for wheelchair access. Materials and styling of wall-mounted lavatories are similar to pedestal lavatories; in fact, some designs are available in either version (Fig. 5.11). Generally speaking, they are the least expensive and most compact sink options, and are relatively easy to install. If installing a wall-hung sink for the first time, plan to tear out part of the wall to add a support ledger.

3. *Countertop or deck-mounted lavatories* are designed for use with vanities and countertops (Fig. 5.9*c*). The majority of lavatory basins made today are cabinet-mounted, and of these, the self-rimming

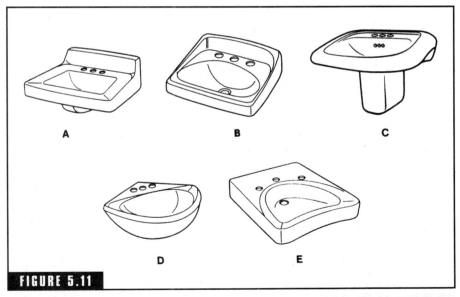

FIGURE 5.11

Different styles of wall-mounted lavatories: rectangular bowl (*a*); asymmetric bowl (*b*); wall-hung with concealed arm carrier for handicapped usage and knee protection (*c*); unique corner bowl (*d*); wheelchair users' lavatory (*e*). (*American Standard.*)

style is generally the easiest to install. These sinks have lots of countertop space around them and can be set into a counter with storage beneath; drawers are more useful than the open space filled with pipes. Their sizes and shapes can be tailored to fit the user's needs and habits (Fig. 5.12).

When planning to install the lavatory, the NKBA suggests a minimum of 4 inches (10 cm) edge to edge between the bowls; 11 to 18 inches (27.9 to 45.7 cm) would be better. At the end of the counter, allow at least 6 inches (15.24 cm) between the ledge of a bowl and the wall—12 inches (30.48 cm) if possible—so as not to feel cramped. Although many homeowners may want to have two lavatories in the same bath, which are customarily placed side by side to utilize the same supply and waste pipes, nothing prevents placement on different walls. If installing two lavatories in the same counter, allow a minimum of 12 inches (30.48 cm) between them and 8 inches (20.32 cm) at each end of the counter. Choose the largest sink to fit with these suggestions; larger sinks are more comfortable to use, and they reduce the amount of water that splashes out of the bowl. If the bathroom is small, avoid using large vanities (even though the storage space is

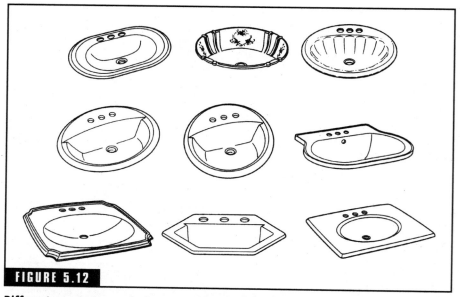

FIGURE 5.12

Different countertop or deck-mounted lavatory shapes. *(American Standard.)*

useful). Instead, choose a pedestal lavatory or a wall-hung style; each takes up less space. Space limitations may cause reconsideration here and although undesirable, perhaps, it may be wise to have one large bowl well situated with ample room around it rather than two small bowls crammed into an inadequate area. Make sure that there is enough room next to each bowl for toiletries and grooming equipment.

The way a lavatory is mounted to the countertop has both aesthetic and practical consequences. There are several different installation styles to choose from when deciding on a lavatory.

1. *Undercounter mount* (*rimless*) lavatories fit tightly, or flush, beneath the countertop opening for a streamlined look (Fig. 5.13*a*). Without any seams or ridges on the countertop at the sink edge its design is sleek and clean. The lavatory is attached to the bottom of the countertop recessed under the countertop and held in place by metal clips. The fittings are mounted through the countertop or directly on the sink. They offer unobstructed countertop surfaces, giving more options for working with color. In some instances they may be difficult to clean at the joint line between vanity and lavatory. This sink is a good choice for use with tile, synthetic marble, and solid-surface countertops.

2. *Flush mounts* (*rimmed*) are held in place through the use of a separate, stainless-steel sink rim and a set of special screw clamps (Fig. 5.13*b*). A surrounding tight-fitting metal frame holds a flush-mount sink to the countertop. With this type, it is difficult to keep the joints between the frame, sink, and countertop clean. The frame comes in several finishes to match the fittings. This style is usually used with plastic laminate countertops.

3. *Top-mount* (*self-rimming*) sinks are the easiest type to install. They have rolled finished edges that can be mounted directly over the countertop opening, with no special tools or techniques required. A self-rimming sink has a molded overlap that's supported by the edge of the countertop cutout (Fig. 5.13*c*). The outside rim is a ridge around the bowl that fits over the countertop to form a tight seal. The specially cut hole in the bathroom vanity is undersized, allowing the sink rim to sit on top of the counter after the sink is dropped into a hole, large enough to accommodate the sink bowl but smaller than the outside rim of the sink. Manufacturers offer a template to give the correct

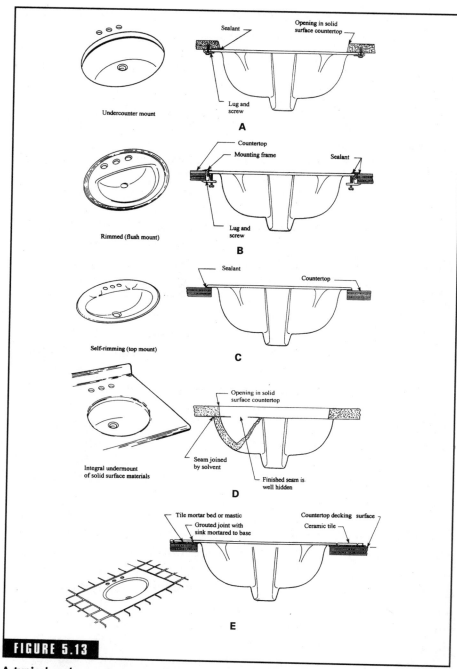

FIGURE 5.13

A typical undercounter mount lavatory (*a*); a typical rimmed or flush-mount lavatory (*b*); a typical self-rimming or top-mount lavatory (*c*); a typical integral undermount of solid surface materials (*d*); a typical tile-in sink (*e*). *(Leon E. Korejwo, Illustrations.)*

shape of hole. Installation is simple because the hole in the countertop need not be perfect because it is hidden once the sink is installed. This style offers the widest range in shapes, including shell, hexagon, and fluted. An additional advantage of the self-rimming sink, which does not require a metal mounting rim to hold it in the cabinet, is that it is easy to replace. Although it's easier to get behind the faucets to clean than with some other types, the joint line between lavatory and vanitytop may be hard to clean.

4. *Integral-bowl sinks,* synthetic composite sinks, can be installed under a countertop made of a matching product to produce a seamless, sleek, sculpted look, molded with no joint or separation between the bowl and countertop (Fig. 5.13*d*). Made of solid-surface material, synthetic marble, vitreous china, or fiberglass, an integral sink and countertop has no joints between the bowl and countertop, so installation and cleaning are easy. Easy to install, this type is set on top of a cabinet and fastened from below; installation costs are about the same for integral units and for separate lavatories and countertops. Some solid-surface units may require factory installation offsite, while some manufacturers advise using bowls of similar materials when joining for the seamless look. However, they can be seam-mounted into the countertop surface, so there is no rim to catch and trap dirt and water. This installation creates a dramatic design and makes cleaning easy. Sink color can either match the countertop or complement it with edge banding and other border options. Other integral sinks are available in synthetic marble, vitreous china, and fiberglass. The main disadvantage to this type of lavatory is that the entire unit, both lavatory and vanitytop, must be replaced if any part of it is damaged. Also available is a pedestal lavatory with an integral countertop.

5. *Tile-in lavatories* feature flat edges and square corners to fit flush with a tiled surface (Fig. 5.13*e*). Whereas self-rimming and rimless sinks are set by a plumber, tile-in sinks are usually installed by a tile setter.

6. *Vanitytop lavatories* are installed so that they will rest above the countertop, presenting a freestanding appearance. They sit fully exposed, on top of a tablelike surface. Manufacturers have created those that are reminiscent of china washbasins or vessels with finished inside and outside walls. This bold step in lavatory styling adds a sleek touch of elegance to any bath or dressing area. They blend the charm of washbasins from the past with the practicality of today, and are designed for use with virtually any countertop material, including colorful glass washbasins (Fig. 5.14). They are available in a variety of colors and textural finishes. Most vessels can be installed with a wall-mounted bracket; some can be installed in a self-rimming application or above the counter. This unique installation extends the design of the lavatory for an individualistic statement in the bathroom.

Sizes and Colors

The revolution in lavatories has added to the homeowner's design freedom (Fig. 5.15). Today, sinks can make a statement with the endless variety of shapes of bowls available—round, oval, square, roundish-squarish sinks, rectangular, triangular (fits nicely in a corner), hexagonal, and other special shapes (Fig. 5.16). Manufacturers have gone to great lengths to give sinks appeal by sculpting their forms; however, the simpler shapes are both more practical to use and easier to keep clean. Some of the more expensive models are adorned with hand-painted designs.

Like other fixtures, lavatories are available in a wide variety of colors. The most popular color, as well as least expensive, is white. The fittings for lavatories are also in a wide variety of styles, colors, and qualities; fittings are purchased separately from the lavatory (see later in this chapter). Vanity bowls are available in almost every imaginable color and style, as well as in several types of materials. Hand-painted finishes can be added to vitreous china sinks to coordinate with tile and other bathroom fixtures. Some manufacturers also offer groups of precoordinated hand-painted (such as with artist editions of flowers, fairy tales, animals, ribbons, etc.) or decorated sinks, tile, and fittings.

Whatever type of lavatory the homeowner chooses, be sure to install it at a

FIGURE 5.14

A unique hexagonal-shaped vanitytop lavatory.
(Kohler Company.)

comfortable height for the adults. Typically, lavatories are mounted 32 inches (81 cm) from the floor (from the top of the lavatory to the floor), but some feel that 34 to 38 inches (86.4 to 96.5 cm) is more comfortable. Lower versions are also available for children. Lavatory bowls range in size from a small 12 × 12 inches (30.5 × 30.5 cm) up to an expansive 22 × 44 inches (56 × 112 cm).

One last important factor when selecting a lavatory is to be sure that it is compatible with the chosen faucets (see later in this chapter). In most cases, it is much easier to hook up faucets and sink flanges before a sink is installed. When applicable, measure the existing vanity countertop to ensure that a comparably sized top will accommodate the lavatory and faucet selection (Fig. 5.17). Lavatories are drilled for faucets with a distance of either 4 inches (centerset), 6 inches, or 8 to 12 inches (widespread) (10.16, 15.24, 20.32, or 30.48 cm) between the hot and cold faucet handles. Many lavatories are also offered with centered single-hole drillings to accommodate single-hole faucets or ones with escutcheons. Holes for spray attachments and lotion and soap dispensers, usually offset to the right or left, must also be taken into account. Some lavatories do not have any faucet drillings; the faucet can be mounted directly on the wall or on the countertop.

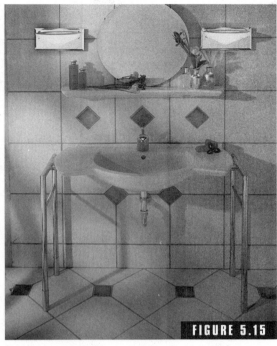

FIGURE 5.15

This exclusive pedestal lavatory can transform any ordinary bathroom into an extraordinary haven of style. *(American Standard.)*

Bathtubs and Showers

Today, more people look to the private escape of a deep, soaking bath to wash away the stress of the day. Although everyone may not have the time to indulge themselves daily, a tub is a prerequisite to relaxation in any bathroom. Even if the homeowner prefers to take showers, there should be at least one bathtub in every home. At some

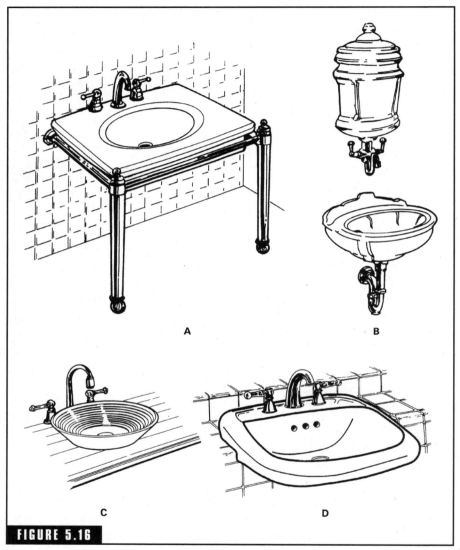

A

B

C

D

FIGURE 5.16

A lavatory with a dramatic design can be the focus of the room and, today, a wide variety of lavatory designs offer attractive alternatives: a unique console tabletop (*a*); cistern (*b*); a vessel-shaped bowl (*c*); a semicountertop lavatory (*d*). (*Leon E. Korejwo, Illustrations.*)

point, they may have to accommodate small children or elderly people who are unable to use a shower. Also, keep in mind the impact it may have on the home's resale value. In response to this demand, manufacturers have created more ways to escape in more sizes, shapes, and colors. As a result, the choice of styles, sizes, materials, and colors is staggeringly diverse. NKBA recommends 21- to 30-inch (53- to 76-cm) clearance in front of the bathtub or shower, 21 to 30 inches (53 to 76 cm) of room in front of the lavatory, and 15 to 30 inches (38 to 76 cm) from the center of the toilet bowl to the wall or fixture on either side.

Here's what you should know before selecting the tub and shower for the new bathroom.

Bathtubs

Inform your clients that before they purchase a tub, they should decide whether they would like a bathtub or a whirlpool and how large a tub—big enough for one or two—and whether they would like to sit across from or next to each other. Then, they should literally

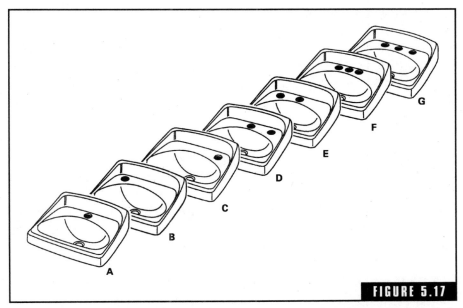

FIGURE 5.17

Lavatory faucet arrangements: single hole (*a*), single hole left offset (*b*), single hole right offset (*c*), single hole with right soap dispenser (*d*), single hole with left offset soap dispenser (*e*), three-hole 4-inch between faucets (*f*), three-hole 8-inch between faucets (*g*). *(Leon E. Korejwo, Illustrations.)*

climb in and try it out. Once they have decided what they would like, you, as the installer, should consider the size. For a remodel, be certain that the new tub will fit the existing space because the homeowner may not want to get involved with the time and expense of having the plumbing and drain lines relocated. Also, take into great consideration how the old tub will be removed and the new one brought into the home. Depending on the material of the existing tub, it may need to be broken apart or part of the wall removed. As far as bringing the new tub in, some styles will not fit through standard doorways, so check the tub's dimensions against the doorways, hallways, and stairways to ensure that you will be able to maneuver it into the bathroom. Getting a new unit in can be easier with a shower-tub kit that comes preformed in sections to fit easily through most doors.

Be cautious when installing a major built-in fixture such as a tub or shower. Its color, if too trendy, will be a problem if the homeowner decides to upgrade an easier replaceable fixture, such as a toilet or sink, because a matching color for the new replacement may no longer be available.

Like other fixtures, tubs are made of a variety of materials and in a variety of shapes and qualities. A white tub without special features is still the least expensive. Most fixtures are style- and color-matched by manufacturers in groups or sets. Keep in mind that if replacing only one of the styling group, consider future availability of the rest of the units.

PORCELAIN ENAMELED CAST IRON

Enameled cast iron, the classic material of old-fashioned, free-standing tubs, offers the greatest quality with excellent long-lasting durability against everyday wear and tear. According to American Standard, for years, despite its tremendous weight, expensive price, and susceptibility to chipping and crazing, cast iron has dominated the market as the preferred material for bathtubs. For bathtubs, cast iron is generally considered to be the best material one can buy; bathtubs of the highest quality are constructed of enameled cast iron. Coated with a heavy layer of baked-on enamel, cast iron makes an extraordinarily smooth and durable tub. Because of its rigidity, cast iron resists chips, dents, and abrasions. Another advantage is that cast iron tubs keep the water warm for a long time.

On the negative side, cast iron does have a few disadvantages. Porcelain enameled cast-iron tubs are extraordinarily heavy—350 to 500 pounds (130.6 to 186.6 kg)—making it more difficult to install, and more expensive than other types. It is a very hard material and can be unforgiving if one happens to fall in the shower; however, the bottoms of new cast-iron tubs have nonskid finishes. Because of its weight, if remodeling, check the joists to make sure that they will support the proposed installation. If the structural framing needs to be strengthened, it may cost substantially more to install.

To improve on these disadvantages and to make an even more perfect product for users, some manufacturers have created a remarkable alternative to cast iron that is more durable, weighs less, and is faster, easier, and less costly to install than cast iron. It even retains heat better (for a longer, more relaxed bathing experience than before) and emits less sound (10 to 12 decibels quieter than cast iron or enameled steel). These products are developed through a patented process bonding a high-quality porcelain enamel surface with an enameling-grade metal and a structural composite backing. Their exclusive bonding process yields a product, as stated, that's tougher than cast iron, weighs less [half the weight of cast iron: 140 vs. 280 pounds (52 vs. 104.5 kg)], and outperforms cast iron in dependability and durability. It consistently resists chips, nicks, and cracks better than do the porcelain surfaces of traditional cast-iron tubs.

ENAMELED STEEL

For many years, the majority of bathtubs sold were made of enameled steel: the familiar boxy, steep-sided units that have one finished side. Enameled-steel (also termed *enamel-on-steel*) tubs are steel-coated with enamel, although the coating is commonly thinner than that applied to cast iron. Today, there are still steel tubs on the market, however, because of its disadvantages, (e.g., they are noisier, are more prone to chipping and denting than other tubs, are cold and slippery, and may deform under the weight of water and bather), they are not highly recommended. Also, water cools down more quickly in a formed steel tub than in one made from fiberglass-reinforced plastic or cast iron. On the positive side, steel is relatively lightweight [they weigh about half what cast iron tubs do—usually between 120 and 125 pounds (44.7 and 46.6 kg)] and is among the least expensive tubs on the market. Before installing the tub, remember to check for the required structural reinforcement.

FIBERGLASS AND ACRYLIC

Acrylic and fiberglass tubs, offered as one-piece models with integral shower surrounds, and the trend toward larger bathtubs, is making fiberglass-reinforced acrylic a popular option. It is comparatively light-weight [most fiberglass tubs weigh between 60 and 90 pounds (22.5 and 33.5 kg)] and therefore lend themselves to remodeling where the structure may not support the heavier fixtures. It also has the added advantage of a large range of contours and sizes; it can be molded into elaborate, comfortable, shapely forms enabling manufacturers to offer a wider variety of forms and surface features, with a wide variety of built-in features, such as built-in arms, headrests, and grab bars. Strong, flex-resistant fiberglass and acrylic baths feature smooth, easy-care finishes that resist chipping and cracking, and their light weight makes them easy to install. Fiberglass is softer than cast iron or steel, a quality that would be welcome in the case of a fall. Plastic is a better insulator than metal so it is warmer to the touch and retains heat well.

Today's fiberglass tubs are available in a wide array of colors and shapes (more than other types); circular, oval, square, as well as the standard rectangle. Many styles are available in apronless models that are easily adaptable to a sunken or raised installation, greatly reducing the former expense of luxury arrangement. The standard rectangle is now deeper than the older cast-iron or steel models by 1 or 2 inches. These tubs are available in the latest colors, neutrals, with a wide range of soft pastels and bold, solid colors, glossy black, and traditional white. The gloss and color of the gel coat finish are similar in appearance to those of enameled or china fixtures.

Acrylic and fiberglass bathtubs are waterproof, durable, and simple to clean, providing an almost carefree surface; acrylic won't grow mildew or mold. Most manufacturers recommend that fiberglass be cleaned only with water, a mild dish detergent, or both. Although this material doesn't chip easily, if at all, abrasive cleaners may damage the surface; they tend to scratch or dull easily. Like cast-iron bathtubs, these tubs keep water warm for a long time.

One disadvantage to these tubs is purely aesthetic—some home-owners still prefer the appearance of cast iron and tile, which is generally perceived as higher quality than fiberglass or acrylic. Many also prefer the solid feel of the solid materials rather than flexible plastic. And overall, they are not as durable as cast iron.

CULTURED STONE

Cultured stone tubs are made of the same materials used to make lavatories. They are materials created by mixing various crushed stones (e.g., onyx, granite, or marble), with polyester resin. The tub's appearance will vary depending on the type of stone used. These tubs are available in every imaginable color and a host of shapes, and are easy to care for. They are far less expensive than tubs made of pure stone; however, they are not inexpensive. With cultured stone, all fixtures can be purchased with the same color and style, which is not always possible with other materials.

Shapes and Sizes

Today's bathtub market offers various styles, constructions, and new and more comfortable shapes. Standard rectangular tubs are 60 inches [5 feet (152.4 cm)] long, 14 to 16 inches (35.5 to 40.6 cm) deep, and 30 to 42 inches (76 to 106.7 cm) wide. Corner units are approximately 48 inches (122 cm) on the wall sides. The tub should be sized according to the available floor space, the level of luxury desired, and the size of the user. For example, if the tub is to serve two people together, the width inside should be at least 42 inches (106.7 cm). The users should be able to stretch out full length to relax, so a 5-foot (152.4-cm) tub would not be adequate for a person who is 5 feet 10 inches (178 cm) tall; also, a heavier person may feel constrained in a 30-inch (76-cm)-wide tub, and the 14-inch (35.5-cm) depth may be insufficient. If thinking of the tub as a place to relax, consider a separate shower and a larger tub; larger sizes are available. In standard tubs, for example, lengths to 6 feet (183 cm) and depths to 20 inches (51 cm) can be purchased. In some cases, there will not be room for a longer tub, but, there may be room for one that's wider and deeper. Increasing these dimensions can add to comfort considerably. When using a standard size tub, even a few inches can help.

Many other sizes and shapes are available in various materials. As stated earlier, before completing a purchase, take careful measurements of the space to make sure the chosen tub will fit through doorways to the bathroom—with room to install it. The standard shape for a tub is rectangular, but there are also corner tubs with a round or oval bathing area, corner-square tubs, recess tubs, square tubs, and oblong tubs. Some common bathtub designs are as follows:

1. *Standard rectangular tubs* are available in recessed and corner styles (Fig. 5.18). Recessed tubs fit between two side walls and against a back wall; they have one finished side. Tubs can be recessed into almost any available nook. Corner models have one finished side and end and may be right or left-handed. Rectangular tubs for recess or for corner installation are typically 5′ (152 cm) long (the most used length), but they are also available from as short as 4′ (122 cm) to as long as 8′ (244 cm). Tubs with widened rims are usually 30 to 33″ (76 to 84 cm) wide; tubs with straight fronts, 28 to 31″ (71 to 96 cm) wide. The tub opening either follows the basic outline or is "contoured"; that is, the oval is angled in the tub shape, providing wider ledges that are useful for seating, especially helpful when bathing children, and for holding bath soaps and oils. Although the standard tub size is 5′ (152 cm) long and 14″ (35.5 cm) deep; however, if space allows, choose a longer model. A 66″- (167-cm)- long tub affords better leg room, and the 16″- (40.6-cm)-deep models are more comfortable to bathe in than the standard 14″ (35.5-cm) ones.

2. *Square tubs* are about 4 × 3½′ or 4′ (132 × 107 cm), and are available for either recess or corner installations. Some styles have one built-in seat; others have two. A square tub is heavier than a rectangular tub and may require additional framing for support. Actually, all built-in tubs or cast iron and enameled steel must be partially supported by the studs to prevent their pulling away from the wall. A 2 × 4″ (5.08 × 10.16-cm) support secured to the studs or special hangers may be used. Fiberglass tubs and shower stalls have nailing flanges and are nailed directly to enclosing stud partitions.

3. *Claw-footed and other freestanding tubs* need adequate clearance on all sides to look their best. An old-fashioned freestanding tub, such as the enduring clawfoot model, makes a nice focal point for a traditional- or country-designed bathroom; reproductions or reconditioned originals are available (Fig. 5.19). These tubs can double as showers with the addition of a Victorian-inspired shower head, diverter, and curtain-rod hardware.

A standard rectangular bathtub with slip-resistant bottom. *(American Standard.)*

4. *Receptor tubs* are approximately 36 to 38″ (91.44 to 96.52 cm) long, 39 to 42″ (99.06 to 106.68 cm) wide, and about 12″ (30.48 cm) high. They are most suitable for shower installations but, because of their lower height, are also convenient for bathing children and others who need assistance.

5. *Platform or sunken tubs* are available in ready-made designs, usually rectangular in shape, or they can be custom-designed. They are most commonly available in enameled cast iron or acrylic, and are either set in a raised platform or sunk in the floor. Building codes should be checked with regard to installation of a sunken tub since some localities require more extensive supporting construction, especially for installation on an upper floor. For relaxation, soaking tubs are hard to beat. *Soaking tubs* are sunken tubs, with deep interiors, in which the bather can soak in a seated position with the water coming up to the neck. In Japan, where the soaking tub, or *furo,* is part of a bath ritual, bathers soap, scrub, and rinse themselves before they enter the

FIGURE 5.19

Combine the charm of the old with the efficiency of the new as you step back in time with this all-new claw-foot bathtub. *(American Standard.)*

tub to soak in hot water. In the United States, this ritual may or may not be followed. Most ready-made soaking tubs are about 40 × 40″ (101.6 × 101.6 cm), and the finished edges for all sides of the unit allow total flexibility in location. Ideal for use in small spaces, they are available in recessed, platform, and corner models, with rectangular or round interiors of fiberglass or acrylic. These tubs do not require an integral heater and take less time to fill than a whirlpool.

6. *Whirlpool tubs* can be thought of simply as bathtubs with air jets (Fig. 5.20). In new installations, whirlpool tubs, available in traditional tub styles and sizes, are in high demand. Jet designs vary with high volume and low pressure with a few strong jets or lots of softer jets. The best whirlpools are adjustable for water volume, air-water mixture, and direction. Because of their extra weight, whirlpools may need special floor framing. They may also require an extracapacity water heater or separate in-line heater. For more on whirlpool tubs, see Chap. 4.

7. *Tub-shower combinations* offer the greatest versatility, are generally less expensive than other bathing receptacles, quite durable, and easy to clean. One-piece bathtub-shower combinations are usually made from fiberglass. The fiberglass construction makes these units light, but their size complicates the installation and removal process. One-piece units are generally installed during the construction process because they are too large to fit through most doors and stairways. Many tub units with showers have glass or plastic doors or shower curtains, which enclose the front of the tub when the shower is in use. Most doors are of the sliding type, but there are folding plastic door units that are very functional and attractive. Amenities such as soap trays, grab bars, and utility shelves are all part of one molded piece.

FIGURE 5.20a

A whirlpool tub can fit into any bathroom scheme (*a, b*). *(American Standard.)*

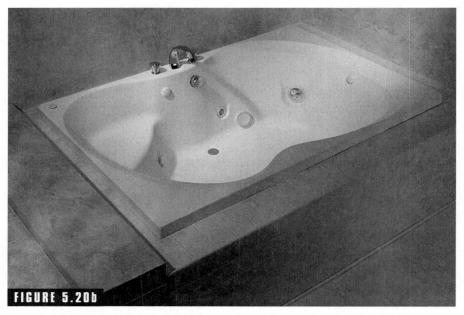

FIGURE 5.20b

A whirlpool tub can fit into any bathroom scheme (*a, b*). *(American Standard.)*

Most tubs have only the front finished, or "aproned." However, they are also available without an apron, allowing a facing to be built in front of the tub. Fiberglass whirlpools can be purchased with a removable apron, which is necessary for gaining access to and servicing the motor. Generally, sides of the tub are straight, but, today all of the new stylings, sloping sides and other configurations (e.g., armrests) may be part of the design. Modern tubs typically have bottoms that are flush with the floor, except for the old-fashioned claw-foot tub, (once again regaining popularity), which has feet and legs to raise it off the floor.

Interior Shape

Another important factor regarding bathtubs is the interior shape of the tub. While one presumably buys a tub to relax in, rather than just to clean one's body, the fact is that 90 percent of the time the tub is really purchased for use as a shower; a standard tub is simply not large enough to relax in. A tub might seem, at first glance, as if it would be very comfortable. But listed overall sizes can be deceptive. When considering styles of tubs, take into account some of the interior amenities manufacturers build into a product. Today's products offer all the personal amenities that help transform an ordinary bath into a rejuvenating bathing experience—lumbar support and beveled head-rests; sloping sides; a slip-resistant patterned bottom for added safety; luxury ledges for increased shoulder and elbow room or for placement of extra bath toiletries; back supports; raised, molded-in armrests; removable metal grab bars; contoured bottoms; and molded-in seats. Finally, be aware of small, attractive, special features, for example, tubs with the drain opposite the faucets, not directly below them.

Safety

When considering what tub to purchase, safety should be just as important as comfort and style. Be aware that, according to safety experts, the bathroom is the most dangerous room in the house, and the tub is the most hazardous part of it. To ensure the safety of every-one using the fixture, keep the following safety factors in mind:

- If the tub is the platform type or is sunken, the user should be able to get in and out of it easily. Steps should be large enough—at least 8″ (20.3 cm) wide with a 7″ (17.8-cm) riser (vertical portion).

- Steps should not be placed right at the edge of the tub.

- Installing a grab bar or two, ideally horizontally, will make it easier and safer for bathers to get in and out of the tub. Any grab bar should be secured to the bath framing (studs) rather than the wall material and be able to withstand a pull of 300 pounds dead weight.

- The bottom of the tub should have a slip-resistant surface, or at least a slip-resistant mat. The bottom itself should be flat rather than contoured.

- Flooring around the tub should have adequate traction.

- Towel rods on the wall adjacent to the tub should be located so that the user doesn't have to stretch to get a towel.

- Soap dishes should be recessed—so that they can't hurt anyone who falls—and can be reached easily. The same is true of wire baskets or other storage units.

A rich assortment of colors is offered in top of the line tubs, including custom tints. For a unique appearance, tubs can be custom-made of ceramic tile or a solid-surface material.

Showers

While many people bathe for relaxation and therapy, almost everyone showers as a part of the daily grooming process; therefore, showers are an important fixture for most households. Today's demand is for larger, more comfortable shower spaces, including two-person showers. With the continuing popularity of the whirlpool bath, many homeowners want a separate tub and shower. Whether the whirlpool tub is elsewhere in the bathroom or nonexistent because of a lack of space, the shower can become the room's focal point, both functionally and aesthetically. Although showering (the most economical way to cleanse the whole body) takes less time than bathing, a luxuriously designed shower with high-tech features, whether part of the tub or separate, allows the user to take a few minutes to relax while grooming (see Chap. 4 for more on luxury showers).

Begin by helping your clients decide what kind of shower suits their needs. Will it be small and functional or large and luxurious? The choice depends not only on the space available but also on how much they want to invest for a custom installation.

A shower can range in size from a compact 32 inches (81 cm) square, up to 48 inches (122 cm). Generally, 36 inches (91.5 cm) is considered the minimum for comfort and safety; anything smaller limits elbow room and the space to jump from the water stream if the water temperature suddenly changes. Allow at least 21 to 30 inches (53.34 to 76.2 cm) of walkway clearance between a shower stall and any opposing wall or fixture. This space should be modified to allow for the swing of the shower door—the wider the opening, the more clearance required.

For the installer, preplanning is important when creating a shower. Starting with the original plans, a plumber should be consulted to determine the amount of work involved and whether the home's water pressure is sufficient to accommodate the desired water features. Certain needs must be accounted for, and will have an impact on the bathroom's plumbing; be sure that it all coordinates and fits with the fixtures.

If space is tight, the most economical way to provide a shower is to add a showerhead over the tub. If the shower fittings are installed at the time the bathroom is built, the pipes for the shower can be concealed in the wall; however, shower fixtures with exposed pipes are available. Also, there are complete fiberglass shower units available that can be set into small niches very nicely as one unit. As a matter of fact, some uncrated shower stalls will pass through the rough framing of a 30-inch (76.2-cm) door. However, for ease of installation, the unit should be on the job during the early framing stages.

Showers can be custom-designed and built on site, or they can be prefabricated.

Custom-Made Showers

With custom enclosures, the possibilities are endless. Custom-made showers are framed like walls and finished with a variety of materials. With ceramic tile, glass block, stone tiles, solid-surface material, or marble, the size and shape of the shower space is completely up to the designer and installer. Custom-made showers may also feature walls and doors constructed of laminated safety glass; seamless glass doors and surrounds are popular. Because most people prefer an open, light shower environment, glass block, which is slightly more expensive than other options, makes for an ideal material for shower enclosures. It transmits light (for a safer, well-lit shower), while providing privacy (the light that shines through is distorted).

Custom building a shower demands more time and expertise, but allows the homeowner choices not available with prefabricated units. The shower can be built into the space available, such as in an out-of-the-way corner, recessed into a wall, or tucked under a steep roof. In addition, floor, wall materials, type of door, and accessories can all be chosen by the homeowner. However, even with this design freedom, a space at least 30 inches (76.2 cm) wide and 36 inches (91.44 cm) deep will be needed to avoid knocking elbows and knees into the walls. See Chap. 4 for more on luxury custom showers.

Prefabricated Shower Units

Prefabricated showers and shower-bath combinations, which are often less expensive than custom-made showers, are generally fabricated of molded plastics such as acrylic or fiberglass, plastic laminate, synthetic marble, and solid-surface material, which provides a durable and nearly maintenance-free shower stall, available as single units molded of fiberglass or cast acrylic and as poly(vinyl chloride) (PVC) wall and floor components that you assemble in place (Fig. 5.21). Walls of the shower stall look like ceramic tile, but they are actually stain- and mildew-resistant gelcoat fiberglass. Foam-back units—including tub-shower enclosures—feature surface texture and simulated grout lines. Acrylic incorporates designs for premolded accessories (shelves, soap dishes, etc.), all things that can't be included as easily with a custom-made tile shower. Prefabricated shower kits are equipped with a base, walls, and door, and are available in a wide range of colors, sizes, styles, and shapes—including rectangular, angular, round, and square.

Many manufacturers have one-piece and sectional versions of showers applicable to any building or renovation requirement. As with tubs, size is extremely important. A one-piece model should not

FIGURE 5.21

A unique corner prefabricated shower with neoangle shower door. *(American Standard.)*

be chosen without first making sure that it will fit through the house. Carefully measure the installation area and the widths of doorways, hallways, and any points to turn corners or stairs. In a remodel, if there are oversize doors in the house, you may be able to use a one-piece molded shower or tub-shower surround. However, these integral enclosures must be placed in the room before the framing is complete, and, therefore, are designed for new houses or additions. Even if working with a small existing bathroom space, a lot of neat things can still be incorporated into the luxury shower. If clearances are insufficient, consider a knock-down type, for example containing a separate tub and four panels for the walls. These units range in floor size from 30 × 30 inches (76 × 76 cm) to 36 × 36 inches (91.4 × 91.4 cm) to 34 × 48 inches (86 × 122 cm). This type can be easily used in new or old baths.

Tub-Showers

Showers combined with tubs save space as well as money. On the negative side, because bathtub bottoms are narrower and curved, tub-showers can be less convenient, and in some cases, not as safe as separate showers.

These popular shower systems, whether custom-made or prefabricated, offer many amenities. Some of the desired features include systems with the traditional shower plus body sprays, fully programmable showers (electronic vs. manual controls) with adjustable multiple-massaging showerheads (providing health benefits as well, e.g., a massage that tones and revives, and stimulates blood circulation), showerheads in different positions (on the ceiling, shower spray bars, rainbars, etc.), adjustable handheld sprayers (also great for cleaning the tub), and cascading waterfalls. Full-bodied steam units can also be incorporated into the shower.

To completely personalize the shower experience, faucets can be preprogrammed for water-temperature and water-volume control, which brings up the issue of pressure balance versus thermostatic valves. Thermostatically controlled valves are important because they actually allow users to personalize the shower by setting to a specific temperature; this is integral to getting the best effect from the shower experience. The pressure balance valve only prevents against scalding; it doesn't hold the temperature. The thermostatic valve has a much better flow and provides enough water to handle several body sprays, rainbars, and so on. Volume of flow, along with safety and control, are what makes thermostatic valves an important part of the luxury shower. Locating the controls near the shower entry allows the user to adjust water flow and temperature before entering.

Homeowners are also interested in items that will make their shower spaces well organized and comfortable. People like fog-free shaving mirrors, built-in shelving, hooks, sturdy decorative grab bars, a seat or bench (one that folds down to save space), armrest rails, soap dishes, and overhead lighting and fan systems. Built-in shower stereo sound systems with radio and CD players are also very popular. In many instances, these individual extras and components can be ordered separately, to create a completely customized space, or they can be purchased in upscale luxury shower packages. Many home-owners prefer the choice of creating their own personal environment. Overall, the design possibilities for a luxury shower are limitless.

Shower Bases

The floors of a custom shower can be site-installed tile over a plas-tic or copper shower floor membrane (receptor base or floor pan) or a prefab base of fiberglass; bases can also be made of acrylic, molded stone, or terrazzo, available in many colors (Fig. 5.22). For example, a pan must be installed below ceramic tile to prevent leakage. Typically, receptors are lead pans that are 5 to 6 inches (12.7 to 15.24 cm) deep, and include a 2-inch (5.08-cm) drain outlet. They are available in stan-dard sizes in rectangular of various sizes up to 60 inches (152.4 cm) long, square, typically 32, 34, or 36 inches (81.28, 86.36, or 91.44 cm), and as corner units, with the two wall sides 36 or 38 inches (91.44 or 96.52 cm) long; all have a predrilled hole for the drain. A shower base can be purchased separately or in a kit that includes a shower sur-round. Finding a base that matches a tub or fixture is very simple; many manufacturers make both. Choosing a prefabricated base elimi-nates the hassles of constructing a watertight floor but limits the shower to the size and shape of the base.

Shower Doors

Unless installing an open or hand-held shower, a curtain or door will be needed. Shower doors are supplied separately from the shower itself and consist of the door and a framework. Doors for showers are

An acrylic corner shower base. *(American Standard.)*

designed for installation in various situations and may be swinging, sliding, folding, and pivoting. For tub-showers, choose sliding or folding doors. They have a metal frame and may be aluminum- or brass-colored. These frames are available in many finishes and can be selected to match the fittings. Doors and enclosures are commonly made of tempered safety glass with aluminum frames. For safety, the glass used must be either tempered or laminated plastic. Curtains are available in fabric and synthetic materials (poly and vinyl), which tend to mildew less than natural materials woven in to fabrics. Of course, each has advantages and disadvantages.

Shower Safety

Safety issues are an important part in the design of a shower. As mentioned earlier in this chapter, it is easier to achieve safe entry and exit in the shower than in a tub; therefore, a shower may be the answer for the aging population, for people with varying physical abilities, and for those planning ahead for accessibility in their later years. For safety, showers should include grab bars, seating, handheld sprays, slip-resistant flooring, and faucets that have scald protection. Safety features are always important with the shower, and universal design will be a concern at some point in almost everyone's life. Eliminate as many protrusions as possible in and around showers and tubs so that they won't be in the way in case of a fall. For more on showers for wheelchair-bound users, see Chap. 4.

Faucets

Fixtures provide the required means for using water. Each has a purpose connected with the homeowner's use of water, and each must have certain features to serve its purpose. Fixtures can be costly plumbing items and should exactly suit the homeowner's needs. A *faucet* is a valve used at the end of a water-supply line. "Fittings" is really a technical name for faucets. Fittings are sold separately from fixtures. When remodeling a bathroom, ask your clients whether they want the existing fixtures and fittings to be cleaned, refinished, or repaired. If not, review with them what features they do and do not like about their existing fittings. Have them evaluate the size, shape, and materials, and the way the faucets turn on and off. Can they adjust the water temperature for the sink and shower as easily as they would like?

In most homes, bathroom fittings receive very heavy daily use; therefore, if assisting your clients when selecting fittings, advise them to consider durability, ease of use and maintenance, and safety, not to choose those that are only aesthetically pleasing. With faucets, the price varies according to material, quality, and design; price, in most cases, is a fairly accurate measure of the quality and level of luxury. A warranty is usually a good indication of a higher-quality faucet.

Faucets are available in a wide (and constantly changing) array of materials, sizes, styles, colors, and accessories to help give every bathroom a custom-made look. Upscale faucets are available in an array of shapes that complement any decor—from strictly traditional to futuristic compression faucets. For instance, ornate fittings along with decorated lavatory bowls, reflecting the styles of earlier eras which combine the charm of the old with the efficiency of the new, are returning in use to give new elegance to the bathroom. Antique-style reproductions, exotic handle shapes, pool-effect faucets with a matching porcelain lavatory, rich colors, and unexpected finish combinations create highly personalized yet functional bathrooms. Be creative—for a cascade of water in the sink or tub, waterfall-style spouts are extremely attractive; also, they produce a gentle flow and fill tubs much faster than do standard fittings. Today's faucets also have features such as sensor-activated faucets which turn on automatically when the user's hands appear under the spout and have digital temperature readouts, and antiscald controls.

Materials

Whatever style is chosen, most bathroom professionals agree that the highest-quality and most durable fittings are constructed of solid brass. They are available in various finishes and designs, including chrome, pewter, solid gold, and bright enamels. Polished brass finishes usually are coated with a baked-on or lacquer coating. Some manufacturers have developed a revolutionary new coating which is a metal-plated surface over brass which affords brass the durability and easy maintenance of chrome, with no tarnishing. Chrome-plated brass is the most common standard finish for most faucets because it is durable and cleans up easily, but there is also chrome-plated plastic (which can be good depending on the brand) and plain plastic faucets (not recommended). Chrome-plastic brass, which may be tubular brass or solid brass, and chrome-plated pot metal are less expensive options; however, they are not recommended because they corrode and pit quickly. No matter what the finish, a faucet is only as good as the material that forms its operating parts. Ceramic- or nylon-disk designs are generally easier to maintain than older washer schemes.

Some brass faucets can contain relatively high levels of lead; lead can damage the nervous system, kidneys, and red blood cells. Manufacturers offer low-lead designs to help reduce exposure to lead in tap water. The Safe Drinking Water Act limits the amount of lead to 8% by dry weight in faucets. Manufacturers have created those at only 1.5% lead. If lead in the water is a concern, look for lead-free brass faucets and inform the homeowner to run the faucet until the water is cold before drinking the water. The first decision when choosing faucets is to select a dual- or single-lever faucet. Both are available with or without drain control levers. Faucets control water flow in the following ways.

Compression (Washer) Faucets

There are two basic types of faucet construction: compression (washer) and noncompression (washerless). The *compression* (also called *stem* or *washer*) *faucet* usually has two levers or handles and one spout. Typically with separate hot- and cold-water controls, they are identified by the threaded stem assemblies inside the faucet body. Compression-type faucets depend on rubber washers (which do eventually wear out and require replacement) to open or close down the water flow. A compression faucet has a stem assembly that includes a retaining nut, threaded spindle, O-ring, stem washer, and stem screw. It closes by a screw compressing a washer against a valve seat. When the faucet is turned on, a threaded spindle with a soft washer on the end, which has been plugging up the hole or seat where the water emerges, comes out. When the handle is turned off, the spindle rotates down until the washer end plugs the hole again, turning the water off. A compression faucet's handle has a "spongy" feel—allowing further tightening—when you close it. These faucets are supplied in many different styles, but all have some type of neoprene washer or seal to control the water flow.

Compression (*dual-handle*) faucets may be used for either bathtubs, showers, or a combination of the two. When used for tub-shower combinations, the tub spout will have a *diverter,* a valve that lets the user switch between shower and faucet. For tub and tub-shower combinations, either single or separate controls can be used. Tub and shower faucets have the same basic designs as sink faucets. Tub-showers need a spout, showerhead, diverter valve, and drain. When a tub and shower are combined, the showerhead and the tub spout share the same hot- and cold-water-supply lines and handles. Combination faucets are available as three-handle, two-handle, or single-handle types. With combination faucets, a diverter valve or gate diverter is used to direct water flow to the tub spout or the shower head. A *gate diverter* is a simple mechanism located in the tub spout. A gate diverter closes the supply of water to the tub spout and redirects the flow to the shower head. On three-handle faucet types, the middle handle controls a diverter valve. A *diverter* is the small rod which is pulled up to divert water from the tub spout to the showerhead. When the diverter rod is lifted, the bulk of the water should come out of the shower head. Two-handle and single-handle types use a gate diverter that is operated by a pull lever or knob on the tub spout.

Three-handle faucets are the same as two-handle faucets, except for the diverter. They have handles to control hot and cold water, and a third handle that controls the diverter valve and directs water to either a tub spout or a shower head. Instead of having a diverter on the tub spout, the center handle diverts the water from the tub spout to the shower head. Most lavatory faucets have a single body with one or two handles. The separate hot and cold handles indicate cartridge or compression faucet designs.

Noncompression (Washerless) Faucets

The other type of faucet is called a *washerless* or *noncompression faucet* (Fig. 5.23). With this type, the flow and mix of hot and cold water is often controlled by a single handle or knob by aligning interior openings with the water inlets (washerless faucets can also have two handles). Types of washerless faucets include rotating-ball, cartridge, and ceramic disk. As compared to compression faucets, washerless faucets have a hard, definite close that doesn't allow further tightening. In some cases, it may be possible to distinguish the type of faucet by the handle; however, to be sure, the faucet should be taken apart.

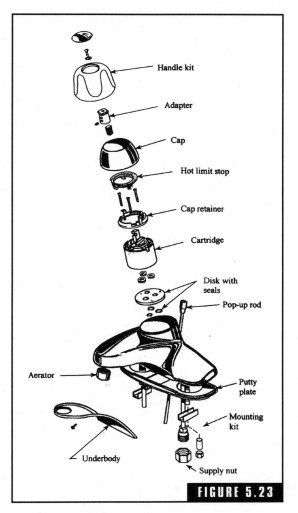

FIGURE 5.23

A washerless cartridge faucet. *(American Standard.)*

A *rotating ball-type faucet* has a single lever which rotates the ball to adjust the water temperature and flow. It is identified by the slotted metal, brass, or plastic ball inside the faucet body atop two spring-loaded rubber seals. Water flows when the openings in the rotating ball align with hot- and cold-water inlets in the faucet body.

A *cartridge faucet* is identified by the narrow metal or plastic cartridge inside the faucet body. Many single-handle faucets and some double-handle models use cartridge designs. This type has a hollow cartridge insert that lifts and rotates to control the flow and temperature of water with a movable cartridge and rubber O-rings. The cartridge controls hot and cold water flowing from the supply tubes into the mixing chamber. Water is forced out the spout and through the aerator.

A *disk faucet* has a single handle and is identified by the wide cylinder inside the faucet body. The cylinder contains a pair of closely fitting plastic or ceramic disks that move up and down to control the flow of water and rotate to control the temperature. The faucet handle controls water by sliding the disks into alignment. Disk faucets usually have a single handle; however, they can also have two levers. In a single-handle type, the handle also controls the mixing of hot and cold.

Lavatory Faucets

An infinite variety of lavatory faucets are available. Figure 5.24*a* illustrates a lever type single hole controlled by washerless ceramic disk valves which mix hot and cold water lifting the lever (left rotation for hot, right for cold). This faucet is attached below the sink deck surface and mixes volume and temperature discharging through a single spout. Action for this fixture can be performed with a single hand. Figure 5.24*b* illustrates a monoblock single-hole, two-handle faucet. This monoblock uses a single hole and two twist handles with valves mixing and discharging through a single spout. The left valve emits hot; the right emits cold. Both hands are required to operate this faucet. Figure 5.24*c* illustrates a two-handle center-set conventional spout. This uses a hot and cold valve and is mounted above the deck surface with a spout centrally mounted in one body. This requires a two-hole opening in the sink and is available with 4-inch (10.16-cm) centers. Figure 5.24*d* illustrates a two-handle minispread faucet. This faucet also has 4-inch (10.16-cm) centers and streamlined styling with separate handles and spout above deck. It is placed on centers fixed by the solid body mounted below the sink surface. Figure 5.24*e* illustrates a two-handle widespread faucet which also has separate valves and spouts above deck, with a flexible center-to-center option. The below deck attachment is with flexible hoses jointing the valves to the spout. Centers from 4 to 12 inches (10.16 to 30.48 cm) are permitted with this type. Sink drains usually are operated by a rod, which may be part of the main body or mounted behind the spout.

Ceramic Disk Valves

Ceramic disk valves cling to each other so tightly that air can't get between them (Fig. 5.25) to effect a tight seal in the valve, ensuring drip-free performance. Each time the faucet is turned on, the disks glide back and forth and become a little more polished. Ceramic disk valves are unaffected by temperature extremes or hard water, handles always stay aligned, and there are no breakable plastic parts. This technology provides ultrasmooth handle operation maximum control and more exit ports for a higher flow rate than do other single-control faucets.

Washerless faucets (which have working parts contained in an easy-to-replace ceramic or plastic cartridge) are more expensive than those with washers; however, they will last longer. Either way, water is directed from the faucet to the tub or shower head by a diverter valve; some have built-in diverter valves, while others have a knob on the tub spout.

Sink Fittings

Fittings for sinks are available in three standard types: center-set, spread-fit, or single controls. Center-set and spread-fit faucets are

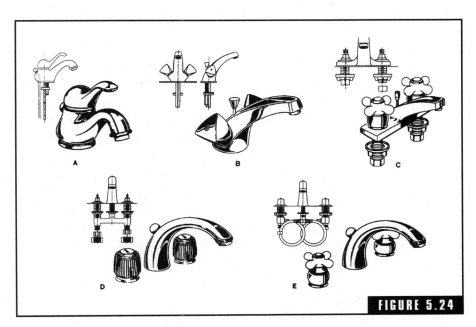

Faucets come in a large variety of sizes, shapes, and finishes. *(American Standard/Leon E. Korejwo, Illustrations.)*

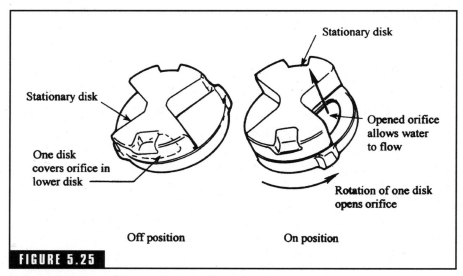

Stationary disk

Stationary disk

One disk covers orifice in lower disk

Opened orifice allows water to flow

Rotation of one disk opens orifice

Off position

On position

FIGURE 5.25

Ceramic disk faucet. *(Leon E. Korejwo, Illustrations.)*

similar. A *center-set control* has separate hot- and cold-water controls and a faucet, all mounted on a base. A *spread-fit control* has separate hot and cold-water controls and a faucet, each independently mounted. The difference between them is that center-set faucets are connected above the sink deck and appear to consist of a single unit. Spread-set faucets have no visible connection between the controls and the faucet because the valves and mixing chamber connect underneath the sink. A single-control fitting also consists of a single unit but has one central control device, a combined faucet and lever or knob that controls the water flow and temperature, instead of two separate control valves.

Most lavatories have holes predrilled in their rims to accommodate standard faucets and plumbing. Remember, before purchasing a faucet set, to make sure that the faucet set is the proper size and design to fit the plumbing fixture. The number of holes in the lavatory and the distances between them, typically, 4, 6, or 8 inches (10.16, 15.24, 20.32 cm) [centers up to 16 inches (40.64 cm) are available], determine which type of fitting can be used. Typically, the further apart the centers are, the easier the faucets are to turn and to clean.

Normally, deck-mounted faucets are positioned in the center of lavatories; except those designed for narrow vanities. In choosing a deck-mounted faucet, be sure that the faucet's inlet shanks are spaced to fit the holes in the lavatory. Be certain that its offset—the distance between these holes, center to center, between the hot and cold taps—corresponds to the holes in the lavatory. Check this by measuring the distance between the center of the hot and cold supply risers from under the basin. If fittings are to be attached to the wall or counter, the holes can be placed to suit the fittings. Lavatory styles that do not incorporate separate openings for faucets offer a means by which to locate faucets anywhere along the vanitytop desired.

Models can be interchangeable as long as the faucet's inlet shanks are spaced to fit the holes of the sink that it will be mounted on. Because bathroom-fixture manufacturers employ their own special designs, not all bathtub-shower faucet handles will fit onto existing valves located just inside walls. This is an important consideration, especially if existing valves are in good condition.

Showerheads

Like other bathroom fixtures, a wide variety of multiple, adjustable, and low-flow showerheads are available (Fig. 5.26). Showers often have two or more showerheads: fixed heads at different levels, hand units on adjustable vertical bars, or one fitted at each end of a double shower. The "surround" designs combine one or more fixed heads with wall-mounted auxiliary jets or adjustable multijet vertical bars. For the shower, look for fixtures that provide a wide spray pattern and a range of pressures, from a mist to a massaging pulse. New diverters may have three or more settings for orchestrating multiple water sources to control all these jets. An alternative to the traditional showerhead is the shower bar, which contains several nozzles arranged in a row.

Shower faucets should be accessible from outside and inside the shower enclosure so that the water flow and temperature can be adjusted from either place. For safety and convenience, the NKBA recommends that shower faucets be offset toward the shower door rather than centered below the showerhead, making it easier to control the water flow without getting wet. Like faucets, showerheads are available in varying degrees of quality and in different styles. Standard shower faucets are available with separate hot and cold controls or with a single-handle control. There are showerheads available that can save water and money with a pause setting which interrupts the flow during periods of shaving or lathering up.

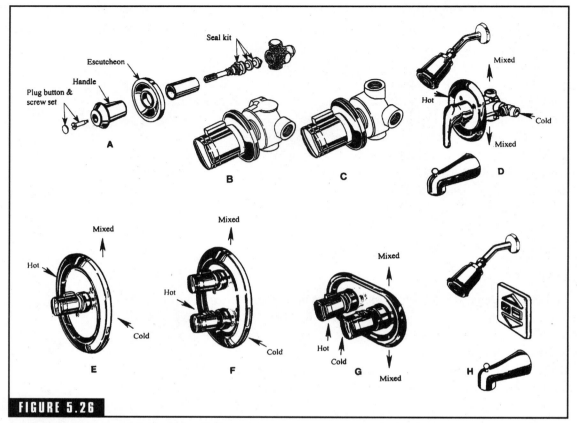

FIGURE 5.26

Several different styles of shower control devices.

Water-Saving Faucets

Depending on the local codes, installing water-saving faucets may be required. Before the federal law changed in 1994, standard shower faucets had a flow rate of 3.4 gallons/minute. Regulations now restrict newly installed showerheads to a maximum flow rate of 2.5 gallons/minute. Although today's showerheads do conserve water, it has been stated in the past that the resulting flow doesn't always feel as luxurious as the older ones. Incorporating a choice of spray patterns helps make up for this lack of water volume. Showerheads are usually made of chrome-plated brass and have swivel joints for directing the spray. Some models also have volume regulators, or both volume and spray regulators.

Tub and Shower Antiscald Controls

Standard shower fittings cannot control a sudden change in water temperature; however, antiscald valves can. Also called *pressure-balancing valves,* these single-control fittings contain a piston that automatically responds to changes in line water pressure to maintain the same temperature, blocking abrupt drops or rises in temperature (with or without digital readouts) (Fig. 5.27). These controls offer faster, more accurate control of water volume and temperature, ensuring that when someone flushes a toilet or turns on the dishwasher elsewhere in the house, the person showering is not suddenly scalded with hot water. Faucets are offered with the opportunity to change from a dual-lever control system for the hot and cold water in the tub and shower to a single-handle, pressure-balanced antiscald valve. Antiscald valves have actually become so effective that they are required by plumbing code for new construction in some states. Pressure-balanced antiscald valves are not significantly more expensive than standard valves and are readily available (Fig. 5.28).

According to American Standard, they offer three levels of antiscald protection. A *hot-limit safety stop* on bath and shower faucets restricts handle movement and reduces risk of accidental scalding, and is simple to set and adjust. High-temperature limit stop single control faucets make it easy to preset a comfortable maximum water temperature to eliminate the risk of scalding. Hot-limit safety stops let the user restrict how far the handle can be pushed to the hot side. Also, thermostatic valves let the user set the temperature so that it's the same every time. The safeguards of the hot-limit safety stop and pressure-balance shower valves offer unique protection against scalding. A pressure-balancing valve system responds to water-supply pressure changes (even the slightest change in water pressure), protecting the user from accidental scalding injury or

FIGURE 5.27

This faucet (with lifeguard system) helps guard against tap-water scaldings. The handle can go only as far to the hot side as it is set. *(American Standard.)*

cold shock in the shower. Temperature-memory single-control faucets allow water to be turned on and off at any temperature setting, conserving time and water.

Handheld Showers

Handheld sprayers, available for sinks, tubs, and showers, are practical as well as stylish. A standard showerhead, typically fixed at approximately 72 inches (182.88 cm) above the floor, doesn't always get the water where it is needed and can be quite inconvenient for

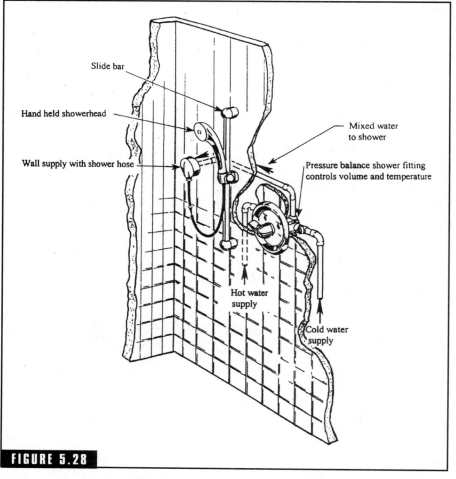

FIGURE 5.28

Pressure-balance shower fitting. *(Leon K. Korejwo, Illustrations.)*

people who are unable to stand while showering. Handheld shower-heads (often equipped with adjustable-flow heads) allow more freedom for directing the spray. Because they are versatile and adjustable, they work well for children and disabled people. Mounted on a flexible hose, these provide the advantage that the user has complete control of the water, such as keeping water off a cast on a leg. The negative to this is that it keeps one hand occupied. To replace a fixed shower with a handheld shower, there are several options. One is to replace the tub spout with a special spout containing a diverter, to which the handheld shower attaches—if the tub does not already have a shower. Another option is to replace the existing showerhead with a handheld model. Some handheld models can be mounted on a vertical bar, allowing the entire spray mechanism to slide up and down.

Comfort

Faucet handles should be shaped so that they are comfortable and easy to grip. If they are small and cylindrical, the user won't be able to turn them as easily as if they were shaped like levers. For the handicapped or elderly who have difficulty using their fingers, single-lever faucets are best, which can be operated by hand without requiring the use of individual fingers. Choose faucets with caution for bathrooms intended for use by either the very young or old.

Tub and Shower Surrounds

Even if there is a backsplash around the tub, it seldom protects the wall from extensive water damage. Walls—whether plaster, drywall, or just insulation and studs—must be protected from moisture; therefore, any surface material selected for the tub or shower surrounds should be applied on top of waterproof, not just water-resistant, wall material. It is useful to install materials that are durable and easily cleaned, both around the tub and on the walls. Most tub and shower surrounds require framing for support; the panel flanges are fastened to the framing.

Various manufacturers offer prefabricated surrounds made of acrylic, fiberglass, vinyl, plastic laminate, or synthetic stone. As with installing bathtubs, remember that with remodeling projects, avoid purchasing a one-piece surround, unless the room has the available openings enabling the large unit to be transported in. Multipiece surround kits, which can be assembled inside the bathroom, are also available. If creating your own bath or tub surround, the following surface materials are available.

Ceramic Tile

Waterproof and durable (when correctly installed), and easy to maintain, tile has long been a favorite material to use in the bath because the adhesive not only holds the tiles in place but also acts as a moisture barrier. Ceramic tiles are an excellent choice for tub and shower surrounds.

The one drawback to ceramic tile is that the grout can mildew, making it difficult to clean. To prevent mildew and dirt from building up, grout must be coated with a special sealer. Ceramic tile performs well in this regard, which is why it is the standard for the heavily used shower rooms in swimming pools and athletic clubs. There is greater freedom in selecting wall tiles than floor tiles, because they will not see the same heavy wear, nor do they need to have a nonskid texture. Since the color, type, and application pattern of the tile will make the major design statement in the room, have the homeowners carefully consider the aesthetic consequences of their choice. Colorful, stylish ceramic tiles are best if applied to tile backer board which is more resistant to moisture damage. Care must be taken, however, to ensure that the adhesive will stick well to the surface. If resurfacing an area, strip off wallpaper or loose paint, or sand the sheen off glossy wall paint.

Plastic Laminate

Plastic laminate tub surrounds are smooth, colorful, and easy to clean; won't leak easily; won't mildew; and are impervious to moisture when properly installed. These panels are available in the same diverse range of colors, texture, and finishes used to make plastic laminate countertops. In vertical applications, however, a $1/32$-inch-thick material can be used rather than the $1/16$-inch stock required for counters. It is durable, but laminate can be scratched. It cleans easily with soap and water or mild detergent. However, the sheets are so bulky that another person must help hold the pieces in place. Install all panels on a smooth, dry surface. Cutouts for fittings need to be made during installation. The panels must fit properly against the tub to prevent leaks—a job more difficult than it may initially seem. To make installation somewhat easier, kits are available with detailed instructions.

Laminate panels can go over any sound, smooth, level surface. Remove loose paint and any wallcoverings. Previously untreated surfaces must have a moisture-resistant finish applied before the laminate panels go up. Laminate kits are made to fit the length of the existing tub; your job is to bond the laminate to the walls with laminate adhesive. To complete the job, you'll need to cut openings for faucets and showerheads, using a hole saw or saber saw.

Fiberglass

Fiberglass tub surrounds are waterproof, durable, and easy to clean (with water and a mild dish detergent). As long as the walls are straight, are plumb, and have been properly prepared, they are easy to install, with no grouting or tiling necessary. These surrounds are ideal if planning to remodel or add to a bath. It will be necessary to cut openings for the fittings with a hole or saber saw. Many companies manufacture tub surround wall units to be installed over existing standard sizes and recessed tubs, and in various sizes—convenient one-piece or flexible three- and five-piece shower designs. Most kits consist of two molded end panels and one or more center panels. Another advantage to fiberglass tub surrounds is that they are supplied with convenient premolded towel bars, soap dishes, ledges, grab bars, shelves, and other accessories.

Solid-Surface Material

Another option for both tub surround and wall surface is solid surfacing. Solid-surface material provides for a durable, stylish, easy-to-care-for shower enclosure, which provide a water-resistant and easily cleaned surface (few joints). Although sometimes expensive, today's options in this category have a lot to offer. This smooth acrylic surface provides for ease in cleaning, and the material lasts a lifetime. It is recommended to be glued to moisture-resistant drywall, cementitious backer board, or marine-grade plywood with its own brand of panel adhesive. The joints between sheets should then be covered with narrow strips or battens of solid surface material. On vertical surfaces, $1/4$-inch-thick solid surfacing can be used (instead of the $1/2$- or $3/4$-inch thick materials required for horizontal surfaces), which, considering the speed of installation, makes this wallcovering competitive in price with tile. For more information on showers, see the luxury shower section in Chap. 4.

Bathroom Cabinets, Storage, and Countertops

One of the biggest problems in bathroom design and decor today is storage. Regardless of the bathroom's size and the arrangement and variety of its fixtures and equipment, it will not function properly unless it has an adequate amount of storage space. In addition to careful planning of fixtures, creating top bathroom efficiency requires prioritizing storage space.

Determine the user's most demanding storage requirements; most frequently used items should always be easiest to access. In the past, when bathrooms had been simple, small, and not much more than a basic utilitarian room, a medicine cabinet above the pedestal lavatory was the extent of bathroom storage available. Today, with the bathroom and master suites expanding into that of a multifunctioning room (by incorporating separate areas for dressing, grooming, laundry, exercise areas, spas, and steam units), the bathroom's storage needs and configurations have also changed. A medicine cabinet just doesn't provide enough space for most families. Although a typical base vanity may still be the only main storage area for some bathrooms, the possibilities have opened up to a host of more elaborate and stylish bathroom cabinet and countertop options (Fig. 6.1).

Bathrooms have expanded beyond the typical single vanity to much more elaborate cabinet layouts. *(Merillat Industries, Inc.)*

Vanities

Vanity cabinets are very popular and still the base of many bath designs, but styles and layouts are becoming more varied all the time. Today, a vanity unit is still one of the best storage ideas for a bathroom, since it permits the uses of the space below the lavatory. The base may be of wood or plastic laminate. Tops can be marble, plastic laminate, cultured marble, slate, pretreated wood, or ceramic tile. Styles range from French provincial to early American to Mediterranean or contemporary.

The standard height for vanities is now typically 28 to 36 inches (71.12 to 91.44 cm) high with depths ranging up to 24 inches (60.96 cm). If there is space available for a long vanity, or for his-and-her vanities, consider adjusting the height for taller, shorter, or seated users. The standard width is 30 inches (76.2 cm), increasing at 3 or 6-inch (7.62- or 15.24-cm) intervals, but some are as narrow as 12 inches (30.48 cm) and as wide as 60 inches (152.40 cm). In a family bath designed for growing children, it is a great convenience to have two vanities, one lower and easier to reach than the other. Or, if they prefer something less permanent, have a pull-out step beneath the lavatory cabinet so that the children can reach the sink without help.

Vanities are supplied as base-only units, a base with an integral basin countertop, or a base with a countertop for a separate basin. The vanity may be fitted with various types of countertops and sinks. Some stock vanities can resemble chests of drawers, while others are simple base cabinets; most combine both drawer and cabinet space. At least 8 inches (20.32 cm) should separate the top of the vanity backsplash from the bottom of the medicine cabinet or mirror. A vanity cabinet can be selected to complement almost any style of bathroom; for example, some vanities are designed to resemble furniture (Figs. 6.2a,b) or with the shape of old pedestal sinks. With vanities, door and drawer combinations are endless, which offers the freedom for you and the client to design a bathroom that is perfect for the homeowner's needs. If the bathroom design is to go beyond the basic vanity with a sink, cabinets similar to those used in kitchens come into play. If your client is unable to find what they want, advise them to search the kitchen departments when cabinet shopping. The kitchen department will have a wider selection, and the differences between kitchen and bath cabinet lines are steadily disappearing.

Cabinets

Cabinets in the bathroom can really help set the bathroom's tone. Before your clients or homeowners select cabinetry, they should determine how they will use the bathroom and what their daily and special storage needs are (these considerations should have been addressed in Chap. 2). This chapter provides the knowledge necessary for assisting your clients in choosing their cabinets. Cabinets are the key element in bathroom storage, as well as one of the most visible features in the bathroom—they can determine how a bathroom looks and functions. Because cabinets are available in many sizes or can be made to order, they provide the flexibility that enables the designer to fit a bathroom to their customers' needs and to the room space.

Remember that cabinets, depending on what type is installed, can be a permanent part of the bathroom; therefore, they should be chosen

FIGURE 6.2a

(a, b) Today, vanities bring the elegance of fine wood furniture to the bath, powder room, or master suite. *(Kohler Company.)*

with care for their quality and lasting value. For those bathrooms with elaborately planned cabinetry, when a portion or all of the cabinets becomes obsolete in usefulness or appearance, the cabinets may not be easily replaced without also disturbing countertops, flooring, wallcoverings, and perhaps the plumbing, wiring, and appliances. As have kitchen cabinet layouts, bathroom cabinet layouts have become very sophisticated (Fig. 6.3).

Bathroom cabinetry can be in the form of built-in wood, base, and wall cabinets. They can be built on the job, built in a local cabinet shop, built as finished prefabricated units by a manufacturer, or purchased completely assembled in a knockdown state or ready-made. Preassembled and prefinished cabinets are the quickest way to finish bathroom cabinets; however, they are also the most expensive way to go. Although there are some well-made cabinets available, beware of budget cabinets held together partly with wire staples in knock-down pieces to be assembled, shelves supported on pins instead of being securely recessed into dadoes, and a coverup coating of thick stain in place of a lasting finish.

Since the number of skilled cabinetmakers is decreasing, and because it is difficult to get a fine finish on job-built cabinets, most builders, designers, and homeowners are relying on prefabricated wood bathroom cabinets. Prefabricated cabinets are manufactured to standard sizes and dimensions, and most cabinet manufacturers do not offer special sizes or shapes.

Cabinets come in a variety of styles, from classic, country, to contemporary, and in a variety of colors and finishes to suit any decorative scheme. Different styles of doors, drawer fronts, and hardware give cabinets their individual character and personality. Although cabinets are available in a wide array of shapes and finishes, their overall basic construction is similar.

As is the case in the purchase of all furniture, good design coupled with expert workmanship and durable materials and finish should be the first criteria in selecting bathroom cabinets. Styles and colors should be ones that can be lived with for many years. The colors that are "in" today can and should be used in the bathroom but should be limited to wall areas and decorative accessories that can be replaced easily and relatively inexpensively tomorrow.

FIGURE 6.2b

(a, b) Today, vanities bring the elegance of fine wood furniture to the bath, powder room, or master suite. *(Kohler Company.)*

Method of Cabinet Construction

As for kitchen cabinets, there are two basic construction styles for bathroom cabinets: framed and frameless.

FRAMED CONSTRUCTION

Framed cabinets provide bathrooms with a traditional look. With framed cabinets, the doors are mounted on a frame, which is then mounted to the front of the cabinet box (Fig. 6.4). They have openings that are completely surrounded by face frames made of stiles (vertical

FIGURE 6.3

Take a second look at this photo—it actually is a bathroom; it could be mistaken for a kitchen because the cabinetry is so sophisticated. Crown moldings and decorative hardware help to create a distinctive look here. *(KraftMaid Cabinetry, Inc.)*

side members) and rails (crosspieces). Better cabinets have adjustable hinges that allow door realignment. With the exception of full-overlay doors, the frame is visible from the front of the cabinet, and can be seen as edges around doors and drawers. Full-overlay cabinetry features oversized doors and drawer fronts built around the frame.

The frame takes up space; it reduces the size of the door opening, so drawers or slide-out accessories must be significantly smaller than the width of the cabinet. The interior size of drawers or roll-out accessories is usually 2 to 3 inches (5 to 8 cm) smaller than the overall width of the cabinet. Although some framed cabinets may not have quite the interior storage space of frameless designs, they are much easier to install, therefore saving you time and your customer installation costs.

Unlike frameless cabinets, framed cabinets have some base cabinet units that are only cabinet fronts. These are most commonly used as sink bases where the back of the cabinet would interfere with plumbing

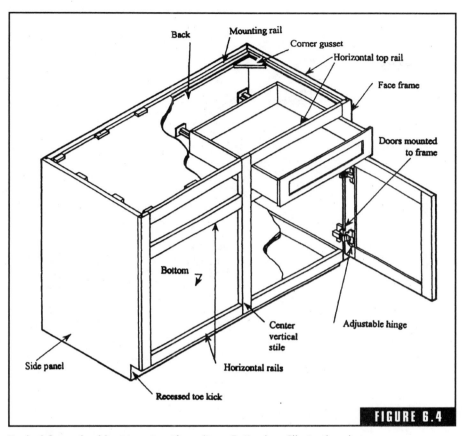

Back

Mounting rail

Corner gusset

Horizontal top rail

Face frame

Doors mounted to frame

Adjustable hinge

Bottom

Center vertical stile

Horizontal rails

Side panel

Recessed toe kick

FIGURE 6.4

Typical framed cabinet construction. *(Leon E. Korejwo, Illustrations.)*

rough-ins at the back wall. They offer somewhat more flexibility in irregular spaces than do frameless units; the outer edges of the frame can be planed and shaped, which is called *scribing,* to conform to unique discrepancies.

FRAMELESS CONSTRUCTION

Frameless cabinets, sometimes referred to as *European-style cabinets,* provide a more sleek, contemporary styling. With frameless cabinets, the doors are mounted directly to the sides of the cabinet box (Fig. 6.5). Core material sides $5/8$ to $3/4$ inch (1.59 to 1.9 cm) thick are connected with either a mechanical fastening system or a dowel method of construction. Because of their thickness, these case parts

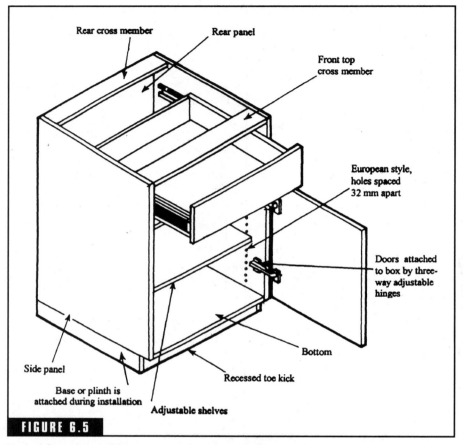

Rear cross member

Rear panel

Front top
cross member

European style,
holes spaced
32 mm apart

Doors attached
to box by three-
way adjustable
hinges

Bottom

Side panel

Base or plinth is
attached during installation

Recessed toe kick

Adjustable shelves

FIGURE 6.5

Typical frameless cabinet construction. *(Leon E. Korejwo, Illustrations.)*

form a box that does not need a front frame for stability or squareness. The hinges on frameless cabinets are screwed directly to the inside of the cabinet, eliminating the need for face frames (hinges are hidden, providing a cleaner look). Because they have no face frames, frameless cabinets offer slightly more storage space than do framed cabinets—for example, they permit easier access to storing larger items—and feature a continuous surface of drawers and door fronts. A simple narrow trim strip covers raw edges; doors and drawers usually fit to within ¹/₄ inch (0.6 cm) of each other, revealing a thin sliver of the trim. Interior components, such as drawers, can be sized larger, practically to the full dimension of the box.

Door hinges are mortised into the sides and the doors usually fit over the entire front of the case flush with each other and with drawer fronts. This method dictates a very tight reveal, the area of cabinet face surface not covered by the doors, usually 1/8 inch (0.3 cm) or less.

Frameless cabinets typically have a separate toespace pedestal, or *plinth,* which allows counter heights to be set specifically to the user's liking, stacking base units, or making use of space at floor level. Because of absolute standardization, every component (shelf supports and connecting hardware) is inserted into standard 1¼-inch (32-mm) on-center predrilled holes. The terms *System 32* and *32-millimeter* refer to the basic matrix of all these cabinets; all the holes, hinge fittings, cabinet joints, and mountings are set 32 mm apart.

The sizes of European styles differ slightly from those of standard cabinets. The depth of the wall cabinet may vary from the 12 to 13 inches (30 to 33 cm) of the standard units.

Cabinet Manufacturing Options

The type of cabinets your customers choose affects the cost, overall appearance, and workability of their bathroom. Cabinets are manufactured and sold in the following different ways.

STOCK

Stock cabinets are literally in stock wherever they are sold. They are made in quantity, in advance, to go into distributor warehouses for quick delivery. They are made in a wide variety of standard sizes (standard width is 30 inches (76.2 cm), increasing in 3- or 6-inch (7.62- or 15.24-cm) increments with heights anywhere from 30 to 36 inches (76.2 to 91.44 cm) that can be assembled to suit the bathroom space. The quality of standard cabinets may be fair, good, or excellent, depending on the manufacturer and price, with a limited number of styles and colors. Stock cabinets are sold mainly to distributors and to builders.

CUSTOM

The word *custom* can be used to describe any cabinetry or manufacturer that builds products to the measurements of a specific project. Custom cabinet manufacturers make cabinets bathroom by bathroom after a bathroom has been designed and sold. Generally, they are made in the same 3-inch (8-cm) modules as stock cabinets, but special sizes are made also for a perfect fit in the bathroom. With custom cabinets, every inch of space can be utilized. Custom producers offer a wide range of wood species, finishes, and special units. Unique ideas can be to curve a custom unit around a corner or plan a floor-to-ceiling storage column.

Because custom cabinets are made to order, delivery may take from 4 to 16 weeks. Place the order well in advance of the date you have scheduled to install the cabinets. Custom cabinets are almost always delivered completely finished, like fine furniture. Prices run from moderate to very expensive. Although it is generally a more expensive approach, custom shops can match old cabinets, build to odd configurations, and accommodate details that can't be handled by stock cabinets.

SEMICUSTOM AND BUILT-TO-ORDER CABINETS

Semicustom cabinets are produced by both stock and custom manufacturers. These usually are produced on a stock basis, but with many more standard interior fittings and accessories than regular stock units, although not as many as are available on custom units.

They are available in a variety of standard sizes, finishes, and styles. Each bathroom is built to order according to the bathroom design and homeowner preference. Custom offers many more choices, special shapes, special sizes, and, usually, better joinery and finishes.

SPECIALTY CABINETS

Speciality cabinet manufacturers are set up to supply specific housing tracts where hundreds of houses might have only three or four bathroom floor plans, and they make cabinets only to fit those floor plans. For example, the specialty manufacturer might take 100 identical single cabinets to fit a wall 96 inches (244 cm) wide that would be the same in 100 houses. A similar wall with stock or custom cabinets would have combinations of cabinets in different sizes.

Cabinet Types

There are three classes or types of bathroom cabinets: base cabinets, wall cabinets, and tall (or floor to ceiling) cabinets (Fig. 6.6).

BASE CABINETS

Base cabinets are usually installed under bathroom counters. They do double duty, combining storage space with working surface. Base cabinets rest on the floor and against the wall and form both the lower storage areas and a base for the countertop and lavatory.

Base cabinets can have only one top drawer or three or four drawers, making them particularly useful. Typically, the front-to-back dimensions are 23 to $24^{1}/_{2}$ inches (58 to 62 cm); 24 inches (61 cm) is the most common (Fig. 6.7). The units are $34^{1}/_{2}$ inches (88 cm) high and support a $1^{1}/_{2}$-inch (4-cm)-thick counter, making the counter surface 36 inches (91 cm) above the floor [4 inches (10 cm) for toespace and base, $30^{1}/_{2}$ inches (77 cm) for the cabinet itself, and $1^{1}/_{2}$ inches (4 cm) for the countertop]. Some homeowners may complain that this height is too low. It can be adjusted upward by increasing the cabinet base or adding another layer to the countertop base material (usually plywood). For people taller than 5 feet 4 inches (163 cm), $37^{1}/_{2}$ inches (95 cm) is a better height. Most base cabinets are equipped with built-in toespace.

This traditionally styled bathroom features two wall cabinets, a base cabinet, and an 84-inch (213.36 cm) vanity linen cabinet. (*Wellborn Cabinet, Inc.*)

Base cabinets range from 9 to 48 inches (23 to 122 cm) in width, increasing in increments of 3 inches (8 cm) from 9 to 36 inches (23 to 91 cm) and in increments of 6 inches (15 cm) after that. Single-door base cabinets are generally available in widths of 9, 12, 15, 18, 21, and 24 inches (23, 30, 38, 46, 53, and 61 cm). Double-door cabinets are usually available in widths of 24 to 48 inches (61 to 122 cm). They are also available in 3-inch (8-cm) increments, but some manufacturers do not provide 39-inch (99 cm) and 45-inch (114 cm) units. Remember that using fewer wider cabinets rather than more and narrower-width cabinets reduces the cost of the installation. Two small cabinets, side by side, each have their own end panels, which take up useful storage space. A carefully chosen single cabinet will use the space for wider drawers or shelves; this also gives a more custom-designed appearance. Base cabinets provide a major portion of the storage needed in the average bathroom.

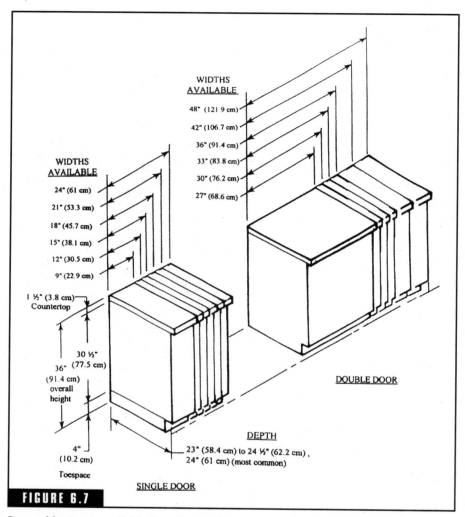

FIGURE 6.7

Base cabinets are available in a variety of sizes. *(Leon E. Korejwo, Illustrations.)*

Other types of base cabinets have several drawers, or pull-out trays, in place of the shelves. For example, the base drawer units have no doors or shelves; they may contain only drawers—usually three. They are available in widths of 12, 15, 18, 21, and 24 inches (30, 38, 46, 53, and 61 cm); the most popular sizes are 15 and 18 inches (38 and 46 cm).

Base corner cabinets are employed to turn a corner where another run of cabinets will join at a right angle. They are blank (no drawer or door) in the area where the other cabinets must butt up against them. Base corner cabinets eliminate the use of base fillers since the cabinets can be pulled away to adjust to add dimensions along the wall. Base corner cabinets are usually blind corner (reach-in) units or rotating-shelf (lazy-susan) units (more often used in kitchens than bathrooms). If equipped with three shelves at least 26 inches (66 cm) in diameter, or two shelves at least 32 inches (81 cm) in diameter, this provides a lot of accessible storage for only 6 inches (15 cm) of frontage. Lazy Susans, while more expensive than other corner cabinets, provide the most efficient use of corner space. However, a blind corner cabinet gives the adjustability to fill a larger range of widths. These units must be installed while the corner is open, usually during initial construction or a major remodeling.

WALL CABINETS

Wall cabinets are upper cabinets that are mounted on the wall or from the ceiling, above the countertops. Wall cabinets are available in singles, doubles, and various speciality configurations. They are available in several heights and widths; they range in width from 9 to 48 inches (23 to 122 cm), increasing in 3-inch (8-cm) increments. Framed single-door wall cabinets (Fig. 6.8*a*) range from 9 to 24 inches (23 to 61 cm) wide; wall cabinets from 27 to 48 inches (69 to 122 cm) wide use two doors, with the center stile included. Frameless single doors range from 9 to 21 inches (23 to 53 cm); double doors begin at 24 inches (61 cm) up to 36 inches (91 cm) without center stile, but 36 to 48 inches (91 to 122 cm) with a stile included (Fig. 6.8*b*).

Wall cabinets are important to supplement the base-cabinet storage. The top shelf should be within 72 inches (183 cm) of the floor. Wall cabinets that extend higher may be desirable for storage of infrequently used items, but no use can be made of shelves that are higher than 72 inches (183 cm) above the floor.

The minimum clearance between the countertop and the bottom of the wall cabinet should be 15 inches (38 cm). Actually, with a clearance of 15 to 18 inches (38 to 46 cm) above a 36-inch-(91-cm)-high counter, the top shelf of a 30-inch (76-cm) wall cabinet with fixed shelves will not be more than 72 inches (183 cm) above the floor. With adjustable shelves in the wall cabinet, the top shelf can be set at an accessible height even if the cabinet is 18 inches (46 cm) above the

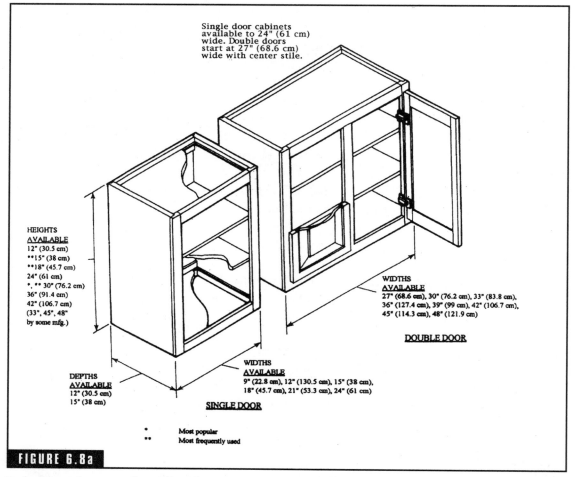

Single door cabinets available to 24" (61 cm) wide. Double doors start at 27" (68.6 cm) wide with center stile.

HEIGHTS
AVAILABLE
12" (30.5 cm)
**15" (38 cm)
**18" (45.7 cm)
24" (61 cm)
*, ** 30" (76.2 cm)
36" (91.4 cm)
42" (106.7 cm)
(33", 45", 48"
by some mfg.)

WIDTHS
AVAILABLE
27" (68.6 cm), 30" (76.2 cm), 33" (83.8 cm),
36" (127.4 cm), 39" (99 cm), 42" (106.7 cm),
45" (114.3 cm), 48" (121.9 cm)

DOUBLE DOOR

DEPTHS
AVAILABLE
12" (30.5 cm)
15" (38 cm)

WIDTHS
AVAILABLE
9" (22.8 cm), 12" (130.5 cm), 15" (38 cm),
18" (45.7 cm), 21" (53.3 cm), 24" (61 cm)

SINGLE DOOR

•   Most popular
••   Most frequently used

FIGURE 6.8a

Typical framed construction wall cabinets. *(Leon E. Korejwo, Illustrations.)*

counter. To prevent the homeowner from being bumped on the head or shoulder, as well as for the look of continuity, wall cabinets should be located over counters, or as a floor to ceiling unit complete with shelves and bins; their shelves tend to be limited and not always easily accessible.

The most commonly used wall units have a front-to-back depth of 12 to 15 inches (30 to 38 cm). The most popular height is 30 inches (76 cm). Although the most frequently used heights are 15, 18, and 30 inches (38, 46, and 76 cm), unit heights range from 12 to 36 inches (30 to 91 cm) or

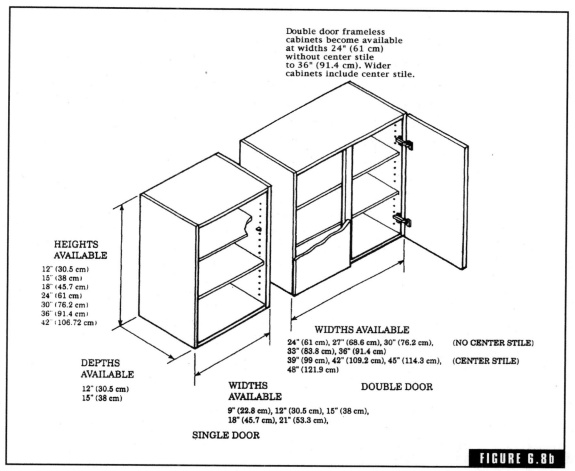

Double door frameless
cabinets become available
at widths 24" (61 cm)
without center stile
to 36" (91.4 cm). Wider
cabinets include center stile.

HEIGHTS
AVAILABLE

12" (30.5 cm)
15" (38 cm)
18" (45.7 cm)
24" (61 cm)
30" (76.2 cm)
36" (91.4 cm)
42" (106.72 cm)

DEPTHS
AVAILABLE

12" (30.5 cm)
15" (38 cm)

WIDTHS AVAILABLE

24" (61 cm), 27" (68.6 cm), 30" (76.2 cm), (NO CENTER STILE)
33" (83.8 cm), 36" (91.4 cm)
39" (99 cm), 42" (109.2 cm), 45" (114.3 cm), (CENTER STILE)
48" (121.9 cm)

DOUBLE DOOR

WIDTHS
AVAILABLE

9" (22.8 cm), 12" (30.5 cm), 15" (38 cm),
18" (45.7 cm), 21" (53.3 cm),

SINGLE DOOR

FIGURE 6.8b

Typical frameless construction wall cabinets. *(Leon E. Korejwo, Illustrations.)*

more. Some manufacturers provide cabinets with heights of 18, 20, and 24 inches (46, 51, and 61 cm). Also, a few companies make cabinets 33, 36, 45, or 48 inches (84, 91, 114, or 122 cm) high. The selection of the height depends largely on the space between the counter surface and the bottom of the cabinet [15 or 18 inches (38 or 46 cm)] and on the height of the top of the door trim, as well as ceiling height.

Single-door wall cabinets are usually available in widths of 9 to 24 inches, in 3-inch increments (23 to 61 cm). Double-door cabinets run from 24 to 48 inches (61 and 122 cm) in width, in 3-inch (8-cm) increments. Cabinets can vary in width from 9 to 60 inches (23 to 152 cm) in 3-inch (8-cm) increments.

There are other forms of wall cabinets. Wall cabinets are available in the blind corner configuration, and in corner cabinets with diagonal front. A few manufacturers make diagonal-front cabinets with rotating shelves [24 × 24 inches (61 × 61 cm)] or, as previously mentioned, with 90° lazy-Susan arrangements.

Tall cabinets are generally constant at 84 or 96 inches (213 or 244 cm) high and are most commonly made in 12-, 15-, and 24-inch (30-, 38-, and 61-cm) depths (front to back). Common frontage widths are 15, 18, and 24 inches (38, 46, and 61 cm); however, larger widths are available. Tall cabinets are very efficient storage units because they use a lot of otherwise empty wall space. There are many different designs available for tall cabinets; for example, a floor-to-ceiling column can provide a lot of storage for towels, bathing supplies, and other items, and even room for a swivel television (Fig. 6.9*a,b*).

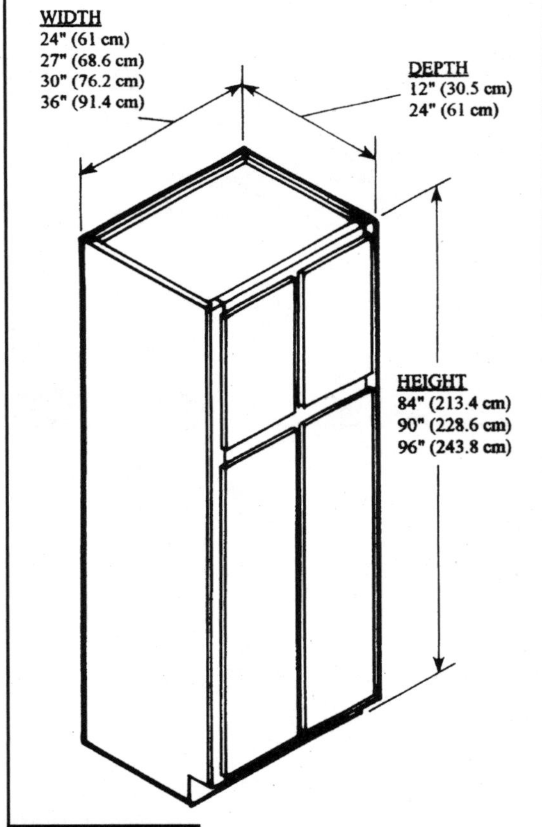

Cabinet Materials

Cabinet manufacturers use a variety of materials for the construction of cabinets. The major classifications used predominantly in the bathroom are wood or wood products covered with decorative laminates (usually on industrial-grade particleboard).

WOOD

Wood is still the most popular of bathroom cabinet materials. Of course, wood cabinet construction varies among manufacturers to some extent, but it is fairly well standardized for stock cabinets.

Oak, birch, pine, maple, ash, walnut, mahogany, and cherry are used in cabinets that are prefinished with the natural look. Moisture resistant woods make it ideal for

WIDTH
24" (61 cm)
27" (68.6 cm)
30" (76.2 cm)
36" (91.4 cm)

DEPTH
12" (30.5 cm)
24" (61 cm)

HEIGHT
84" (213.4 cm)
90" (228.6 cm)
96" (243.8 cm)

FIGURE 6.9a

Tall cabinet. *(Leon E. Korejwo, Illustrations.)*

FIGURE 6.9b

The tall vanity linen cabinet topped with classic crown and rope molding is ideal for storing towels. *(KraftMaid Cabinetry, Inc.)*

the bathroom's steamy environment. The cabinets are stained and finished with clear lacquer or other plastic finishes that are sprayed on.

Plywood has always had a prominent place as a basic material for cabinets. In recent years the use of particleboard has become more prominent. Particleboard has proved particularly useful as a base for cabinets finished with wood or plastic laminates.

LAMINATES

The use of laminated panels for cabinets has become popular in recent years. They are available in a wide variety of colors, patterns, performance characteristics, thicknesses, and prices. Particleboard is the predominant core stock for this kind of cabinet. However, some plywood is still used as a core material in cabinet construction.

Today, with new technology and improved resin and glue methods, the best interior surface for many cabinet applications is some type of artificial board that has been covered with either a laminate solid-colored surface or a laminated wood-grain surface.

Cabinet Construction

The major components of typical cabinets, regardless of type of construction, are the front frames, end panels, backs, bottoms, shelves, doors, drawers, and hardware.

CASE PARTS

The front frames usually are made of hardwood, $1/2$ to $3/4$ inches (1 to 1.9 cm) thick. Rails, stiles, and mullions are doweled (or mortise-and-tenoned), as well as glued and stapled for rigidity. Lap joints and screw joints are also used.

End or side panels typically consist of $1/8$- or $1/4$-inch (0.3- or 0.6-cm) plywood or hardboard, glued to $3/4$-inch (1.9 cm) frames, or $1/2$-inch (1-cm) and thicker plywood or particleboard without frames. The end panels frequently are joined by tongue-and-groove (Fig. 6.10*a*) or dovetailed (Fig. 6.10*b*) into the front frames. The mortise-and-tenon (Fig. 6.10*c*), butt joints, rabbet (Fig. 6.10*d*), dado (Fig. 6.10*e*), and dowell (Fig. 6.10*f*) are also used to affix the end panels to the front frames. Furniture-grade plywood and particleboard with veneer facings are the most common materials for end panels.

The backs of cabinets range in thickness from $1/8$ to $1/4$ inch (0.3 to 0.6 cm) and are of plywood or hardboard construction. The backs are fastened to the side panels by insertion and with glue blocks that are pinned with staples. The ledger at the back of the cabinet provides a solid surface through which screws are driven to anchor the unit to the wall.

The tops and bottoms of cabinets also vary from $1/8$ to $1/2$ inch (0.3 to 1 cm) in thickness, and they are let into the sides (dadoed) and fastened with glue blocks. Base cabinets seldom incorporate tops; however, some manufacturers still use the dust caps as cabinet tops on the base units. Of course, plumbing will occasionally require penetration of these panels.

Shelving in both the base and wall units vary in material composition from plywood to particleboard with or without wood or plastic-banded edges. Thickness varies from $3/8$ to $3/4$ inches (0.95 to 1.9 cm). Shelving in wall cabinets is either fixed or adjustable, with the trend toward adjustability, using either plastic or metal hardware.

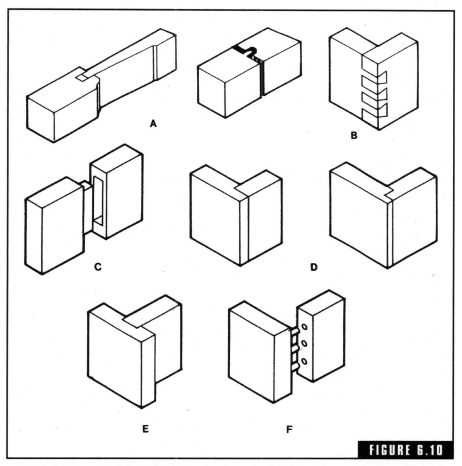

Wood joining methods include tongue and groove (*A*), dovetail, (*B*), mortise-and-tenon (*C*), rabbet (*D*), dado (*E*), and dowel (*F*). *(Leon E. Korejwo, Illustrations.)*

DOORS

The doors and drawer fronts are the most visible parts of cabinets; therefore, they determine the style of the cabinets. There is a wide array of cabinet door and drawer styles from which to select. Actually, hundreds of variations exist; however, the construction of doors is of two types: flush and panel. The flush doors may be hollow or may have a particleboard, wood, high-density fiber, or foam-plastic core. Veneer overlays may be wood or plastic.

Cabinet door panels may also be decorated with vinyls, brass grilles, cane, spindles, reinforced plastic, colored glass, or glass mullion doors. The panel doors consist of stiles, rails, and panel fillers of various types. These flush panels or raised panels with beveled edges may be shaped to fit openings that are rectangular or curved.

A number of producers are now using doors and drawer fronts made primarily of plastics. A wood frame with a foam-plastic core and laminated plastic face is a common type. Complete assemblies consisting of vacuum-formed plastic faces assembled over a foam core are increasing in popularity because of the ease of molding grain and trim patterns. Such material can be cleaned easily.

Doors and drawers are fit in one of three ways: flush with the frame (inset), partially overlaying the frame (offset), or completely overlaying the frame (full overlay). Doors are $3/4$ to $1^1/4$ inches (1.9 to 3.175 cm) thick.

DRAWERS

Drawers frequently have hardwood lumber sides and backs and plywood bottoms. There is as wide a variation in drawer-front styling as there is in door design. Drawer construction also varies depending on cabinet quality. In some cabinets, the sides are connected to the front and back with multiple dovetail joints. In others, they are connected with lock-shouldered or square-shouldered joints. Refer back to the joining methods illustrated in Fig. 6.10. Drawer bottoms are dadoed into the sides, front, and back for more rigid construction. Some drawer units are one-piece molded polystyrene plastic (except for the front), with rounded inside corners for ease of cleaning.

Drawer slide mechanisms are manufactured in several levels of sophistication. Cost is the controlling factor. Simple ones have a single central slide; others use two slides, one on each side of the drawer. Still others allow a drawer to be pulled out to the full length with added slides. Some have steel ball bearings, for smooth operation. Weight of the things stored in the drawer affect the slides. A heavy drawer or loaded drawer can easily derail on the economy slides.

Cabinet Hardware

Cabinet hardware includes pulls or handles, knobs, hinges, catches, and slides. Hardware is available in various materials, finishes, and designs to meet the needs of almost any style of cabinet. Many manufacturers permit customers to select the design and finishes of knobs and pulls or handles they desire.

Cabinet Finishes

Most natural finishes on wood cabinets consist of a penetrating stain and seal followed by spray-applied clear finishes. Acrylic and polyester have largely replaced nitrocellulose lacquer for this application. Other manufacturers use curtain coating or immersion finishing systems.

New finishing systems are being developed to meet environmental standards. Manufacturers are under much pressure to introduce water-based environmentally friendly finishes, and new ones appear and disappear as the products face the buying public's need for a durable product. Some products will need development time, but look for those that have some proven time in the field. Replacing a failed finish is costly. The water-based finish is inevitable, and when the system is worked out, it will be more widely available.

Finishing is a factor in cabinet quality and price; it should be easy to clean and resist moisture well. Some of the fine custom producers have 12 or more steps in the finishing process. The high-gloss finishes might be polyester or enamel. Achieving a high-gloss polyester finish is very time-consuming and expensive. High-gloss enamel is easier but is less durable. Glossy high-pressure (HP) laminate is often considered quite acceptable at a much more acceptable price. However, glossy finishes require more care than matte finishes.

Probably the most durable finish is produced by a plastic laminate. Such a finish is usually limited to slab doors or plain panels, although decorative moldings are sometimes applied over the laminate.

New materials and finishes are constantly being developed to improve cabinets and gain advantages in material availability. Therefore, the specifications for materials and finishes given here are subject to change at any time. One final note when placing cabinets. It would be wise not to place any permanent attachments to walls that would block access needed by a plumber to reach behinds showers, etc.

Plan for Additional Bathroom Storage

One of the biggest problems in bathroom design and decor today is storage. Bathroom storage does not have to be purely utilitarian; it can also be beautiful. In bathrooms, as in kitchens, there can never be too much storage space. Cabinetry, vanities, and shelves provide maximum storage in a minimum of space. Refer back to the worksheet in Chap. 2 (Table 2.1) to review what the user's needs are; consider what they need to store, how much space they need for it, and how best to organize the space. The answers to these questions should help determine the most efficient combination of cabinet space and drawers.

Depending on the kind of bathroom being built or remodeled, as you create storage space in the bathroom, there are a number of principles you should try to follow to ensure maximum use from the storage units available. First, there should be easy access to grooming and toiletry supplies (makeup, shaving gear, dental accessories, etc.) right near the lavatory, tub, shower, or toilet.

Different manufacturers provide a wide variety of accessories which may be added to cabinets. Inform your clients to look at the kitchen cabinetry possibilities to include in their bathroom design. They can include elements such as a pull-out wastebasket, pull-out towel racks, slide-out shelves, roll-out wire bins, and swing-out bins for easy access to items, tilt-out drawers, a built-in tilt-open clothes hamper, or lazy Susans for supplies (Fig. 6.11). Appliance garages store frequently used items out of sight and keep the countertop clean. Nooks for storing toothbrushes, razors, and other grooming aids can also be built in. Locate pegs, hooks, or bars made of wood, ceramic, plastic, or metal on walls near their point of use. If electric items are used, such as toothbrushes, electric razors, and hair dryers, be sure to plan ahead to locate them near a ground-fault circuit interrupter (GFCI)-protected outlet.

The advantages to using drawers is that items can be stored out of sight when not in use, and all items can be easily accessible (if the homeowner doesn't pack things on top

FIGURE 6.11

A wire vanity hamper provides for a unique and effective method of bathroom storage. *(KraftMaid Cabinetry, Inc.)*

of each other). To avoid cluttered drawers, select shallow drawers for small accessories, such as cosmetics, and use the deep drawers for larger items, such as curling irons and hair dryers; store rarely used items in the more out-of-way spots. Another handy idea is to install pull-out, removable drawer units so that the whole drawer can be pulled out and, if necessary, moved to the site of an ailing or handicapped person.

Shelves, whether open or enclosed, can be added almost anywhere in the bathroom. They offer easy access and make good use of shallow spaces or in walls. Narrow shelves work better than deep ones; things can get buried in deep shelves, making them hard to reach. Open shelves can display decorative items such as bottles, soaps, and linens and add to the decor as well as provide storage. If mounted on adjustable clips, the height of shelves may be repeatedly changed. Shelves can be shallow or deep, but a greater number of shallow shelves are apt to be more useful than a lesser number of deep shelves. Corner shelves take advantage of frequently wasted space. Shelving units that glide out work better than drawers, because storage items stay neat and undisturbed.

Most bathrooms are full of items that should be stored out of sight and out of the reach of children or pets, such as medicines and cleaning supplies. In households where there are small children, provide a separate cabinet, one that can be locked for medicines. Medicines should be quick and easy to find when needed, where adults can get at them, but where young children cannot. The odd-shaped space below the sink in a vanity cabinet is convenient for storing cleaning supplies as long as children do not have access. The plumbing below a sink should be easily accessed for service. When a leak occurs, anything under a sink will sustain water damage. It is nice to be able to inspect the plumbing easily.

Not only can the right accessories add that special touch, but they can save a lot of time, effort, and space. In addition to the cabinets, some manufacturers have decorative wall and base shelves, valances that can be used as decorative trim across windows between two cabinets, molding for trim work around cabinet installations, end panels to finish runs of wall and base cabinets, and filler strips. The strips should not be used except to take up, or fill in odd dimensions, at the end of a given run or in conjunction with corner base cabinets to provide drawer clearance. Optional extras allow you to help customize your client's new bathroom cabinets in any manner that suits them. The newest modular wire shelving systems offer maximum flexibility and also provide ventilation for linens; modular units are made for curves, and so on.

Medicine Cabinets

A frequently used method of storage in the bathroom is the medicine cabinet. Medicine cabinets are available in two basic styles: recessed units designed to fit between walls framed with 2 × 4s, and those meant to be surface-mounted. From the functional medicine cabinet that is merely a box with a mirrored door, you can go to large mirrors that slide to expose storage behind, or decorative mirrors in rectangular or oval shapes that are actually the doors of a medicine cabinet. Some units have a mirror in the center mounted on the wall, with mirrored medicine cabinets at each side. When the mirrored doors of the cabinets are open, they form a three-sided mirror. Most medicine cabinets are mounted over the lavatory, but some are designed to be mounted in the wall beside the vanity. These are generally used when the wall behind the vanity is completely mirrored. They range from an invisible door, one covered with the same wall covering as the walls; to louvered or paneled doors. Some medicine cabinets are equipped with lights, but lighting should be considered separately. Medicine cabinets to blend with any design of bathroom are available in a variety of styles.

Cabinets are, of course, the most common storage area, but there are many possibilities for imaginative and practical storage in the bathroom. A few additional suggestions are as follows:

1. *Use furniture from other rooms.* For example, antique kitchen cupboards, an antique dresser, chest of drawers, and china cabinets add a unique style while providing storage space. If including this type of wood furniture, remember that it needs to be finished with a moisture-resistant sealer to prevent warping.

2. *Put in a drink or wet-bar cabinet.* For the frequent entertainer who wants a wet bar in the bathroom, it is fun, and much more convenient when the drink ingredients, glasses, and the rest of the necessary supplies are right at hand in a single storage unit.

3. *Add a dressing table adjacent to the bathroom.* Provide additional space outside the bathroom for grooming routines that don't require water, such as makeup application and hair drying. A dressing table with shallow drawers in an adjacent area or bedroom can help to unclutter the bathroom.

4. *Add a closet or large cabinet just for bulky items and towels, blankets, and so forth.* A built-in linen closet offers lots of shelf space and can hide clutter very efficiently. Seasonal linens such as holiday towels and bedding can be stored in the linen closet, as well as guest linens. Since seasonal items are accessed only a few times a year, they can be put in those areas at the higher levels, or corners where convenience is not essential.

5. *Utilize the space above the toilet tank.* This area is the one area most often overlooked. Cover the wall area with built-in storage shelves. Items needed for use at the lavatory should be kept in a cabinet that is large enough to hold them and placed so that the door can be opened and reached without moving from in front of the lavatory. The cabinet may be either straight ahead or on a side wall, or have cabinets in both locations. A low-profile toilet, with a tank that rises only slightly above seat level, opens up more wall area for storage. Remember to consider the elbow room. When seated and twisting to reach something, make provisions so that the user's elbow will not knock things over. Also, a shelf too close to a toilet may be an annoyance to a user when rising from the toilet.

6. *Soffits.* The soffit area, the space between the top of the wall cabinet and the ceiling, can be utilized as extra space. It can be left open for plants. Add shelves or rails to display items, or close it completely, with either drywall or more cabinets. Many soffit areas are closed to hide ductwork. Check to see that it is the case before tearing them out.

7. *Plan around obstacles.* Do not let the chimney, clothes chute, heating ducts, or pipes interfere with storage plans. Locate a cabinet to house necessary things, but let it also be just a bit larger for valuable additional storage.

Note: Remember to ventilate storage space in a moisture laden bath area. Trapped moisture from a shower or sink can cause mildew.

Reading Manufacturer-Supplied Instructions

Understanding the system used to identify the cabinets and accessories you will install is important. The Kitchen Cabinet Manufacturers Association established a generic cabinet coding system more than 20 years ago to standardize the nomenclature used for identifying and specifying kitchen, bathroom, and other specialty cabinets. The National Kitchen and Bath Association has customized this coding system somewhat; this is the system explained here. The system has been adopted and used by most cabinet manufacturers, providing standardized definitions for sizes and types of cabinets. The system is based on an 11-character code that explains each cabinet category, type of cabinet, width of cabinet, and height. Although this is primarily a kitchen-based system, discussion here provides guidance if you decide to use kitchen-style cabinets for some bathroom projects.

The first character defines the general type of cabinet. There are six general cabinet categories, one accessory category, and one molding/trim category. The six general categories are W, all wall cabinets; T, all tall cabinets; B, all base cabinets; V, all vanity cabinets; D, all desk cabinets; P, all peninsula cabinets; and F, all furniture cabinets. For some cabinet manufacturers, vanity and desk cabinets are interchangeable; therefore, the V designation is used in both applications. A D designation is applied only if sizing between the two systems differs. Molding and trim pieces are identified by a separate code that describes each piece. There is no major category that sets them apart from the other groupings.

The second set of characters identifies the type of cabinet. For example, a BB is a blind base corner cabinet. A BC is a base corner cabinet. It may have fixed, adjustable, or rotary shelving, which is designated by a letter. A BD is a base cabinet that features a stack of drawers. A standard B is assumed to have a drawer above the door. A WO is a wall cabinet that has no doors; therefore, it is called an open cabinet.

The next two numeric symbols identifies the width of the cabinet. This dimension is always listed because the widths are variable. Most manufacturers have 3-inch (8-cm) modules, ranging from 9 to 48 inches (23 to 122 cm).

The next two numeric symbols identify the height of the character. These two digits are used only if varying heights are available. For example, in wall cabinets, choose from heights of 12 to 30 inches (30 to 76 cm). Some manufacturers offer additional heights. This is not the case in base cabinets where one standard height is used throughout the room, so no height dimension is a part of that code.

The last two characters identify any nonstandard configurations within that specified cabinet unit. For example, a D would identify a diagonal corner unit, a GD identifies glass doors, D3 means three drawers, PC means pie-cut, TO means tilt-out drawer head, and so forth.

Accessories to be added to the cabinet are designated following the cabinet code: HU for hamper unit. Miscellaneous trim and finish pieces with no specific category heading have individual codes: VP is a valance panel, VP-C is a valance panel with contemporary styling, and VP-T is traditional. A corbel bracket is indicated by CB, outside corner molding by OCM, and crown molding by CM.

Here are a few examples to demonstrate reading manufacturer-supplied instructions:

1. W 30 12 indicates a wall cabinet, 30″ (76 cm) wide and 12″ (30 cm) high.

2. W 30 15 24 D indicates a wall cabinet, 30″ (76 cm) wide, 15″ (38 cm) high, and 24″ (61 cm) deep (D).

3. WB 24/27 30 is a wall blind, 24 to 27″ (61 to 69 cm) adjustable width, 30″ (76 cm) high.

4. WC 24 30 PC is a wall corner, 24″ (61 cm) wide, 30″ (76 cm) high, pie-cut.

5. BD 12 D4 indicates a base drawer, 12″ (30 cm) wide, with four drawers.

Evaluating Cabinet Construction

Regardless of the type and style of cabinets, quality construction is of utmost importance. If you are assisting the client in choosing new cabinetry, look for the following features as indicators of quality construction:

1. Front cabinet frames should be glued and fastened with steel reinforcements. They should be of the same wood species as the door to insure a uniform finish match.

2. Wood doors should be manufactured from solid wood or a combination of solid wood and wood veneers.

3. All interior surfaces should be well finished, including adjustable shelves, which should be vinyl-clad to make cleaning easier.

4. Penetrating finish stains should be hand-wiped to enhance the depth and clarity of the wood grain.

5. Quality cabinets have doors that swing freely and latch securely and drawers that roll on metal tracks.

6. Shelves should be a minimum of $5/8''$ (1.6 cm) thick to prevent warping and bowing. Shelves should also be adjustable to maximize storage flexibility. Hinges should be solidly mortised, concealed, adjustable, made of materials that will not corrode, and covered by a lifetime warranty. Keep in mind that excessive moisture promotes swelling of doors and drawers.

7. Drawer boxes should be full-depth, constructed of solid wood and feature either doweled or dovetailed joints that are backed by a warranty. The drawer suspension system should have a guarantee and feature captured, epoxy-coated slides with ball-bearing rollers.

Upgrading Bathroom Cabinets

For those bathroom remodeling projects that have already existing elaborate cabinetry, it is very likely that they are still structurally sound and perfectly serviceable. Cabinet refacing is a middle ground between redecorating and major remodeling. Most types of cabinets can be refaced. Refacing existing bathroom cabinets can be an excellent, less expensive choice, rather than replacing the entire cabinet system, with results that look essentially the same. However, if the homeowner doesn't like the present layout of the bathroom or if it seriously lacks storage space or countertop area, refacing is not a good idea.

Changing the existing pulls, hinges, knobs, and other hardware designs can give a quick change to the appearance of existing cabinets. The range of manufactured hardware styles is great and can create interesting design and period changes.

Many refaced bathrooms are indistinguishable from bathrooms with all new cabinets. The downside to refacing cabinets is the lack of design flexibility; space cannot be reapportioned within the room. However, the refacing job can be combined with some minor cabinet modifications that can make a big difference in how efficient the bathroom is.

Countertops

Review with your client whether they have ample counterspace in their existing bathroom, and if not, discuss with them where they would like to add more counters. Would they prefer a different type of countertop material than they have in their present bathroom, or are they satisfied with what they are using now?

Residential bathroom countertop depth is normally 25 inches (64 cm) deep, front to back, to cover base cabinets. With typical 24-inch (61-cm) base cabinets, this counter depth provides a 1-inch (2.54-cm) overhang. Normally, they are $3/4$ inch (1.9 cm) thick. In most cases, they have an added $3/4$-inch (1.9-cm) builddown strip in front to conceal the joint where they are fastened to the base cabinets. For frameless cabinets, a buildup strip is used to raise the countertop, because the doors come all the way to the top of the cabinet front. The backsplash (vertical extension of the countertop surface between the horizontal countertop proper and the wall cabinet overhead) might fit against the back wall, approximately 4 or 5 inches (10 or 13 cm), or go all the way up to the wall cabinets. End splashes usually are fitted where countertops fit against side walls. Countertops are used as a general work surface, as well as a storage area. The material used to surface the countertop must therefore fill a variety of requirements. Remember—space to put things on is just as important as space to put things in. Plan an area large enough for appliances such as electric razor rechargers and waterpics, so that they do not get bumped into a water-filled basin sink.

First, consider the decorative aspect. Since it is one of the most prominent of the bathroom's design, the countertop should blend with the cabinets, yet add its own note of beauty, texture, and pattern to the bathroom. At the same time, it must harmonize with the floor and wall colors. Adding front edge accents, such as wood edges, contrasting color, or rolled front edges, will dramatically change the look of the countertop. If a vintage atmosphere is sought, a contemporary solid surface with bold stripes would be out of place, whereas a plain color would be more harmonious with that period style.

As for the functional aspects of the countertop, remember the important fact that the countertop will take almost as much wear and abuse as the floor. Therefore, above all, it has to be durable, easy to clean, and resilient. When selecting the countertop material, the additional factors that should be considered are resistance to moisture, water, heat, sharp blows, scratching, staining, and fading, as well as be resistant to soap, toothpaste, cosmetics, and alcohol- and acetone-based liquids. The intended use of the counter area determines those factors most important to your client. Discuss with your client whether the bathroom will require any specialized countertop surfaces.

Countertop Materials

A number of countertop surface materials are available in a wide range of colors and prices. As the builder, you need to know the types of countertops available and all their advantages and disadvantages. In addition, you will need to know how to fabricate and install the various countertop types (see Chap. 10), and how to provide proper substrate (base materials) for countertops.

The most common materials used for countertops include decorative plastic laminates, ceramic tile, solid-surface composites, marble and granite, and wood. Any one of these surfaces can be installed throughout the bathroom. The countertop can be used to bring together a mixture of materials used throughout the rest of the bathroom by combining elements of those other surfaces into a harmonious blend. A tile floor and wooden cabinets can be represented by a row of tile or strip of wood in the counter.

LAMINATES

Laminated plastic is the most popular countertop material, since it is tough, easy to care for, long-lasting, and water-resistant and offers the widest possible range of colors, textures, and patterns (including wood grain, marblized effects, simulated brick or slate, and geometric designs). It is also cost-effective. These surfaces are not affected by soaps, detergents, or hot water. They resist stains, fading, and moisture and therefore are ideal for use in most bathrooms. Some disadvantages are that although it withstands high temperatures, plastic laminate is not totally heat-resistant; however, this should not be as much of a concern in the bathroom as it is in the kitchen. Some laminates may scratch and chip. Most laminate has a dark backing that shows at seams, or when chipped.

There are two types of decorative laminates widely used for bathroom countertops: high-pressure decorative laminates and color-through laminates.

High-pressure decorative laminates are plastic laminates composed of a decorative paper that is bonded to several layers of phenolic resin–treated kraft paper, then covered with a translucent, melamine-resin paper that becomes clear during processing. The laminate material is then bonded to a substrate (plywood or particleboard) to form a countertop. Typically, laminate sheets are $1/16$ inch (1.6 mm) thick and range in width from 30 to 48 inches (76 to 122 cm). High-pressure decorative laminate countertops are relatively inexpensive and can be fabricated quickly. The majority of decorative laminate countertops are custom-produced. A countertop made with laminates can be tailored to fit any space. Custom laminate countertops are built by gluing sheet laminates to particleboard. Custom edges add a decorative molding to a standard laminate countertop, creating a customized design statement with thousands of design options.

There are two basic types of laminated plastic countertops: post-formed and self-edged.

Postformed countertops are one continuous sheet rolled at the back-splash and front edge with a curved sweep from the bottom of the front vertical edge to the top of the backsplash (Fig. 6.12a). Because they are all one piece, postformed tops make a smoother, cleaner surface. Postformed countertops are made of sheet laminates glued to particleboard, and come from the factory cut to length and ready to install. They are manufactured in a variety of colors and styles, are available in stock lengths, and are cut to fit your client's bathroom space. Premitered sections are available for two- or three-piece countertops that continue around corners. Since the prefinished

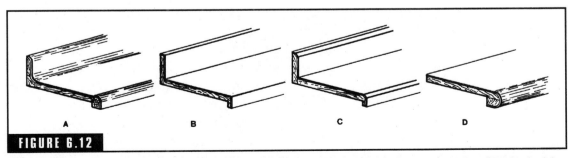

FIGURE 6.12

A   B   C   D

Post formed with an integral and rolled front (*A*), self-edged with backsplash in front (*B*), self-edged with beveled corners (*C*), and self-edged with laminate surface rolled over with additional builddown (*D*).
(Leon E. Korejwo, Illustrations.)

backsplash and front edges are already in place, curved turns in corners are not possible.

Self-edged tops offer a straight-line effect achieved by 90° corners at the backsplash and the front edge. They are flat with the edge of the same material and a separate 4-inch (10 cm) backsplash; separate strips of matching laminate are applied to the edges (Fig. 6.12*b–d*).

Both self-edged and postformed countertops can be obtained with a standard 4-inch (10 cm) backsplash or with a full-fixed backsplash. Self-edged are also available as a flat top with no fixed backsplash. Where the backsplash is not an integral part of the countertop, there are wall materials that can be used in its place. A good backsplash also has a practical side; if properly installed, it seals the area from moisture penetration, and therefore makes the wall a lot easier to keep clean. Postformed, pre-molded, and prefabricated, are the least expensive options; a custom top with a built-up lip and backsplash looks best but is more costly. If unusual shapes with curves are desired, laminate sheeting can be glued to a particleboard countertop and cut to shape. Curved edges are easily made by gluing a strip to the curved surface finishing with a router.

Color-through laminates are similar to standard high-pressure decorative laminates, except that the melamine color sheets are used throughout the material instead of the phenolic-core kraft paper layer. The laminate contains color throughout, and joint lines are difficult to detect after fabrication. Solid-color laminates do not show dark lines at the trimmed edges, but they chip more easily than do traditional laminates and must be handled carefully. Color-through laminates can be used for the total countertop installation. They are also used for special edge treatments where the surface is engraved or routed to produce unique edge profiles or reveal other colors. This material is more expensive than ordinary high-pressure decorative laminate. The fabrication takes more care and attention.

The core stock of decorative laminate surfacing materials is either $3/4$-inch (1.9-cm) industrial-grade plywood or particleboard (also known as *flakeboard*). A $3/4$-inch-(1.9-cm)-thick wood frame is attached to the bottom of the substrate material to give the countertop rigidity. The countertop is attached to the base cabinets by screwing into this wood frame. Laminated plastics usually are available in sheets a few inches larger than standard 4 × 8-foot panels to allow for the edge trimming that is necessary. When figuring the amount of material needed, remember to avoid joints as much as possible by using the maximum lengths available. For example, if a countertop is to be built 9 1/2 feet (290 cm) long, a 10-foot (30.5 cm) length of base core and laminate is needed rather than joining an 8-foot (244 cm) piece with a 1 1/2-foot (45.7) added piece. If the countertop has to turn a corner, it is probably best to join pieces. Provide for thermal growth expansion in long countertops, which may buckle if boxed in.

CERAMIC TILE

For elegance and durability, few countertop materials can touch or emulate ceramic tile (Fig. 6.13). To produce a profitable job and a satisfied client, you need to have a solid understanding of the product, its installation methods (see Chap. 10), and care recommendations. Keep in mind that ceramic tile installation requires fewer tools and less working room than plastic laminate installation.

Ceramic tile is durable and heat-resistant. It is available in a wide variety of sizes, colors, textures, and patterns (along with decorative tiles that have colorful pictures and patterns on them for use as border or accent tiles), and therefore offer great design flexibility. Tiles can be magnificently decorative for counters, backsplashes, walls, or as

FIGURE 6.13

A ceramic tile countertop is still one of the most popular bathroom countertop materials. *(American Standard.)*

display inserts in another countertop material. A variety of edge treatments are also used.

The differences between raw materials, manufacturing methods, and surface finishes make some types of tile more durable in heavy-use areas than others. The firing method also affects the absorption rate of different types of tile, making some more appropriate than others for high-moisture areas.

Although you may not be specifying the tile selection, you should carefully review the type you will be installing on countertops, as well as the installation methods (Chap. 10). Setting ceramic tile is a skilled trade and may require the services of another contractor. The most commonly specified tile for bathroom installations are glazed tile, quarry tile, decorative tile, and mosaic tile.

Glazed tiles are available in high-gloss, abrasive slip-resistant, and matte finishes. These tiles are an excellent choice for vertical surfaces; however, their susceptibility to scratching may make them a poor choice for bathroom countertops. Keep in mind that glazed tile should have a matte finish for better resistance to scratching.

Quarry tile may be very soft and irregular in shape, so breakage and installation time is increased. Quarry tile is extremely porous and requires a penetrating sealer to protect the surface. Unglazed tile is too porous for bathroom counter use. Nonporous glazed tiles do not soak up spills and stains.

Decorative tile (*deco*) may include a painted design or raised or recessed relief pattern. Deco tiles are recommended for use for vertical applications only, not as a countertop surface.

With *mosaic tiles,* color goes all the way through the porcelain or clay material. Because they are baked at higher temperatures, they have a harder, denser body. Mosaic tiles are quite suitable for countertops. They are impervious, dentproof, and stainproof.

For the installation project, be certain the type of tile specified is manufactured with all the specially designed edge and trim pieces required to put together a countertop. Installed correctly, ceramic tile is resistant to just about everything, including water, alcohol, and common chemicals, and as stated earlier, it is not affected by heat. Ceramic tile is nearly indestructible in normal use; however, a sharp, hard blow can crack or chip the tile. It is noisy and has a hard surface. If a ceramic cup or toothbrush holder is dropped on the tile, the object will most likely break. Problems with the tiles themselves are rare—most tile countertop problems stem from improper installation of the underlying decking material. If an area is damaged, individual tiles can be replaced, rather than having to replace the entire countertop.

A major drawback of ceramic tile is that the grout that fills the spaces between tiles is porous and stains easily if not sealed. This problem can be minimized by sealing the grout lines.

Although costs generally vary, ceramic tile countertops cost approximately $2^{1}/_{2}$ times more than standard decorative laminate countertops and are approximately equal in price to solid-surface countertops. Prices range from modest to extravagant, depending on style, accents, and accessory pieces.

SOLID-SURFACE MATERIALS

Solid-surface materials are artificial composites made of acrylics or polyester resins blended with additives. These materials offer a number of advantages for the bathroom and have become increasingly popular in recent years. These synthetic surfaces have much of the visual elegant look and feel of natural stone for virtually seamless surfaces (Fig. 6.14).

Solid-surface edge treatments are varied. A classic edge is achieved with an ogee cut with a router. Two layers may be different colors. The lower layer may be recessed to add depth.

The most desirable aspects of solid-surface materials are their workability and durability. These products are thick and strong enough to serve as the entire counter; no substrate is required. Many different manufacturers have a variety of solid-surface materials on the market and have produced their own varieties and blends of natural mineral fillers and resins to create an exceptionally strong and resilient solid-surfaced material. Each of these manufacturers varies in quality, durability, and composition; however, they share many of the same advantages.

All solid surfaces have no pores (making it resistant to most stains) or seams, so bacteria and mold have nowhere to collect and grow. They are very easy to care for (surfaces can be cleaned with mild soap and water), smooth, extremely durable, and water-resistant. Solid surfaces can withstand higher temperatures than most other countertop materials. The surface is durable because the color is blended

FIGURE 6.14

The integral solid-surface design is a lavatory bowl and vanitytop molded together into one seamless, easy-to-clean piece. *(American Standard.)*

completely through the material, so minor scratches and stubborn stains (e.g., cigarette scorches) can be repaired easily by lightly sanding with 320- or 400-grit sandpaper to restore the original look. Deeper damage often can be filled with matching color fillers. Solid-surface countertops are more resilient than some other countertops. Delicate items are less likely to break if they fall on a solid-surface countertop than on other materials.

The design possibilities are endless with this adaptable, flexible product. Styling options include a wide variety of sink mountings, different colored borders, and edge treatments, including integral units. The fabricator can make almost indistinguishable joints between sheets, create curved shapes, design intricate inlays with similar surfacing in contrasting colors, and sandblast patterns into the material.

More ornate selections imitate the random patterns found in natural materials; some even have deep, translucent, marble veining patterns. Solid surfacing is fabricated to the specifications of the individual design. Solid-surface sinks enhance the individualized look. They are made in many solid colors, with a range of patterns or patterns that resemble natural stone (marble, granite, etc.). In comparison with laminates, colors are sometimes limited and costs increase for inlays and other fancy edge details.

For countertops, use $1/2$-inch (1-cm) material. Use $3/4$-inch (1.9-cm) material for built-up edge treatments. To form corners and long countertops, sheets are welded together with color-matched joint adhesive. Solid surfaces have characteristics of wood; they can be cut, shaped, sanded, and installed with woodworking tools. They allow for a variety of sink installations, including integral units.

All companies offer sheet goods in $1/2$- to 3-inch (1- to 7.6-cm) thicknesses. Some are also available in thinner form, approximately $1/4$ inch (0.6 cm) for backsplashes or other wall applications. Other thicknesses are available and vary by company. All manufacturers recommend that unsupported overhangs not exceed 12 inches (30 cm) with $3/4$-inch (1.9-cm) sheets or 6 inches (15 cm) with $1/2$-inch (1-cm) sheets. Solid-surface countertops are expensive (they can cost five times as much as a basic self-edged laminate countertop and at least three times more than a bevel-edged laminate countertop, according to industry figures) and require firm support from below. When properly fabricated, the seam between two pieces of the solid-surfacing materials is almost imperceptible. However, you should never promise an invisible seam.

The quality of solid-surfacing installation is fabricator-sensitive. All manufacturers stress the importance of retaining only qualified or certified fabricators. You will work with fabricators who take the solid-surface sheet stock and customize it for the home. Handling solid-surface material often requires the services of another contractor. It takes special training to shape, cut, and handle them. Most manufacturers of solid-surfacing materials offer seminars on working with their materials. In most instances, it is necessary for you to take a training course before the materials are purchased. Before establishing a relationship with a solid-surfacing fabricator, you should ask to see proof of training certification. Be aware that mixing solid-surface manufactured sinks with that of another brand of solid-surface countertop may void any warranties.

Once the solid-surface countertop is delivered to the project site, you must handle it with great care. It can be easily broken in the field. Be sure that it does not fall over, because it is often susceptible to breakage. Often, large solid-surface countertops are delivered to the site in sections which must be joined in the field. You may find it wise to use "biscuits" (three biscuits per joint) for most installations to allow for accurate alignment of the sections being joined.

The following materials can also be used as complete countertops but are probably more efficient and useful if used as small inserts in countertops of some other materials.

STONE

Marble and granite are beautiful natural materials for countertops. Clients must be aware that because stone is a natural material, there will be slight variations from slab to slab. Generally, marble and granite are regarded as heatproof (marble counters never burn), water-resistant, easy to clean, and incredibly durable. Some of the disadvantages of these beautiful materials are that solid stone slabs are very expensive; stone tiles, including slate and limestone, are less expensive alternatives. Oil, alcohol, and any acids can stain marble or damage its high-gloss finish. Granite, however, is usually resistant to these because of its extremely low absorption rate; it is also less prone to scratching than marble. Its coarse grain also makes it more slip-resistant than marble. Marble counters need to be waxed and polished to prevent damage. Granite also can take a high polish. Repairs are difficult, if not impossible.

Marble, granite, slate, and other natural stones require specialized tools and skills for proper installation. The base cabinets have to be constructed with enough bracing and structural integrity to support the weight. Measuring granite countertops for installation is a precise process that can be completed only when the base cabinets have been installed. Accurate field dimensions are imperative, since granite countertops are prefabricated and delivered to the job site ready for installation. Installation costs are generally less for granite than for solid-surface countertops, because the fabrication is simpler and is completed at the factory. For most granite countertops, the optimum thickness is 1¼ inches (3.18 cm). The difference in cost over the more fragile ¾-inch (1.9-cm) slabs is minimal and the added thickness gives more strength for extensions, while reducing the risk of breakage during transport and installation. Keep in mind the weight of these countertops as you plan the installation. Inspect the delivered materials for cracks or damage before signing for acceptance.

Granite slabs for countertops can measure up to 4 to 6 feet (122 to 183 cm) wide and up to 9 feet (274.32 cm) long, allowing flexibility in countertop design. Should more than one piece be necessary, the slabs can be matched for color and grain consistency and then cut to butt squarely against each other. Plan seams at the most inconspicuous location. However, avoid seams in the vicinity of the sink cutout because of the possibility of moisture infiltration.

Marble is extremely brittle and must be handled like glass during installation. It is rated according to an A-B-C-D classification based on the fragility of the stones. A and B marbles are solid and sound. C and D marbles are the most fragile, but also the most colorful and decorative. The grade of marble affects its pricing; the more fragile and decorative it is, the more expensive. Clients should understand the durability aspects of marble before using it on a project. Many slabs of marble are available in 1¼ inches (3.18 cm) thick. Other suppliers stock ¾-inch (1.91-cm) thicker countertops. Some carry 1½-inch-(4-cm)-thick slabs. In addition to slab countertops, marble tiles can be installed by a tile setter following specifications developed by the Ceramic Tile Institute. Marble is soft and porous, which means that it will stain easily if it is not sealed with at least two coats of penetrating sealer. It must be frequently resealed.

Natural stones are not the counter choice for an active family. Suggest to your client a slab of one of these materials as an accent counter, rather than installing marble countertops throughout the bathroom, while using with ceramic tile or other complementary countertop surfaces in the rest of the bathroom.

WOOD

Wood is handsome, natural, and easily installed. Although not a widespread choice for the bathroom, wood countertops offer very pleasing visual and textural effects. Selected woods, either natural or laminated, are highly recommended for the kitchen (food-preparation areas) and are excellent, durable cutting surfaces.

Countertops made from laminated wood products are commonly referred to as "butcher block." Maple butcher block can be used as a countertop material in the bathroom as well as in the kitchen. Butcher block consists of hardwood laminated under pressure and sealed with oil or polymer. Custom bathrooms may feature the entire countertop in butcher block. When this type of surface is planned, it is necessary to know what type of wood will be used, what type of finish is to be applied, and what water and heat protection the block will receive.

Maple butcher block, the most popular choice, is sold in 24-, 30-, and 36-inch (61-, 76-, and 91-cm) widths. The installed price is comparable to ceramic or top-of-the-line laminates. Constructed of oak, redwood, teak, sugar pine, birch, alder, or other hardwood, they are almost completely indestructible, and even after years of use they can be renewed by sanding or planing. Countertop installations should be of thick butcher block, which means that the counters will weigh a great deal. Because it is thicker than other materials, it raises the counter level $3/4$ inch (1.9 cm) above standard height; plumbing connections will need to be modified accordingly. The edges of the plumbing fixtures must be sealed to prevent water seeping in and causing wood rot. The wood tops may be finished in several ways. The intended use of the block should determine the finish selection. Unfinished wood is most desirable if the entire counter surface is wood and local fabrication of seams or miters is required. Care and maintenance of unfinished wood includes protecting the wood from standing water, scraping with a steel scraper or spatula, and oiling the top weekly with mineral oil. For prefinished wood, the factory finish includes a penetrating sealer and a nontoxic clear finish. The combination of sealer and varnish ensures a waterproof surface and prevents scratches; however, it will not stand up to heat. No oiling is necessary, and a damp cloth may be used to wipe the board clean. Wood treated with urethane sealer is very good on countertops that will be exposed to moisture or liquids.

The disadvantages of wood countertops are that because they are porous, they can sometimes be difficult to keep clean, can soak up grease, are very susceptible to water damage (most bathroom surfaces are often exposed to water), and can scorch from excessive heat. However, if the wood is oiled occasionally, it will serve faithfully for years, and the surface can be easily repaired (sanded down). Additional drawbacks are the cost and upkeep. Doing an entire bathroom with real butcher-block counters can be quite expensive. Unfinished blocks require weekly cleaning and finishing with mineral oil.

Laminated hardwood countertops are available in a wide range of standard sizes from 12 to 120 inches (30 to 305 cm). They are usually a full 1½ inches (4 cm) thick and 25 inches (66 cm) deep and come with or without a 1-inch (2.54-cm)-thick backsplash. They come ready for installation on top of the base cabinets.

Backsplashes

The *backsplash,* the wall surface surrounding the countertop, can be used to make an aesthetic statement. If properly installed, a good backsplash also has practical advantages; it seals the area from moisture, and makes the wall easier to keep clean. In the past, the average countertop, typically laminate, had a 4-inch (10.16-cm) lip on the back. More and more backsplashes are being installed at greater heights. Hand-painted accent tiles, stone tiles, solid-surface materials, glass block, and mirrors are a few backsplash ideas.

Scheduling the Countertop Installation

As soon as you have signed the contract for an installation job, contact the countertop fabricator regarding the specifications for the surfacing materials and approximate date needed; therefore, the fabricator can be prepared to schedule your job and produce the countertops. Generally, countertops are produced by countertop fabricators from measurements you supply. In most cases, they are not cut to fit in the field. For this reason, measurements that are supplied to the countertop manufacturer must be accurate for proper fit. Some manufacturers come to the site and take field measurements. It is generally recommended that measurements be taken only after all the base cabinets have been set. Plan for, and make customers aware of this when scheduling this part of the job. In situations in which the same bathroom configuration is being installed in a number of homes, countertops may be ordered in quantities without waiting for field measurements. Standard-size bathroom vanity countertops are often available in stock without having to be custom-manufactured.

Depending on the manufacturer, the countertop material, and the level of difficulty required to construct the countertops, lead time for countertops can range from a few days to 2 weeks. You may need to use one fabricator for laminate and solid-surface countertops and a different fabricator for other countertop materials such as natural stone. It is important to establish a relationship with a countertop fabricator who is reliable and has a reputation for prompt delivery.

Getting the Bathroom Ready

It is time to get the bathroom ready for installation. The cabinets, countertops, fixtures, and other components are all on order, and the plans are in place. It is time to tear out the old bathroom and prepare for the new one. Certified plumbers are required to perform these tasks in most areas, but knowledge of the procedure will allow a remodeling contractor to smoothly interface with him.

As mentioned in Chap. 2, be certain that you and the client are clear on what existing materials will be removed and discarded. If items are to be saved—such as plumbing fixtures, and vanity countertops—be sure that the client provides an area where these items can be stored. A lot of rough treatment occurs during an installation project, and it is easy for items to be ruined, even when you are trying your best to keep everything intact. Decide who is responsible for the removal of any salvaged items. Don't leave these items vulnerable to damage. Have a plan as to how you are going to transport and remove broken cast-iron parts, wall tile, drywall, and floorcovering materials.

The bathroom remodeler must be on the lookout for design and structural traps. For example, work put in by amateurs is often overengineered (and hard to remove) and often ignores codes (which makes it harder to get the job accepted) and standard practices (so studs, pipe, and wires may not be where one would expect them). Drain lines, vent piping, and plumbing may be deteriorated, as well as out-of-code compliance. The main thing to remember is to work carefully. The goal is to remove the old bathroom with as little damage to the surrounding areas as possible, to minimize unintended reconstruction work.

The bathroom is basically dismantled in the opposite order in which it is assembled. The first items to remove are the fixtures and plumbing fittings. Before beginning, locate the water supply at the main shutoff valve, as well as the electric service panel. Verify that the water and electric are off before continuing. Shutting off a supplied service may require notifying the utility providing that service. Not informing them may be a violation. In addition, remember that drain and vent lines that are affected by the project disturb the other bathrooms that remain in use during remodeling. Vent gasses must be dealt with during this period, and the flow of waste cannot be blocked.

Removing Existing Plumbing and Fixtures

When one is equipped with the proper tools and techniques, removing existing plumbing should go smoothly. Evaluate each circumstance and proceed with caution. Good planning is the key to a successful removal of old plumbing. It is extremely important before you begin work to check all code requirements for any of the following described removals. Before removing any plumbing, turn off the water at the fixture shutoff valves or main shutoff valve. Check the flow at the faucet to ensure that the shutoff still functions well. A slow flow may not be immediately apparent.

Note: Throughout the removal process, it is imperative to always wear safety goggles. Unless installing a new floorcovering, be sure to protect the bathroom floor with a piece of cardboard or plywood. Always be prepared to have any necessary replacement parts on hand if a pipe or fixture is damaged in removal or if the water is to be turned back on immediately.

Removing the Toilet

Removing a toilet or bidet is not very complicated. During major remodeling involving the floor or walls, remember that toilets and bidets are the first fixtures to remove and the last to install. As with the removal of all fixtures, be certain to turn off the water supply at the main shutoff valve, even if the fixture has a separate shutoff valve. To begin, flush the toilet twice to empty the bowl and tank. Towel or sponge any remaining water from the tank and bowl. For a two-piece toilet, the tank will be removed first, followed by the bowl. For a one-piece toilet, the tank and bowl are removed at the same time. A small siphon pump and bucket will come in handy.

With an adjustable wrench, disconnect the riser, shutoff valve, and escutcheon. Disconnect the toilet from the floor. Remove the protective caps from the hold-down bolts and unscrew the nuts with an adjustable wrench. If the bolts are too corroded to come loose, soak them with penetrating oil or cut them off with a hacksaw.

Bowl-mounted toilet tank. To remove a bowl-mounted toilet tank, detach the empty tank from the bowl by removing the two bolts holding it in place under the rear rim of the bowl. Lift the tank off the bowl. These bolts are most likely beyond future use. If the existing unit is to be reinstalled, you should have new bolts on hand.

Wall-mounted toilet tank. If the tank is mounted on the wall, remove the L-shaped spud pipe securing the tank to the bowl by removing the slip nuts at either end of the pipe. Reach inside the tank with a wrench and unscrew the nuts on the hanger bolts, which attach the tank to the hanger bracket on the wall. The tank can then be removed. At the base of the bowl near the floor, pry off the metal or ceramic caps covering bolts that secure the bowl to a flange on the floor. Unscrew the nuts from the bolts. Gently rock the bowl from side to side to break the wax seal underneath (between the bowl and the floor). Keeping the bowl level to prevent remaining water from spilling from its trap, lift the bowl straight up off the drain (lifting the toilet can put strain on your back; use caution). Plug the floor waste opening to prevent any escaping sewer gases.

Removing a Bidet

Typically, a bidet is not difficult to remove. However, unlike a toilet, a bidet has a sink-type drain and trap and is plumbed for hot and cold water. With this type of removal, two water-supply lines, a drainpipe, and the hold-down bolts will be disconnected. To completely drain all remaining water, open all faucets and unfasten the coupling nuts on the hot- and cold-water-supply lines. These lines are either attached to the wall behind the bidet or are freestanding. Some bidets may be plumbed with mixing valves in the wall and a single water-supply line running to the fixture. For those bidets which may have a mixing valve and a hammer device inside the wall, these items will need to be removed. Figure 7.1 shows a deck- or shelf-mounted bidet with hot- and cold-water lines to a "spout" with a mixing valve, a drain similar to a drain below the floor.

Find the drainpipe connection and, in most cases, a pop-up drain assembly located behind and under the back of the bidet. Loosen the clevis screw and disconnect this assembly. Next, loosen the slip nuts on the trap and remove it.

Pry the caps off the flange at the base of the bidet and remove the nuts underneath them. If the nuts have rusted, the bolts can be soaked with penetrating oil or cut with a hacksaw. Rock the fixture back and forth gently to break the caulk seal around the base and free the fixture from the floor. The bidet can now be lifted straight up off the hold-down bolts which were securing it to the floor. To prevent debris from falling into the opening, stuff a rag into the drainpipe.

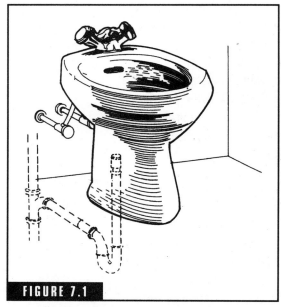

FIGURE 7.1

A typical shelf- or deck-mounted bidet. (*Leon E. Kore-jwo, Illustrations.*)

Removing a Shower

Most showers consist of three walls with waterproof wallcovering, such as tile or panels, and a separate base, mounted in a wood frame. Therefore, removing a shower is a three-step procedure: disconnecting the plumbing, removing the wallcovering, and removing the base. If the shower is a one-piece unit, you will also have to cut a hole in a wall to get it out, unless you cut the unit into pieces. If changing the location of a shower or permanently removing the shower, you will probably want to dismantle the wood frame and remove the plumbing.

DISCONNECTING THE PLUMBING

First remove the rod, curtain, or shower door. Then turn off the water supply at the fixture shutoff valves or at the main shutoff valve. Open the faucets to drain the pipes; sponge the shower base dry.

Remove the faucet handles and other trim parts, leaving the faucet stems. Then remove the showerhead with a pipe wrench (wrapped to avoid scarring the fixture).

Unscrew and pry up the drain cover. With a pair of pliers and a small prybar, unscrew the cross piece. If removing a one-piece shower enclosure, you will also have to disconnect the drainpipe and remove protruding faucet stems and fittings that, when you tip the unit to pull it out, might get in the way. Finally, plug the drain opening with a rag to prevent debris from falling into it.

REMOVING THE WALLCOVERING

The removal procedure you will follow depends on whether you are removing a tiled shower, walls covered with fiberglass panels, or an older metal shower.

Ceramic tile. Ceramic tile is the most difficult wallcovering to remove. If the existing tile is clean, smooth, and securely attached, you can avoid removing it by using it as a backing for a new tile surface. To remove tile set in mortar, you must break up the tile, mortar, and any backing with a sledgehammer. Remove it down to the wood frame, being careful not to hit and damage the wall studs. If the tile is set on wallboard with adhesive, use a cold chisel and soft-headed steel hammer to chip away small sections of tile and backing. Then insert a prybar and pry off large sections of tile and backing until the entire frame is exposed.

Caution: If the tile is set with mortar and metal lath, it will be rusty and sharp. Be cautious and wear heavy gloves.

When remodeling, if you want to salvage old ceramic tile (walls, floors, countertops) make sure that you can replace the tile with exactly the same tile. If it is not possible to find exact replacements, attempt to break out the tile in a pattern so that it can be replaced with a different tile and still look acceptable. This also gives it a different look.

Fiberglass panels. First remove any molding or wallboard covering the panel flanges. Then pry panels, along with any backing and nails, off the wood frame. If removing a one-piece enclosure, you may have to cut it apart with a reciprocating saw. Use a dust mask, goggles, and gloves when sawing the fiberglass; it can be toxic and an irritant.

Metal showers. Metal shower walls are removed by unscrewing them at the edges, at the front and at the back corners. These screws hold the shower walls to each other and, in some cases, to a wood frame. If the screws are rusted, cut the screw heads off with a hacksaw, cut off tool, grinder, or cold chisel; then separate the walls with a hard pull.

After the wallcovering has been removed, check for moisture damage to the frame and to any soundproofing insulation secured across the inside of the frame. Repair or replace if necessary. Always beware of old asbestos and use approved procedures for its removal.

REMOVING THE BASE

The base may be tile on a mortar bed, or it may be a fiberglass unit. Tile is difficult to remove because it is laid in mortar; fiberglass bases are simply pried out. After the base has been removed, inspect the subfloor and framing for moisture damage, and repair where necessary. As with tile walls, check first to see if the new tile can be installed over the old. If not, use a sledgehammer to break it up and remove all tile and mortar down to the subfloor. You may be able to pry up one side of the base and slip a sledge under it to make it easier to break up. For fiberglass units, remove all nails or screws from the flange around the top of the base. Pry the base off the floor with a prybar; lift it out.

Removing Old Faucets

The two types of faucets which are widely used in bathrooms are deck-mounted models for lavatories and wall-mounted models for bathtubs and showers. Before removing the faucet, turn off the valves in the hot and cold supply pipes below the basin. If there are no valves, turn off the water supply at the main shutoff valve. Place a bucket under the valves and use a wrench to remove the coupling nuts connecting the water-supply lines to the valves. Open the faucet and allow the water to drain from the lines. Disconnect the faucet tailpieces from the supply risers with a basin wrench.

REMOVING A DECK-MOUNTED LAVATORY FAUCET

If the lavatory contains a drain control, it needs to be disconnected before removing the faucet. With a pair of pliers, loosen the clevis screw and the spring clip that secure the pivot rod to the pop-up rod, then free the pivot rod from the drain. Separate the pivot rod from the pop-up plug; remove both pieces.

With an adjustable or basin wrench, reach up behind the lavatory and remove the supply nuts (where the supply tube is connected to the inlet shanks on the faucet). Turn the faucet mounting nuts and washers counterclockwise and remove from the shanks. Because of their location, the mounting nuts, the ones that hold the faucet onto the lavatory, are hard to see and reach, and can be difficult to remove. They often rust and become difficult to turn. Even with a good basin wrench, there may be times when the nuts will not turn. In this instance, cut the nuts off the faucet inlets. There is ordinarily a ridged washer between the nut and the lavatory. Take off the washers, lift up the faucet and remove it from the lavatory or countertop. If necessary, insert a putty knife under the baseplate to remove the faucet from the basin. Remove any remaining caulk or adhesive.

REMOVING WALL-MOUNTED MODELS FOR BATHTUBS AND SHOWERS

The faucet body is mounted directly on the water-supply pipes inside the wall. Turn off the water at the bathtub or shower shutoff valves or at the main shutoff valve. Preliminary inspection of the adjoining rooms may indicate electrical outlets or wiring in the wall. It is prudent to shut off circuit breakers before cutting into a wall.

Replacing a complete bathtub or shower faucet involves cutting away the wallcovering and removing the faucet body from the supply pipes with wrenches or a small propane torch.

Caution: When working with a torch, put a piece of sheet metal between the pipe and wall (or any combustible surfaces). Keep an extinguisher handy and inspect any possible sources of fallen or smouldering materials inside the walls. It is possible to ignite when left overnight.

To gain access to the faucet body, remove the faucet handles, trim, and stem parts; then remove the diverter. Remove the tub spout or shower head with a tap-wrapped pipe wrench. To work on the faucet body and the pipes behind the wall, open the access panel, if available.

If not available, cut a hole in the bathroom wall large enough to allow you to work on the faucet body and pipes. The faucet body may be attached with either threaded or soldered connections; if the latter, unsolder them, using a small propane torch; the former, unscrew them. Use one wrench on the supply pipe to hold it steady, and one wrench on the coupling, turning it counterclockwise.

Removing Lavatories

In the fixture industry, a bathroom "sink" is technically referred to as a *lavatory*. Before removing the lavatory, be sure to protect the bathroom floor with a piece of cardboard or plywood, unless installing a new floor covering. Also have a supply of sponges or rags and a bucket close by to soak up any excess water. Always use a flashlight to light the area below the vanity because if water drips down onto the alternating-current (ac)-powered light (such as a drop or trouble light) and causes a short circuit, you could be injured.

Lavatories are fairly easy to remove; however, procedures for the removal do vary somewhat, depending on the type of lavatory. The first step, for all lavatories, is to turn off the water at the lavatory shutoff valves or at the main shutoff valve. Disconnect the supply lines at the shutoff valves, and open the faucets to let any trapped water escape. Supply lines connect up underneath the basin with a pair of coupling nuts; many have a second set of connections down below, where water lines exit from the wall. There may be shutoff valves located there, as well. If the lavatory doesn't have shutoff valves, disconnect the supply lines at the faucet inlets. Reinstalling the plumbing shutoffs should be discussed with your clients. It is an extra feature and, therefore, an added expense.

Before removing the trap, set a bucket underneath to catch any water standing in the trap. To disconnect the trap from the lavatory's tailpiece, with a basin wrench, loosen the slip nuts at one or both ends of the trap and twist them loose. If you plan to reuse the trap, wrap the jaws of the wrench so that you don't mar the plated finish. However, the trap can be easily broken, and you should plan on having to replace it. Disconnect the pop-up drain assembly by loosening the clevis screw and then remove the spring clip that connects the stopper and pivot rod to the pop-up rod on the faucet. The tailpiece, drain body, lavatory flange, and faucet will now come out with the lavatory.

Caution: Safety glasses are important when working under the lavatory. They protect you from falling rust and other foreign objects.

When the waste and water connections are disconnected, you are ready to remove the lavatory bowl.

REMOVING WALL-HUNG LAVATORIES

Wall-hung lavatories are fairly easy to remove. First unscrew the legs, if any, that support the front of the lavatory. If the lavatory is wall-hung, it rests on a bracket or cleat at the rear, where it also may be secured with a couple of bolts. When the waste and water lines are free, inspect underneath for any lag bolts securing the bowl to the mounting bracket on the wall. Loosen the bolts, if any, and the bowl should lift off its bracket without much trouble.

REMOVING A ONE-PIECE (INTEGRAL) COUNTERTOP WITH MOLDED LAVATORY

Lavatories for vanity cabinets can be molded as part of the countertop or installed separately into holes cut in the countertop (see the next paragraph, on removing a deck-mounted lavatory). An integral lavatory is molded as part of the countertop. The unit is secured to the top of a vanity cabinet. Metal clips or wooden braces securing the unit can be removed. This allows the whole unit to be lifted off. If this gives you some difficulty, insert the end of a small prybar in the joint between the countertop and vanity cabinet at a back corner. Carefully lift up the prybar to break the sealing material between the countertop and vanity. If the joint is too narrow, cut through the sealing material with a hot putty knife, then pry or lift up the countertop.

REMOVING A DECK- (OR COUNTERTOP)-MOUNTED LAVATORY

There are three basic types of deck-mounted lavatories used in vanity countertops: self-rimming lavatories, recessed (undercounter mount) lavatories, and flush-mount (or mounting frame) lavatories. All may be secured to the countertop with lugs or clamps that must be unscrewed before you remove the lavatory.

1. *Self-rimming lavatories.* Self-rimming lavatories have a smooth, rounded edge, and no metal lavatory rim. Nothing holds them in place except a bead of sealant between the underside of the lavatory rim and the counter, plus their own weight. To remove them, with a hot putty knife, cut through the sealant around the rim of the lavatory (between lavatory and countertop). When the caulked seal is broken, pry up from below the bowl to remove the lavatory from the countertop.

2. *Recessed (undercounter mount) lavatories.* A recessed lavatory is secured to the underside of the countertop. The easiest way to remove the lavatory is to first take off the countertop. Check underneath for any brackets attaching the countertop to the cabinet and remove them. Then insert a prybar into the joint between the countertop and the vanity cabinet near a rear corner, and pry it up. Turn the countertop bottom side up and rest it on a padded surface. Undo the lugs or clamps securing the lavatory, and lift it off the countertop. Many tiled-in lavatories are set on the countertop decking and then held in place with tile. Look underneath; if you don't see any clips or brackets, you will need to chip off the tile to completely expose the rim of the lavatory. With a soft-headed steel hammer and cold chisel, remove enough tile so that you can lift the lavatory from the countertop.

3. *Flush-mount (mounting-frame) lavatories.* A surrounding metal frame holds a flush-mount sink to the countertop. Flush mounts have a metal rim as a separate piece. The screws and clips hold the lavatory, the rim, and the counter all sandwiched together. It is imperative that you suspend the weight of the lavatory from above or find a helper to support it while you remove the last of the lugs or clamps. Remove the lugs or clamps that secure the lavatory's metal rim to the counter's underside. Cut through the sealing material between the rim and the countertop with a hot putty knife. This will allow you to pry up the rim to free the lavatory.

REMOVING A PEDESTAL (FREESTANDING) LAVATORY

Most pedestal lavatories are made of two pieces—the lavatory and the pedestal or base—installed after disconnecting the drain and supply plumbing. Look in the opening at the rear of the pedestal to locate a nut or bolt holding the lavatory down. If you find one, remove it. Lift off the lavatory and set it aside. The pedestal is usually bolted to the floor. You may find the bolts on the base, or on the inside of the pedestal. Undo the bolts and remove the pedestal. If you can't move it after removing the bolts, rock it back and forth, and then lift it out. If the pedestal is recessed into a ceramic tile floor, you may have to remove the surrounding floor tiles with a cold chisel and soft-headed steel hammer. Rock the pedestal back and forth to break any remaining seal with the floor. Lift the pedestal up and set it aside.

After you have removed any style of lavatory, stuff a rag into the open line to keep sewer gases out of the house. If your fixture doesn't have shutoff valves, be sure the supply lines are capped off.

Removing the Bathtub

Removing the bathtub can be quite a difficult task. When planning the space and selecting fixtures, it is imperative to construct a plan for removing the old tub or shower as well as installing the new unit. Keep in mind that doors and stairways can be major hindrances when it comes to taking a tub out of the house. Tubs were often installed before walls were finished; when the house was built. Openings in the partition wall framing made tub installation easier, and the wall was closed after the tub and plumbing was installed and inspected. You will need helpers to move the old tub, especially if it is a one-piece fiberglass tub or a heavy cast-iron fixture. If your client has chosen a unit that cannot be moved into the bathroom through existing hallways or doors, plan ways to move it through the outer wall, such as removing a first-floor window or a portion of the wall on the second or third floor. Be certain not to disturb vital structural members (see later in this chapter).

DISCONNECTING THE PLUMBING

When disconnecting the plumbing, turn the water off at the fixture shutoff valves or at the main shutoff valve. Typically, the tub valve will be replaced with the tub, but even if you don't anticipate replacing the tub valve, cut off the water. Open the faucets to drain the pipes.

Remove any fittings (spout, faucet parts, showerhead, and diverter handle) that will be in the way. Unscrew and remove the overflow cover and drain lever and slowly pull the linkage rod coil assembly out. By pulling out this fitting, you will also remove the bathtub drain assembly if it is a trip-lever type. If a pop-up stopper, pull it out with the rocker linkage after removing the overflow cover. If there is an access door or access from the basement or crawlspace, use a pipe wrench to loosen the slip nuts that hold together the drain, trap, and overflow tube, and remove these components. You can work from inside the tub if unable to get access to the drain plumbing.

REMOVING THE WALLCOVERING

Most bathtubs are surrounded by walls on three sides (recessed). Depending on whether you want to replace the tub only, or the tub and wall covering, you need to remove all or part of the surrounding tiles or panels. Sometimes working through an adjacent closet wall will be a way to go.

Ceramic tile. If there are wall or floor tiles along the edge of the tub, free the tub by chipping out approximately 4" (10 cm) to the nearest grout joint. On the walls, remove the plaster wallboard backing at the same time so that several inches of the wall studs are exposed. Use a cold chisel and soft-headed steel hammer to remove the tile, and as stated before, remember to wear safety goggles when removing tile. Remove enough tile and other obstructions from the floor and walls to be able to slide the tub out of its recess.

Fiberglass panels. Take out the wall panels by first removing the wallboard or molding from the panel flanges. With a prybar, pry the panels, along with any backing, off the studs. Once the end panels are removed, back panels can be removed leaving the exposed wall studs.

Glass block. Glass block is usually held in place with mortar or lead, similar to leaded glass, since the mortar seldom bonds to the glass as it would to the cement block. If you break out one glass block, you should be able to loosen the others. Although it seems like common sense, be certain to always start at the top.

REMOVING THE BATHTUB FIXTURE

If the tub is steel, it will need to be removed in one piece. In this case, you will need additional help. A standard-size tub (30 × 60 inches) will fit through doorways, when turned on its side. Larger tubs may require you to remove them through windows or openings in walls. Since cast-iron tubs commonly weigh in excess of 400 pounds and can't be removed in one piece, breaking the tub into pieces is the easiest way to remove it. Safety glasses are extremely important for this type of removal because cast iron shatters (like a piece of pottery) and is dangerously sharp. Use a sledgehammer, applying only as much force as necessary. To get the tub out, you may first have to remove the bathroom door or even cut a hole in the wall opposite the tub plumbing.

When the wall sections are removed, you will be able to see that the tub is sitting against stud walls. Locate and remove from the wall studs any nails or screws at the top of the tub's flange that may be holding the tub in place. With at least one helper (most likely you will need more than one), have the helpers use a 4-foot section of a 2 × 4 stud as a lever. Rock the tub up so that the helpers are able to place the stud under the tub. Use the lever to force the tub out, little by little. Although a slow removal process, this will work, as well as reduce the risk of personal injury.

To remove a fiberglass or plastic tub, pull out all nails or screws driven into the wall studs through the flange. Reach between the studs and grasp the tub under the flange; with the aid of a helper, if necessary, pull the tub up off its supports and out of the recess.

Removing One-Piece Bathtub-Shower Combinations

One-piece bath-shower units are usually made from fiberglass. The fiberglass construction makes these units light, but their size complicates the removal process; they are generally installed during the construction process. These large units will not fit through most doors and stairways. To remove this large unit from the house, it will need to be cut into pieces with a reciprocating saw. Again, take precautions by using a dust mask, gloves, and goggles; fiberglass has some very irritating properties.

Removing a Vanity

Vanities are usually attached to the walls with nails or screws. Enlarge the openings around the water shutoff valves to enable you to pull the vanity free. Drill a pilot hole, then use a keyhole saw to enlarge the holes. Once all piping is disconnected, remove any nails or screws holding the vanity in place and pull the cabinet away from the wall. Vanitytops are glued in place or attached to frames with screws from underneath.

Removing Cabinets and Countertops

Although many bathrooms are still equipped with the typical base vanity, today bath storage areas have become more stylish by integrating built-in cabinets like those found in the kitchen. The differences between kitchen and bath cabinet lines have diminished.

The removal of existing cabinets and countertops can be accomplished fairly easily, once they are empty, and all doors and drawers have been removed. Be certain that the water was turned off at the shutoff valves. The plumbing fixtures should have been disconnected and removed. Usually it is most efficient to remove the upper cabinets first. If the cabinets are modular, you will find that they are screwed together through the edges of the face frame. These should be the first screws to be removed. Next, any screws holding the cabinets to the wall must be removed. In some cases, nails are used instead of screws. Use a nail puller to get under the head and raise the nail; then remove it with a hammer. If salvaging them, be careful to avoid damage to the cabinets. Always take caution to avoid damage to the surface of the wall.

Once all the upper cabinets have been removed, the countertops are next. In some cases you will find that screws have been driven up through cleats on the top of the base cabinets, into the underside of the counters. Simply remove the screws. Remove any screws or brackets holding the countertops to the cabinets, and unscrew the takeup bolts on mitered countertops. A utility knife can be used to cut caulk beads along the edge of the countertop and backsplash. Remove trim moldings at the edges and tops of cabinets with a flat prybar or putty knife. Use a flat prybar to lift the countertop away from the base cabinets, as well as to remove base shoe moldings and baseboards. If the countertop cannot be pried up, use a reciprocating saw or jigsaw with a coarse wood-cutting blade to cut the countertop into manageable pieces for removal. Be careful not to cut into the base cabinets.

To remove ceramic tile, chisel the tile away from the base with a ball-peen hammer and masonry chisel. A tile countertop that has a mortar bed can be cut into pieces with a circular saw and abrasive masonry-cutting blade. It is imperative to always remember to wear eye protection, dust mask, and heavy gloves while breaking tile.

When the counters have been removed, the base cabinets can be taken out. Unscrew them as you did with the upper cabinets, remove the doors, take out the screws from the face frame, and then remove the screws from the wall.

Some older styles of cabinets were built on site when the house was constructed. These cabinets, in many cases, have no backs, and there is little to be done to salvage them. Begin by unscrewing and removing the doors. Using a hammer from the inside of the cabinet, knock the face frame free of the shelves. Depending on how the cabinets were originally built, either remove the sides to completely free up the shelves or pry the entire cabinet off the wall or off the cleats. Beware that these types of cabinets were assembled with a number of finishing nails.

Built-in cabinets should be cut into pieces and discarded. Old cabinets can be salvaged if they are modular units that were installed with screws. Remove trim moldings at the edges and tops of cabinets with a flat prybar or putty knife. Remove vinyl base trim. Work a prybar or putty knife underneath to peel off the vinyl, as well as to remove base shoe moldings and baseboards. During this removal process, wall surfaces can be protected with scraps of wood. Keep in mind while removing valances that some are attached to cabinets or soffits with screws, while others are nailed and must be pried loose. Any screws holding the cabinets to the wall must be removed. Cabinets can be taken apart piece by piece with a hammer and prybar or cut into manageable pieces with a reciprocating saw. Once the old counters and cabinets are removed, remove them from the work area.

Removing Flooring

If the old flooring is in good condition and adheres well to the floor, you may be able to lay the new flooring right over it. In most cases, a better overall finish will be achieved by removing the old flooring (Tables 7.1 to 7.3).

If you find an instance in which the fixtures or cabinets were installed first, followed by underlayment, and then flooring, you will find large gaps in the underlayment when they are removed. The best thing to do in this situation is to simply remove the underlayment, flooring, and all. Remove the base trim. Use a prybar to remove the baseboard and base shoe from where the wall meets the floor. As you pry each portion outward, insert a wood shim behind it to keep the molding away from the wall so you can insert the prybar at the next position. When prying the baseboard away from the wall, place a block of wood behind the bar to protect the wall from dents.

To remove resilient sheet goods, slit them with a utility knife, work a spade underneath, and then peel up the flooring. Old resilient floorcoverings that are embossed or cushioned should be removed or covered with plywood underlayment before installing new flooring (see section on preparing for resilient flooring at end of this chapter). Be sure to remove the felt backing entirely by moistening the glued felt with soapy water and with a floor scraper or drywall knife. Ceramic tile that is damaged or loose must be removed by breaking the tiles with a heavy hammer or sledgehammer and prying up the pieces with a cold chisel. Remove baseboards and base shoe with a drywall knife (protects wall surfaces) and prybar. Bathroom carpeting is almost always glued down. It must be scraped off completely to prepare for the new flooring.

When all the plumbing fixtures, cabinets, countertops, and flooring have been removed, study the proposed layout to prepare for what else needs to be removed. If the walls need to be opened up (e.g., to provide for access for new plumbing or wiring), do as much of this as possible now. Finally, completely clean the bathroom, sweep up all the debris, and remove all the old items to their proper designated area.

The Structural System

When a bathroom is being assembled in a new house, structural problems should not arise. However, when planning to remodel an old bathroom, problems commonly arise. Even if the home is only a few years old, it always seems that the windows are never quite where they ought to be, or the chimney flue forms a jutting corner right where your client wants you to add a cabinet. And, just about as common are problems that already exist in the wall, such as plumbing lines, wiring, and the doors that never seem to be where they should be. Electrical lines and outlets can be moved or added with little trouble, but reworking existing piping and ductwork involves more complicated solutions (see Chap. 9). As was discussed in Chap. 2, be certain that you had a preliminary inspection. As a result of this inspection, you should have discussed with the client the cost of the desired changes. Inform your client of the expense of taking out and putting in new fixtures. Replacing fixtures also means renovating the electrical, plumbing, and heating lines that serve the bathroom. Keep in mind that a strong floor-framing system is extremely important near the bathtub or whirlpool. A cast-iron tub of average size can weigh a minimum of 300 pounds. Filling it with water and the bather adds several hundred more pounds. This will put quite a strain on the supporting structure. It is very important to look carefully for any hidden structural weakness.

In existing homes inspect areas where plumbing penetrates the floor. Often, a large drain enters the floor immediately above a floor joist or a wall into a wall stud. The worker may solve the dilemma by butchering up the structural member, rather than redesign, move, or reroute the line. Remodeling may require moving these lines, taking care not to further weaken a member, and also repairing the damage done. Analyze the problem to avoid unpleasant surprises to the homeowner, as well as yourself.

Before you begin work, it is extremely important to analyze the house structural system. Do not assume that the architect or the dealer or designer has provided all this information for you. You need to be able to identify bearing and nonbearing walls, study the floor and ceiling framing, and determine in which direction the members are oriented (important in determining locations for plumbing and ductwork runs and recessed light fixtures). Architectural drawings generally show only schematic layouts, with locations and, hopefully, sizes of pipe to be used. The routing is left to be done "in the field."

If the design does not provide the required structural support (e.g., for a masonry floor), immediately notify the architect or the dealer or designer that it is okay to modify the plans and that the client can be made aware of the additional working costs.

Extensive Framing

Before you begin any framing work, have your plan worked out, to scale, on paper. Since most of the other interior work depends on the framing, it is crucial that you get the planning and framing work done properly.

Existing floor and ceiling structural members can present problems. Floor joists and subflooring could be rotted. Repairing damaged framing generally is not a big deal, but it is extremely important that the existing joists be strong enough to handle the live load of the planned space.

The term "wall framing" includes primarily the vertical studs and horizontal members of interior and exterior walls that support ceilings, upper floors, and the roof. The wall framing also serves as a nailing base for wallcovering materials (see Chap. 10).

The wall framing members used in conventional construction are generally nominal 2 × 4-inch (5 × 10-cm) studs spaced 16 inches (41 cm) on center (Fig. 7.2). Depending on the thickness of the covering material and the purpose of the wall, 24-inch (61-cm) spacing is sometimes used. Top plates and sole plates are also a nominal 2 × 4 inches (5 × 10 cm) in size. Headers over doors or windows in load-bearing walls consist of doubled 2 × 6-inch (5 × 15-cm) and deeper members, depending on the span of the opening. Ceiling height for the first floor is 8 feet (244 cm) under most conditions. It is common practice to rough-frame the wall (subfloor to top of upper plate) to a height of 8 feet $1^{1}/_{2}$ inches (248 cm). In most construction, precut studs are often supplied to a length of 7 feet $8^{5}/_{8}$ inches (244 cm) for plate thickness of $1^{5}/_{8}$ inches (4.13 cm). When dimension material is $1^{1}/_{2}$ inches (4 cm) thick, precut studs would be 7 feet 9 inches (236 cm) long. This height

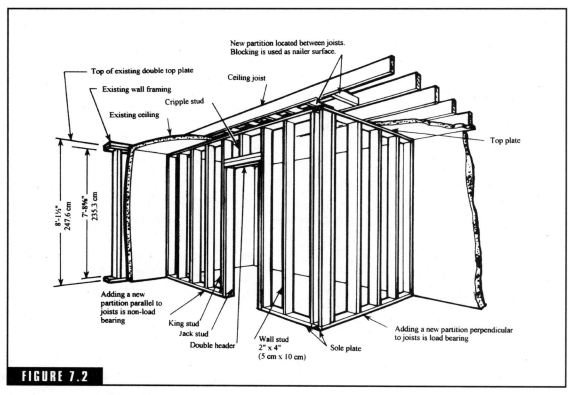

FIGURE 7.2

Framing members of partition walls. *(Leon E. Korejwo, Illustrations.)*

allows the use of 8-foot- (244-cm)-high drywall sheets and still provides clearance for floor and ceiling finish or for plaster grounds at the floor line.

You are likely to encounter three types of framing systems: platform-frame construction, post-and-beam construction, and balloon-frame construction. Each system has its own set of unique characteristics which makes it generally easy to identify. While the platform method is more often used because of its simplicity, you may encounter any one of these systems when remodeling a home.

PLATFORM-FRAME CONSTRUCTION

The wall framing in platform construction is erected above the subfloor, which extends to all edges of the structure (Fig. 7.3). A combination of platform construction for the first-floor side walls and full-length studs for end walls extending to end rafters of the gable ends is commonly used in single-story houses.

One common method of framing is the horizontal assembly (on the subfloor) or "tilt-up" of wall sections. This system involves laying out precut studs, window and door headers, cripple studs (short-length studs), and window sills. Top plates and sole plates are then nailed to all vertical members and adjoining studs to headers and sills with 16-penny (16d) nails. Let-in corner bracing should be provided when required. The entire section is then erected, plumbed, and braced.

POST-AND-BEAM CONSTRUCTION

The post-and-beam form of building can be seen in historical structures dating back to the earliest European influence. Gaining popularity in current rural structures, it presents a different set of circumstances for the remodeler. Massive wood members carry the loads, leaving open spaces in the wall normally taken up by the wall studs. These open areas between the beams and posts, referred to as *glazed areas,* are free to be remodeled without weakening the wall, although side loads (created by wind, called *shear* or *racking*) require diagonal bracing. Braces may be diagonal wood members. Bracing may also be achieved by using sheathed framed walls or solid masonry in the glazed areas. These braces must not be removed. Areas below interior beams within the house can remain open or can be closed in. In post-and-beam houses, all the building's loads are carried on heavy lumber posts.

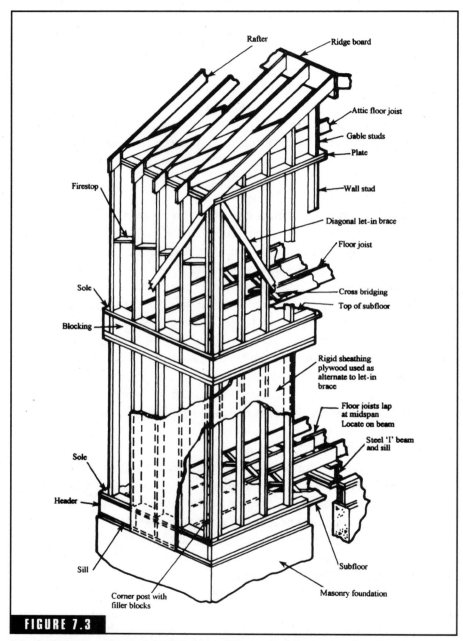

FIGURE 7.3

A typical platform-frame (also known as _Western-frame_) construction._(Leon E. Korejwo, Illustrations.)_

This type of construction, while not adaptable to many styles of architecture, is simple and straightforward.

Today, specialists in timber framing can combine post-and-beam construction with panels filled with insulation. Many have drywall on the inside and siding on the outside. The insulating values of these nonbearing panels is very good. Without making any structural changes to the houses, these panels can be removed. Historical buildings used pegs or other wooden attachments to join the members. Current modern methods of steel angle and straps and plate systems ease assembly or reconstruction for today's carpenters.

BALLOON-FRAME CONSTRUCTION

The main difference between platform and balloon framing is at the floor lines (Fig. 7.4). The balloon wall studs extend from the sill of the first floor to the top plate or end rafter of the second floor, whereas the platform-frame wall is complete for each floor. Balloon-frame construction uses wood studs rather than posts. Because the studs extend continuously from the top of the foundation to the roof, the stud cavity makes it easy to pull new wiring or reroute plumbing supply lines. The use of firestops, however, creates blockages that may be in areas difficult to see and penetrate for new wiring or plumbing.

In most areas, building codes require that firestops be used in balloon framing to prevent the spread of fire through the open wall passages. These firestops are ordinarily 2 × 4-inch (5 × 10-cm) blocking placed between the studs or as required by local regulations.

In balloon-frame construction, both the wall studs and the floor joists rest on the anchored sill. The studs and joists are toenailed to the sill with 8d nails and nailed to each other with at least three 10d nails. The ends of the second-floor joists bear on a 2 × 4-inch (5 × 10-cm) ribbon that has been let into the studs. In addition, the joists are nailed with four 10d nails to the studs at these connections. The end joists parallel to the exterior on both the first and second floors are also nailed to each stud.

Walls

Sometimes major bathroom remodeling entails removing all or part of an interior wall to enlarge the space. Frequently, you will run into the problem of a wall not being where it should be in the new plan.

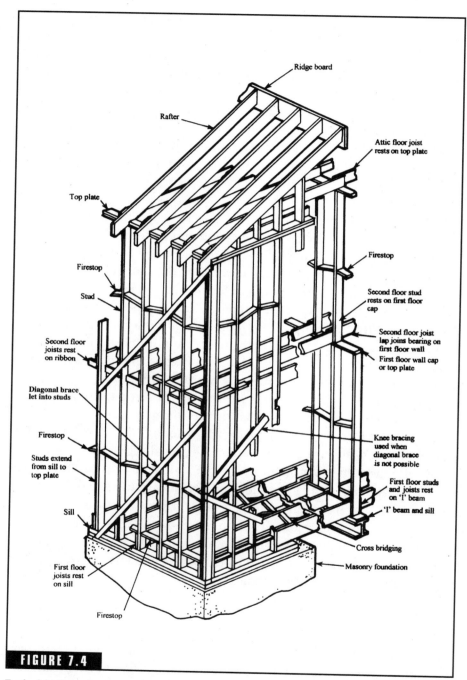

FIGURE 7.4

Typical balloon-frame construction. *(Leon E. Korejwo, Illustrations.)*

Before starting demolition, check the wall carefully. It may be a load-bearing one. Load-bearing walls carry the weight of the roof or upper floor down to the foundation. The entire stability of the house is dependent on these bearing walls. Any bearing wall must be replaced with a beam at ceiling level supported at the side walls or alternative support system. Nonbearing walls are independent of the structural system, and some serve merely as partitions separating interior spaces. They are relatively easy and inexpensive to remove, provided they don't carry drain and vent lines.

About the only visible difference between a bearing and nonbearing wall is that the bearing wall has a double top plate. It can be identified by drilling a small hole in the wall a few inches from the point where it meets the ceiling. Even better, go to the basement or attic and note the direction in which the floor joists run. Nonbearing walls usually run parallel to joists; bearing walls run perpendicular to joists. Double joists or extra members built into a floor under a wall indicate that it is load-bearing.

Any openings to exterior walls (i.e., doors and windows) which are load-bearing have structural framing (headers) above them. Headers distribute weight from above to the vertical framing at either side of these openings.

In some cases, a wall may need to be added. Doing so is quite simple and can be accomplished by following standard construction procedures.

Removing Existing Walls

In a remodeling job, a few walls might need to be torn out. In most cases tear-out is not too difficult, but some circumstances can make the removal of walls a bit more challenging. Finding insects or animals, such as a colony of honeybees, snakes, or rats, can give you major complications when tearing out walls.

Beware of electrical wires, plumbing, or heating piping, which are usually located in interior walls. It is always best to open walls with a hammer rather than a saw. If you rip into a wall with a reciprocating saw, you might wind up shocking yourself. Turn off the circuit breaker for that area and test the outlets and lights. Other areas may be affected by that circuit. Hitting a wire with the face of a hammer is not likely to electrocute you.

Plumbing pipes can also be hidden in existing walls. Cutting through a water pipe can really cause severe problems. If a drain or vent pipe runs through a wall you want to remove, the pipe must be relocated. As with electrical wires, using a hammer to open existing walls is a lot safer than a saw when working around plumbing pipes. Heating, ventilation, and air-conditioning (HVAC) ducts can also present a challenge when remodeling a bathroom. Electrical wires are fairly easy to relocate. Plumbing is tougher to move than electrical wires, but it is easier to relocate plumbing than the heating and air-conditioning ducts. Always consider codes and remember the slope of drains, placement of traps, vents, and access to fixtures. When involved with a large remodeling project, you are probably going to be rearranging most of the mechanical systems (see Chap. 9).

REMOVING DRYWALL OR PLASTER

You can usually tell the difference between drywall and plaster by knocking on the wall. Drywall has a hollow sound between the studs; plaster is more solid. Removing plaster requires a slightly different procedure than removing drywall. Tearing out either type of wall is a messy job. Be sure to move any furniture, protect the floor by covering it with drop cloths, and hang plastic or damp sheets in all doorways. Always wear a filter mask, goggles, gloves, and head protection when you take out a wall. Cut out the drywall between studs with a circular saw, reciprocating saw, or handsaw. Expect to make lots of dust at this point. Cut the studs in half and wrench out the pieces. For plaster over metal lath, use a metal-cutting blade or simply batter the plaster with a crowbar or sledgehammer until it falls off the wall in chunks, then pry away the lath. Use caution in removing the metal lath and nails. It is usually corroded, and sharp edges result from cutting them.

REMOVING INTERIOR PARTITIONS

Removing interior partitions is a basic procedure. Once you get around the mechanical obstacles, ripping out non-load-bearing walls is easy. A reciprocating saw, a hammer, and a nail puller make the job simple.

REMOVING LOAD-BEARING WALLS

Load-bearing walls present more complications than do simple partition walls. Structural walls can be removed, but some concessions must be made. You might have to install an I-beam, or some other form of support. Instead of removing a wall, consider opening it up using a beam and using portions of the existing wall to support the load.

When opening a load-bearing wall, you must reinforce it to support the weight bearing on it (Fig. 7.5*a*). A temporary support on both sides of the wall is erected with studs and top and bottom plates. It should be slightly higher than the existing wall and wedged up to raise the joists and relieve the load. Shut off the circuit breaker that supplies the wiring. In addition, shut off the water-supply valves. Plan ahead to rewire or change piping while this wall is open. Have all supplies on

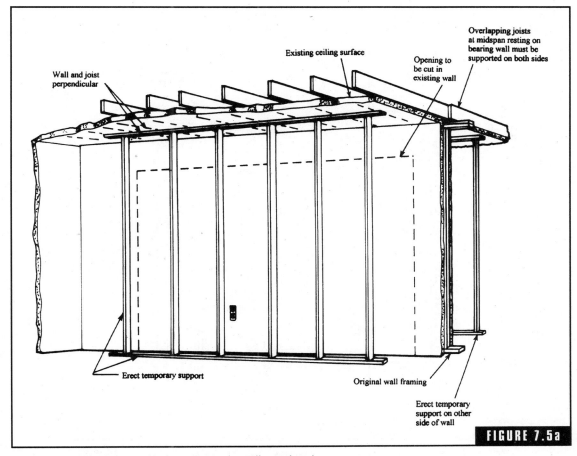

Overlapping joists at midspan resting on bearing wall must be supported on both sides

Existing ceiling surface

Opening to be cut in existing wall

Wall and joist perpendicular

Erect temporary support

Original wall framing

Erect temporary support on other side of wall

FIGURE 7.5a

Opening a load-bearing wall. *(Leon E. Korejwo, Illustrations.)*

hand. Cut away the existing wall and ceiling surface, being careful not to damage wiring or piping inside the framework (for clarity, the temporary bracing is only partially shown in Fig. 7.5b). Remove the unwanted studs by cutting them at midspan and twisting the halves while using a prybar. The top plate must remain intact. Rewire or move the pipe. Figure 7.5c shows a new beam properly sized to support the load for the span. The beam members should be sized by an architect to sufficiently support the load. Double studs at the corners are cut to fit and nailed to the existing sole plate. Cut away the unused sole plate. If the span is wide, support the beam with extra pairs of studs by extending the beam further into the wall. The extra leverage gained

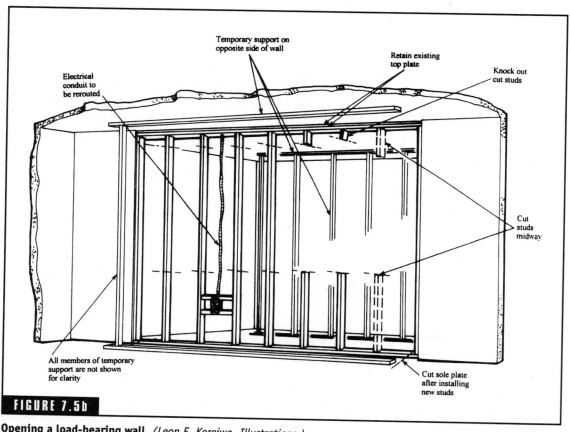

FIGURE 7.5b

Opening a load-bearing wall. *(Leon E. Korejwo, Illustrations.)*

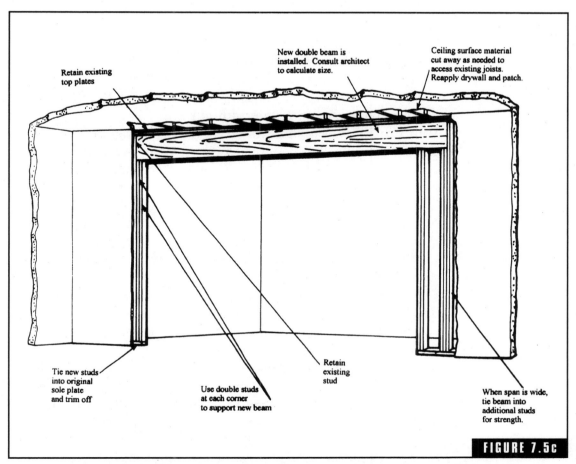

Retain existing
top plates

New double beam is
installed. Consult architect
to calculate size.

Ceiling surface material
cut away as needed to
access existing joists.
Reapply drywall and patch.

Tie new studs
into original
sole plate
and trim off

Use double studs
at each corner
to support new beam

Retain
existing
stud

When span is wide,
tie beam into
additional studs
for strength.

FIGURE 7.5c

Placing a new beam properly sized to support the load for the span. *(Leon E. Korejwo, Illustrations.)*

by extending over support studs will create less deflection in the new beam. Finish the wall with drywall.

Before you start removing support walls, talk with an engineer, architect, or contractor. Experienced carpenters can do a good job designing support systems, but this approach may be risky. If a problem shows up later, the individual who made the decision on what to use as a replacement for bearing walls can be held responsible. Therefore, it is most important to consult an engineer or architect.

Wall Preparation

If the bathroom installation includes the removal and replacement of wall finishes, check the insulation in the walls. Because the designer or architect has not had the opportunity to look inside the walls, you should report your findings so that the designer or architect can determine whether additional insulation is warranted.

Wall insulation is manufactured in several R (rigidity) values, or insulating values, corresponding to the thickness of the wall studs. Walls with 2 × 4-inch (5 × 10-cm) studs can accommodate R-11 batting insulation and, in some cases, R-13 or R-15, while 2 × 6-inch (5 × 15-cm) stud walls can accommodate R-19 batting insulation.

Figure 7.6 shows a room with a variety of options that apply to construction and insulation types—how a variety of insulations may be applied to different conditions (see explanation of segments *A–G* in the following paragraphs).

Blanket insulation is sold in rolls of widths made to fit between wall studs of either 16 or 24 inches (41 or 61 cm) between centers (Fig. 7.6, segment *A*.) The rolls are fitted with allowances for the studs. The installer only cuts it in lengths to fit from floor to ceiling. It comes in thicknesses of 1 1/2 inches (4 cm), 2 inches (5 cm), or 3 inches (8 cm) for 2 × 4-inch (5 × 10-cm) studded walls. Thicker widths are available for 2 × 6-inch (5 × 15-cm) studded walls, although attempting to compress thicker insulation of higher R value into a 2 × 4-inch (5 × 10-cm) wall does not yield that higher R value. Figure 7.7 shows the proper method to install insulation backed with kraft paper.

The rolls usually have instructions printed on the backing to ease installation. Blanket facings have a paper "flange" that, when scored, folded, and stapled, fits into the studs with a dead-air space and vapor barrier.

Batt insulation is sized to fill the space between studs spaced 16 or 24 inches (41 or 61 cm) on center and can be purchased faced or unfaced. It is sold in precut lengths of 4 or 8 feet (121.9 or 243.8 cm). Faced insulation has a vapor barrier installed on the warm side of the wall, and it can be stapled to the face of the studs (Fig. 7.6, segment *B*). Unfaced insulation is stuffed between the studs, but a separate vapor barrier, such as a sheet of polyethylene, must be installed over this insulation on the warm side of the wall (Fig. 7.6, segment *C*).

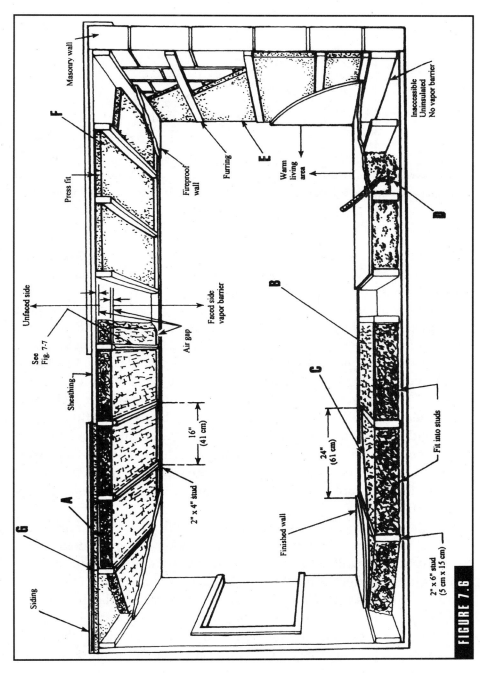

FIGURE 7.6

Several possible methods to insulate walls. *(Leon E. Korejwo, Illustrations.)*

Masonry wall

Press fit

Fireproof wall

Furring

F

E

Inaccessible
Uninsulated
No vapor barrier

Warm living area

D

Unfaced side

See Fig. 7-7

Sheathing

Faced side vapor barrier

Air gap

B

C

16"
(41 cm)

24"
(61 cm)

2" x 4" stud

A

G

Fit into studs

Finished wall

Siding

2" x 6" stud
(5 cm x 15 cm)

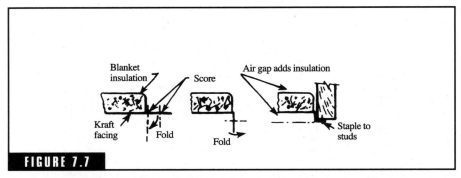

Blanket insulation   Score   Air gap adds insulation

Kraft facing   Fold   Fold   Staple to studs

FIGURE 7.7

The proper method to install kraft-paper insulation. *(Leon E. Korejwo, Illustrations.)*

Insulation should be installed in all new wall construction, facing an outside surface. Even when not required for structural reasons, many homes are now being constructed with 2 × 6-inch (5 × 15-cm) studs to accommodate R-19 wall insulation to meet more stringent energy codes. When reviewing installation plans, check the wall sections to verify the size of the studs being used in the exterior walls.

In existing homes with no insulation, blown-in loose-fill insulation is an option if the wall finishes are not being removed (Fig. 7.6, segment *D*). However, it is expensive if a limited wall area is being insulated. It is best done as a part of a complete house insulation project.

Rigid-foam or Styrofoam insulation can be used to insulate the interior side of a concrete or concrete block wall. The sheets are mechanically fastened to the wall, and studs or furring strips provide a means to install a fireproof layer of drywall over the insulation (Fig. 7.6, segment *E*).

Rigid-foam insulation sheets may be used on frame walls; some have a foil facing. This facing, placed adjacent to a dead-air space toward the living area, provides further insulation (Fig. 7.6, segment *F*). Rigid insulation is available as an exterior sheathing material and adds R value to a wall, but because it has little structural value, it must be supplemented by diagonal bracing at the corners of walls. Diagonal braces at the corners of the walls must be cut and nailed into the studs, or a sheet of plywood may be used on each side of the corner instead of the insulation sheet (Fig. 7.6, segment *G*). Often plywood is used in place of the insulating panels at the corners to brace a wall.

Doors, Windows, and Skylights

Doors, windows, and skylights can turn a dull bathroom into a bright, cheerful place. Bathrooms almost always benefit from more natural light. Surveys have indicated that homebuyers are favorably impressed by rooms that have an abundance of natural light. To some extent, the existing construction of the bathroom can affect the options, but most buildings can be adapted to accept a wide variety of windows, doors, skylights, and roof windows.

Adding a lot of natural light to a small bathroom can make it appear larger and more appealing. If the area doesn't allow room for tall or wide windows, there are alternative solutions. If wall space is at a premium because of the bathroom cabinets or counters, and there is attic space or only a roof, above the bathroom, skylights can be installed. Privacy dictates the use of opaque glass. Currently, glass areas are becoming larger, especially where the view can be enjoyed from a hot tub or whirlpool. This trend can demand creative solutions from designers.

Doors

When installing a new bathroom, or remodeling an existing one, additional interior doors, exterior doors, or moving or closing up an existing door may be required. Almost every modern wooden door has a vertical stile and horizontal rail framework. This construction helps counteract the tendency of wood to shrink, swell, and warp with humidity changes.

SOLID-PANEL DOORS

With a solid-panel door, you can see the framing. Spaces between frame members can be paneled with wood, louvered slats, or glass (Fig. 7.8a).

FLUSH DOORS

Flush doors (hollow-core or solid-core doors), which have no panels, hide their framing beneath two or three layers of veneer. Alternating the direction of the veneer minimizes warping.

HOLLOW-CORE DOORS

A hollow-core door, usually 1³/8 inches (3 cm) thick, may be filled with a lighter material, such as corrugated cardboard (Fig. 7.8b).

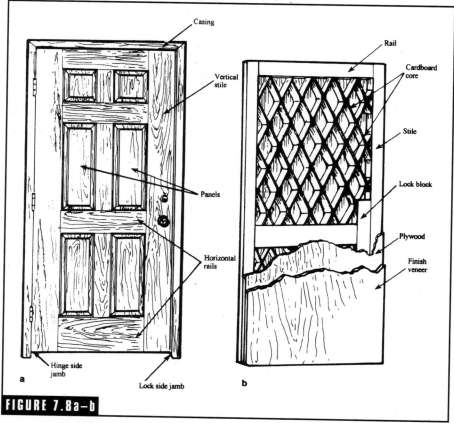

Casing

Rail

Vertical stile

Cardboard core

Stile

Panels

Lock block

Horizontal rails

Plywood

Finish veneer

Hinge side jamb

a

Lock side jamb

b

FIGURE 7.8a–b

(*a*) **A typical solid panel door; (*b*) a typical hollow-core flush door.** *(Leon E. Korejwo, Illustrations.)*

SOLID-CORE DOORS

A solid-core flush door, usually $1^3/_4$ inches (4 cm) thick, has a dense center of hardwood blocks or particleboard glued together within the internal stile and rail framework that is hidden under the veneer (Fig. 7.8*c*). Closet or linen storage areas are often closed off with bypass doors, which come in pairs. Panel or flush, solid or hollow-core, they roll along an overhead track and are guided by metal or nylon angles screwed to the floor and header (Fig. 7.8*e*). Folding doors are hinged together. One slides along a track, and the other pivots on fixed pins (Fig. 7.8*f*). If two doors are installed together, the unit is

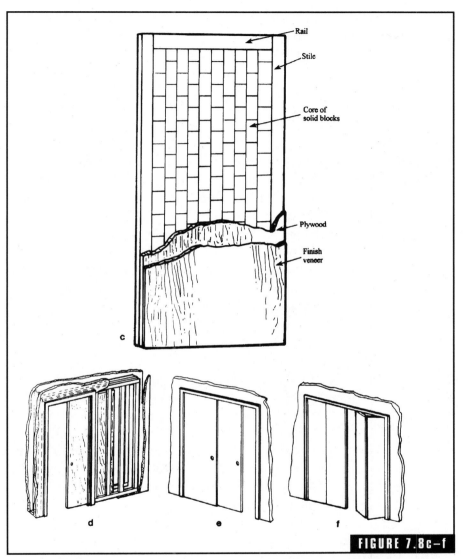

Rail

Stile

Core of
solid blocks

Plywood

Finish
veneer

c

d

e

f

FIGURE 7.8c–f

(c) A typical solid-core flush door; **(d–f)** doors useful in bath closets; **(d)** pocket door;
(e) bypass door; **(f)** bifold door. *(Leon E. Korejwo, Illustrations.)*

referred to as *French doors.* With French doors or other pairs of doors, one door is classified as *inactive.* Be sure you know which panel is to be the inactive door before the door is ordered.

INTERIOR DOORS

Interior doors are manufactured in wood, flat panel, six-panel composite, and French doors. They do not need to be as sturdy as exterior doors. Hollow-core flush interior doors are common. In areas where space is limited, the design may call for you to install a pocket door. A *pocket door* can be either a panel door or a flush door. It is made to slide into a pocket in the wall (Fig. 7.8*d*). A number of door manufacturers make pocket door units that can be framed right into the wall during construction. Have the framing, door track, and door as an assembly. In this case, be careful to keep plumbing and wiring clear of the area of the wall where the pocket will be located. Unless plywood or furring has been provided under the drywall, cabinets cannot be hung on a wall containing a pocket door.

Although bathrooms rarely use exterior doors, wood, fiberglass, metal-insulated, sliding-glass, or terrace doors may be used to fill some design requirements. They provide weather protection and security while allowing people to move from the inside to the outside. While wood doors are still the most prevalent, steel and fiberglass doors are gaining popularity. Fiberglass and steel doors seal tightly, in most cases are filled with a high-R-value foam insulation, and seldom warp. A wood door may have an R value of 1 to 5 compared to R-6 to R-12 of a steel door. To keep out cold air and rain, doors must seal tightly. Over time, old-fashioned wood panel doors can become leaky because they expand and contract with changes in weather. This problem can be remedied by providing weather stripping.

PREHUNG DOORS

Installing prehung doors is highly recommended. Prehung units do not cost much more than slab doors and the components needed to make them operational, but they can be installed in a fraction of the time needed to fabricate a complete door unit.

A prehung door usually comes complete with a split jamb and prefabricated trim (Fig. 7.9). The door can have either lower-cost fingerjoint trim or solid trim. Either trim is fine if it is to be painted, but fingerjoint trim looks out of place when it is stained.

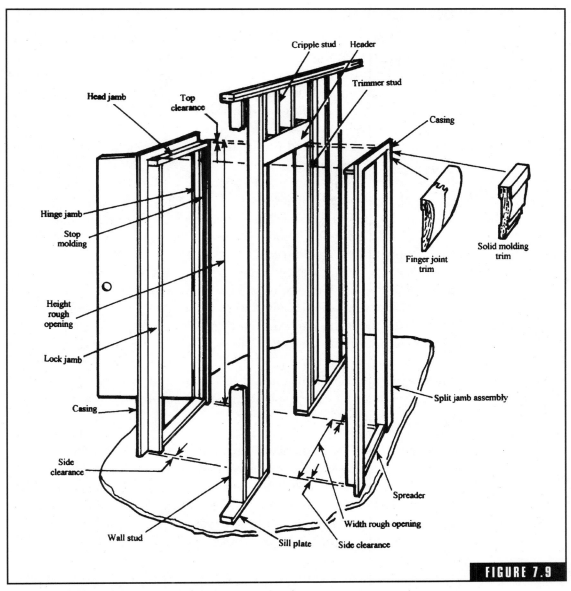

A prehung door assembly. *(Leon E. Korejwo, Illustrations.)*

FIGURE 7.9

Door Installation

When framing rough openings for door installations, you must allow room for shimming the door (Fig. 7.10). Rough openings should generally be 2 to $2\frac{1}{2}$ inches (5 to 6 cm) larger than the width of the door to allow enough room for the jamb. The header is normally framed 3 inches (8 cm) higher than the door height. This height must consider the type and thickness of floor material being used. The door must be hung straight and plumb to operate properly. Different styles of prehung door assemblies are shown in Fig. 7.10. Interior door frames are made up of two side jambs and a head jamb and include stop moldings on which the door closes. The most common of these jambs is the one-piece type. The two- and three-piece adjustable jambs are also standard types. Their primary advantage is in being adaptable to a variety of wall thicknesses.

Doors are either right-handed or left-handed. Your clients can determine the handedness by facing the door as it is swinging toward them. A door that is left-handed has the latch on the left, while a right-handed door has the latch on the right. The swing of the door can be crucial in bathroom projects. It is possible to solve a swinging door problem with bifold doors, swinging café doors, or pocket doors. The moisture content in baths should be considered in material selection. Check the manufacturer's specification for applications.

Windows

Sometimes it is necessary, or at least desirable, to replace existing windows. Adding windows is a job that anyone with basic carpentry experience can usually handle. However, the process can get difficult at times. Ductwork, a plumbing vent, or a chaseway for electrical wires may be located in the same place you want to put a new window. Local code requirements might insist that new windows be added as the use of space is changed.

There is a wide variety of window styles from which to choose. Double-hung windows are the most common type; single-hung windows are not used very often. Casement windows, awning windows, fixed-glass windows, and sliding windows are some additional types.

Window Installation

Cutting in the rough opening for a new window can be a little tricky. However, once the wall is opened up, framing the window

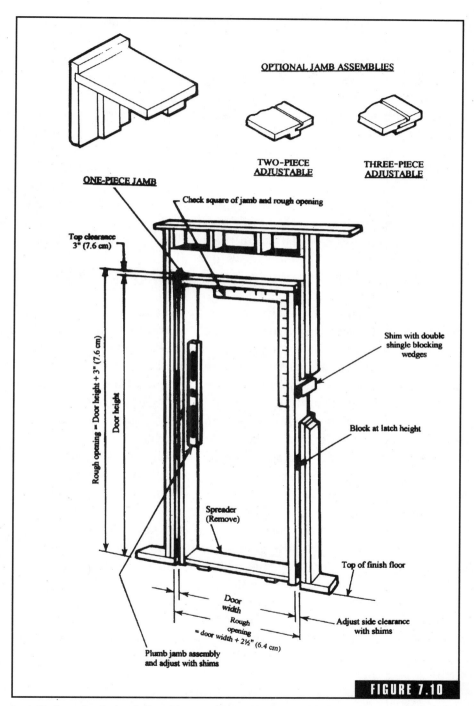

OPTIONAL JAMB ASSEMBLIES

TWO-PIECE
ADJUSTABLE

THREE-PIECE
ADJUSTABLE

ONE-PIECE JAMB

Check square of jamb and rough opening

Top clearance
3" (7.6 cm)

Rough opening = Door height + 3" (7.6 cm)

Door height

Shim with double
shingle blocking
wedges

Block at latch height

Spreader
(Remove)

Top of finish floor

Door
width

Rough
opening
= door width + 2½" (6.4 cm)

Adjust side clearance
with shims

Plumb jamb assembly
and adjust with shims

FIGURE 7.10

Installation of a prehung door in a rough opening. *(Leon E. Korejwo, Illustrations.)*

opening is pretty simple. Examine the structure of the wall before including major wall changes.

Some windows are held in place with a nailing flange. The flange is set against the exterior wall sheathing and screwed in place. The wall studs of balloon-framed houses carry the load of the second floor and roof; cutting into them may be best handled by a subcontractor. Siding is installed over the flange. Not all windows have nailing flanges. Some windows are made so that they are nailed into place through their sides. Follow the manufacturer's recommendations when installing any window.

When preparing to cut in a new window, it is important to remember to start on the inside of the building. If you work from the inside and discover an obstacle that could prevent the window installation, you need to only patch the interior wall, but if you start the work from the outside, you have to repair the siding and sheathing, which is a much larger project.

Once the window hole has been cut out on the inside wall, you can see if there will be any problems installing the windows in the desired location. If there is no reason to change plans, you can continue with the process. This process entails the alteration of existing framing to accommodate a header, jack studs, and cripple studs. Some of the exterior siding and wall sheathing also must be cut away (Fig. 7.11).

The space for the new window is termed *rough opening*. Its dimensions are supplied by the manufacturer of the window. These are usually inches larger to provide for thermal expansion and contractions, as well as building settling, shrinkage, or binding, which can distort the new frame. This space is shimmed with tapered slivers of wood shingles to adjust, level, and fasten the window inside the rough opening.

The last step, when the rough opening is completed, is installing the window. This step usually goes smoothly. It is the early stages of this job that present you with the most problems. Remember, to keep the risk to a minimum, work from the inside out.

Double-hung windows include heavy sash weights concealed behind the frame's side jambs (Fig. 7.12). Connected via a rope-and-pulley system, the weights provide a counterbalance that not only makes the sashes easier to open but also holds them in any vertical position you choose.

A series of stops fitted to the jambs provides channels in which the sashes slide. Check the top view and note that although the outside

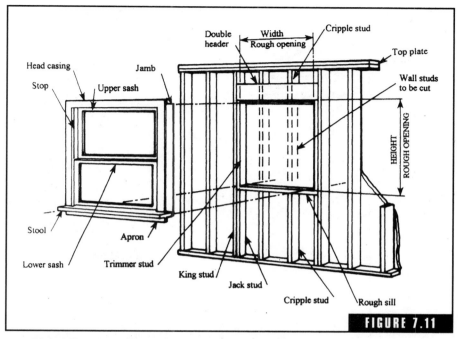

Installation of a window in an existing wall. *(Leon E. Korejwo, Illustrations.)*

bind stop is more or less permanently affixed, the parting stop and inside stop can be pried loose if you want to remove the sashes.

Newer double-hung windows replace the weight-and-pulley mechanisms with a pair of the spring-lift devices. With both types, the lower sash comes to rest behind a flat stool; its outside counterpart, the sill, slopes so water can run off. Trim—called *casing* at the sides and top, and an *apron* below—covers any gaps between the jambs and the wall material. Casement windows open and close door-fashion, usually with the help of a crank-type operator (Fig. 7.12). With some double-glazed casements, though, the muntins (or grilles) snap to the inside of the window to facilitate cleaning or are absent altogether.

As with double-hung windows, sliding-sash windows open up only 50 percent of the total window area for ventilation (Fig. 7.12). Some have one fixed and one sliding sash; with others, both sashes slide along continuous tracks. Sliding windows may have wood or metal construction.

Awning-sash windows tilt outward, under the direction of a scissors- or hinge-type cranking system (Fig. 7.12). Some awnings slide

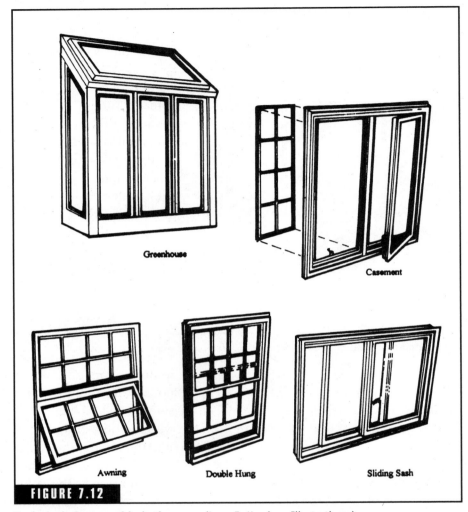

Greenhouse

Casement

Awning

Double Hung

Sliding Sash

FIGURE 7.12

Typical windows used in bathrooms. *(Leon E. Korejwo, Illustrations.)*

downward as they tilt, so they can be opened to an almost horizontal position for maximum airflow.

Jalousie windows also let in lots of air; each turn of the crank pivots a series of glass slats for maximum flow control. The frames here consist of short metal channels at either end of the slats. Those glass-to-glass joints tend to leak air, so jalousies are usually found only in breezeways, porches, and other zones not normally heated. Glass-enclosed greenhouse windows (Fig. 7.12) open an area without major structural remodeling. If the bathroom will be moved to an outside wall facing a public street or neighboring home, this may limit selection; also building codes may dictate certain restrictions.

Installing a Skylight

A skylight brings light and an open feeling into windowless interior bathrooms or those where uncovered windows would be a privacy problem. Cutting a skylight into an existing roof is not a big problem, unless the home is next to a high rise. However, the location of a skylight may be restricted by barriers such as electrical lines, heating ducts, or structural framing. Moving the location is less costly than rerouting utility lines or making structural changes. Skylights can be purchased in a size that allows them to fit between existing rafters. A rule of thumb concerning size is to buy a skylight with an area 10 to 15 percent of the area of the floor in the room. To install them, you simply cut a hole in the roof, set the skylight in place, and seal around it. In vaulted ceilings, the job is not complicated at all.

If there is attic space between the roof and living space, the task takes on a few twists—a lightbox must be built (Fig. 7.13). Building a lightbox is really quite simple. Once you have located a place for the skylight, a plumb bob is used to find an appropriate spot on the ceiling below (done in the attic). A hole is then cut in the roof for the skylight, and the ceiling is also cut out, providing you with a hole in the roof and a corresponding hole in the ceiling below. Lumber is then used to frame the lightbox. The framing can be attached to the rafters on either side of the holes. The inside of the lightbox should be framed so that the skylight can give maximum light. Once the framing is complete, drywall can be hung and finished.

Larger skylights may span two or more rafters. To install these, rafters must be cut and new framing installed to maintain the roof's structural integrity.

Skylights are available in many different shapes and sizes. Some are operable—they can be opened—and others are fixed. Operable and fixed skylights look much the same. They both allow the same amount of light to enter a home, but operable skylights also provide ventilation. Improvements in glass permit the use of large areas of glass without *mullions,* which are the support strips used between the panes of glass. Glazing options in good-quality glass skylights provide insulation,

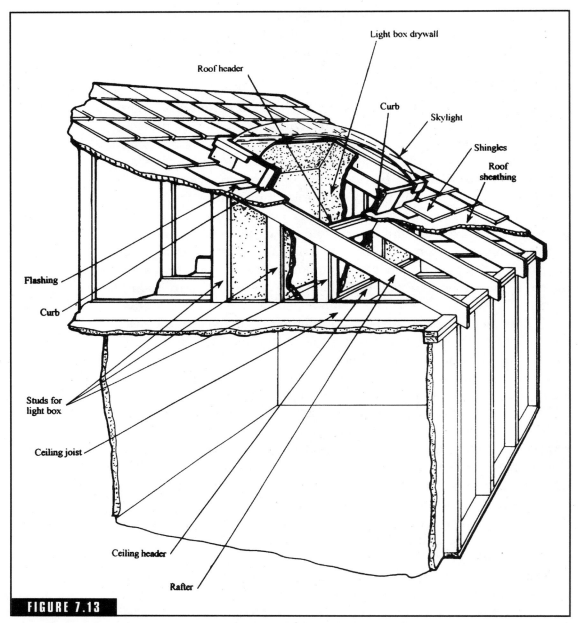

Light box drywall

Roof header

Curb

Skylight

Shingles

Roof sheathing

Flashing

Curb

Studs for light box

Ceiling joist

Ceiling header

Rafter

FIGURE 7.13

A skylight with a light box through the bathroom ceiling. *(Leon E. Korejwo, Illustrations.)*

shield rooms from the sun's ultraviolet rays, and create a buffer against outside noise.

Floors

The choice of flooring style affects several construction factors that must be dealt with early on. Figure 7.14*a* shows a floor and its supporting structure for a typical platform-framed house. Wood floor systems and concrete slab floors are the two most common types of floor systems. Concrete slab floors are used when there is no basement or

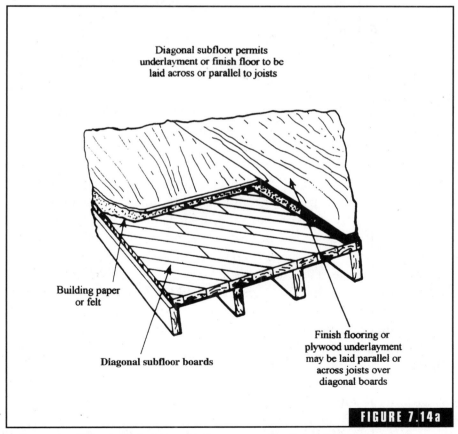

Diagonal subfloor permits underlayment or finish floor to be laid across or parallel to joists

Building paper or felt

Diagonal subfloor boards

Finish flooring or plywood underlayment may be laid parallel or across joists over diagonal boards

FIGURE 7.14a

A diagonal subfloor permits the underlayment or the finish floor to be laid across or parallel to joists. *(Leon E. Korejwo, Illustrations.)*

crawlspace. Wood floor systems are used when a house has a basement or crawlspace.

Wood Floors

A *wood floor system* can be thought of as a wood platform on which the house is built. The platform is usually built of structural wood or engineered joists. Both types of joists are covered by subflooring. Subflooring is a panel material, such as plywood. The structure of a wood floor system generally does not need to be altered unless you were installing a new piece of equipment that would exceed the bearing or weight capacity of the existing wood platform.

Before ordering materials or beginning the preliminary work of preparing the subfloor for new flooring, check the basic floor and supporting structure. In older homes, you may find that the wood flooring system has sagged because of settling and shrinkage, creating a dip in the flooring surface. This settling does not necessarily mean that a structural weakness exists. A number of nonstructural changes may be required. Thoroughly inspect the existing flooring for indications of problems. If the existing floor is being removed as a part of the project, you can examine the subfloor. If the finish flooring is to remain, you need to inspect the subflooring from the underside by going into the crawlspace or basement. From this vantage point, you should be able to examine the floor joists, foundation, and subfloor, and determine the extent of any water damage and estimate how much subflooring needs to be replaced. Look especially for signs of a spongy or deteriorating subfloor. Spongy or deteriorated subfloor may indicate more extensive damage due to leaks in the plumbing or the walls and roof.

Insects, such as termites and carpenter ants, as well as animal nesting, is unseen from above the floor. Termites build tunnels across masonry to reach the wooden framework. The surface appears solid while they consume the centers of the wood members. Professional exterminators and structural repairs affect time and costs. During this inspection, check the plumbing and electrical runs for condition or modification problems. If you find any indication of structural damage, notify the client of the damage and the anticipated cost to correct the problem.

The masonry foundation should be sound, with no crumbling mortar or loose or missing bricks or stones. Block or poured concrete foundations are more obvious, and cracking in mortar, while common, can worsen as a result of frost and moisture penetration. Repointing is advisable. Large separations or cracking may indicate a problem in the footer. Changing fixtures, tubs and showers, or adding a partition over an uneven floor makes installation more time-consuming. Proper structural repairs may actually be more cost-effective, requiring fewer cosmetic coverups.

If the finish flooring is sheet goods, the entire existing finish floor has to be removed and replaced. If the floor is ceramic or vinyl tile, it may be possible to remove only the affected portion and replace it once the subfloor has been repaired. Once the floor surface has been leveled, you can install a new finish floor.

If you are installing a new finish floor material, it is generally best to remove the existing flooring materials rather than overlaying the existing flooring with new flooring. Many installers install new underlayment regardless of whether they remove the old flooring. Existing imperfections in the old finish flooring usually end up showing through the new flooring material at some point. The advantages of laying new flooring over old are that you bypass the messy job of removing old flooring, and you gain some soundproofing and insulation. Avoiding the sound of a toilet flushing near the guests in the dining room may take a little planning. Some disadvantages are that you are unable to inspect the subflooring and make corrections, and there may not be enough space left above to install certain fixtures. Check with the flooring manufacturer for specific instructions and requirements for flooring underlayment. Keep in mind that failure to follow specific recommendations can void some manufacturers' warranties.

An extremely important matter to be aware of is that a variety of old flooring materials were manufactured with asbestos in them. Today asbestos is no longer used in flooring materials, but if you are remodeling a house, it may already exist in the flooring. If you have reason to believe that the existing flooring contains asbestos (which is a recognized health hazard), leave the flooring in place. Do not sand it. If you have any doubts about the composition of the existing flooring, consult with a flooring expert before removing the flooring. In addition, check with the local state health department or local Environmental Protection Agency (EPA) office. These agencies require an approved method of disposal, and undoubtably there will be additional asbestos removal costs.

Concrete Floor Slab

In a house with a concrete floor slab, the problems are somewhat different. Concrete slabs are prone to cracking as a result of stress on the slab or soil movement beneath the slab. If you are to install a new finish floor on an existing concrete slab, an existing crack might cause a tile floor to crack along the line of the existing crack. If you are installing sheet goods, the crack might telegraph through the new finish flooring. A crack can be masked by using a cleavage membrane material manufactured for this purpose.

Regardless of whether there are problems with the concrete slab, completely remove the existing finish floor before installing a new floor. Old adhesive from the existing flooring needs to be completely removed to ensure a good smooth surface for the new flooring.

Because plumbing, piping, and sometimes heating ductwork or piping are installed before pouring the concrete slab, any additional or relocated plumbing rough-in will probably require cutting or breaking out part of the existing floor slab. Obviously, this needs to be done before any new finish floor work begins. When the concrete slab is patched, feather the joint between the existing slab and the patch so that the joint does not telegraph through the new finish floor.

Finish flooring must be compatible with the materials beneath it. Not all types are suitable for all kinds of conditions. Almost any kind of flooring material can be used over a wood floor system, including ceramic tile (use a thick-set mortar base or a backerboard), vinyl, and hardwoods (in strip or parquet patterns). Wood is affected by moisture, so only laminated products should be considered for rooms below grade.

The best finish floor materials over a concrete slab are sheet goods or vinyl, ceramic tile installed with an organic adhesive, and hardwood parquet flooring (but only if installed with a moisture barrier). If installing wood strips over a concrete slab, the best approach is to place the floor on sleepers or screeds. *Sleepers* are treated 2 × 4s laid flat on the slab. The sleepers must be protected from moisture by a vapor barrier. If the slab has no existing vapor barrier beneath it, ground moisture will penetrate to the sleepers. A layer of mastic, covered by 15-pound, asphalt-saturated felt paper, and finally another coat of mastic is needed. A layer of poly sheet between sleepers and final flooring is advised. For air circulation, a gap $1/2$ inch (1 cm) between the last board and nail works well. Rows of staggered sleepers 12 to 16 inches (30 to 41 cm) on center are placed at right angles to the flooring. Also consider drain slopes and vent runs when placing the sleepers.

Putting the floor on sleepers will allow a strip wood flooring system, but the floor will be at least 2 inches (5 cm) higher than in adjacent rooms. Either use finish floor materials that can be installed directly on the concrete slab or find a transition between adjacent flooring materials.

Do not make any final flooring decisions until you know the kind and condition of the subfloor and underlayment the new floor will cover. With proper preparation, a concrete subfloor, because it is rigid, can serve as a base for almost any type of flooring. Other subfloors are more flexible and are not suitable for rigid materials, such as masonry and ceramic tile, unless they are built up with extra underlayment or floor framing. Keep in mind that too many layers underneath can make the bathroom floor awkwardly higher than surrounding rooms.

The finished floor will be only as good as the material over which it is laid, so it is essential that the subfloor be properly prepared to guarantee a smooth surface. Assuming that the substructures are sound and sturdy, the subfloor must be adequately prepared to receive the new flooring.

Types of Subflooring

Subflooring is used over the floor joists to form a working platform and base for finish flooring. It usually consists of square-edge or tongue-and-groove boards no wider than 8 inches (20 cm) and not less than 3/4 inch (2 cm) thick or plywood that is 1/2 to 3/4 inch (1 to 2 cm) thick, depending on species, type of finish floor, and spacing of joists.

Subflooring boards may be applied either diagonally (most common) or at right angles to the joists. When subflooring is placed at right angles to the joists, the finish floor should be laid at right angles to the subflooring. Diagonal subflooring permits finish flooring or butt joints to be laid either parallel or at right angles (most common) to the joists (Fig. 7.14a). End joints of the boards should always be located directly over the center of the joists. Plywood subfloor is nailed to each joist with two 8d nails for widths under 8 inches (20 cm) and three 8d nails for 8-inch (20-cm) widths.

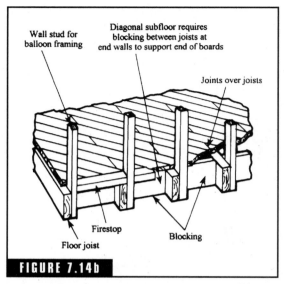

Wall stud for balloon framing

Diagonal subfloor requires blocking between joists at end walls to support end of boards

Joints over joists

Firestop

Floor joist

Blocking

FIGURE 7.14b

Balloon-frame blocking. *(Leon E. Korejwo, Illustrations.)*

The joist spacing should not exceed 16 inches (41 cm) on center when finish flooring is laid parallel to the joists or where parquet finish flooring is used, nor should it exceed 24 inches (61 cm) on center when finish flooring at least $25/32$ inch (2 cm) thick is at right angles to the joists. Where balloon framing is used, blocking should be installed between ends of joists at the wall for nailing the ends of diagonal subfloor boards (Fig. 7.14b).

Plywood should be installed with the grain direction of the outer plies at right angles to the joists and be staggered so that end joints in adjacent panels break over different joists (Fig. 7.15). Plywood should be nailed to the joist at each bearing with 8d common or 7d threaded nails for plywood that is $1/2$ to $3/4$ inch (1 to 2 cm) thick. Space nails 6 inches (15 cm) apart along all edges and 10 inches (25 cm) along intermediate members. When plywood serves as both subfloor and underlayment, nails may be spaced 6 to 7 inches (15 to 18 cm) apart at all joists and blocking. Use 8d or 9d common nails or 7d or 8d threaded nails.

If necessary, lay an underlayment of untempered hardboard or plywood directly over the subfloor to raise the surface of new flooring to the same height as the old. Be sure to ensure a level transition between the new floor and adjacent rooms and make it unnecessary to trim door casings, doors, or moldings. In some instances, the addition of new flooring and plywood underlayment may interfere with the replacement of cabinets or fixtures. In these cases, be sure to remove the old flooring. Carefully examine the old flooring to determine what preparation, if any, must be completed before the new flooring is installed.

Underlayment

Correctly installed, underlayment provides a flat, uniform surface; eliminates irregularities in the subfloor; strengthens the floor; and creates a more secure and stable surface for laying finish flooring. It is

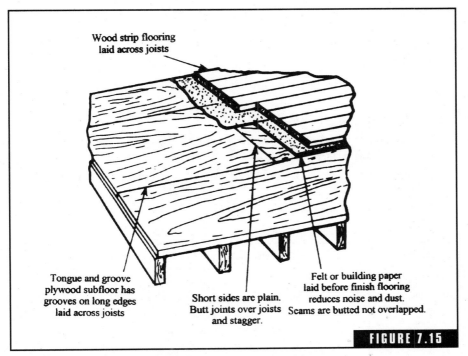

Wood strip flooring
laid across joists

Tongue and groove
plywood subfloor has
grooves on long edges
laid across joists

Short sides are plain.
Butt joints over joists
and stagger.

Felt or building paper
laid before finish flooring
reduces noise and dust.
Seams are butted not overlapped.

FIGURE 7.15

Plywood subfloor laid across joists. *(Leon E. Korejwo, Illustrations.)*

available in 4 × 8-foot sheets. For underlayment, choose either ¼-inch (0.6 cm) plywood or hardboard or up to ½-inch (1-cm)-thick particle board. Do not install underlayment in exceedingly moist or humid weather or at times when the atmosphere is usually dry. Techniques for installing underlayment vary, depending on whether the subfloor consists of plywood sheets or individual boards. Check the subfloor for uneven areas with a long, straight 2 × 4 laid on edge. Correct the low spots by shimming from below; protruding joints or fasteners will be revealed later on a new glossy surface. Loose joints will later crack through.

A new type of underlayment on the market which is gaining popularity is a fiber-reinforced underlayment, which provides an excellent base for a variety of floorcoverings. This type of underlayment is smoother, more durable, and more moisture-tolerant than conventional wood-based underlayments. It is made by blending cellulose fiber and gypsum throughout the panel, giving it a uniformly smooth surface. Its high-density surface provides superior indentation resistance compared to traditional plywood underlayment. In addition, it is fire-resistant. It makes a perfect base for reapplying resilient floorcovering, vinyl tiles, carpet, ceramic tile, quarry tile, and wood flooring.

Preparing for Resilient Flooring

The preparation work required before installing sheet vinyl is crucial to success (Table 7.1). Since most resilient flooring is so pliable, it conforms to irregularities in the subfloor. For this reason, it is essential that

Table 7-1 Preparation Guidelines for Resilient Flooring

Surface applied over	Preparation steps
Concrete slab (on or below grade)	Be sure the slab is smooth, level, and clean. Newly poured concrete floors need at least 90 days to dry. Check that it is completely dry and take steps to ensure it stays dry. Any moisture coming through the concrete will eventually cause the flooring to loosen. Be sure to remove grease, oil, and other foreign material. Remove old paint or sealer. Fill any low spots, cracks, or joints in the surface with latex underlayment compound. Cover the surface with a sealer or other moisture barrier. If the slab is too uneven to be completely leveled by patching, lay a new plywood subfloor (on screeds) or pour a new thin concrete slab over the old.
Plywood subfloors	If the subfloor is new, make sure that the panels are securely attached with ring-shank nails, cement-coated nails, or screws and that the nail or screwheads are flush with the surface. Remove every bit of old surface flooring, including cushioning, felt backing, and grout. A layer of underlayment is advised. If old flooring is too difficult to remove, cover the floor with a new underlayment of plywood or untempered hardboard (at least $1/4$" thick). Leave a $1/8$" (0.3 cm) gap between panels to allow for later expansion.

Table 7-1 Preparation Guidelines for Resilient Flooring (*Continued*)

Woodboard subfloors	It is extremely difficult to make wood board subfloors smooth and level to properly install a resilient floor covering. Cover with $1/4''$ (0.6-cm) (minimum thickness) underlayment-grade plywood or untempered hardwood.

New resilient flooring can be applied only over an old floor surface that has been properly prepared to provide a clean, level base only.

Old resilient flooring	If the old flooring, cushioning, or underlayment is damaged, remove it. If old floor is completely smooth, solid (not cushioned), and firmly secured, new resilient flooring can be installed directly over old resilient flooring. Clean the surface of the old flooring thoroughly, removing old wax or finish. Do not sand the old floor covering. It may contain asbestos fibers (see text). Solid vinyl tile should not be laid directly over existing resilient flooring; install plywood underlayment first.
Old wood flooring	This can be laid directly over hardwood floor only if it is completely level, smooth, and in good condition. If old wood flooring is in poor condition, install plywood or hardboard underlayment. Otherwise, joints may show through. A wood floor makes a good base for vinyl tile only if there is an adequate ventilation space or crawlspace beneath it, at least $24''$ (61 cm) above the ground level.
Old ceramic tile, slate, or masonry flooring	If possible, remove old flooring. If the old floor is level, it can be covered with a plywood subfloor laid on screeds, a latex underlayment compound, or a cement-base leveling compound. Resilient flooring should never be installed directly over old ceramic tile, slate, or masonry flooring with an uneven surface. Solid masonry-type floors can be covered with a new concrete slab.

care be taken to prepare the subfloor properly to guarantee a smooth surface. If the surface that is to be covered with new flooring is rough, the finished job will not look good. When preparing an old floor for new vinyl, always install new underlayment. Hardboard or plywood that is ¼ inch (0.6 cm) or thicker works well. It provides a clean, porous base for the adhesive that secures the vinyl in place. It is best to have the old floor removed before adding the underlayment. Research material specifications for manufacturers' recommendations in wet or moist areas.

It might be necessary, even when new underlayment is installed, to fill cracks that form between the sheets. It is also important to make sure that nails and screw heads are not protruding from the underlayment. Any that stick up will show in the new vinyl.

Be sure that you are clear about the manufacturer's installation recommendations and any restrictions that may apply to the flooring selected. Most of today's resilient flooring can be installed on any grade. A few, though, should not be laid on concrete in contact with soil. Refer to Table 7.1 for the information necessary to properly prepare a concrete slab, a wood subfloor, or an existing floor for new resilient flooring.

Preparing for Ceramic Tile

Unless it is installed over a perfectly sound subfloor, the most carefully laid ceramic tile floor will eventually reveal flaws, and cracks will appear. Inspect the subfloor from above and below for any necessary repairs. Inspect the floor structure and joists, and look for loose boards or a random low spot in a subfloor, which indicate defects. If the subfloor and structure are sound, you can lay ceramic tile over subfloors made of plywood panels or individual boards (Fig. 7.16a).

Use an underlayment suitable to your selected adhesive, such as the fiber-reinforced concrete. Traditionally, ceramic tile was installed on floors using the *mud-set* method—the tile was set in a bed of mortar. The mud-set method allows the ceramic tile to be set level even if there are dips or imperfections in the subfloor when using plywood. Fiberglass-reinforced board is currently recommended. When using these underlayments, a thin-set adhesive method may be recommended by the tile manufacturers. Since you will be raising the level of the floor itself, check the bottoms of the door for adequate clearance. If necessary, trim the door. A wood base is suitable if the boards or panels are securely fastened to the joists. Baseboard trim, heating elements, and existing cabinetry will also be affected. Figure 7.16*b,c*, briefly illustrates a method of installing ceramic floor tiles.

Ceramic tile can now be installed much more simply than the mud-set method using a thin layer of adhesive applied with a trowel. It requires a very flat, rigid surface, meaning that wood board floors or damaged resilient tile must be covered with underlayment such as the fiber-reinforced concrete before the tile can be laid. Adhesives have been developed that permit installation of ceramic tile in an area with some moisture, making it an appropriate choice to cover a below-grade concrete slab. Refer to Table 7.2 for the information necessary to prepare a concrete slab, a wood subfloor, or an existing floor for new ceramic tile flooring.

Table 7-2 Preparation Guidelines for Ceramic Tile Flooring

Surface applied over	Preparation steps
	Ceramic tile should be installed over subfloors no less than 1 1/8" (2.9 cm) total thickness.
Concrete slab	A concrete slab will make the best possible base for the tile. New or old, the concrete must be completely dry, clean, and level before you can begin preparing it for tile installation. Once dry, ensure that it is clean and free from grease, oil, and old paint of other finishes. Fill any holes, low areas or cracks in the slab with a concrete patching compound or mastic compound.
Plywood subfloors	For best results, an underlayment of reinforced panels is recommended. Be certain that plywood panels are securely attached to joists with no protruding nails. If plywood panels move when walking on them, reinforce the floor with second layer of plywood or underlayment. Plywood underlayment panels should be at least 3/8" (0.9 cm) thick if using mastic, 5/8" (1.6 cm) thick for epoxy adhesive. Stagger second layer of plywood panels or underlayment to be sure joints do not fall directly over those in the layer below. Leave 1/8" (0.3-cm) gaps between panels. Drive nails through panels into the joists before applying second layer.

Table 7-2 Preparation Guidelines for Ceramic Tile Flooring (*Continued*)

Wood board subfloors	If subfloor is made of individual 4″ or 6″ (10 or 15 cm) boards, be sure that each board is securely attached.
	To prevent warping, cover subfloor with underlayment before installing ceramic tile.
	Strip, plank, or parquet floors in good condition can be covered with ceramic tile using underlayment.
	If old floor is sound and level, you only need to give it a rough sanding to remove the old finish and smooth the rough areas.

Whenever possible, old flooring should be removed before installing new ceramic tile flooring. Not only is it easier to examine the subfloor, and make necessary repairs, but also the new floor will be level with the floors in adjacent rooms. Underlayment for ceramic tile floors must resist moisture and be rigid enough to prevent flexing, which cracks tile and grout. Several types are available, including $1/4$″ (0.6-cm) exterior-grade plywood, reinforced-concrete panels and reinforced gypsum board specially designed for tile. Check manufacturer recommendations.

Old resilient flooring	Well-bonded resilient flooring, if level and in good condition, can be successfully covered with tile. Underlayment is recommended.
	Resilient flooring that is severely damaged should be removed or covered with a layer of underlayment.
	Cushioned resilient flooring (sheet or tile) is too springy to be used as a base for ceramic tile and must be removed.
	Old resilient flooring may contain asbestos—*use caution!* Consult local codes for approved removal and disposal methods.
Old wood flooring	Wood floors, wood strip and parquet flooring are not smooth enough to serve as backing for ceramic tile. Cover with a layer of underlayment.
Old ceramic tile, slate, or masonry flooring	Tile can be applied over old ceramic tile if the old tile is in good condition, clean, and well bonded; otherwise, remove it. It will raise the floor level excessively.
	If there is evidence of water damage, the tiles and backing may have to be removed and the moisture problem corrected.
	Clean the old tile with a degreasing agent.
	An underlayment layer, or new concrete laid over the old, is the best. The subfloor must be level for a good bond.

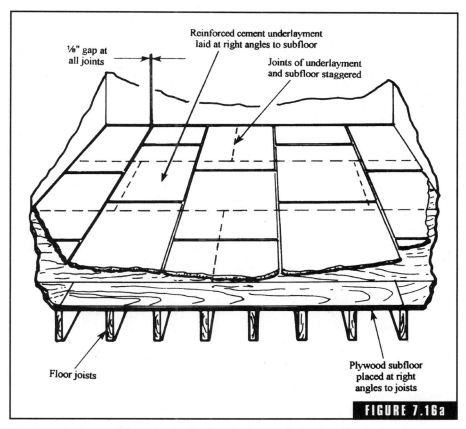

Placing underlayment for ceramic tile flooring. *(Leon E. Korejwo, Illustrations.)*

Note: Ceramic tile should be installed over subfloors no less than 1$\frac{1}{8}$ inches (3 cm) total thickness. Thinner subflooring may flex, causing the tiles to break or the grout to crack.

Preparing for Wood Flooring

Preparing a proper base for any type of wood flooring can be more demanding than putting in the new flooring itself. It is important to check an on-grade concrete slab carefully for moisture before installing wood flooring; be certain that it will stay dry over the years. Similarly, the space below a standard floor supported by joists and beams should be properly ventilated and protected from moisture for wood flooring to be laid over it.

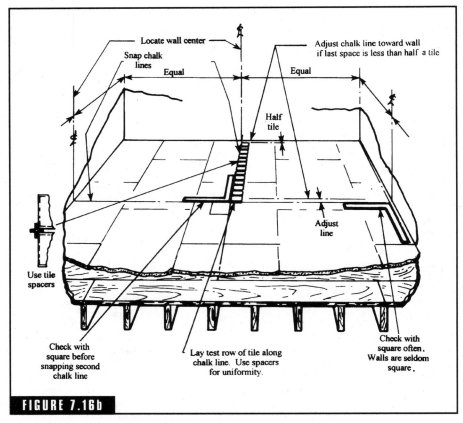

FIGURE 7.16b

A test row of tile and layout chalk lines. *(Leon E. Korejwo, Illustrations.)*

If there is already an old floor in place, the best approach is to expose the subfloor. Leaving the old floor surface there will increase the weight of the system and will detract from the headroom. If you want to leave an old floor in place, cover it with asphalt felt, as you would a wood subfloor.

Strip flooring is laid lengthwise in a room and normally at right angles to the floor joists. A subfloor of diagonal boards or plywood is normally used under the finish floor (Fig. 7.17). Strip flooring of this type is tongued-and-grooved and end-matched (Fig. 7.18). Strips are random lengths and may vary from 2 to 16 feet or more. The tongue fits tightly into the groove to prevent movement and floor squeaks. All these details are designed to provide beautiful finished floors that

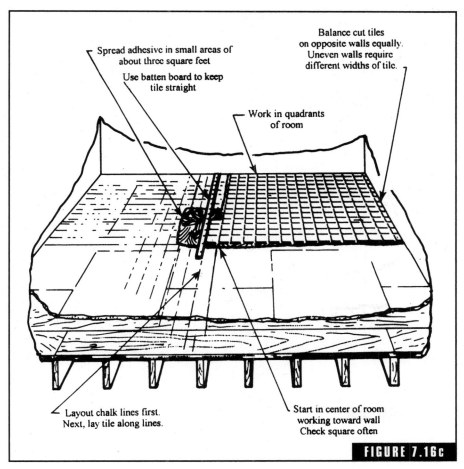

Spread adhesive in small areas of
about three square feet

Use batten board to keep
tile straight

Balance cut tiles
on opposite walls equally.
Uneven walls require
different widths of tile.

Work in quadrants
of room

Layout chalk lines first.
Next, lay tile along lines.

Start in center of room
working toward wall
Check square often

FIGURE 7.16c

Laying ceramic tile. *(Leon E. Korejwo, Illustrations.)*

require a minimum of maintenance. Blind-nail boards without damaging the finish. Drive nails into the tongue with the nail set. Use a block and bar to tightly force board tongue into the groove without damaging it (Fig. 7.19).

Parquet (*block*) *flooring* is made in a number of patterns. Blocks may vary in size from 4 × 4 inches (10 × 10 cm) to 9 × 9 inches (23 × 23 cm) and larger. Solid wood tile is often made up of narrow strips of wood splined or keyed together in a number of ways. Wedges of the thicker tile are tongue-and-grooved, but thinner sections of wood are

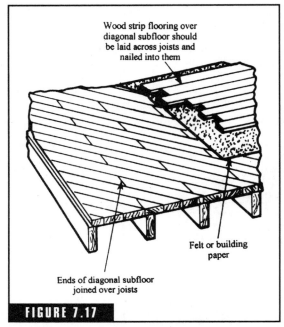

Wood strip flooring over diagonal subfloor should be laid across joists and nailed into them

Felt or building paper

Ends of diagonal subfloor joined over joists

FIGURE 7.17

Wood strip flooring installed over diagonal subfloor-ing. *(Leon E. Korejwo, Illustrations.)*

usually square-edged. Plywood blocks may be $3/8$ inch (1 cm) and thicker and are usually tongued-and-grooved (Fig. 7.20). Many block floors are factory-finished and require only waxing after installation.

Whichever of the three types of wood flooring your client has chosen, preparing a reliable base requires the same steps. Wood floors are typically laid over a con-crete slab, over a wood subfloor supported by joists and beams, or, in some cases, over an existing floor, depending on the old floor's composition and condition and on the kind of wood flooring you plan to install. Strips or planks can be fastened to a wood floor or subfloor or to plywood or 2×4-inch sleepers (or screeds) installed over a dry, level, concrete slab (Fig. 7.21). See Table 7.3. If the concrete is uneven, it is best to build a subfloor suspended over the concrete base. Parquet flooring requires a solid, smooth, continuous subfloor,

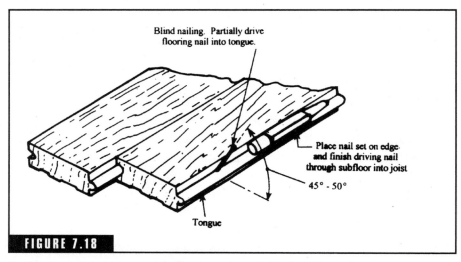

Blind nailing. Partially drive flooring nail into tongue.

Place nail set on edge and finish driving nail through subfloor into joist

45° - 50°

Tongue

FIGURE 7.18

Nailing tongue-and-groove strip flooring. *(Leon E. Korejwo, Illustrations.)*

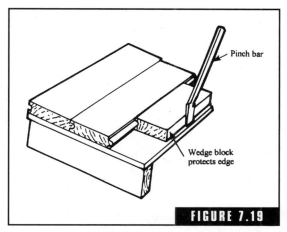

FIGURE 7.19

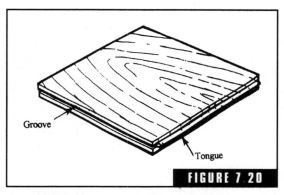

FIGURE 7.20

Tongue-and-groove wood block flooring. *(Leon E. Korejwo, Illustrations.)*

Lay each succeeding course by fitting the groove edges of flooring pieces into the tongue edges of the preceding course. Use a block and bar to force board tongue into groove without damaging flooring. *(Leon E. Korejwo, Illustrations.)*

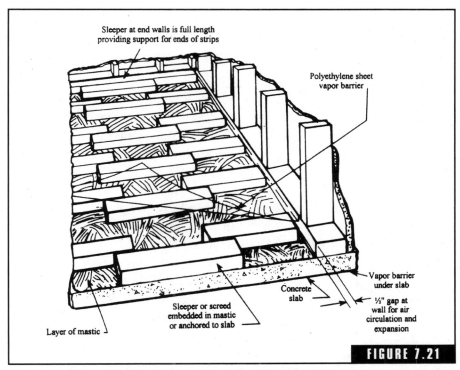

FIGURE 7.21

Sleepers over a concrete slab with a vapor barrier underneath. *(Leon E. Korejwo, Illustrations.)*

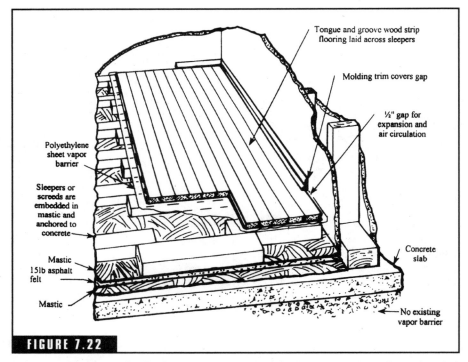

Labels on figure:
- Tongue and groove wood strip flooring laid across sleepers
- Molding trim covers gap
- ½" gap for expansion and air circulation
- Polyethylene sheet vapor barrier
- Sleepers or screeds are embedded in mastic and anchored to concrete
- Mastic 15lb asphalt felt
- Mastic
- Concrete slab
- No existing vapor barrier

FIGURE 7.22

Tongue-and-groove strip flooring over a concrete slab. *(Leon E. Korejwo, Illustrations.)*

whether of boards or plywood panels, concrete, or even resilient floor-ing. Laminated wood tiles can be laid directly in mastic on a thor-oughly dry concrete slab that has a waterproofing membrane below or above to keep it dry, but blocks of solid wood pieces are best installed over a plywood base built over the slab.

Unlike parquet tiles, strip-and-plank flooring can't be cemented directly to concrete. If you don't want to build a subfloor, lay a poly-ethylene vapor barrier, fasten down 2 × 4-inch (5 × 10-cm) sleepers, and then nail the flooring to the sleepers. Be sure the concrete is prop-erly sealed against moisture. If the floor is cold, lay rigid-foam insula-tion between the sleepers. Allow some space above the foam for air circulation. A single layer of polyethylene film laid under new wood flooring is usually considered adequate moisture protection for a dry slab floor (Fig. 7.22).

A wood subfloor, either plywood or boards, should be covered with a plywood underlayment. The combined thickness of subfloor and underlayment should be $1\frac{1}{4}$ inches (3 cm) with underlayment at least $\frac{3}{8}$ inch (1 cm). If the combination is not thick enough, cover it with a layer of $\frac{3}{8}$-inch (1-cm) exterior-grade plywood.

The laying of wood strip flooring should be completed after the other interior wall and ceiling finish is completed (see Chap. 10), windows and exterior doors are in place, and most of the interior trim, except base, casing, and jambs, is applied, so that the flooring will not be damaged by construction activity. Board subfloors should be clean and level and covered with a deadening 15-pound asphalt-saturated felt. This felt stops a certain amount of dust, somewhat deadens sound, and, where a crawlspace is used, increases the warmth of the floor by preventing air infiltration. Because of the potential for expansion and contraction, always allow a gap at the wall, finishing with molding to conceal the gap.

In some cases, tongue-and-groove flooring needs no additional subflooring and can be nailed directly to the joists. When installing over this type of existing floor, eliminate loose or squeaky joints before installing a new surface.

Refer to Table 7.3 for information necessary to prepare a concrete slab, a wood subfloor, or an existing floor for new wood flooring.

Table 7-3 Preparation Guidelines for Wood Flooring

Surface applied over	Preparation steps
Concrete slab	Be sure that the slab is smooth, level, and clean.
	Check that it is completely dry and take steps to ensure it stays dry. Any moisture coming through the concrete will eventually cause the flooring to loosen, rot, or mildew.
	Sweep the slab clean to remove dust and dirt. Do not clean the floor with water. Use a chemical cleaner that will remove grease and oil.
	Even if a below-grade or on-grade slab appears dry, apply a good vapor barrier (polyethylene) under the floor to safeguard against future moisture problems.

Table 7-3 Preparation Guidelines for Wood Flooring (*Continued*)

	Except for glue-down parquet or laminated planks, wood flooring cannot be secured directly to a concrete slab.
	Lay sleepers (strips of wood) with a plywood subfloor of 3/4" (1.9 cm) tongue and groove exterior plywood (required for wood block floors), as a vapor barrier. This allows for air circulation, preventing moisture buildup.
Wood subfloor supported by joists and beams	Plywood common pine or fir 1 × 4 or 1 × 6 boards provide a suitable base for wood flooring.
	3/4" (1.9 cm) plywood is considered the best subfloor material.
	Lay subfloor boards or planks diagonally across the joists and nail them in place using a 1/16" gap between them for expansion.
	Plywood subflooring with interlocking tongue-and-groove joints have those edges on the 8' sides only. They are laid across the joists, while the 4' lengths are laid over the centerline of the joists.
	It is possible to lay wood flooring over an old floor that is in good condition. For the most reliable base, remove the old flooring to get down to the subfloor and make any necessary repairs, or install underlayment.
Old resilient flooring	If in good condition, flat, and securely fastened down, this can serve as a base for new wood block—not strips or planks.
	If damaged, the flooring should be removed or covered before installing a new wood block floor.
	If too difficult to remove old vinyl flooring, cover with 1/4" (0.6 cm) underlayment plywood or hardboard.
Old wood flooring	The flooring must be structurally sound and perfectly level. A wood floor will make a good subfloor if there are no seriously damaged or loose boards.
	Examine the old floor and support structure carefully for damaged members or moisture damage.
	If installing new wood block flooring, remove all wax, varnish, or other finish from the old floor.

Preparing for Masonry Flooring

Masonry flooring can be laid over a ground-level concrete slab or a suspended wood floor. However, putting masonry over a suspended floor in a frame home can be complicated because of the weight. If setting masonry over a wood floor, the floor must be protected by a moisture barrier of asphalt felt.

Masonry exerts tremendous weight and should be laid over concrete. A concrete slab provides the best possible subfloor. Make sure the slab is clean so that mortar will bond to it. Slate or flagstone may be set in a bed of mortar on a concrete slab or in mastic or adhesive over a wood subfloor. Preparing a base for masonry flooring is simple, if the flooring is to be laid over a concrete slab at ground level. If masonry flooring was planned as part of the original building, allowances will have been made for the extra weight, and the support system will have been planned accordingly. But if brick or stone flooring is being laid in an older home as part of a remodeling project, the old floor, in most cases, will need reinforcing. Always consult a building design professional before putting masonry flooring over any subfloor other than a ground-level concrete slab.

Stone is available in rough-hewn pieces (irregular thickness and shape) or in uniform tiles. You will need a thick mortar base over a concrete slab to lay a flooring of rough-hewn stone. The irregularity of the material makes it necessary to provide a cushion of mortar that compensates for the differences in thickness from piece to piece.

You can use thin-set mortar for stones that can be cut into pieces of uniform thicknesses, such as slate and marble. Keep in mind that the thickness of these stones, plus the mortar bed, raises the height of the floor considerably. Although most bricks can be used for both walls and floors, *pavers* are intended specifically for floors. Pavers are available in regular or slightly less than regular thicknesses, or as splits, which are half as thick as regular bricks. Full pavers can be laid on a concrete slab; splits require a concrete slab topped with a mortar bed or spread with thin-set adhesive. Wooden subfloors require the lighter weight splits. Because this precut material is a lighter floor, it requires less structural support than rough-hewn stone in a full bed of mortar. The subfloor requirements are the same as those for ceramic tile. If installing a masonry floor, particularly one of natural stone, be sure to check the local building code for subfloor requirements.

Installation of Cabinets, Countertops, and Fixtures

Once the room is thoroughly prepared, you are ready to begin installation of the cabinets, countertops, and fixtures. All the plumbing and electrical wiring should be complete; all rough carpentry should be out of the way; and all floor, wall, and ceiling preparation work should be accomplished. The bathroom should be completely clean. Remove any debris and unneeded materials, and lay out your tools where they are accessible, but not in the way. Protect all finishes that have been completed prior to this point.

Whether the installation of the bathroom equipment is troublesome or easy depends on good preparation and proper installation techniques. Out-of-square walls, insufficient clearances, and incorrect installation procedures can create costly problems and delays. Take care to avoid these problems.

Bathroom Cabinets

Today with homeowner's changing lifestyles and bathrooms becoming more elaborate and expressive (gyms, spas, grooming centers, etc.), storage needs and configurations are also changing. Some bathrooms may still have the typical base vanity, while others will have complete custom cabinetry, with wall cabinets, base cabinets, and floor-to-ceiling units, as in the kitchen. In fact, kitchen and bath cabinet lines have very few differences anymore.

All cabinets, hardware, moldings, and other materials must be on hand; verify that the shipment is complete. Most manufacturers perform rigid quality inspections; however, damage may occur through shipping and handling. Carefully compare the cabinets you received with the bathroom plan, ensuring the proper type of cabinet and that quantities are correct for the installation. Store the cabinets in an out-of-the-way place where they will be safe and protected, such as in the client's basement or garage. Keep the cabinets in the room overnight to allow them to adjust to the temperature of the room.

Checking for Square and Plumb

All cabinets must be installed perfectly level and plumb from a standpoint of function as well as appearance. Because each floor and wall has uneven spots that will affect the installation, it is necessary to locate these uneven areas and shim or cut the cabinetry to make the installation plumb, true, and square. Never assume that a room is perfectly square and plumb; in most cases, no two walls intersect at a corner with a perfect 90° angle.

The first step in laying out the bathroom for cabinet installation is to determine whether the floor under the cabinets is level. To check the floor, lay a long, straight 2 × 4 with a 4-foot (122-cm) or longer carpenter's level on top of it (Fig. 8.1). Examine the room in any area where cabinets will be installed, paying particular attention to the area between the wall and about 24 inches (61 cm) out. If the floor is uneven, which is common, determine where the highest point is. Measure up from this high point to draw the reference lines. Mark a continuous level line on the wall along the floor. This line, called the *baseline,* indicates where the bottom of the base cabinets will rest and gives you an idea of where shimming will be needed and in what amount. If the subfloor or finish floor is to be replaced and will extend under the area where the base cabinets are installed, the rough-in work should be completed before checking for level. Protect the floor with cardboard or tarps during the rest of the installation.

The next step is to determine whether the ceiling is level. This step is very important if you are installing cabinets that run all the way to the ceiling or if planning to build soffits above the wall cabinets. Perform

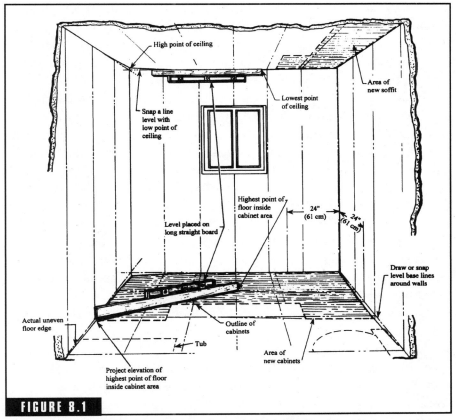

FIGURE 8.1

Find high point of floor and low point of ceiling. *(Leon E. Korejwo, Illustrations.)*

the same process as you did for the floor, but rather than determine the high point, determine the low point of the ceiling. From the low point, mark a continuous level line on the wall along the ceiling.

Probably the most common installation problem is the out-of-square wall. It is most troublesome at the end of a wall or base cabinet run and can prevent drawers and sliding shelves from being opened their full length, cabinet doors from being opened a full 90°, and countertops from being properly fitted. If an existing wall is out of square with the cabinets, a filler strip should be used at that wall, which brings a finished look to the shimmed cabinet. It moves the cabinet door or drawer away from the out-of-square wall enough to allow the full use of the cabinets.

To check the squares of the corners of a room, use the triangulation method often referred to as the "3-4-5 rule." Measure 36 inches (3 feet) (91 cm) from a corner along one wall, make a mark; measure 48 inches (4 feet) (122 cm) out from the corner along the second wall and make a mark (Fig. 8.2). If the diagonal distance between the two marks is exactly 60 inches (5 feet) (152 cm), the corner walls are square. If it measures less than 60 inches (5 feet) (152 cm), the walls intersect at less than 90°, and the cabinets must be shimmed at the corner. If it is more than 60 inches (152 cm), the walls intersect at an angle greater than 90°, and the cabinets are shimmed at the far end from the corner. Mark the actual cabinet outlines of all wall cabinets on the wall to check wall dimensions against the layout. Be accurate in the layout and include any fillers you will be using to make up odd inches.

Next, check the walls for uneven spots. Wall unevenness can cause cabinets to be misaligned, resulting in racking or twisting of doors and drawer fronts after they have been screwed tight against the wall. Some high spots can be removed by sanding. Otherwise, it will be necessary to shim the low spots to provide a level and plumb installation. Stretching string across a wall from corner to corner is a quick reference to the unevenness of a wall.

The tops of wall cabinets are generally installed 84 inches (213 cm) above floor level. Locate this height from the baseline, which is the highest point of the floor. Check the width of the room first at the high point. Next check the level of the floor at this point, 24 inches (61 cm) from the wall (which is the width of the wall cabinet). If the floor is higher than 24 inches (61 cm) away from the wall, mark this height on the wall. Then, proceed up the wall and mark off the 84 inch (213 cm) height and, using the level and straightedge, continue this line around the room. This line will show the location of the tops of the wall cabinets at 84 inches (213 cm) above floor level. Mark another horizontal line on the wall at 34$\frac{1}{2}$ inches (88 cm) above the high point to locate the tops of the base cabinets. Mark the walls for each cabinet. Begin at any corner and fix the position of each cabinet by marking its exact location.

On the walls where cabinets are to be installed, remove the baseboard and chair rail for a flush fit. If the bathroom is utilizing tall cabinets, they require a full 84 inches (213 cm) in height. If the room has an existing soffit and the height from the baseline to the soffit is less

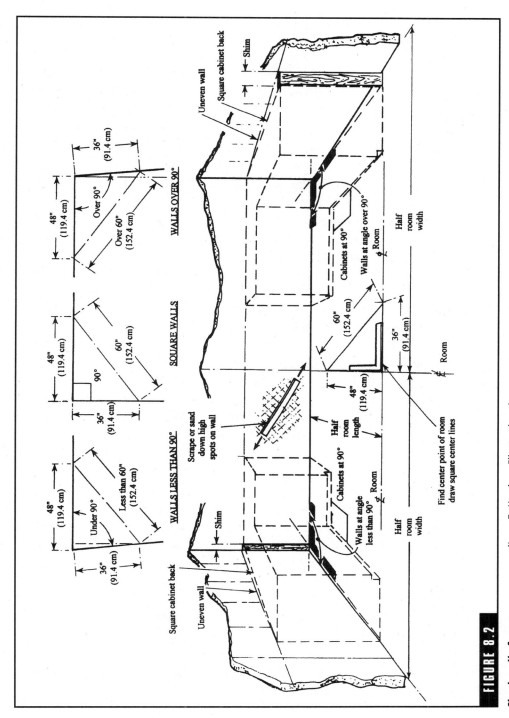

Over 90°

Over 60"
(152.4 cm)

48"
(119.4 cm)

36"
(91.4 cm)

WALLS OVER 90°

90°

60"
(152.4 cm)

48"
(119.4 cm)

36"
(91.4 cm)

SQUARE WALLS

Under 90°

Less than 60"
(152.4 cm)

48"
(119.4 cm)

36"
(91.4 cm)

WALLS LESS THAN 90°

Uneven wall

Square cabinet back

Shim

Cabinets at 90°

Walls at angle over 90°

Room

Half room width

60"
(152.4 cm)

36"
(91.4 cm)

Room

48"
(119.4 cm)

Half room length

Cabinets at 90°

Walls at angle less than 90°

Room

Half room width

Find center point of room draw square center lines

Scrape or sand down high spots on wall

Shim

Square cabinet back

Uneven wall

FIGURE 8.2

Check walls for square corners. *(Leon E. Korejwo, Illustrations.)*

329

than 84 inches (213 cm), you need to work to the soffit and trim off the bottom of the tall units to make the adjustment.

Again, take several measurements and use the highest mark for the reference point. When the typical 1$\frac{1}{2}$-inch (4-cm) countertop is added, the top of the countertop should be 36 inches (91 cm) above the finish floor. Use a level to mark a reference line on walls. Base cabinets will be installed with top edges flush with the 34$\frac{1}{2}$-inch-(88-cm)-high line.

Lay out the entire cabinet arrangement on the walls and floor. Doing so helps you visualize the configuration of the cabinets and quickly points out dimension problems or conflicts. Marking full plumb lines for each cabinet unit is not necessary. Start with a vertical plumb line using an accurate level and double-check with a plumb bob. Use this line as a reference point. It may not be necessary to repeat the leveling for all your lines. Because the face frames extend slightly beyond the sides of most base cabinets, there will be about a $\frac{1}{4}$-inch (0.64-cm) space between the lines drawn for each base cabinet.

It is important to take the time to draw the cabinet layout on the walls and floor, measuring carefully the entire bathroom before you just jump in and start installing the first cabinet or fixture. Knowing where to start installing the cabinets, and in what order they will be installed, is vital to a successful installation.

Wall cabinets are installed with top edges flush against the 84-inch (213-cm)-high line. Measure down 30 inches (76 cm) from the wall cabinet reference line and draw another level line where the bottom of the cabinets will be (Fig. 8.3). Temporarily, ledgers (or cleats) can be installed against this line. Double-check this point by measuring up from the baseline. The measurement should be 54 inches (137 cm).

If you are working tight to the ceiling or a soffit, make sure to have established a level line at the low point. There is generally 16 to 18 inches (41 to 46 cm) between the countertop and the underside of the wall cabinets, but this distance must be checked to ensure that the wall cabinets align with the top of the tall cabinets. With the bottom line of the wall cabinets established, mark vertical lines for each wall cabinet unit in the same manner as the base cabinets. Allow for the required clearances of fixtures and equipment in the layout of the room.

You need to check for vertical-alignment relationships between the base and wall cabinets, especially where a base and a wall cabinet abut a tall cabinet. Because it is extremely important to support wall

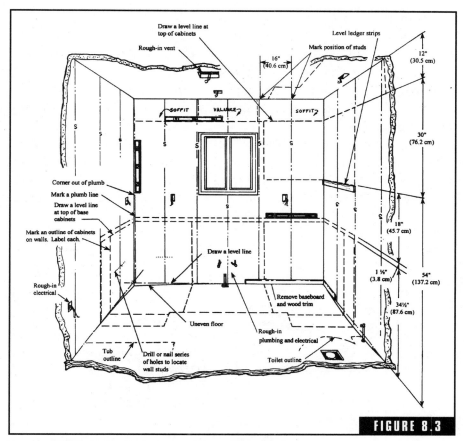

Lay out cabinets on wall. *(Leon E. Korejwo, Illustrations.)*

cabinets with a solid mounting, you also need to determine the layout of the wall studs to which you will be attaching the cabinets. Cabinets must be attached to studs for full support. Remember that studs are usually laid out at 16 or 24 inches (41 or 61 cm) on center. If you know the location of any studs from the rough work you did earlier, measure out on 16-inch (41-cm) centers to locate the rest of them. If you don't know the location of any of the studs, use a stud finder.

Soffits

To close the gap between the tops of the wall cabinets and the ceiling, soffits are frequently employed (Fig. 8.4). They are framed with

2- × 3- inch (5 × 7.6-cm) soffits. A ceiling plate is spiked to the joists above, and the wall cleat is spiked to the studs. The short 2 × 3s between the main members are toenailed in place. Afterward, the face of the soffit is covered with wallboard or any convenient sheet material. When the cabinets are hung, gaps remaining between the bottom of the soffit and the tops of the cabinets are hidden by a cove molding that is the last item to be affixed.

If soffits are to be built, they should be constructed and installed before installing the cabinets. Soffits in a room with 8-foot (244-cm) ceilings are normally 12 inches (30 cm) in height and 14 inches (36 cm) in width. If the wall cabinets are to be against an existing ceiling

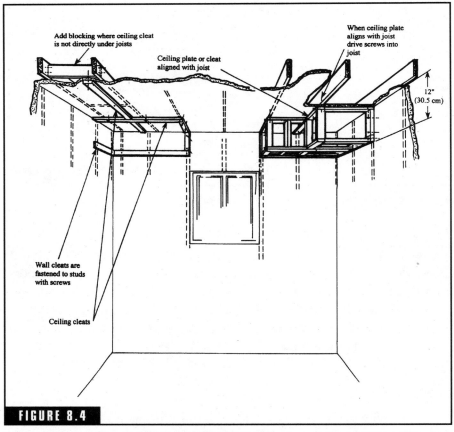

FIGURE 8.4

Soffits or ceiling-mounted cabinet attached to joists. *(Leon E. Korejwo, Illustrations.)*

soffit, the soffit should be examined to determine whether it is level. Use a straightedge and level much the same as you did when looking for the lowest spot (closest to the floor) on the ceiling. Corner cabinets should be shimmed down to this "lowest" height. By comparing measurements from the base-level line, you can locate any unevenness in soffit height.

The Installation

Proper installation means better performance of fixtures and equipment, a less costly installation, and few service complaints.

Ceiling-Mounted Cabinets

Not all wall cabinets are mounted to the wall. Although more often used in kitchens than bathrooms, peninsula wall cabinets must be hung from the ceiling or from overhead soffit construction. If there is existing ceiling framing, determine whether the layout of the framing aligns with the location of the cabinets. To adequately support the cabinets, it may be necessary to open up the ceiling and install additional blocking. If constructing a new soffit, lay out the soffit framing to provide a proper means of connection. Peninsula wall cabinets must be fastened to the overhead structure with at least four screws, as close to the outside corners as possible.

Most manufacturers recommend installing wall cabinets before base cabinets. The reason most prefer this order is because working around the wider base cabinets to hang the wall units may be awkward. Also, to support the wall cabinets on jacks during installation the installer needs to have the floor space free below the wall cabinets. There is also the risk of damaging the base cabinets if a wall cabinet or a tool is dropped during the installation of the wall cabinets.

Some installers do, however, prefer to begin with the base cabinets. With this approach, once the base cabinets are set, the vertical relationships between the base and wall cabinets can be established and the wall cabinets installed. Countertops cannot generally be measured for or ordered until the base cabinets are set. Therefore, while the countertops are being fabricated, the wall cabinets can be installed. Installers who prefer to install base cabinets first can still use jacks to install wall cabinets. In this instance, shorter jacks are used. Be sure to protect the base cabinets. Plywood sheets serve this purpose and also provide a surface to support the jacks.

If a full-height backsplash is specified, the best fit is achieved by installing the base cabinets first. Once the base cabinets and backsplash have been set, the wall cabinets can be installed to sit tight against the backsplash.

Whether you choose to begin installing wall cabinets or base cabinets first is up to you. One way is not necessarily better than the other, although each has its merits. Consider all the options and choose what makes the most sense for each individual project.

Wall Cabinet Installation

To make the installation of wall cabinets easier, install a 1 × 2- or 1 × 3-inch (2.5 × 5- or 2.5 × 7.6-cm) strip of wood as a temporary support cleat or ledger strips at the 54-inch (137-cm) cabinet line mark. Check the trueness of the ledger after the screws are tightened to the wall. This ledger strip allows you to align and support the wall cabinets as they are being installed. Attach ledgers with 2 1/2-inch (6-cm) wallboard screws driven into every other wall stud. Mark stud locations on ledgers. Cabinets rest temporarily on ledgers during the installation, which are then removed. If, however, you are working against a wall that has already been finished or one that will not later be covered with a backsplash, you should not use a ledger strip, since the holes will show. Use the 54-inch (137-cm) line as a visual reference point, a location to raise the cabinets to, and use a floor T-brace.

Remove doors from cabinets to ease access to hanging strips, lighten the load, and ease handling. If possible, remove the cabinet doors by their hinge pins and interior shelves from the cabinet unit before lifting the cabinets into position. However, it is important to bundle the shelves and mark them so that you know which cabinet unit they came from.

Start the cabinet installation from an inside corner and work outward. If you have a diagonal corner wall cabinet, it is an excellent cabinet to install first (Fig. 8.5). The back of a corner wall cabinet is usually beveled at a 45° angle so that it can be fitted into nonsquare corners. This angled back can make corner wall cabinets very awkward to set in place. Check with the manufacturer for pull spacing, as alignment may require a space behind. Ledger strips help keep the

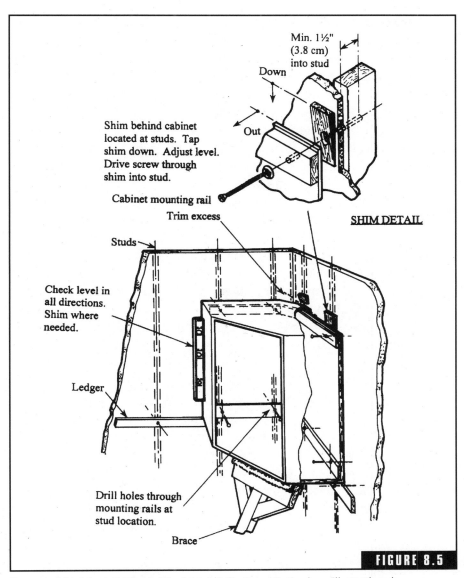

Min. 1½"
(3.8 cm)
into stud

Down

Out

SHIM DETAIL

Shim behind cabinet
located at studs. Tap
shim down. Adjust level.
Drive screw through
shim into stud.

Cabinet mounting rail

Trim excess

Studs

Check level in
all directions.
Shim where
needed.

Ledger

Drill holes through
mounting rails at
stud location.

Brace

FIGURE 8.5

Corner cabinet installation with shim detail. *(Leon E. Korejwo, Illustrations.)*

unit from shifting. Once the cabinet is supported, measure from the corner to the first stud mark and transfer this measurement to the inside of the cabinet to be installed in the corner. Mark the next stud, and so on. Drill through the hanging strips (or mounting rails), which are horizontal strips built into the backs of the cabinet at both the top and bottom. Locate holes about 3/4 inch (1.9 cm) below the top shelf and 3/4 inch (1.9 cm) above the bottom shelf from inside the cabinet. Holes can also be marked on the back of cabinets and holes drilled before cabinets are raised into place. When drilling, be sure not to split the finished face of the inside of the cabinet.

A variety of jacks and props are available to assist in holding the wall cabinets in place for a one-person job. However, some installers choose to have a helper brace the cabinet while checking for plumb and level. Wooden shims can be driven between the cabinet and the wall, as needed, to bring the cabinet perfectly into position. C-clamps can be used to connect cabinets together to obtain proper alignment.

Lift the first cabinet into place atop the ledger strip and brace it. Drill through previously located marks (if you have not already done so). Loosely attach the cabinet to the studs with installation screws long enough to extend minimum 1 1/2 inches (4 cm) into the studs. Depending on the thickness of the hanging rail, cabinet back, and drywall or plaster wall surface, the screws should be between 2 1/2 and 3 inches (6 and 8 cm) long. Some manufacturers supply installation fasteners; others do not. (If walls are plaster and thicker than normal, run a test screw and remove it to see its depth of engagement.) In most instances, the fasteners used are nos. 8 and 10 screws, with the recommended head types varying by cabinet manufacturer. Drywall or wood screws are two popular choices, and a power driver can speed the work.

Wall cabinets are generally attached to wood studs with no. 8 or 10 wood screws or drywall screws of sufficient length. If you were not able to locate a wall stud, or if a stud does not exist at the point where the cabinet is being mounted, install what you can and then use the next cabinet to add support. Toggle bolts can be used in some cases in lieu of attaching to a stud, but in no case should a wall cabinet be installed without being secured to at least one wall stud. Masonry walls may require use of expansion anchors. Adjust the screws only loosely at first so that the final adjustments can be made after the cabinets have been checked with a level. A minimum of two screws should be placed in the top and bottom mounting rails. Each cabinet under 24 inches (61 cm) wide should receive four screws, a minimum of two screws per stud: one top rail and one bottom rail. Cabinets larger than 24 inches (61 cm) should receive two screws per stud. Cabinets over 42 inches (107 cm) wide should have six screws, depending on the stud layout. Since studs are usually 16 inches (40 cm) apart center-to-center, a 24-inch (61-cm) cabinet should be located over at least two studs. Occasionally studs are 24 inches (61 cm) apart; then toggle bolts must be used through the wall. Always keep in mind that careful attention to detail will ensure a first-rate installation.

Remember that the increased weight of bathroom storage can pull fasteners through wallboards. Use good judgment in adding toggle bolts or fasteners. Use fasteners with finishing washers to prevent the screw from sinking into or splitting the wood and to provide a professional finish. To adjust and align cabinets, use shims made from tapered wood such as shake shingles, which can be driven between wall and cabinet back. Adjust by tapping wedges and loosening or tightening screws until everything is plumb and level.

Place the shims at the stud locations. Drill them, running mounting screws through them after final adjustment to prevent them from working loose. Trim off the excess with a handsaw. When tightening, look for gaps behind the cabinets. Do not tighten a screw that is at an unshimmed gap. Tightening screws can cause the cabinet to bow. Shim as needed (refer to Fig. 8.5). The first cabinet sets the accuracy for the entire row—time spent here saves time later. Before screwing the cabinet to the wall, recheck the sides of the cabinet to ensure that they are level and plumb.

A blind corner cabinet must be adjusted horizontally to line up with the row of cabinets it abuts (Fig. 8.6). The manufacturer recommends a dimension. Mark the required distance on the wall, and locate the studs. Lay the cabinet in place on the cleat, adjust the position, referred to as *pull,* away from the wall, and proceed as before.

Note: Cabinets must always be attached to walls with screws. Never use nails.

With the first cabinet and any necessary fillers in place, the second wall cabinet in the run is placed in position next to the first (Fig. 8.7). Set it on the cleat or prop it into place; then carefully align it with the

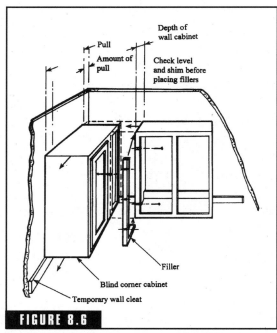

FIGURE 8.6

Blind corner wall cabinet positioning. *(Leon E. Korejwo, Illustrations.)*

first cabinet. When the bottoms and faces of the stiles are flush, use C-clamps (or handscrew clamps) to clamp the two cabinets together. (Use pads with the clamps so that the cabinet finish will not be damaged.) Drill through the first stile with a diameter just wide enough to allow the screw to slide in without binding its threads. Countersink this hole slightly to recess the screw head. Connect the cabinet with two screws in from one side at the top and bottom and one in from the other side in the center. Two screws are usually adequate for wall cabinets up to 36 inches (91 cm) high. When the cabinets are secured to each other, check the second cabinet for plumb and level, and shim it as necessary. Drill through the upper and lower nailing

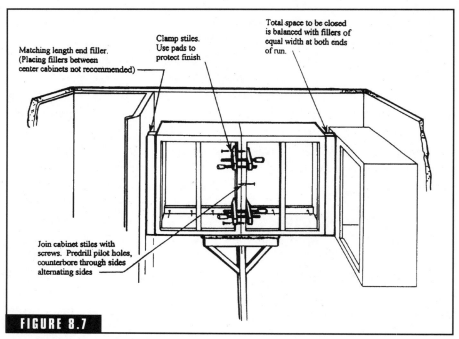

FIGURE 8.7

Continue run of wall cabinets. *(Leon E. Korejwo, Illustrations.)*

strips into the studs and screw the cabinets to the wall. Once again, do not fully tighten the screws. The seams between the cabinet units are not generally covered by any trim or molding, as it is imperative that the alignment of the face frames is exact and that the fasteners pull the units snugly together.

Most manufacturers recommend the use of electrician rails or some type of lag-bolt system for mounting to masonry walls, with the quantity required being the same as for regular screw installations. Alternatively, lag-bolt a hanging rail to the masonry wall first, and then mount the cabinets to the rail. The hanging rail is usually a 1 × 4-inch (2.5 × 10-cm). Some installers notch out the wall finish so that the rail can set directly against the masonry and thus reduce the gap between the back of the cabinets and the wall.

To attach adjacent wall cabinet units, fasten with no. 8 $2^1/4$- or $2^1/2$-inch (5.7- or 6.4-cm) wood screws or drywall screws through the vertical stile of one cabinet into the vertical stile of the adjacent cabinet. The length is dependent on the thickness of the stiles, which varies from manufacturer to manufacturer. Two screws per pair of wall cabinets being connected are generally sufficient for cabinets up to 36 inches (91 cm). Taller cabinets should have three screws.

This process continues until the full run of wall cabinets has been installed. Check often during the installation to make sure that the face of the cabinets are aligned, plumb, and level. It might be necessary to shim at the wall and between cabinets to correct for uneven walls or floors. When everything looks correct, finish tightening the screws. Finish installing all the wall cabinets before beginning the base runs. A series of two or three wall cabinets can also be attached together before lifting them into place, allowing the alignment work to be done without having to support the weight of the cabinets. The use of jacks is recommended for this installation method.

Base Cabinet Installation

Base cabinets should be installed next, in the same manner as wall cabinets, starting at the same inside corner and working outward in each direction from that point. Before you begin installing them, remove any baseboard, moldings, or wall base that might interfere. Since support is not a problem for the base cabinet, it is a good idea to bring in all the cabinets for one run and set them together. If a base

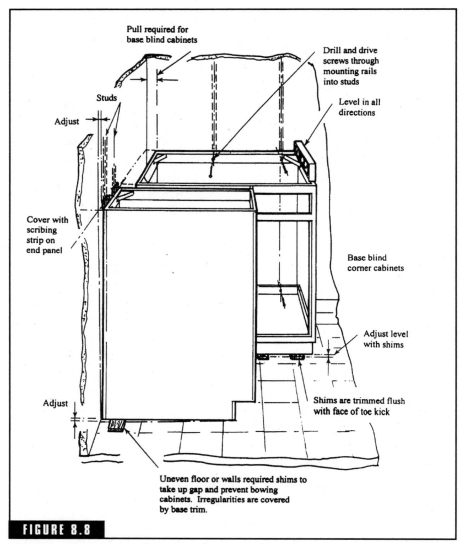

Pull required for
base blind cabinets

Drill and drive
screws through
mounting rails
into studs

Studs

Level in all
directions

Adjust

Cover with
scribing
strip on
end panel

Base blind
corner cabinets

Adjust level
with shims

Adjust

Shims are trimmed flush
with face of toe kick

Uneven floor or walls required shims to
take up gap and prevent bowing
cabinets. Irregularities are covered
by base trim.

FIGURE 8.8

Adjusting level of cabinets with wood shims. *(Leon E. Korejwo, Illustrations.)*

blind corner cabinet is used, pull it out of the corner to the proper dimension as shown on the bathroom layout. Position the cabinet so that the top is flush with the reference line. Measure the cabinet carefully for level and plumb: from side to side and front to back. If necessary, adjust by driving wood shims under cabinet base (Fig. 8.8). Scribing strips may be included along the sides to allow full alignment with the wall. Both shims and irregularities in the floor can be hidden by baseboard trim, vinyl wall base, or new flooring. Be careful not to damage flooring.

Fasteners for base cabinets are similar to those used for wall cabinets. However, because base cabinets are resting on the floor surface, fasteners are used basically to secure the unit in place once it has been leveled. If the base cabinet backs up to only one wall surface, two screws placed through the center of the mounting rail into wall studs are generally sufficient to stabilize the unit. Adjacent units are screwed together through the vertical stiles or through the adjoining cabinet side panel, depending on whether they are framed or frameless cabinets. Brads or other suitable types of nails are recommended only for use with wood trim, panels and other types of molding. Nails are not considered sufficient fasteners for either base or wall cabinets.

Attach cabinets loosely to the wall with screws. If necessary, attach filler strip to adjoining cabinets. Clamp adjoining cabinets to corner cabinet. Make sure that the cabinet is plumb, and then join the cabinets with screws. In some cases the filler may not be required, specifically, where a drawer unit is the adjacent cabinet or where the full opening of doors on adjacent cabinet is not necessary. Use a jigsaw to cut any cabinet openings needed for plumbing, wiring, or heating ducts. If you need to cut access holes in a cabinet's back or bottom for plumbing supply and drain pipes or for electric wire serving the sink complex, do so before installing the cabinet.

Most of us think of a lazy Susan as used only in kitchens; they can also be used quite effectively in bathrooms. If using a base lazy Susan-type cabinet in the bathroom, apply a 1 × 2 or 1 × 3-inch (2.5 × 5- or 2.5 × 7.6-cm) strip to the wall at the proper height. To support the countertop, apply strips to both walls at right angles. This frame should be nailed or screwed to the studs and will provide support for the countertop once it is installed into the corner. It is usually better to fasten at least one cabinet in both directions to the base lazy Susan cabinet and be sure that they are shimmed properly before attaching the wall cleat.

Drill holes through the mounting rail into each stud, then drive no. 8 flathead wood screws that are 2½ inches (6 cm) long. Two screws are usually sufficient to secure the base cabinet in place. If the spot where you need to screw the base cabinet is not flush with the wall, place a shim between the cabinet and the wall so that as the screw is tightened, the cabinet is not pulled out of square.

Adjacent base cabinets are installed in the same manner as the wall cabinets. Continue installing base cabinets one next to the other, and at the end of the cabinet run, where necessary, attach filler strips. Continue to shim up the base cabinets so they are all level and follow the base cabinet line on the wall. Set the second cabinet, level, align, and then screw it to the first cabinet through the adjoining stiles. The second cabinet then can be screwed to the wall. Once again, if necessary, adjust by driving wood shims underneath the cabinets. Place wood shims behind cabinets near the stud locations wherever there is a gap. As you tighten the wall screws, be sure that face frames remain square and in exactly the same place.

Frameless Cabinet Installation

Frameless cabinets originated from a European technology that centered on portability and a metric standardization. The standard was based on unitized 32-mm modular spacing of components. Domestic frameless cabinets combine features of the European unitized manufacturing with American practice.

The difference between framed and frameless cabinets is that framed cabinets have a face frame attached to the cabinet sides, and the doors are hinged to the frame. With frameless cabinets, doors and drawers cover the entire front of the cabinet, and doors are attached directly to the sides of the cabinet with concealed hinges.

Frameless cabinets are essentially an open-front box with large doors and drawers that cover the entire front. Multiadjustable concealed hinges and mounting hardware present different installation procedures for some of these cabinets and vary among manufacturers. Refer to the manufacturer's instructions for specific details.

In general, the wall cabinets are mounted on a wall track. The track is leveled and screwed to the studs; then the cabinets are hung on the track. Adjustments in the hanging clips allow the cabinets to be raised or lowered to level them. Most frameless wall cabinets attach to the wall similarly to framed wall units. But some frameless manufacturers' wall cabinet units themselves are not permanently attached to the wall.

A hanging rail (or track) of steel that is approximately $1^1/4$ inches (3 cm) wide holds the wall cabinets. It has an offset channel that is designed to accept the adjustable hooks on the back of each wall cabinet unit. The hanging rail is drilled and screwed to wall studs. Holes that are $1/4$ inch (0.6 cm) in diameter are predrilled in the rails for mounting. Use no. 14 $2^1/2$-inch (6-cm) panhead screws to attach the rails to the wall studs.

Some cabinets have the hanging rail behind the wall cabinet or run above the wall cabinets. Crown molding or trim can conceal the hanging rail. If the hanging rail runs behind the wall cabinets, the backs of the cabinets should be notched so that the cabinets will sit tight against the back wall. Do not notch the end panel of a wall cabinet at the end of a run of cabinets; stop the rail at the inside end panel.

When the alignment of cabinets is complete, they can be bolted together with the partially drilled holes for this purpose. Finish drilling the holes for screws or hardware included with the cabinets. This specialized hardware has connectors that are threaded to pull the cabinets tight. The holes are then covered with plastic caps (Fig. 8.9).

Attach the doors to the cabinets and adjust them. Hinges provide for slight adjustment and can move the doors up, down, in, and out, and side to side for perfect alignment, but not enough to correct an out-of-square condition.

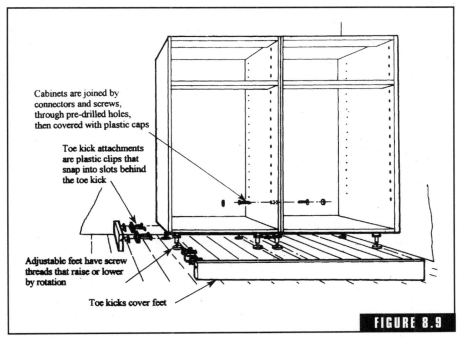

Cabinets are joined by connectors and screws, through pre-drilled holes, then covered with plastic caps

Toe kick attachments are plastic clips that snap into slots behind the toe kick

Adjustable feet have screw threads that raise or lower by rotation

Toe kicks cover feet

FIGURE 8.9

Leveling frameless base cabinet. *(Leon E. Korejwo, Illustrations.)*

Frameless Base Cabinet Installation

Some styles of base cabinets have exposed screw legs, which simplify leveling. These legs allow the cabinets to be leveled and adjusted during installation without the use of shims. The leveling legs are slipped into plastic sockets on the underside of the base cabinets. They are adjusted with a screwdriver through holes located in the bottom of the cabinet. You can also twist the legs by hand when more than a minor adjustment is required. After the cabinets have been leveled and screwed to the wall, the toekick cover panel is simply snapped in place to provide a very clean, finished look.

Both upper and lower cabinets are screwed together as conventional cabinets are, but the screw heads are recessed and then concealed with decorative snap-on tops that match the surrounding laminate finish. Final adjustment of the doors is done with the hinges, which can move up, down, in, out, and side to side for perfect alignment.

Mount the cabinets to the wall or a continuous blocking strip behind the cabinets. European frameless base cabinets are not as deep, and standard countertops extend beyond the face more than usual. Blocking behind the cabinets moves them out to 24 inches (61 cm) from the wall and also provides a means of attaching the cabinets to the wall. You need special end panels on exposed cabinet ends to cover the gap between the wall and the base cabinets.

Note: If you choose to screw the base cabinets to the wall, make sure you use washers or some other means of keeping the screws from pulling through the back of the cabinet.

Toekicks are supplied in long sections. You need to rip the toekick to the proper width once the cabinets are in place. Scribe the toekick right to the flooring, and seal it to the floor using a vinyl strip, similar to weather stripping, that is usually supplied with the cabinets.

End caps are generally provided for the connection of inside and outside corners. If corners meet at angles other than 90°, abutting corners need to be mitred and glued. When the toekick has been assembled, the clips that attach it to the legs are inserted in a groove in the back of the toekick to correspond to the locations of the legs. Some side-to-side adjustment is possible once these clips have been attached to the toekicks.

Tall Cabinet Installation

Tall cabinets, which usually follow the wall and base cabinets, can add difficulty to the installation and must be planned for in advance. If the tall unit is at the end of a run of cabinets, which is most often the case, the installation methods previously explained are still acceptable. However, if the tall cabinet unit is in the middle of a run of cabinets, it may be necessary to install the base cabinets, along with the tall cabinet unit, before installing the wall cabinets. This order of installation ensures that the wall cabinets and the tall cabinet unit are perfectly aligned.

Tall cabinets are mounted in the same manner as base and wall cabinets (Fig. 8.10). The screws are driven through the cabinet mounting rails into the wall studs. The position of the mounting rails will vary by manufacturer, so follow the manufacturer's instructions closely.

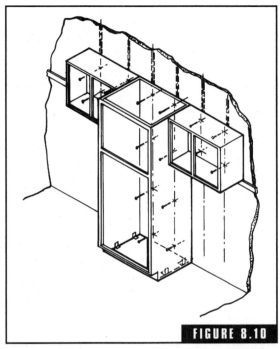

FIGURE 8.10

Tall cabinet installation. *(Leon E. Korejwo, Illustrations.)*

Vanity Cabinets

If your client does not want a bathroom full of base and wall cabinets, installing a vanity cabinet is a less complex route to take and is still one of the best storage ideas for a bathroom. To install a prefabricated vanity cabinet with a countertop, complete with backsplash, finish, and cutout for a separate basin, and to install a multibasin unit, use the following installation procedures.

A vanity cabinet should not be installed until any necessary alterations to the wall surface, that is, putting up new drywall, have been made. Any moldings, baseboard, or wall base that might interfere must be removed at this point. Measure up 34 1/2 inches (87.63 cm) from the floor—the height of a standard vanity cabinet. Take several measurements and use the highest mark for your reference point. Draw a level line through the mark and across the wall. To minimize plumbing work, try to place the vanity so that the basin will align with the existing plumbing. Outline the opening for the water shutoff valves and drainpipe on the back panel of the cabinet. The holes for the drainpipe and water-supply pipe can be cut using a saber saw. For open-back vanities, locate and mark all wall studs in the wall above where the vanity will be installed. Move the vanity into place.

Level the top of the vanity, front to back and side to side, shimming as necessary. To obtain a snug fit without shims, mark and place the vanity so that it hugs the floor. Shims and irregularities in the floor can be hidden by baseboard trim, scribing strips along the sides. Or decorative panels can be used to finish the end of a cabinet run. Studs can be located in the wall behind the cabinet. Install two $2^1/2$-inch (8.85-cm) wood screws, one at the top and one at the bottom, through the back panel or mounting rail and into the two studs closest to the ends of the cabinet. Pilot holes need to be drilled up through the corner braces and into the particle board of the countertop; drive $1^1/4$-inch (3.175-cm) wood screws through the braces.

Once the top is secured, a strip of masking tape should be placed $1/4$ inch (0.64 cm) above the backsplash, and another strip on the top of the backsplash, $1/4$ inch (0.64 cm) away from the wall. Run a bead of silicone caulk along the joint between the backsplash and the wall inside the two strips of tape. Tool into a smooth, concave profile with your finger. Carefully strip off the masking tape. After you have secured the vanity cabinet, install the countertop and sink. The water-supply lines, trap, and pop-up drain can now be installed.

Cabinet Accessories

A wide range of accessories are available to customize bathroom cabinets. The construction and installation procedures for each of these accessories varies according to the manufacturer; therefore, follow manufacturer-supplied instructions closely. Take note of the clearances that each of these accessories requires. Make certain that adjacent cabinets, fixtures, and equipment will not interfere with the accessories.

Fillers

Planning a bathroom on paper is one thing; on the job site you may run into some realities. Fillers are placed at the end of a run of cabinets that will abut an irregular wall surface. The filler can then be attached to the cabinet stile and scribed to the wall. They are also used to make up odd inches in a run of cabinets and to adjust the portion of wall that remains exposed around doors and windows. Some manufacturers offer cabinets with extended or side stiles that eliminate the need for fillers in many cases. Be certain to plan for and lay out all fillers shown on the plans. The need for fillers varies with the size of the cabinet's face frame and the depth of the handles being used (Fig. 8.11).

For runs that start in a corner and end at a window or door, place all the fills at the starting corner. If the cabinet run goes from corner to corner, fillers should be evenly divided and placed at each end of the run, rather than placing them all at one end or in the middle.

Additional Trim and Finishing

To complete the cabinet installation, use moldings to cover gaps between the cabinet and the wall or floor, as well as to provide an attractive transition. Finish trim offers a custom look to any type of cabinet.

Prefinished moldings are usually available from the same manufacturer that supplied the cabinets. Some cabinets are supplied with decorative panels that finish the visible end of a cabinet run, and some are designed with scribing strips along the sides. Both include extra material to be shaved down to a perfect fit between the end cabinet and an irregular wall.

Scribe moldings are flat trim pieces that have relatively little profile and can be applied along the edges of cabinets where they meet the walls. They help conceal the gaps that occur because of shimming and irregular wall conditions. Trim or scribe molding is recommended to hide small gaps between the top of the cabinets and the soffit or ceiling.

Batten molding is a flat trim available to mask joints between adjacent cabinets where desired or required. The edges of this trim are usually chamfered.

Outside corner molding, used to seal joints between two panels at right angles to one another, is an L-shaped molding tacked onto the corner of the cabinet like an edge band or edge strip.

Inside corner molding is available to mask open joints between cabinet units or cabinets and wall surfaces. This molding is often milled with a concave cove profile.

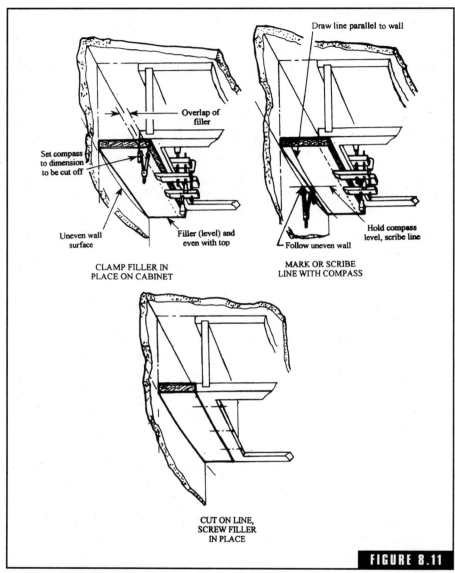

Draw line parallel to wall

Overlap of filler

Set compass to dimension to be cut off

Uneven wall surface

Filler (level) and even with top

CLAMP FILLER IN PLACE ON CABINET

Hold compass level, scribe line

Follow uneven wall

MARK OR SCRIBE LINE WITH COMPASS

CUT ON LINE, SCREW FILLER IN PLACE

FIGURE 8.11

Scribing filler. *(Leon E. Korejwo, Illustrations.)*

Trim can be used with considerable impact at the top of wall cabinets, at either the ceiling or the soffit, depending on the type of construction and the method of installation. Many cabinet manufacturers provide one- and two-piece crown moldings expressly for this purpose. The trim is factory-finished to match the cabinet finish. Crown molding is generally sold by the lineal foot, and can be quite expensive. Special care must be taken in the cutting and fitting together of crown molding to produce tight-fitting joints. The joints for this type of molding are usually mitred and coped. Some manufacturers produce specialty trim such as window and door trim, which can integrate all the wood trim used in the room. This trim is prefinished to match the cabinet finish. Because trim pieces have to be nailed onto the cabinets in most cases, the manufacturer-applied finish will need to be touched up when the trim has been installed. You may find a few areas on the face of the cabinets that require touchup also. Manufacturers provide finish touchup kits in all the various finishes they produce for this purpose. Include touchup kits in the cabinet order so that you have it on hand during installation.

Handles and Pulls

Many manufacturers provide hardware for drawers and doors. Because the homeowner may not like the hardware selections available from the manufacturer, cabinets usually are ordered with the least expensive hardware, and later discarded for hardware purchased from another source. Few manufacturers predrill the holes required for the hardware installation because the orientation and position of the handles and pulls varies according to the personal taste of the end user and the designer. Quite often the hardware supplied with the cabinets is not used at all. If the holes were predrilled for the hardware provided, the substituted hardware might not work in the same holes.

Jigs are available to aid in the consistent alignment of hardware holes. Some installers who have a large quantity of holes to drill will make a template to ensure that the holes are consistent. Typically, one template would be required for doors and another for drawer fronts. Some handles and pulls require one hole each, while others require two or more. Review the hardware carefully before you begin any drilling. Check the spread between holes on all hardware requiring multiple holes. Do not assume that the spread is the same for all hardware on the entire job, although generally that would be the case.

Use a punch or awl to mark the hole before drilling to keep your drill from drifting. You do not want to damage the face of the cabinet. Always drill from the finished face of the door or drawer to avoid any splintering of the wood or chipping of the finish. Installation of the handles and pulls should be the last step in the cabinet installation process. If the handles have a protective coating, leave this in place until you are ready to do the final cleanup.

Installation of Countertops

You need to know how to install the various countertop types as described in Chap. 6 and how to provide proper substrate (base materials) for them. Generally, countertops are fabricated by countertop fabricators from measurements you supply. However, some manufacturers visit the project site and take the field measurements themselves. Because countertops are not usually cut to fit in the field, measurements must be accurate for proper fit. If a manufacturer is fabricating the countertops and does not take the field measurements, the most accurate method is for you to draw a rough sketch to scale, showing the exact dimensions. This sketch can then be given to the manufacturer to fabricate the countertops to your exact measurements. It is generally recommended that measurements be taken only after all the base cabinets have been set.

Depending on the countertop material, the level of difficulty required to construct the countertops, and the manufacturer, lead time for countertops can range from a few days up to two weeks. It is important for you to establish a good relationship with a countertop fabricator who has a reputation for reliability and prompt delivery. It is common to use one fabricator for laminate and solid-surface countertops and a different fabricator for other countertop materials, such as marble or granite.

Before beginning the countertop installation, be certain that all cabinets have been properly prepared to receive the countertop. All cabinets must be level, and the bathroom measured carefully, especially from corner to corner and up to window and door openings.

Unless the countertops are being fabricated in the field, as with ceramic-tile countertops, the countertop section or sections will be installed onto the base cabinets. Be certain that the substrate or support system is in place for the type of countertop being installed.

In most cases, base cabinets have triangular corner struts (or gussets) at the four upper corners of the cabinet (Fig. 8.12). The countertop frame is screwed to these struts from below. Be careful to measure the distance and select the proper-length screws. Also, be extremely careful to drill the proper-depth hole into the countertop. Do not drill through the countertop.

If the countertop is in multiple sections, the sections should be set in place to determine proper fit and alignment of edges and patterns. To install the countertop sections, start with the section that fits into a corner, if applicable, and work outward in the same way that the cabinets were installed. The sections of countertop should be joined with connecting bolts that fit into a special slot under the countertop surface (Fig. 8.13). Remember to follow any instructions provided by the countertop fabricator.

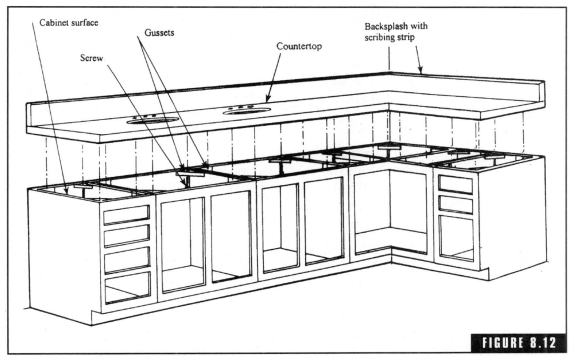

FIGURE 8.12

Attaching the cabinet to the countertop with gussets. *(Leon E. Korejwo, Illustrations.)*

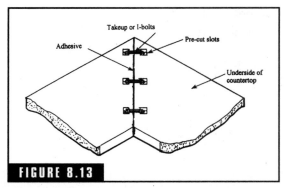

FIGURE 8.13

Take-up bolts. *(Leon E. Korejwo, Illustrations.)*

Backsplashes

Typically, 4-inch (10-cm)-high standard backsplashes are not attached to the wall. Backsplashes, which are not an integral part of the countertop, should be installed after setting the horizontal portion of the countertop. To provide proper alignment, the standard 4-inch (10-cm)-high backsplash is often provided with thin, oval-shaped disks, called "biscuits." These biscuits slide into slots in both the countertop and the backsplash. They are also sometimes used between sections of countertop being joined together to aid in alignment. The backsplash is joined to the countertop surface with the same adhesive used to join sections of the countertop.

Full-height backsplashes, which often extend from the countertop surface to the underside of the wall cabinets, are attached to the wall surface. Solid-surface and laminate materials are adhered directly to the wall surface with an adhesive. Other backsplash materials, such as ceramic tile, are field-assembled and installed. The techniques and types of adhesives for preparing the edges to be joined vary according to the type of countertop material. Closely follow the recommendations provided by the material manufacturers.

Installing Plastic Laminate Countertops

The most critical step with laminate counters is the measuring; order the counters to exact size to minimize cutting on the job site. If possible, as with all countertops, it is best to wait until the base cabinets are installed before taking the measurements. If not possible, order the counters long and cut them after the cabinets are installed and you are able to verify the measurements. As explained earlier, in most instances, most of the work has already been done by the manufacturer. However, if your dealer has a backlog, there may be a delay of several days in the installation, so you may have no choice but to make the order beforehand. In either case, measure the bathroom very carefully, especially from corner to corner and up to window and door openings. If planning to have all the cutouts done for you, provide the exact location and sizes of the sink. Once the countertops arrive, you need only assemble the pieces and attach them to the base cabinets.

Plastic laminate countertop sections have a wood framework already attached to the underside of the countertop. This framework supports the countertop and provides a way to attach the countertop to the base cabinets without screwing into the laminate surface. There are two types of plastic laminated countertops: postformed and self-rimming.

POSTFORMED

Postformed countertops are premolded, one-piece tops, from curved backsplash to bullnosed front (Fig. 8.14). They are bought as blanks in stock sizes, are made to order, and cannot be reshaped because of the forming. Since postformed countertops are manufactured only in standard sizes, you normally need to buy one slightly larger than needed and cut it to length. (To cut the countertop with a handsaw, cut from the top side of the counter. If using a power saw, or any saw that cuts on the upstroke, make the cut from the back side.) If the countertop has an exposed end, you need an endsplash kit that contains a preshaped strip of matching laminate. For a precise fit, the backsplash must be trimmed to fit any unevenness in the back wall (a process called *scribing*). Postformed countertops have a narrow strip of laminate on the backsplash for scribing.

Measure the span of the base cabinets, from corner to outside edge of the cabinet, to determine the size of the counter needed. The standard overhang on a laminate top varies between 3/4 and 1 inch (1.9 and 2.5 cm) in front and on open ends. Add these dimensions to the dimensions of the cabinet.

If you are planning to include an endsplash at one or both ends, check the endsplash kit. Since most endsplashes are assembled directly above the end of the cabinet, generally subtract 3/4 inch (1.9 cm) from the length of the countertop on that side. Endsplashes are assemblies used at the cut or exposed ends of the countertop (Fig. 8.15). They consist of added strips of material called *battens*, which are screwed to the underside of the countertop. The

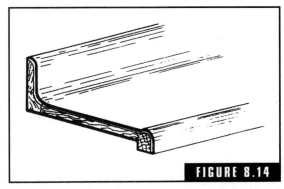

FIGURE 8.14

Postformed countertop. *(Leon E. Korejwo, Illustrations.)*

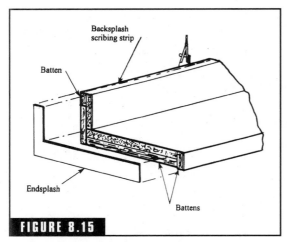

Backsplash
scribing strip

Batten

Endsplash

Battens

FIGURE 8.15

Endsplash kit. *(Leon E. Korejwo, Illustrations.)*

edge is covered by an *end cap,* a preshaped section of laminate joined to the exposed end by silicone sealant or adhesive recommended by the manufacturer. Holding the endsplash in place with C-clamps, drill pilot holes, if needed, and drive in the screws. File the edges of the new strip flush with the top and front edges of the countertop, or use an electric router and laminate-trimming bit.

If you have installed new base cabinets, as explained earlier in this chapter, they should be level. Older cabinets may have settled somewhat. Lay a level at several points along the front, rear, and sides to see if you need to shim under the new countertop or realign the cabinets.

Position the countertop on the base cabinets. Make sure that the front edge of the countertop is parallel to the cabinet face and check for level. It is difficult to adjust drawer alignment once countertops have been fastened in place. Therefore, before installing tops, check drawer alignment in all base cabinets to be sure that drawer fronts meet the face frame evenly all around. All drawers and doors must open and close freely. Test-fit one of the counters to be certain the overhanging front lip does not interfere with the drawers.

If needed, adjust the countertop with wood shims. Remove the countertop. Use a belt sander to grind the backsplash to the scribe line.

If the manufacturer has not already cut out the area for the lavatory, and you are installing a self-rimming lavatory, mark the cutout for the lavatory. Position the lavatory upside down on the countertop and trace an outline. Draw a cutting line $5/8$ inch inside the lavatory outline. Cutouts for the lavatory can be made with the counters out and sitting on sawhorses or after the counters have been installed, provided there is enough clearance within the cabinets for the saw blade to move.

Carefully measure and mark the cutout. Position the metal frame on the countertop, using the lavatory rim as a template or manufacturer's instructions to establish the exact size, and trace an outline around the edge of the vertical flange. Remove the frame. Drill pilot holes just inside the cutting line. Make cutouts with a jigsaw. Support the cutout area from below so that the falling cutout drops down before the cut is finished, ruining the laminate or bending the saw.

Precut laminate and postformed tops have miter joints at their corners. Lay the pieces upside down on a soft surface to prevent scratching them. If the cabinets are U- or L-shaped, you need mitered countertop sections. The mitered sections should have small slots along the bottom edges. They are connected with takeup or draw bolts. Coat the edges with silicone sealant, align them carefully, and tighten the bolts. Fasten the backsplashes together with wood screws. As mentioned earlier, countertops, like cabinets, rarely fit uniformly against the back or side walls because the walls rarely are straight. Use a scribing strip that can be trimmed to the exact contours of the wall. Apply adhesive caulking to the edges of the miters, and press them together. From underneath the cabinet, install and tighten miter-takeup bolts. As always, check the alignment before tightening each bolt. To set the assembled counter in position, you may need assistance. Push the backsplash tightly up against the wall. Temporarily shim underneath if the cabinet tops are not perfectly level. Any high spot (bulge or unevenness) on the wall's surface will create a gap between the wall and backsplash or either side of the bulge.

Measure to be sure that there is at least $34\frac{1}{2}$ inches (88 cm) in height between the underside of the counter and the floor. If the counter is less than $34\frac{1}{2}$ inches (88 cm) above the floor or if its front edge interferes with the operation of drawers, you need to raise the counter with riser blocks: 2-inch-square spacers located about every 8 inches (20 cm) around the perimeter. When the counters are correctly in place, secure them by drilling pilot holes up through the corner braces into the countertop's underside. Be careful that these holes do not penetrate more than two-thirds of the counter's thickness. Finally, drive no. 10 wood screws through the braces into the countertop. To prevent moisture from seeping behind the counter, once the top is secured, run a bead of tile caulking along the joint between the backsplash and wall.

SELF-RIMMED

The term *self-rimmed* simply means that the laminate is applied over an old countertop or new core material (Fig. 8.16). Although postformed countertops are simpler to install, a self-rimmed countertop

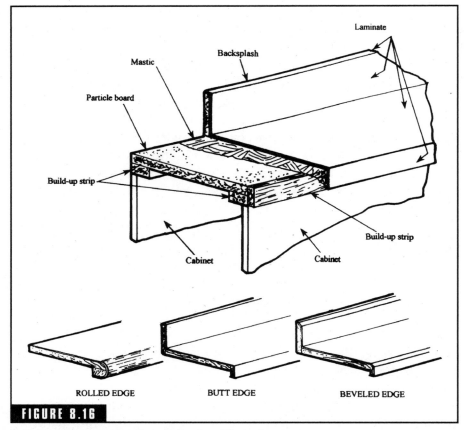

ROLLED EDGE **BUTT EDGE** **BEVELED EDGE**

FIGURE 8.16

Self-rimming laminate. *(Leon E. Korejwo, Illustrations.)*

can be tailored to fit any space and can be customized with a decorative edge treatment. They are made on the job and are easily shaped into curves.

Laminates are sold in lengths of 6, 8, 10, or 12 feet (183, 244, 305, or 366 cm). These laminates are about $1/16$-inch (0.16 cm) thick (standard) and range in width from 30 to 48 inches (76 to 122 cm).

Cut the core material to size from $3/4$-inch (1.9-cm) plywood or high-density particleboard. The perimeter is built up with strips of particleboard screwed to the bottom of the core. Laminate pieces are bonded to the countertop with contact cement. Edges are trimmed and shaped with a router.

Measure along the tops of the base cabinet to determine the size of the countertop. Allow for overhangs by adding 1 inch (2.54 cm) to the length for each exposed end and 1 inch (2.54 cm) to the width.

The substrate surface must be clean, dry, and smooth. Cut 4-inch (10-cm) strips of particleboard for the backsplash and for joint support where sections of countertop core are butted together, and 3-inch (8-cm) strips for edge buildups. Join the countertop core pieces on the bottom side using $1^{1}/4$-inch (3-cm) wallboard screws.

To determine the size of the laminate countertop, measure each surface to be laminated, adding at least $^{1}/4$ to $^{1}/2$ inch (6 mm to 1 cm) to all dimensions to allow for trimming after bonding. Mark and cut the laminate by scoring and breaking it. Place masking tape over the cut line and cut through the tape and laminate; the masking tape prevents chipping. Cut with a fine-toothed saw, face down with a circular or saber saw, face up with a table saw or handsaw.

Build down edges of the core with 1 $\times$ 3 battens. Laminate the countertop, sides, and front strips first, and then the top surface.

Apply contact adhesive to both the laminate back and the substrate to be joined, and allow to dry according to manufacturer's instructions. Check alignment carefully before joining the two; once joined, the laminate cannot be moved. Press the laminate into place and bond with a J-roller.

Trim all the laminate with an electric router flush with core's edge. Where the router can't reach, trim with a file. File all edges smooth with downward strokes to avoid chipping. Make cutouts for the lavatory. Use templates provided to mark the top, make straight cuts, and then radius corner cuts with a router or keyhole saw. Install the lavatory according to manufacturer's instructions. Apply back- and end-splashes as needed. They should be cut from the same core material as the main countertop and butt-joined to the countertop with sealant and wood screws.

Installing Solid-Surface Countertops

Installation of subsurface countertops requires fine tools, care, and expertise. Solid surfaces can be sawed, drilled, and shaped with customary woodworking tools and carbide-tipped blades. To form corners and long countertops, sheets are welded together with color-matched joint adhesive. Some of these materials are sold only to distributors or other qualified firms with trained fabricators on staff. One slip with a saw or router can ruin a very expensive piece of material. It is important to know that many distributors will not sell solid-surface materials unless they do both the fabrication and the installation. They recommend that only factory-trained fabricators install the tops. However, as the bathroom installer, you should be familiar with some key factors.

This type of countertop surface is made from $1/2$-inch (1-cm) solid-surface material. The countertop edges are built up with $3/4$-inch (1.9-cm) solid-surface strips attached with special joint adhesive (Fig. 8.17). Prior to installation, blocks are usually bonded to the surface of the tops with silicone on either side of the joint. A notching-joint adhesive is applied to the joint, and clamps are then slipped over the blocks and tightened. After the joint has set, the blocks are pried off and the joint area is sanded smooth. Cutouts can be cut with a scroll or saber saw, especially where curves are needed, or a portable circular saw for straight cuts. The edge is then shaped with a router, and the surface is smoothed with sandpaper. The $1/2$ inch (1 cm) thickness must be continuously supported by the cabinet frame or closely spaced plywood blocks.

Unsupported overhangs should be kept to a minimum. A maximum overhang of 6 inches (15 cm) for a $1/2$-inch (1-cm)-thick sheet or 12 inches (30 cm) for a $3/4$-inch (1.9-cm)-thick sheet is recommended. For more than that, add corbels or other additional support.

To install the top, attach three 1×3-inch (2.54×8-cm) wood strips to the cabinets for the length of the run. Install cross-supports to frame

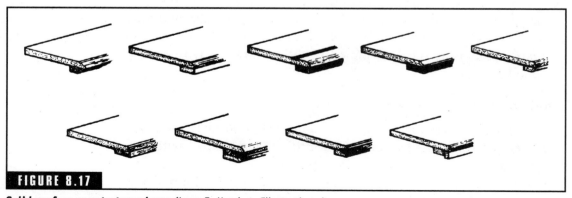

FIGURE 8.17

Solid-surface countertop edges. *(Leon E. Korejwo, Illustrations.)*

each cutout and to support each seam. Run a bead of neoprene adhesive along the top of the frame and on any supports. A full-height backsplash of solid surface should be installed before the top is installed; it is placed behind the top. The backsplash is attached to the wall with panel adhesive and sealed with silicone caulk. A standard backsplash should sit on top of the countertop, affixed with silicone sealant, and must be sealed to the top, not to the wall.

When installing a solid-surface top between walls, allow 1/8 inch (0.32 cm) for expansion every 10 feet (304.8 cm). The countertop can be edged with wood trim, strips of solid-surface material, or a combination thereof.

Tiling a Countertop

Of all the countertop options, ceramic tile is the longest-lasting. Problems with the tiles themselves are rare. Most tile countertop problems stem from improper installation of the underlying decking material. A ceramic-tile countertop installation is only as good as what is installed below the tile surface. Although stated many times before, the cabinets must be level and plumb and the substrate set level as well. If this is not done, the backsplash grout will not be straight.

Tiling a countertop does not necessarily require the services of a professional tile setter. The most common choice for countertops is glazed ceramic tile. Wall tiles—which are lighter and thinner than floor tiles—are the normal choice for countertops and backsplashes. A variety of sizes and thicknesses are available. Ceramic tiles are available individually, or connected with mesh backing to form mosaic sheets. Do not use pregrouted sheets of tiles. This type may contain a mildewcide that is not FDA-approved for food-preparation areas. A client who invests in ceramic tile expects it to last, which means that it must be properly installed. Proper planning promotes a quality installation and reduces time and labor spent.

Ceramic-tile countertops are installed directly on a deck or substrate by one of two installation methods: mastic (organic adhesive) or conventional mortar bed (mud).

Mastic

With the mastic method, generally referred to as a *thin-set installation,* tile is directly applied to the substrate material with troweled-on mastic (Fig. 8.18). The surface is raised only by the thickness of the

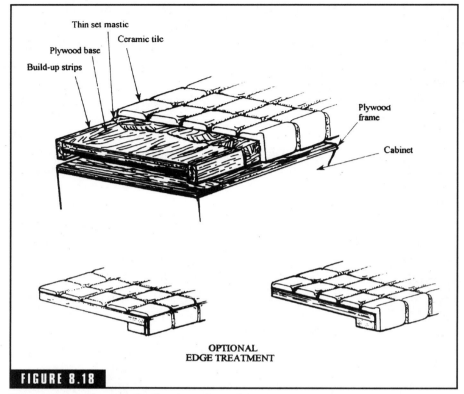

FIGURE 8.18

Thin-set method—ceramic tile. *(Leon E. Korejwo, Illustrations.)*

tile. A mastic installation may use any of the following base surfaces: existing tile, gypsum board, fiberglass, wood, paneling, brick, masonry, concrete, plywood, or vinyl—virtually any sturdy surface, as long as the surface is structurally sound, level, and moisture-free. However, most countertop installations are done over plywood. A mastic installation does not hide any dips or bows in the substrate material; any imperfections will show up in the finished tile installation.

For an installation using mastic on plywood, before laying tile, remove any old countertops; then install an underlayment of $3/4$-inch (1.9-cm) exterior-grade plywood, cut flush with the cabinet top, screwing it to the cabinet frame from below. If the cabinets were installed correctly, the plywood top should be level. If it is not, shims can be placed on top of the cabinets to level the decking. Test-fit a piece of cap tile on the front edge of the plywood to be certain that drawers and fixtures will clear the tile. If they don't, block under the plywood as necessary to raise it. Make all necessary cutouts in the decking for lavatories, and test-fit them for accuracy. Double-check that the decking is level and secure and that the cut ends of the decking around any openings are adequately supported to carry the weight of the lavatory. Because bathroom surfaces are exposed to moisture, use moisture-resistant adhesive, followed by a layer of cement backerboard on top, and glazed tiles. Surfaces may need to be primed or sealed before tile is applied.

CONVENTIONAL MORTAR BED (MUD)

For many years, the standard installation method was to first lay a thick, level mortar base, allow it to dry, and then adhere the tile to that base. Traditional decking is often used to provide flexibility under the tile. In this method, the tile is installed on a bed of mortar $3/4$ to $1^1/4$ inches (1.9 to 3.2 cm) thick. This procedure is still the method preferred by professional tile setters; however, perfectly acceptable results can be obtained working with adhesive over a plywood base (Fig. 8.19). With this method of installation, the countertop height is raised to the thickness of the tile and the mortar bed.

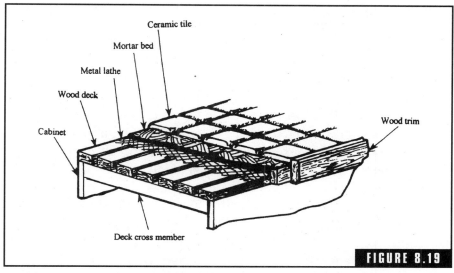

Mortar method—ceramic tile. (*Leon E. Korejwo, Illustrations.*)

For *surface preparation,* the wood base is installed over the top of the base cabinets on which the tile rests; this is called the *deck.* Its proper installation is essential for a good job. Solid decking and careful planning and layout are the keys, along with selecting the proper materials for each particular job.

For a mortar-base installation, the decking is done with grade 1 or grade 2, kiln-dried, 1 × 4- or 1 × 6-inch (2.54 × 10 or 2.54 × 15-cm) Douglas fir. The decking boards can be applied either parallel or perpendicular to the face of the cabinets, with a spacing of about ¼ inch (0.64 cm) between the boards. Fasten the boards securely to the tops of the cabinets, using screws (preferred) or ring shank nails. Plywood should be avoided as a decking under mortar-base tile. However, its use is necessary in some cases, such as on wide overhangs. The decking should be delivered to the project site several days before the installation to allow the wood to reach the relative humidity of the room. The decking should overhang the cabinets and should be flush with the face of the drawers and doors. Fixture cutouts are made during the tile-decking installation. Actually place the fixture in the cutout to ensure a proper fit. When possible, any cutout should be a minimum of 2 inches (5.08 cm) away from a wallboard or plastered backsplash.

Before you start laying the tile, you must decide how you want to trim the countertop edge and the lavatory. Ceramic tile is available with several edge trim options—for the lavatory area, install sink cap tiles that have a raised edge to prevent water from dripping on the floor. In some installations, wood furring strips are used to frame the tile surface. If using wood trim, seal the wood and attach it to the cabinet face with finishing nails. When in place, the wood strip's top edge should be positioned at the same height as the finished tile.

Trim pieces are available with a ¾-inch (2-cm) radius for conventional mortar installations and a ¼-inch (0.64-cm) radius for organic-adhesive installations. These trims are generally more expensive than field tile.

Elimination of stress is critical when countertop overhangs are planned. The tile must have a solid base. If any movement occurs when pressure is placed on the top, the tile or grout will crack. The underside of the decking should be finished to match the cabinets or correspond with other products used in the project. The wall backing up the ceramic-tile backsplash must be solid.

To support the top, install cross-braces measuring either 1 × 2 inches (2.5 × 5 cm) on edge or 2 × 4 inches (2.5 × 10 cm) laid flat. Do not place the braces more than 3 feet (0.91 m) apart. Drill two pilot holes, evenly spaced, into each brace. Then, working from below, screw each brace to the top. To hold an apron or other drip-edge trim, nail a 2 × 2-inch (5 × 5-cm) furring strip to the front edge of the top. This strip will also be covered with tile.

DRY TILE LAYOUT

Carefully lay out the tiles on the top to determine the best location for the cuts. Dry-laying tiles shows how many tiles are needed and which tiles must be cut to fit and to make sure that the finish layout is pleasing to the eye.

The row that falls between the edge trim and the last full row of field tile is cut to fit. Work from the front to the back so that cut tiles are the last row, with the cut edge against the back wall. Find the center point of the area and snap perpendicular chalk lines through it to divide the space to be tiled into equal quarters. Check the intersection of the angles to make sure that they are perfectly square.

Lay out one vertical row and one horizontal row in a quarter, allowing for even grout lines. If the end tiles are less than one-half a tile wide, reposition the vertical centerline. Pieces smaller than one-half the width of a tile are difficult to cut. When possible, try to position cut tiles in an inconspicuous area. Measuring from end to end, locate and mark the center of the countertop. Lay the edge tiles out on the countertop, starting from the mark.

To allow for grout lines, some tiles have small ceramic lugs molded onto their edges to keep spacing equal; if not, use plastic spacers. Use a carpenter's square to check that the courses are straight. Carefully position the rest of the field tiles on the countertop. Observing the layout, make any necessary adjustments to eliminate narrow cuts or difficult fits.

If the countertop has a backsplash or turns a corner, be sure to figure the cove or corner tiles into the layout. Mark reference points of the layout on the plywood base; then remove the tile.

PLACING THE TRIM AND SETTING THE TILE

Set all trim tiles before spreading adhesive for the field tiles. Keep the dry-laid tiles in place while you adhere the edge trim along the front of the lip. Use the countertop tiles to maintain the spacing you have decided on. With a notched trowel, apply adhesive (thin-set adhesive mixed with latex additive is water-resistant and easy to use) along the front edge of the furring strip. Then cover the backs of the tiles with adhesive and press into place, aligning them with the reference marks. Next apply adhesive to any back cove tiles and set them against the wall. With the edge complete, install any trim tiles for the lavatory openings or corners. Be sure to caulk between the lavatory and the base before setting the trim.

Next, spread adhesive over a section of the countertop with a notched trowel. Begin laying the field tiles, working from front to back. The installation will begin at the center point and progress outward, one quarter at a time. Cut tiles to fit as necessary. As you lay the tiles, check the alignment frequently with a carpenter's square. Mark and cut all partial tiles prior to applying any adhesive. Doing so saves time because you can then tile in one uninterrupted operation. Press firmly so that only beads of adhesive from the trowel notches (forming ridges for better adhesion) are evident on the surface. Spread no more adhesive than you can cover before it starts to harden. If the adhesive starts to skin over before you have a chance to lay the tile, scrape it off and apply new adhesive. Periodically check to see that all joints are straight and even.

Place the first tile at the intersection of the lines. Press into position with a slight twisting motion to ensure a good bond. To set the tiles and level their faces into the adhesive, use a block of cloth-covered plywood over them and gently tap the scrap with a hammer. Lay all the full tiles and leave spaces for the cut tiles.

In the case of a lavatory set parallel to the wall, work from the center of the lavatory toward the ends of the top. An L-shaped countertop with a corner lavatory must be handled differently from other settings. Since there is no way to avoid very odd cuts of tile around the lavatory, work from the ends of each leg of the top toward the lavatory opening.

Because of variations in wall runs, each tile should be butted, measured, and cut individually, rather than taking a single measurement and cutting a number of tiles at once. To make straight cuts, place the tile face up in the tile cutter to score a continuous line on the tile; then press down on the cutter's handle to snap the tile. Smooth the cut edges of tile with a tile sander. To cut irregular or curved lines, score a crosshatch outline of the cut with a tile scoring tool. Use tile nippers to gradually break away small portions of the tile until cutout is complete.

Bullnose tiles, which have rounded edges, are used to cover edges of the countertop and backsplash. Use them to finish off the side-wall installation, creating a smooth, round edge. Backsplash tiles can be installed over a separate plywood core or directly to the wall behind the countertop.

TILING THE BACKSPLASH

If the backsplash area is to be tiled, it must be patched and solid. To set the backsplash, begin one grout joint space above the cove tiles or countertop tiles. Cover the area with adhesive. Also, for a better grip, cover the back of each tile, and set the tiles in place. If desired, finish off the backsplash top edge with trim pieces, or continue tiling up to the undersides of the wall cabinets or window sill. Run a wide strip of masking tape along the underside of the front trim tiles to keep the grout from dripping out before it has a chance to set up. Also mask any surrounding wood surfaces to protect them from grout stains. Turn off the circuit breaker, or remove the fuse in the line that feeds any light switch or fixture before setting tiles around it.

APPLYING THE GROUT

Before grouting, make sure that adhesive is set and tiles are held firmly in place. Grout lines can be as thin as $1/16$ inch (0.16 cm) and up to $3/8$ inch (0.95 cm) or more. These lines look better with small tiles, while $1/4$-inch (0.635-cm) lines look better with larger tiles (i.e., 6 inches square).

Carefully remove any spacers and clean the tile surface and grout joints until free of adhesive. Joint depth should be at least two-thirds the thickness of the tile. Check to see that all tiles are level. Wait at least 24 hours for the tile to set. Work the grout diagonally across the grout lines to fill the tiles completely. Mix the grout and apply it with grouting trowel, working at an angle to the grout lines. Once the grout has set, use a damp sponge to remove any excess grout. Caulk the seams between the tile and the lavatory. After the grout has dried, approximately 24 hours later, thoroughly wipe (in a diagonal direction) the tile with a soft, lightly dampened sponge. Lightly buff the tile to a shine.

Grouting procedures are the same for mastic or mortared tile. Grout is porous and can absorb moisture and stains. After installation, seal the tile and grout with a quality silicone sealer to prevent water damage. Sealing it prevents this absorption and should be periodically reapplied.

Installing Natural-Stone Countertops

Traditionally, marble used for countertops is supplied in large slabs. Suppliers differ on the size and thickness of countertops that they stock. Many slabs are available in thicknesses of $1^1/4$ inches (3.18 cm). Other suppliers, however, stock $3/4$-inch-(2-cm)-thick countertops. Some carry $1^1/2$-inch-(3.81-cm)-thick slabs. The appearance of a $1^1/2$-inch (3.81-cm)-thick counter can be achieved by joining the $3/4$-inch-(2-cm)-thick counter to a $3/4$-inch (2-cm) edge treatment in much the same manner as solid-surface countertops are constructed. The pieces of marble can be glued together so that the seam is unnoticeable. For proper installation of natural stones, specialized tools and skills are required.

Installation of Fixtures

The installation and connection of major fixtures is one of the final tasks in the installation process. Because they are difficult to work around and can easily be damaged, it is best to keep fixtures out of the bathroom area as long as possible. Connection requirements, of course, vary according to the type of fixture and its features. Manufacturer-supplied instructions usually describe the installation process at length and should be followed closely.

The installation of countertops and fixtures happens near the end of the bathroom installation. However, it is extremely important to plan for these installations early on in the project. All the necessary clearances, cutouts, and rough-ins must have been determined and provided for well before the installation. If subcontractors are needed to return to the job site to assist with final hookups and connections of plumbing fixtures, be sure to have planned ahead and scheduled for their visits. These details are all critical to the timely completion of the project. Mistakes at this point in the project (such as having to order additional cabinets) are very costly for you, as well as disturbing to your client. Although situations do occur, with proper planning, the majority of problems can be avoided.

Appliance Delivery Inspections

At the time it is accepted from the carrier, the installer should carefully inspect the unit for visual, as well as concealed, transportation damage. File a damage claim immediately with the carrier's claim agent if visual damage is evident; transportation damage is the responsibility of the carrier. It is important that the claim agent see both the appliance and the crate it arrived in.

The exterior finish of most bathroom appliances, with proper usage, lasts indefinitely. However, some are more fragile to impact and bending strains than others (e.g., porcelain). Therefore, all appliances should be uncrated and moved with extreme care. The appliance is usually packaged in a carton-type crate and fastened to a wood base by four shipping bolts (the range-leveling feet). Cut the bottom metal band, then lift the carton off the appliance. With the appliance on its back, remove the wood base, and install the leveling feet. Careful handling of the appliances in the user's home is also very important since most bathroom floorcoverings scratch easily.

Most appliances are supplied with manufacturers' installation instructions; therefore, in all cases, be sure to read and abide by them. The following information is based on general conditions. Some fixtures may require other installation procedures.

Lavatory Installations

Before you begin, unpack the new lavatory and inspect it carefully for damage. Immediately notify the distributor of any damage. Replace the lavatory in its original packing carton to protect it until you are ready to begin the installation.

A bathroom lavatory must be installed in accordance with local plumbing codes. In remodeling work, the location of existing plumbing is important in deciding where to place the lavatory in the new bathroom. Unless the remodeling plans call for a new vent stack, the lavatory should be located within the limits of the existing stack. One way of increasing the distance between the lavatory trap and the vent stack is to increase the drain-line pipe size. Often, depending on the job, it's easier to install the faucet before mounting the sink in the cabinet.

As described in Chap. 6, a variety of bathroom lavatories are available. Each has its own method of installation. Therefore, before beginning, read the manufacturer's instructions. The procedure for installing a sink depends partly on what the counter is made of and partly on the type of sink being installed. With laminate countertops, install the counter first, then make a cutout for the sink. With a tile counter, make the cutout and, in some cases, install the sink before tiling.

If you can handle the installation, it saves the time and expense of scheduling the plumber to come back to the job again. If you must use a plumber, carefully schedule the work to avoid delays in completing the job. If you have an integral sink that is a part of the countertop, or if the sink was undermounted by the countertop fabricator in the shop, all that is left to do is hook up the plumbing. Check to make sure that all holes or cutouts required for installation of the faucet and any other accessory items have been made before you schedule the plumber.

INSTALLATION OF WALL-HUNG LAVATORIES

If installing a wall-hung lavatory, the first step is to install the wall bracket; the bracket is screwed to the wall. A piece of wood backing should have been installed in the wall during the rough-in. Refer to the fixture instructions for the proper height of the bracket; usually an inch or two below the finished sink height is sufficient. Check that the back wall of the sink is level. To support a (single or double) bracket solidly, provide a horizontal 1×8-inch (2.54×20.32 cm) board firmly anchored to two studs and embedded flush with the wall behind where bracket will be. When the bracket is properly installed, the lavatory is simply hung on it (or them) against the wall. Press down on the back rim of the bowl to seat it onto the bracket. Some models will have flanges and holes below the lavatory to allow the installation of extra screws. These screws are a safety precaution to prevent the lavatory from being knocked off the bracket.

INSTALLATION OF PEDESTAL LAVATORIES

Pedestal lavatories tend to be a bit more difficult to install than others. The bowl is mounted to a wall bracket, just like a wall-hung lavatory. Be sure to provide suitable reinforcement behind the finished wall for the lavatory anchor screws (Fig. 8.20a). Determine the horizontal center-line location of support from the fixture (Fig. 8.20b).

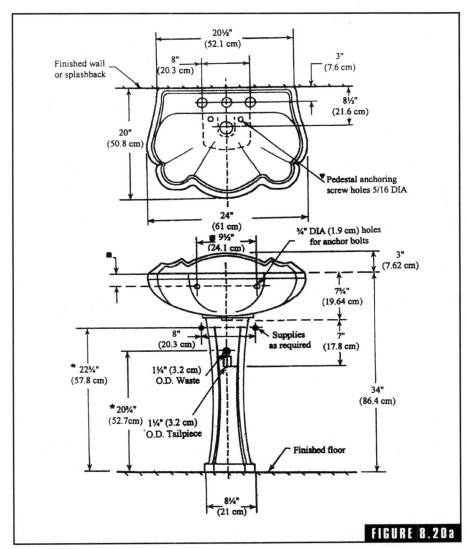

Manufacturer's rough-in drawing for a pedestal lavatory. *(American Standard.)*

Note: If replacing an existing lavatory, be certain to shut off water supply before removing the old lavatory.

Next, place the lavatory and pedestal into the installed position, the pedestal is placed under the bowl to hide piping and to help support the bowl. Level and square the lavatory and pedestal assembly. Use one or more bumper cushions to level and cushion the lavatory

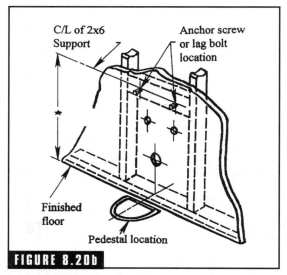

FIGURE 8.20b

Provide suitable reinforcement in wall for pedestal lavatory installation. *(American Standard.)*

slab to the pedestal (Fig. 8.20*c*). Mark the lavatory and pedestal screw locations through the mounting holes. Remove the lavatory and pedestal from the installed position. Drill pilot holes for the lavatory and pedestal anchor screws or lag bolts. For an anchor screw installation, install lavatory anchor screws leaving $1\frac{7}{8}$ inches (4.78 cm) threaded and exposed (Fig. 8.20*d*). For lag bolt installation, use lag bolts to secure the lavatory (Fig. 8.20*e*).

Following manufacturer's instructions, install the faucet-and-drain assembly (see "A" on Fig. 8.20*f*). Be certain to apply a bead of sealing putty on the underside of the drain in order to ensure a watertight seal between the lavatory and drain. Remove excess putty after installing the drain on the lavatory. Return the fitted lavatory and pedestal to the installed position. Connect the trap to the drain assembly hand tight to check alignment. It may be necessary to cut off part of the tailpiece (see "B" on Fig. 8.20*g*) or part of the horizontal leg of the trap (see "C" on Fig. 8.20*g*). Secure the lavatory to the wall as illustrated in Fig. 8.20(*d* and *e*). Install washers and hand-tighten the nuts or lag bolts. Level and square the unit. Connect

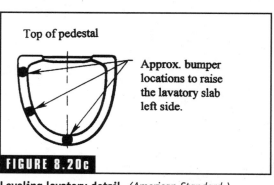

FIGURE 8.20c

Leveling lavatory detail. *(American Standard.)*

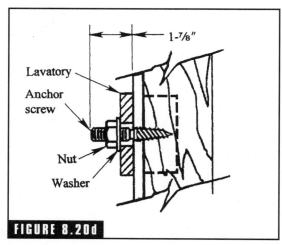

FIGURE 8.20d

Anchor screw installation. *(American Standard.)*

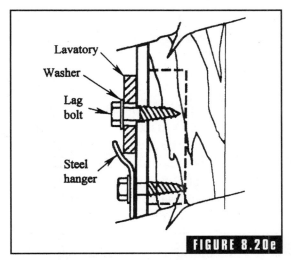

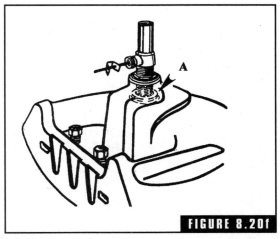

Lag bolt installation. *(American Standard.)*

Attaching drain assembly to bowl. *(American Standard.)*

the hot and cold supply lines to the shutoff valves. Tighten trap joints for watertight assembly (Fig. 8.20*h*). At this point, install the pedestal screws. Securely tighten the lavatory anchor nuts or lag bolts.

The complicated part of a pedestal sink is when making the trap and supply connections. There is very little room to work and a minor miscalculation will ruin the effect of the pedestal. Some pedestals have a hole in the base to allow you to screw them to the floor. Others depend on the weight of the bowl to hold the pedestal in place. With any of these specialty fixtures, refer to the installation instructions and rough-in book.

INSTALLATION OF COUNTERTOP LAVATORIES

1. *Self-rimming.* If making a cutout is necessary (e.g., if the basin is not an integral part of the countertop or the countertop piece wasn't ordered with the cutout already made), locate the position of the lavatory. Provide proper clearance under the countertop for the faucet supply lines, drain assembly, and the structural parts of the cabinet. If self-rimming, turn upside down and trace perimeter of the lavatory. The template provided by the supplier can be used. Determine the dimensions of the cutout from the basin or the manufacturer's instructions. Drill a clearance hole ½ inch (1.27 cm) inside the perimeter line of the lavatory. Cut an

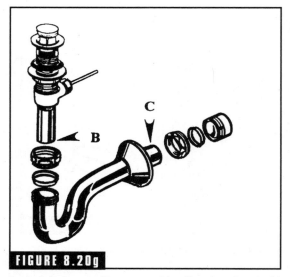

FIGURE 8.20g

Drain tailpiece and trap assembly. *(American Standard.)*

opening $^1/_2$ inch (1.27 cm) inside the perimeter of the lavatory. If your basin is metal rimmed, lay the metal trim over the countertop and use it as a template to mark the cutout. The faucet-and-drain assembly should be mounted on the lavatory following the faucet manufacturer's instructions. Be certain to apply a bead of sealing putty on the underside of the drain in order to ensure a watertight seal between the lavatory and the drain. Remove excess putty after installing the drain on the lavatory. Before applying the sealant, place the lavatory temporarily into the cutout. Check for alignment and clearance. Then mark the lavatory and countertop in several places as a guide for the installation location. Again, after checking fit and alignment, turn the lavatory upside down and apply a generous portion of sealant around the underside of the rim, near the edge. Carefully lower the lavatory into place, align with marks made earlier, and press down firmly. Remove excess sealant for a smooth even line of sealant around the edge of the lavatory. Allow the sealant to set before connecting supplies and drain. At this point, connect the supply line to the faucet (fingertight) and carefully bend tubes to engage with the supply shutoff valves. Tighten all the connections at the faucet and shutoff valves for a secure seal. Connect the trap to the drain assembly hand tight to check alignment. It may be necessary to cut off part of the tailpiece or part of the horizontal leg of the trap. Finally, secure joints for watertight assembly.

2. *Mounting-frame lavatories (steel-rimmed).* When locating the cutout for the lavatory, follow the mounting frame manufacturer's instructions for proper clearances. Most frames require 1-inch (2.54-cm) clearance on all sides for installing the frame clips. Always use the lavatory-mounting frame as a template for marking the cutout.

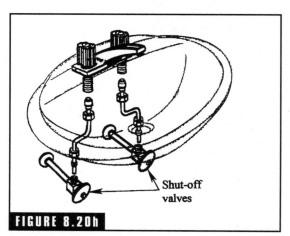

FIGURE 8.20h

Connection of hot and cold supply lines. *(American Standard.)*

Place the frame on the countertop face up in the exact installation location. Provide proper clearance under the countertop for the faucet lines and the structural parts of the cabinet. Draw a guideline around the outside edge of the vertical leg of the frame (not the outer edge of the frame). Drill a clearance hole on the inside edge of the cutout line. Using a saber saw, carefully make the lavatory cutout. Mount the faucet-and-drain assembly on the lavatory following the faucet manufacturer's instructions. Be certain to apply a bead of sealing putty on the underside of the drain in order to ensure a watertight seal between the lavatory and the drain. Remove any excess putty after installing the drain on the lavatory. Using plumber's putty, place a bead around both the inside and outside edge of the mounting frame. Attach the mounting frame to the lavatory following manufacturers' instructions. Most frames are secured to the lavatory by bending tabs with a screwdriver around the edge of the lavatory. Lower the lavatory and frame into the cutout. Check for alignment. From underneath, hook the mounting fasteners to the mounting frame. Begin with one fastener in the middle of each side and position the balance uniformly around the frame. Tighten the fasteners evenly and firmly until the mounting frame is seated with no gaps. Be careful not to overtighten, as this could damage the lavatory or mounting frame. Wipe off excess plumbers' putty on the countertop. Connect the supply lines to the faucet (fingertight) and carefully bend tubes to engage with the supply shutoff valves. Tighten connections at the faucet and shutoff valves for a tight, secure seal. Connect the drain assembly hand tight to check for alignment. It may be necessary to cut off part of the tailpiece or part of the horizontal leg of the trap. Secure joint for watertight assembly. If you have an integral lavatory which is a part of the countertop, or if the lavatory was undermounted by the countertop fabricator in the shop, all that is left to do is hook up the plumbing. Check to make sure that all holes or cutouts required for installation of the faucet and any other accessory items have been made before you schedule the plumber. When using a top with the bowl already molded into it, all you have to do is place the top on the cabinet. The lavatory bowl is an integral part of the countertop and requires no additional installation.

FAUCET AND DRAIN HOOKUPS

Before lowering the lavatory into the opening, it is a good idea to make the faucet and drain-assembly hookups. Faucets sometimes come with the lavatory; other times only holes are punched in the lavatory so that faucets can be purchased separately. There are many different styles of faucets available—standard two-faucet types, single-lever types, color-coordinated faucets, and so on. Other attachments such as sprays and hot-water dispensers may also be installed in the lavatory unit.

Roughing in a Toilet

The toilet bend and toilet floor flange must be roughed in first, as shown in Fig. 8.21*a*; the floor flange must then be positioned at the level of the eventual finished floor (otherwise you could be faced with a toilet that leaks at its base), as shown. Pipes that are required for roughing in a toilet include $1/2$-inch riser tube, a cold-water-supply stubout with shutoff valve, and a flexible riser tube above the shutoff valve.

Installing a toilet or bidet is not very complicated, especially when the plumbing is already in place. During major remodeling involving the floor or walls, remember that toilets and bidets are the first fixtures to remove and the last to install.

The amount of work needed to install a new toilet depends on whether it will be in a new location. Hooking up a toilet in a new location is a challenging project because you must extend supply, drain, and vent pipes. Replacing an old fixture with a new one at the same location is a simple procedure (Fig. 8.21*b*). The only crucial dimension you need to check on a new toilet is its roughing-in size: the distance from the wall to the center of the drainpipe [most are 12 inches (30.48 cm)].

You can usually determine roughing-in size before removing the old bowl—just measure from the wall to one of the two hold-down bolts that secure the bowl to the floor. (If the bowl has four hold-down bolts, measure to one of the rear bolts.) The new toilet's roughing-in size can be shorter than that of the fixture you are replacing, but if it's longer, the new toilet won't fit.

Once you've determined that the fixture will fit, it's time to install it.

Installation of a Toilet

These installation instructions are generic in nature and are for general information only. Refer to installation instructions packed

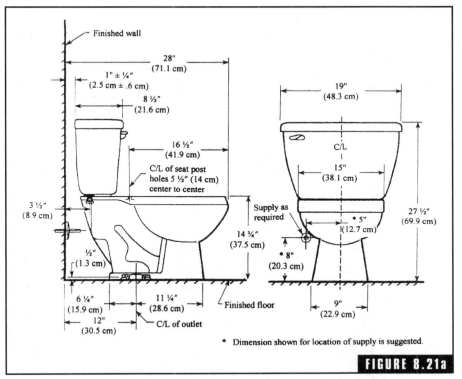

FIGURE 8.21a

Manufacturer's rough-in details of a two-piece toilet. *(American Standard.)*

with the product for more detailed information. When mounting the toilet, the center of the floor drain and floor flange should be 12 inches (305 mm) from the rear wall. Install closet bolts in flange channel, turn 90°, and slide into place 6 inches (152 mm) apart and parallel to the wall (Fig. 8.21c).

Note: If replacing an existing toilet, be certain to shut off the water supply before removing the old toilet.

Using a closet flange for plastic pipe, apply plastic cement to inside of the flange and outside of closet bend. Insert closet bolts through the round end of slot. Slide the flange over closet bend and rotate flange to position the bolts along centerline of the drain. Screw the flange to the flooring using round holes. Invert the toilet on the floor (cushion to prevent damage), and install wax ring evenly around the waste flange (horn), with tapered end of the ring facing the toilet. Apply a thin bead

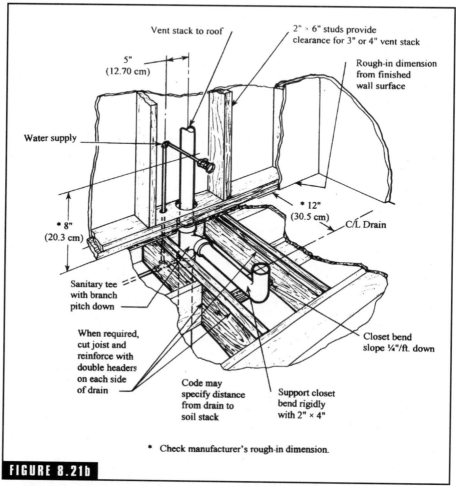

Vent stack to roof

2" × 6" studs provide
clearance for 3" or 4" vent stack

5"
(12.70 cm)

Rough-in dimension
from finished
wall surface

Water supply

* 12"
(30.5 cm)

C/L Drain

* 8"
(20.3 cm)

Sanitary tee
with branch
pitch down

Closet bend
slope ¼"/ft. down

When required,
cut joist and
reinforce with
double headers
on each side
of drain

Code may
specify distance
from drain to
soil stack

Support closet
bend rigidly
with 2" × 4"

* Check manufacturer's rough-in dimension.

FIGURE 8.21b

Plumbing details for toilet installation. *(Leon E. Korejwo, Illustrations.)*

of sealant around the base flange (Fig. 8.21*d*). To position the toilet on the flange, unplug the floor waste opening and install the toilet on the closet flange so the bolts project through mounting holes. Loosely install retainer washers and nuts. Side of washers, as are marked, must face in "up" position (Fig. 8.21*e*).

To install the toilet, position the toilet squarely to the wall and, with a rocking motion, press the bowl firmly down fully on the wax ring and flange. Alternately tighten nuts until the toilet is firmly seated on the floor. Be cautious and DO NOT overtighten the nuts or base may be damaged. Install the caps on the washers. If necessary, cut bolt height to size before installing the caps. Smooth off the bead of sealant around the base. Remove execess sealant.

INSTALLING THE TOILET TANK (NOT REQUIRED FOR ONE-PIECE TOILETS)

To install the tank, install the large rubber gasket over threaded outlet on bottom of the tank and lower the tank onto the bowl so that the tapered end of the gasket fits evenly into the bowl water inlet opening. Insert tank-mounting bolts and rubber washers from inside tank, through mounting holes, and secure with metal washers and nuts (Fig. 8.21f). With the tank parallel to the wall, alternately tighten nuts until the tank is snugged down evenly against the bowl surface. Again, DO NOT overtighten the nuts more than required for a snug fit.

Connect a flexible supply tube to the water control shank, and hand tighten. Connect the other end with the supply shut-off valve. Tighten the connections at the shut-off valve and water control shank. Inside the tank, insert the refill tube into the overflow tube through the small hole on top of the tube. Open the shut-off valve slowly and check for watertight connections. Set to indicated water level inside tank by adjusting the water-level screw. Set flow rate for tank to fill in 30–60 seconds by adjusting flow-rate screw (Fig. 8.21g). Finally, open the stop valve, fill the tank with water, flush the toilet, and check for leaks.

Installation of a Bidet

A bidet is usually installed next to the toilet and is floor-mounted with hold-down bolts. Before you plan to install a bidet in

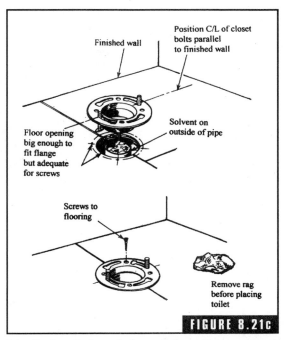

Installation of closet bolts and closet flange. *(American Standard/Leon E. Korejwo, Illustrations.)*

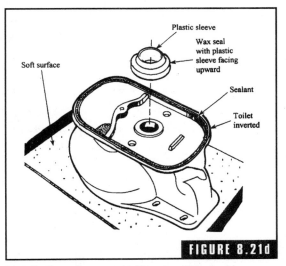

Installation of wax seal. *(American Standard.)*

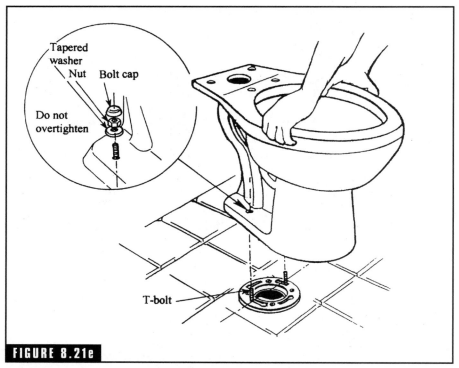

FIGURE 8.21e

Position of toilet bowl on closet flange. *(American Standard.)*

the bathroom, you must be certain enough room exists and that access is available for the under-floor plumbing. Drain plumbing is set up just like that for a toilet; however, unlike a toilet, the bidet has a sink-type drain and trap and is plumbed to include both hot and cold water-supply lines.

When hooking up a new bidet in an existing location and planning to use the existing floor bolts, the distance between bolt holes must be the same as for the original fixture. It is also important that new bidet fittings be compatible with the existing water-supply and drain lines. When installing the bidet in a new location, plan on needing to extend water-supply pipes and drainpipes.

After you have unpacked the new bidet, place the fixture's drain opening directly over the drainpipe. When you are installing a new bidet rather than replacing an existing one, use the holes in the bidet's flange as guides to mark the locations for the hold-down bolts on the floor. Once complete, remove the bidet, drill holes appropriately sized for the bolts, and screw the bolts through the floor. Turn the bidet upside down and apply plumber's putty around the bottom edge.

As with toilet installation, remove the rag from the drainpipe and set the bidet back in position, using the bolts as guides. Level the bidet, from side to side and from front to back. If necessary, use brass or copper washers to shim beneath the bottom edge; or shimming it may be necessary to reseal the fixture to the floor. Hand-tighten washers and nuts onto the hold-down bolts; you will tighten them further after the plumbing connections are made. If applicable, connect the pop-up drain assembly.

Connect the drain and the two water-supply lines. Once all connections are made, use a wrench to tighten the nuts on these lines, as well as the nuts on the hold-down bolts. Don't overtighten the hold-down bolts, or you will crack the fixture. Fill the caps with plumber's putty and place them over the nuts on the bidet flange. Turn on the water and check for leaks.

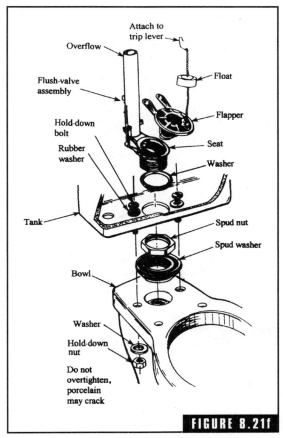

FIGURE 8.21f

Installation of tank and flush valve. *(American Standard/Leon E. Korejwo, Illustrations.)*

Installation of a Bathtub

A bathtub is the only fixture that should be installed before the walls and floors are finished. Always check local building codes for support requirements prior to installing a tub in a new location. A bathtub filled with water is extremely heavy and needs plenty of support. Also check the plumbing code requirements for extending the water-supply and drain-waste-vent (DWV) systems. When replacing an existing bathtub, carefully inspect the subfloor for moisture damage and level; make any necessary repairs or adjustments. When installing a tub in a new location, the framing and rough-in of plumbing will be done first; bathtubs are installed during the rough-in stage of the job.

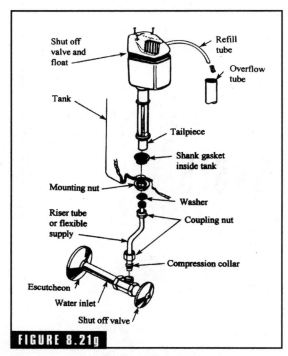

Shut off valve and float

Refill tube

Overflow tube

Tank

Tailpiece

Shank gasket inside tank

Mounting nut

Washer

Riser tube or flexible supply

Coupling nut

Compression collar

Escutcheon

Water inlet

Shut off valve

FIGURE 8.21g

Connecting water supply and shutoff valve. *(American Standard/Leon E. Korejwo, Illustrations.)*

Carefully uncrate and inspect your new bath for any shipping damage. If such damage is found, report it immediately. After inspection and during installation, protect the bath from construction damage. After installation, and before enclosing with wallboard, tile, and other materials water-test the unit and check for leaks. If a whirlpool, do not make modifications to the whirlpool system or remove pump from the factor mounting. This could adversely affect the safety and performance of the whirlpool and void the warranty. Do not handle or move the whirlpool by the pump, motor, or piping system.

Mechanical Systems

A bathroom builder must be familiar with the mechanical systems, such as plumbing; gas; electrical; heating, ventilation, and air-conditioning (HVAC). Generally, you use trained subcontractors (most likely required by local building code) for much of this work; however, as the builder, you need to have a clear understanding to accurately plan, coordinate, and install a bathroom. If you are not a licensed plumber, electrician, or other specialist, where codes allow, you should have the knowledge and ability to disconnect and tear out plumbing fixtures and electrical outlets (do all wall opening and other rough work) in order to streamline the installation process for the subcontractor. It is important to always have a plumbing plan to help determine the type and quantity of each fitting required, whether only adding a single faucet or planning a major remodeling project. When planning any plumbing addition, you must balance the limitations of the existing system's layout, design considerations, your own plumbing abilities, and most importantly, code restrictions.

Bathroom Plumbing

The most fundamental of all bathroom elements is the plumbing system; however, home plumbing is neither mysterious nor overly complicated. The plumbing system of the home provides a means of bringing water to an outlet and a means of taking used water away with consideration to venting. In today's bathrooms, water is needed at many places; water must be supplied to the lavatories, tubs, showers, toilets, whirlpools, and any other fixtures and equipment installed in the bathroom that use water. It is also necessary to provide a means of draining wastewater away from each of these fixtures.

Once installed, the plumbing system is relatively permanent. Changes to existing systems (especially when the new fixture is to be located far from any existing plumbing) are usually expensive because they require walls to be opened and holes to be cut in floors and ceilings, as well as costly work on vent stacks and supply pipes (especially if the home is on a concrete slab foundation). The effect that changes may have on rooms located below or above the bathroom, or both, can also increase costs considerably.

To minimize costs and keep work simple, when adding or moving bathroom fixtures, arrange a fixture or group of fixtures so that they are as close as possible to existing plumbing, for example, placed adjacent to existing upstairs plumbing (if any), or directly above or directly below an existing room on the first floor that contains plumbing (e.g., existing bathroom or kitchen). The level of difficulty of the installation is determined by the location with existing plumbing and availability of usable space. Existing drain lines and vent stacks already have a path through the walls and floors. Creating a new vertical penetration requires much work, which may include reventing through upper floor attic and roof. Replacing an old bathtub, lavatory, or toilet with a new one in the same location is a fairly simple job. On the other hand, roughing in (installing) plumbing for fixtures in new locations requires skill and planning and, as previously mentioned, a plumbing license. The farther away you move from the existing stack and water lines, the more expensive it will be because framing members may need to be cut through to run water and waste lines.

The total plumbing system includes all pipes, fixtures, and fittings used to convey water into and out of the homes. It can be divided into three basic areas:

1. The water-supply system
2. The drainage system
3. The fixtures and appliances

The object of it all, of course, is to make water available where it is wanted in the home, and to get rid of water, plus wastes, after it has served its purpose.

Water-Supply System

In every plumbing system, there must be a source of water, and pipes to carry the water into the house and distribute to all the plumbing fixtures (Fig. 9.1). This water-supply system must be adequate to ensure that the homeowner has pure water for drinking, to supply a sufficient quantity of water at any outlet in the system (at the correct operating pressure), and to furnish the homeowner with hot or cold water, as required.

The main supply line (regulated by a main shutoff valve) coming into a house carries cold water. This source is provided by either a

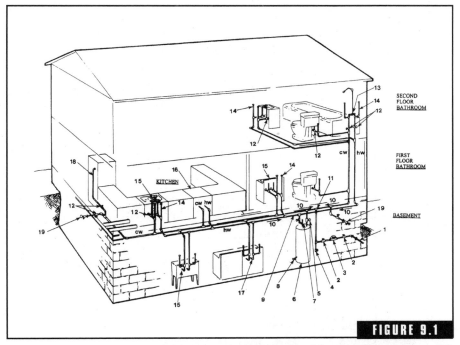

FIGURE 9.1

A typical water-supply system: (1) main supply to house; (2) main shutoff valve; (3) water meter; (4) system draincock; (5) cold-water supply to hot-water heater with shutoff valve; (6) hot-water heater; (7) hot-water supply to house; (8) hot-water heater drain valve; (9) main hot-water supply line; (10) pitch of pipe down $^1/_4$ inch/foot; (11) low point of line for drainage; (12) fixture stop valve; (13) shower fixture; (14) air chamber; (15) sink fixture; (16) dishwasher; (17) clothes washer; (18) refrigerator cold-water supply; (19) hose bib with inside shutoff. *(Leon E. Korejwo, Illustrations.)*

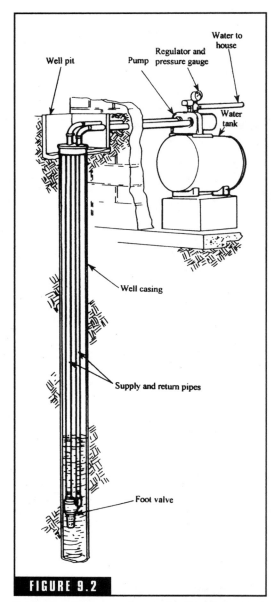

Well pit

Pump

Regulator and
pressure gauge

Water to
house

Water
tank

Well casing

Supply and return pipes

Foot valve

FIGURE 9.2

Jet-pump well system. *(Leon E. Korejwo, Illustrations.)*

municipal water company or a private underground well. Figure 9.2 shows a typical jet-pump-type private underground well. If the source is a municipal supplier, the water passes through a meter that registers the amount of water used. This main supply line splits and divides in two—one line branches off and is joined to a hot-water heater, while the other remains as cold water. From this point, branches lead off from these pipes to the various fixtures and faucets in the home. The two pipes usually run side by side below the first-floor level until they reach the vicinity of a group of fixtures, then lead up through the wall or floor. Not all fixtures need both of the supply lines; for example, a toilet has only a cold-water line. In some cases, the water supply is treated by a filter or water treatment to soften or correct chemical conditions in the well. This equipment is located at the supply line before entering the house main.

The water supply to fixtures and appliances is controlled with faucets and valves. The supply mains should be graded to one low point in the basement so that a draincock will permit complete drainage of the entire supply system. Any portion of the piping which cannot be so drained must be equipped with a separate draincock. As a rule, a pitch of $1/4$ inch (0.6 cm) to each foot of pipe is sufficient to permit proper drainage.

The water-supply system should deliver water to the various fixtures in the quantity and rate needed. The size of pipe, number of fittings, the length of pipe from the main, the pressure available, and the number of other fixtures in use at the time determine the rate at which water will flow from the faucet. In remodeling projects, if new plumbing fixtures are added, the pipe size of risers and main arteries (or branches) might need to be increased.

Water travels under pressure, which is measured in pounds per square inch (lb/in^2; psi). Water pressure is very important when adding or changing fixtures. For example, if installing new fixtures on the second floor, the installer must be certain the pressure will be strong enough to push the water to the required height. The amount of water delivered is also important and must be checked. Pipes must be large enough to supply sufficient water to the existing and new fixtures. In an average home, supply pressure ranges from 20 to 45 psi.

The service from the main or well should be underground to avoid freezing or mechanical damage. A valve to control the water (main shutoff) should be located inside the house near the entrance of the water-service pipe. On municipal supply systems, the water meter (if installed) is usually located at this point.

The size of the water piping from the main to the individual fixtures is determined by the number and type of fixtures served by the pipe. Pipe is measured by its inside diameter. The following relationship can be used as a general rule of thumb:

- For service to three or more fixtures, use 3/4-inch (2-cm) pipe.
- For service to two or fewer fixtures, use 1/2-inch (1.3-cm) pipe.

Each fixture is supplied by a fixture-supply pipe. Table 9.1 shows the minimum sizes of supply pipes for specific fixtures. This table is a good starting point. For most fixtures, a 1/2-inch (1.3-cm) pipe should be run to the fixture's cutoff valve. Of course, depending on applicable codes, the main line coming to the house is usually 1 1/4 or 1 1/2 inches (3.17 or 3.1 cm), while the branch water lines are 3/4 inch (1.9 cm). The larger water pipe allows for future expansion and provides a higher volume of water to the interior system. Each supply pipe should be equipped with a valve or "stop" so that repairs can be made to an individual fixture without interrupting service to other fixtures in the house.

WATER HEATERS

Hot water is obtained by routing cold water through a water furnace. This heater may be part of the central heating plant or a separate unit. When part of a central system, a separate hot-water storage

Table 9-1 Minimum Sizes for Fixture Water-Supply Lines

Fixture	Supply pipe size
Clothes washer	3/4″ (2 cm)
Lavatories	1/2″ (13 mm)
Toilets	1/2″ (13 mm)
Bathtubs	1/2″ (13 mm)
Showers	1/2″ (13 mm)
High-volume bathtub or shower	3/4″ (2 cm)*
Hot-water heater	3/4″ (2 cm)
Laundry tub	1/2″ (13 mm)

*Stipulated by manufacturer, if necessary.

tank is generally provided to hold the heated water. On the other hand, when a separate heater is used, the water is stored within the unit (Fig. 9.3).

A separate heater unit may be electric, oil-fired, or gas-fired, but all are automatically controlled by a preset thermostat. Each style of heater is available in a wide variety of sizes. All automatic heaters have the necessary internal piping already installed, and the only connections required are the hot- and cold-water and fuel lines. Oil- or gas-fired water heaters also require flues to vent the products of combustion.

A new hot-water heater might be necessary when new plumbing is added to the present system. Even if the present water heater is functioning properly (not scaled up or rusted out), there may not be sufficient hot water available for the family. Actually, the size of the hot-water storage tank needed in the house depends on the number of persons in the family, the volume of hot water that may be needed during peak-use periods, and the recovery rate of the heating unit.

Because gas water heaters can produce hot water more quickly than electric heaters, the size of the gas hot-water heater is generally smaller. A good rule to follow when estimating the capacity of the tank required is 10 gallons per hour for each member of the family. For a family of four, for example, the electric hot-water demand is 40 gallons of hot water per hour. However, a 40-gallon gas hot-water heater will usually

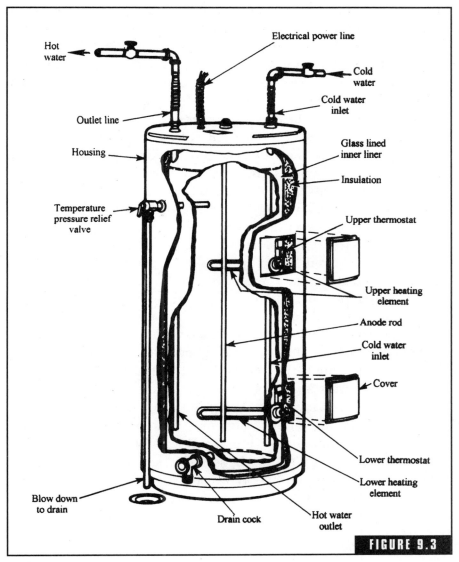

Hot water

Electrical power line

Cold water

Cold water inlet

Outlet line

Housing

Glass lined inner liner

Insulation

Temperature pressure relief valve

Upper thermostat

Upper heating element

Anode rod

Cold water inlet

Cover

Lower thermostat

Lower heating element

Blow down to drain

Drain cock

Hot water outlet

FIGURE 9.3

Electric water heater. *(Leon E. Korejwo, Illustrations.)*

serve a family of six. This does not mean that the system operates continuously at that capacity, but it must be capable of producing that amount of hot water to keep up with normal usage. If any unusual demands are anticipated, a larger capacity should be provided. For example, if an extra shower is being added, a larger or even additional water heater may be required. Because a whirlpool or spa bathtub requires a very large amount of hot water, it is recommended that a separate water heater be provided for these fixtures.

The recovery rate of water heaters varies with the type and capacity of the heating element. Temperature and pressure-relief valves are on all hot-water heaters and hot-water storage tanks. Their function is to relieve pressure in the tank and water pipes should any other piece of control equipment in the system fail and the water temperature reach a point high enough to cause a dangerous pressure that would rupture the tank and pipes. Another important device on the heater is the draincock or valve. Located at the bottom of the storage tank, the draincock or valve allows for the draining of the tank. A shutoff is also located on the cold-water intake pipe.

In some houses, the distance from the water heater to the point of use may be significant and may result in long waiting periods for hot water. A circulation line can be installed to ensure that hot water is always available at each fixture. As an alternative to the circulating system, a separate water heater should be considered for the remote area. Or, in some instances, it may be convenient to install a small hot-water booster if the primary source of hot water is too small in storage or recovery capacity to provide sufficient hot water.

To prevent users from experiencing sudden temperature drops and from being scalded, lower the setting on the water heater, and install a temperature-limiting mixing valve or a pressure-balanced valve. To save energy, the water heater, pipes, and walls should all be appropriately insulated. Energy can also be saved by reducing the water heater's temperature setting from the average 140°F to 110 or 120°F. If in the market to replace a water heater, look into the many energy-efficient models available.

WATER SOFTENERS

In some areas of the country, it is necessary to make hard water soft by piping the domestic water supply through a device called a water softener. Most water softeners have few moving parts and consume little power (Fig. 9.4). The water is treated as it flows through a special chemical that removes the objectionable minerals that make the water hard. Depending on the hardness of the water, the rate of consumption, and the unit's capacity, periodically the chemical must be regenerated or the equipment must be cleaned and renewed. Different types of chemicals and equipment may be required to treat a specific water-hardness problem. For this reason, the water should be analyzed. This test may be performed by various local agencies or with a kit that can be obtained from a plumbing supplier.

Drainage System (Drain-Waste-Vent System)

After the water is used in lavatories, tubs, and toilets, it leaves the house through the *drain-waste-vent* (DWV) system. Drainage (strictly

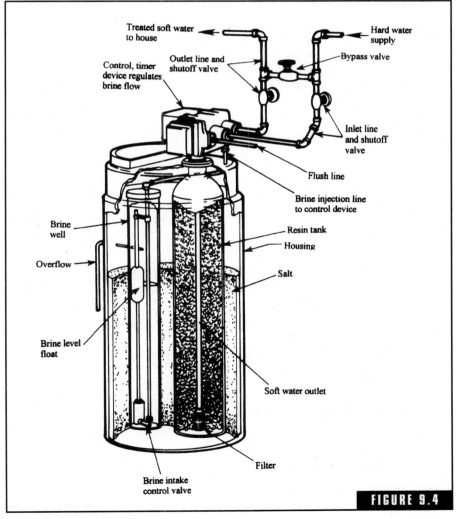

FIGURE 9.4

Water softener. *(Leon E. Korejwo, Illustrations.)*

controlled by code in most localities) is the complete and final disposal of the wastewater and the sewage it contains. A drainage system, therefore, consists of (1) the pipes that carry sewage away from the fixtures (Fig. 9.5) and (2) the place where the sewage is deposited (Fig. 9.8).

The concept of plumbing centers on two physical principles: pressure and gravity. When water is delivered to an outlet, some provision must be made to drain away waste or excess water. The drainage system differs from the water supply in one very important respect.

In supply lines, water flows under pressure. In the drainage lines, flow is entirely by gravity, and the pipes must be designed and installed carefully to ensure flow at a velocity adequate to keep the pipes clean. Because supply lines are small in diameter and depend on pressure rather than gravity, they are easily rerouted. The drainage system is also more complex than the supply system in that it consists of three parts, all of which are needed in every installation, even if only one fixture is served. The flow of wastewater starts at the fixture trap, the device that stops sewer gases from entering the house. It flows through the fixture branches to the soil stack. It continues through the house drain and the house sewer and finally reaches the city sewer system, or, in a private system, a septic tank. Waste stacks carry only water waste. These parts are as follows:

1. *Traps.* These are water seals that carry the wastewater to the drain lines and prevent the backflow of air or sewer gas into the house. Figure 9.6a shows a trap as its liquid is being siphoned out by suction in the drain line. Other drains downstream can also draw the liquid when they are drained. Figure 9.6b shows how gasses pass over the low water. Figure 9.6c illustrates how adding a vertical vent pipe breaks the vacuum in the horizontal drain, thereby allowing liquid to remain in the curve of the trap. The liquid seal blocks rising sewer gases from entering the room. Traps should be accessible and as close as possible to each fixture. Sometimes they are part of the fixture. Plumbing codes restrict the distance that a sink trap can be located from its drain or vent line. The trap never empties and retains enough water to maintain the seal. Trap styles are S-trap, deep-seal P-trap, and running trap (Fig. 9.6d), P-trap (Fig. 9.6e), or P-traps using a J-bend fitting (Fig. 9.6f) which connect the fixture and the drainpipe. When the fixture drains, water flows through the trap and into the drainpipe. Most traps used today are P-traps, which drain into the wall by way of a 90° trap arm. On existing installations, you might also find S-traps,

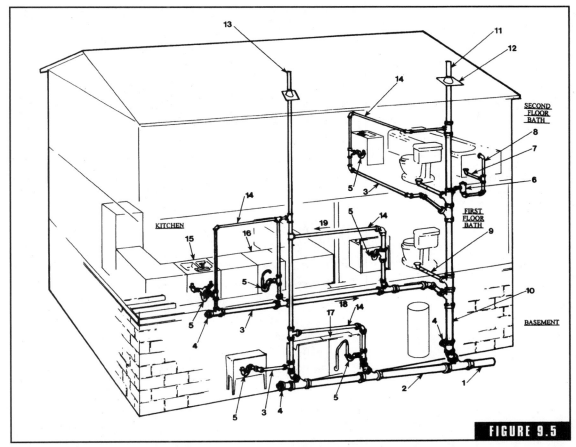

FIGURE 9.5

A typical drainage system: (1) house sewer; (2) house drain; (3) branch drain; (4) cleanout; (5) trap; (6) drum trap; (7) tub drain; (8) tub overflow; (9) closet bend; (10) main soil stack; (11) vent stack; (12) flashing; (13) secondary vent soil stack; (14) vent run; (15) sink; (16) dishwasher; (17) clothes washer; (18) drain pitch down $^1/_4$ inch/foot; (19) vent pitch up $^1/_4$ inch/foot. *(Leon E. Korejwo, Illustrations.)*

which drain into the floor via a 180° trap arm. (This type is no longer allowed by code in many areas.)

2. *Drainage lines.* These are pipes, either vertical, called *stacks,* or horizontal, called *branches,* that carry the discharge from the fixtures to the house sewer (see Fig. 9.1). They are usually concealed in walls or floors. The pipes receiving the discharge from the toilet are known as *soil lines.* Those receiving the discharge from other fixtures (lavatories, tubs, showers, etc.) are known as *waste lines.*

3. *Vent lines.* These are pipes extending upward through the roof. They allow air to flow into or out of the drainage pipes, thus equalizing air pressure in the drainage system and protecting the water seal in the traps. Without a vent pipe, the rush of water down a drain could cause a siphoning action that would pull the water seal out of the trap and let sewer gases enter the home. The vent pipe is generally located right behind the sink.

The relationship between the trap, the drainage line, and the vent line is very important and will have a great influence on the location of plumbing fixtures, particularly in remodeling work where the relocation of fixtures is desired. Actually, the required maximum distance from a trap to a vent does not usually present any problems in residences (except when lavatories are of a freestanding design, such as an island type). This problem can usually be solved by using a drainage line large enough for the distance to the nearest vent. The actual span varies from one locality to another, but generally speaking, a sink cannot be moved more than 3 to 4 feet without either adding or extending branch lines; in some situations an entirely new run of piping from basement to roof may be needed. Remember that some plumbing code regulations do not permit sinks or other water-using appliances anywhere other than along a wall.

All vents must terminate outside the house. The vent terminal must be carried through the roof full size. It must be at least 3 inches (8 cm) in diameter to prevent clogging by frost. The minimum extension above the roof is 6 inches (15 cm). *Individual vents* serve one fixture with a trap (Fig. 9.7*a*). A *common vent* serves two fixtures (Fig. 9.7*b*). When a fixture discharges through its drain to the soil stack, it is called a *wet vent* (Fig. 9.7*c*). A *dry vent* does not act as a drain (Fig. 9.7*d*).

Each trap installed in a drainage system must be vented. Traps (refer to Table 9.2 for trap size guidelines) may be provided with individual vents (sometimes referred to as *back vents* or *continuous vents*) or a common vent. The latter is useful when lavatories are located side by side or when a new fixture is to be added to an existing drainage system. A new fixture could be added below or above an existing fixture as long as the lower fixture is the one with the greater flow.

The drain and waste lines from each fixture or group of fixtures are connected to the building drain. The building drain takes the waste material to the sewer system or septic tank. The building drain must be installed with the proper slope: $1/4$ inch (0.6 cm)/foot (Fig. 9.7*e*). Steeper slopes provide higher velocities, increasing the carrying capacity of the pipe, and tend to keep the drainpipe clean.

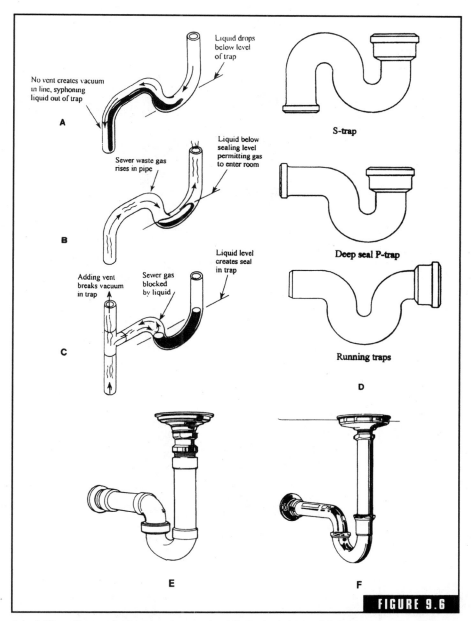

Liquid drops below level of trap

No vent creates vacuum in line, syphoning liquid out of trap

A

S-trap

Liquid below sealing level permitting gas to enter room

Sewer waste gas rises in pipe

B

Deep seal P-trap

Liquid level creates seal in trap

Adding vent breaks vacuum in trap

Sewer gas blocked by liquid

C

Running traps

D

E

F

FIGURE 9.6

(*a–c*) **The effects of vents on trap seals.** (*d*) **Typical traps.** (*e*) **Typical P-trap.** (*f*) **Typical P-trap with a J-bend fitting.** (*Leon E. Korejwo, Illustrations.*)

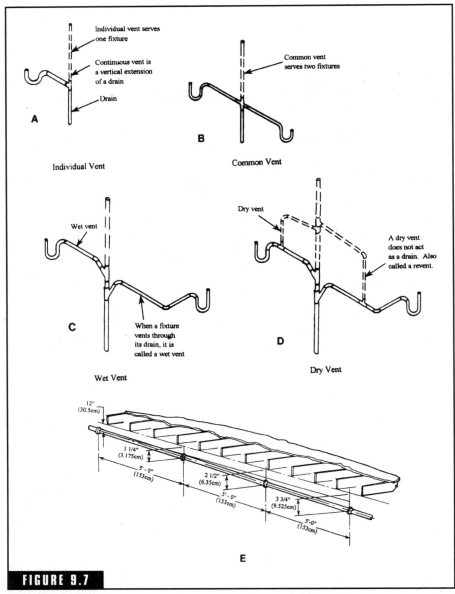

Individual vent serves one fixture

Continuous vent is a vertical extension of a drain

Drain

A

Individual Vent

Common vent serves two fixtures

B

Common Vent

Wet vent

When a fixture vents through its drain, it is called a wet vent

C

Wet Vent

Dry vent

A dry vent does not act as a drain. Also called a revent.

D

Dry Vent

12"
(30.5cm)

1 1/4"
(3.175cm)

5'- 0"
(153cm)

2 1/2"
(6.35cm)

5'- 0"
(153cm)

3 3/4"
(9.525cm)

5'-0"
(153cm)

E

FIGURE 9.7

(*a–d*) **Various methods of venting:** (*a*) **individual,** (*b*) **common,** (*c*) **wet,** (*d*) **dry vents.**
(*e*) **The proper pitch for drain lines.** (*Leon E. Korejwo, Illustrations.*)

A septic tank treats waste right on the property in an enclosed tank. They are watertight receptacles that receive the discharge of the drainage system. The liquids are discharged into the soil outside the tank in an area referred to as a *tile field* (or *drain field*); the solids in the waste biodegrade in the septic tank (Fig. 9.8).

The city sewer system carries waste away from the property. If adding new fixtures to the bathroom, double-check that the capacity of the septic system can handle the additional fixtures. If the residence is hooked up to a city sewer system, be sure that the waste line is properly sized to handle the total fixtures.

To be safe, the drainage system has to meet five basic requirements:

1. All pipes in this system must be pitched (slanted) down toward the main disposal so that the weight of the waste causes it to flow toward the main disposal system and away from the house. Because of gravity flow, the waste lines must be larger than the water-supply lines, in which there is pressure.

2. Pipes must be fitted and sealed so that sewer gases cannot leak out.

3. The system must contain vents to carry off the sewer gases to where they can do no harm. Vents also help equalize the air pressure in the drainage system.

4. Each fixture that has a drain should be provided with a suitable water trap, so that water standing in the trap seals the drainpipe and prevents the backflow of sewer gas into the house. The trap for the toilet is built into it.

Table 9-2 Minimum Trap Size Requirements for Various Fixtures

Fixture	Minimum trap size, inches (cm)
Lavatories	1¼ (3.175)
Bathtubs	1½ (3.81)
Showers	2 (5.08)
Toilet (one- and two-piece)	Internal trap in fixture
Bidet	1¼ (3.175)
Laundry tub	1½ (3.81)

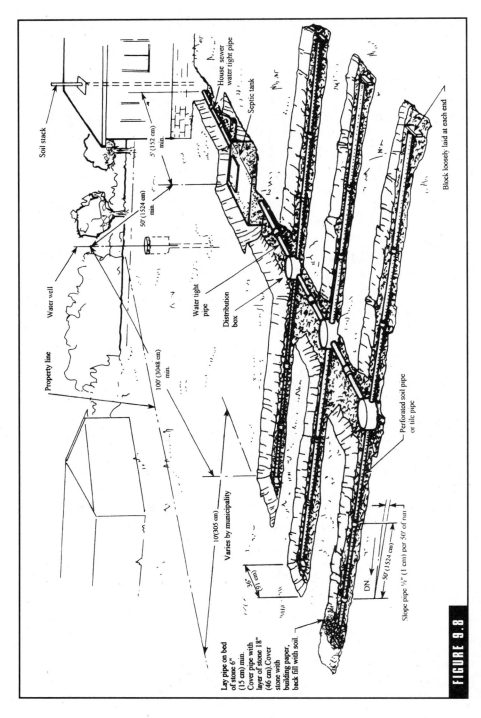

Soil stack

House sewer water tight pipe

Septic tank

5' (152 cm) min.

50' (1524 cm) min.

Water well

Water tight pipe

Distribution box

Property line

100' (3048 cm) min.

10'(305 cm)

Varies by municipality

Perforated soil pipe or tile pipe

Block loosely laid at each end

36" (91 cm)

DN

50' (1524 cm)

Slope pipe ½" (1 cm) per 50' of run

Lay pipe on bed of stone 6" (15 cm) min. Cover pipe with layer of stone 18" (46 cm).Cover stone with building paper, back fill with soil.

FIGURE 9.8

Septic-tank tile field. *(Leon E. Korejwo, Illustrations.)*

5. Revents should be provided wherever there is danger of siphoning the water from a fixture trap or where specified by local codes.

Although the water-supply system is basically the same for sinks regardless of whether they are in the kitchen or bathroom, there are some differences in the waste system. Lavatory basins have a smaller-diameter drain hole and are typically installed with a pop-up waste, whereas kitchen sinks have a basket strainer. Kitchen sink traps are required by code to have a minimum diameter of $1^1/2$ inches (3.81 cm), and lavatory basin traps are required to have a minimum diameter of $1^1/4$ (3.17 cm) inches. Except for this factor, the trap assembly is basically the same regardless of the sink type.

Fixtures

The fixtures provide the required means for using the water (Fig. 9.9). In this sense, a faucet on the outside of the house (for attaching a hose) is a fixture, as well as a laundry tub in the basement, or a dishwasher, or toilet. Each has a purpose connected with the homeowner's use of water, and each must have certain features to serve its purpose. Fixtures can be costly plumbing items and should exactly suit the homeowner's needs.

Plumbing Codes

Be aware that most building codes require plumbers to have a special license, so unless you have that license, you need to hire a plumbing contractor. Some areas have exceptions; however, the work must still be approved and checked by the local building inspector. Although most plumbing systems are based on national codes, local building codes may vary from those in an adjoining city or town.

When installing a bathroom, all plumbing work must be done in accordance with local plumbing codes. However, few code restrictions apply to simple extensions of hot- and cold-water-supply pipes (provided the home's water pressure can handle the addition). Material and diameters for supply pipes serving each new fixture or appliance are described in the plumbing code. Codes can be very specific about the size of drainpipes, stacks, and vents serving any new fixture that requires drainage; the critical distance from fixture traps to the stack; and the method of venting fixtures. Plumbing regulations do vary among different regional areas with regard to DWV systems. Some require venting at every fixture and others rely on various distances

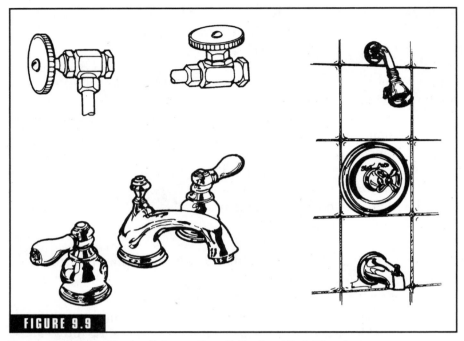

FIGURE 9.9

Various types of bathroom fixtures. *(Leon E. Korejwo, Illustrations.)*

from vents before requiring additional vents. The primary purpose of a plumbing code, as well as of a building code, is to protect the health and safety of the homeowner.

Three major plumbing codes are used in the United States: the BOCA National Plumbing Code (used primarily along the eastern coast), the Uniform Plumbing Code (most prevalent in the western United States), and the Standard Plumbing Code (primarily in the southern states). Other codes are used, but these are the three major ones. If plumbing work is done in accordance with the codes, the homeowner is protected against improper fixtures, materials, and installation (against contamination of the water supply, contamination of the air, and undesirable odor due to escape of sewer gas).

Plumbing Materials

Regional preferences and area building codes generally dictate what type of pipe must be used for both new construction and remodeling projects. However, builders should be familiar with the major types of plumbing pipe used.

Plastic piping is lightweight and one of the easiest pipings to use. In new construction, it is becoming the water piping choice. However, it is important to be aware that its use is restricted by some building and plumbing codes. As with all plumbing, be sure to check all codes before using these materials. Some types of plastic piping include polybutylene (PB), chlorinated PVC (CPVC), polyethylene, acrylonitrile butadiene styrene (ABS), and poly(vinyl chloride) (PVC).

PB and *CPVC* are used in water-supply systems. PB is very flexible and extremely durable (Fig. 9.10*a*). This pipe is available in long rolls, eliminating the need for joints. It is flexible and resistant to damage from backfilling. If comparing costs, ease of installation, and effectiveness, polybutylene pipe is hard to beat. When installed properly, it is one of the best materials for carrying water. CPVC is a rigid pipe which tends to be brittle and is prone to cracking under stress (Fig. 9.10*b*). But once it is installed correctly, CPVC gives reasonably good service, as long as it is not subjected to abuse, and can last a long time. CPVC and PB are suitable for both hot- and cold-water applications. Whenever feasible, it is best to eliminate joints in underground piping, and with CPVC, you cannot eliminate the joints in long runs.

Polyethylene pipe has long been used as a water-service pipe (Fig. 9.10*c*). It also is supplied in large rolls, eliminating the need for underground joints. The plastic pipe is durable and resistant to backfilling accidents. Polyethylene is probably one of the most frequently used pipe for modern water-service installations.

ABS and *PVC* are both commonly used in drain (DWV) systems (Fig. 9. 10*d,e*). They are very simple material to work with and can be cut with any fine-toothed handsaw. ABS and PVC are, in some instances, used together in the same system.

Note: The home electrical system is possibly grounded through metal water pipes. When adding plastic pipes to a metal plumbing system, be certain that the electrical ground circuit is not broken. Use ground clamps and jumper wires to bypass the plastic transition and complete the electrical ground circuit. Clamps must be firmly attached to bare metal on both sides of the plastic pipe.

Copper (technically called *tubing,* not *pipe*), although somewhat more expensive than others, is lightweight, versatile, and highly resistant to corrosion, and gives many years of good service (Fig. 9.10*f*). It

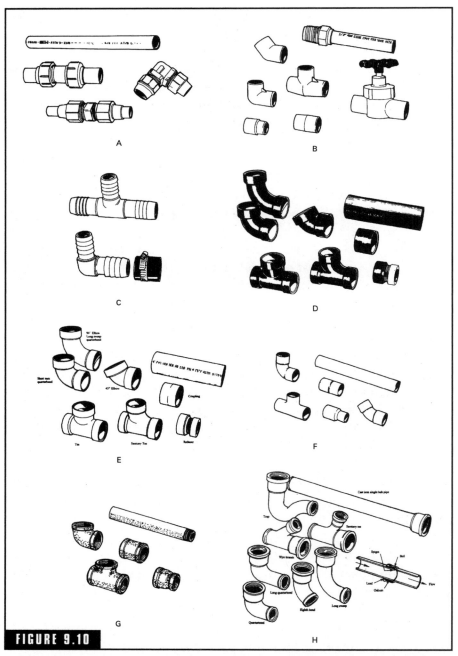

(*a*) PB piping; (*b*)CPVC piping; (*c*)PE piping; (*d*)ABS piping; (*e*)PVC piping; (*f*)copper piping; (*g*)galvanized-steel piping; (*h*)cast-iron piping. (*Leon E. Korejwo, Illustrations.*)

is most commonly used for water supply for remodeled bathrooms and kitchens. It is good water-service pipe, unless the water supply contains a high acid content. Be certain to verify that the pipe thickness is sufficient to meet all building codes. Many times, building codes specify the use of copper piping.

Galvanized-steel piping (found in houses built before 1935) is notorious for its tendency to rust out and clog up, and it is heavy (Fig. 9.10*g*). Whether used for drain, vent, or water service, all galvanized-steel pipes should be replaced. It is outdated and serves no purpose in modern plumbing installations. It increases the risk of rust, leaking joints, and restricted water flow.

Cast-iron piping has a long life with few problems and is basically satisfactory for continued service (Fig. 9.10*h*). However, it is one of the heaviest and most difficult pipings to work with. It does only DWV duty, although no-hub clamps do somewhat facilitate smaller jobs for an amateur.

Checking Plumbing

Because of the inaccessible routing of plumbing, inspection of the plumbing system is not easy. Be sure to look under any cabinets that have plumbing (e.g., under the sink) to find out the types of materials used for water pipes, drains, and vents. It might also be possible to inspect some of the plumbing from the basement, cellar, or crawlspace.

After completing the plumbing evaluation procedure, the condition of plumbing systems and how the problems can be corrected can be accurately assessed.

Lead in Plumbing

Lead has become a serious problem, and one that must be addressed by builders doing bathroom remodeling projects. Its presence depends on when the house was built, what kind of plumbing pipes it has, and what types of water mains connect the building to the water-supply system. If you discover any lead bends, traps, or pipes, they should always be replaced when remodeling a bathroom. Many homes also have lead waste pipes; although these are less cause for concern, some jurisdictions will require you to replace them as part of any home remodeling project. However, lead water pipes should always be removed when remodeling a bathroom. In addition, any repairs or additions to existing copper pipes should not be made with lead solder.

Unsightly Pipes

When remodeling a bathroom in an older home, unsightly pipes running up the walls can be a problem. There are two relatively simple solutions.

- Enclose the pipes in the wall. You must cut the pipe and install elbows to move the pipe into the wall itself, which means cutting a slot in the wall for the pipe, then patching the wall afterward. It is a lot of work, but it is the most satisfactory solution. If drains from upstairs bathrooms pass into the remodeled area, a 2 × 6″ (5 × 15-cm) wall may provide adequate (Fig. 9.11*a*).

- Box in the pipes. This solution is easier. Simply build the wall out around the pipes using a simple wooden-box construction.

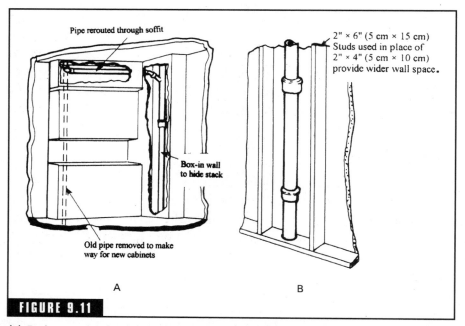

FIGURE 9.11

(*a*) **Enclose unsightly pipes.** (*b*) **One method of concealing pipes.** (*Leon E. Korejwo, Illustrations.*)

Then paint or paper the addition to match the rest of the wall. This method is more of a compromise solution, and it does leave a corner jutting into the room. Drain lines are usually larger than the 2 × 4″ (5 × 10.16-cm) framing in most walls (Fig. 9.11b).

To reach a second story from a basement or crawlspace, you can often route pipes unobtrusively through a closet. Then no enclosure is needed. An enclosure can take the form of a soffit, corner cabinet, room divider, or closet.

Heating, Ventilation, and Air-Conditioning (HVAC) System

Heating, ventilation, and air-conditioning (HVAC) systems are designed to maintain comfort in the home. HVAC systems may be affected by the proposed bathroom project. Changes are governed either by the local plumbing regulations or a separate mechanical code. As with plumbing, a special trade license is usually required in this area of work. Therefore, unless you are a skilled HVAC technician, you should plan on hiring a competent subcontractor to work with these systems.

It is always important to make your client aware of two important factors when installing a heating-cooling system: (1) the cost of the purchase and installation and (2) the cost of actually operating the various systems.

As the installer, you are not responsible for the design of the system, but you need to review the design before the project begins for any potential problems. Kitchen and bath builders must check the type of heat and make sure that the designer or architect took the existing system and ducts or radiators into consideration in the design and layout of the room. Probably the most difficult task in providing heating and cooling for a kitchen or bathroom is finding a suitable location for the terminal device of the heating-cooling system.

Both air-conditioning and heating ducts are fairly easy to reroute, as long as you can gain access from a basement, crawlspace, garage wall, or unfinished attic. Radiant-heat pipes or other slab-embedded systems may pose problems. Ductwork and plumbing may compete for existing routing, so plan ahead with subcontractors early.

When remodeling a bathroom, in most cases, the existing system can be used or modified. If you want to extend the existing heating system to a new bathroom, check with a specialist to be sure that the system can handle the added load.

The various heating systems used in a home will not be discussed in complete detail here. However, suggestions as to how they can be employed and installed in a bathroom—new or remodeled—are given here.

Heating Systems

Home heating systems can be classified by the fuel they use or by a heating medium. The medium can be warm air, hot water, or steam. Fuels are natural gas, fuel oil, or electricity. Water and steam heat the house with radiators piped from a boiler. Warm air is generated by a furnace and is widely favored because it is easy to add a central air-conditioning unit and a central humidity control. Electric resistance heaters are easy to install, but electric rates make them expensive to operate. Warm-air systems deliver heat to a room through wall, floor, baseboard, or ceiling registers or diffusers (Fig. 9.12a). Air returns to the furnace through return grilles.

WARM-AIR SYSTEMS

Registers for warm-air systems and small electric resistance blower-operated units can be located in the vanity kickspace by changing the ductwork beneath the floor; ducts for wall registers can be rerouted in the stud wall. These units are acceptable for heating, but registers in the toe space present problems of proper air distribution for cooling applications. If they are used, they should be considered for heating use only, and provision should be made so that they may be closed with a damper in summer when the cooling system is in operation. If the bathroom being remodeled does not have a register, one can be added in a kickspace with a duct elbow to route heat into the room through a toekick grille; locate it where the ductwork can be extended easily from the existing system and where wall space will not be sacrificed.

In new construction, provisions can be made for using toespace registers for heating and auxiliary registers located on the side walls for cooling, if the installed system is one that provides both heating and cooling (Fig. 9.12b). For remodeling work, the relocation of ductwork can sometimes present serious difficulties, particularly if the

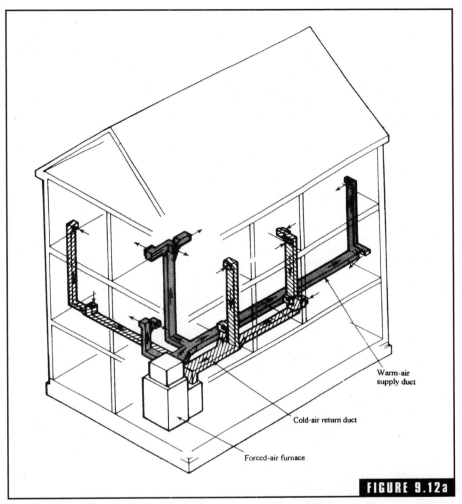

Warm-air
supply duct

Cold-air return duct

Forced-air furnace

FIGURE 9.12a

(*a*) **A typical forced-air heating system.** (*b*) **Placement of heating or cooling registers in bathroom.** (*c*) **Possible furnace clearances.** *(Leon E. Korejwo, Illustrations.)*

house is built on a slab or if there is a finished ceiling in the basement below the bathroom. If the "new" bathroom is located in an addition to the house, it is possible to extend the ductwork to provide for heating and cooling the addition. Before this is done, the existing furnace should be checked to ensure that it has sufficient heating and/or cooling capacity for the addition. Generally, heating the entire space of an average-sized bath will require an additional 1500 watts of power. The blower unit must also be checked to ensure that it is capable of delivering the additional air needed in the new room. It may be necessary to replace the blower assembly or the blower motor in order to increase the air-handling capability of the system, even though the furnace burner has sufficient heating capacity. It is also possible to

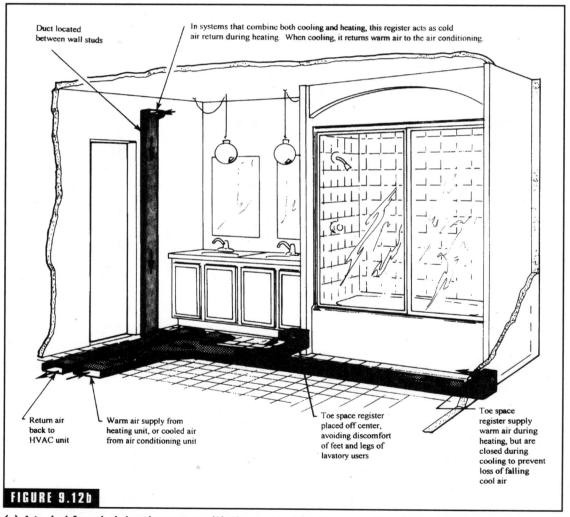

Duct located between wall studs

In systems that combine both cooling and heating, this register acts as cold air return during heating. When cooling, it returns warm air to the air conditioning.

Return air back to HVAC unit

Warm air supply from heating unit, or cooled air from air conditioning unit

Toe space register placed off center, avoiding discomfort of feet and legs of lavatory users

Toe space register supply warm air during heating, but are closed during cooling to prevent loss of falling cool air

FIGURE 9.12b

(*a*) **A typical forced-air heating system.** (*b*) **Placement of heating or cooling registers in bathroom.** (*c*) **Possible furnace clearances.** *(Leon E. Korejwo, Illustrations.)*

increase the air-handling capacity of the system by speeding up the blower. In general, this is not a good practice, since the increased blower speed normally increases the noise level from the furnace.

Be aware that when remodeling for a bathroom or room adjacent to a heating unit, moving walls or surfaces too close to the heater or duct-work is hazardous. Each heating unit has minimum safe clearances, which are included with the manufacturer's installation information or, in some instances, shown on a sticker on the unit (Fig. 9.12c). If in question, consult the subcontractor or manufacturer before planning to move a partition. A heater must have adequate air for combustion. It must not be enclosed in such a way that cuts off its air supply or impedes its flue or exhaust.

Most forced-warm-air systems can support another register or two if the furnace is centrally located. A zoned heating system designed to

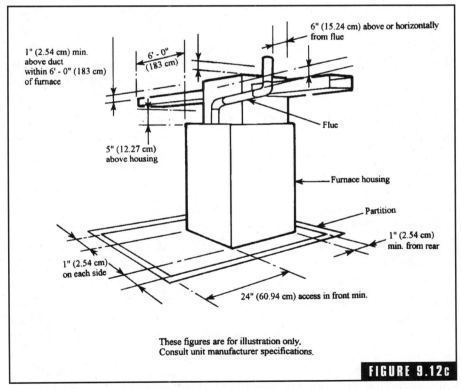

6" (15.24 cm) above or horizontally from flue

1" (2.54 cm) min. above duct within 6' - 0" (183 cm) of furnace

6' - 0" (183 cm)

5" (12.27 cm) above housing

Flue

Furnace housing

Partition

1" (2.54 cm) min. from rear

1" (2.54 cm) on each side

24" (60.94 cm) access in front min.

These figures are for illustration only.
Consult unit manufacturer specifications.

FIGURE 9.12c

(*a*) A typical forced-air heating system. (*b*) Placement of heating or cooling registers in bathroom. (*c*) Possible furnace clearances. (*Leon E. Korejwo, Illustrations.*)

heat the addition may be the best answer. Quite often, the HVAC plan you receive with design plans may be very schematic, and the dedicated areas for running ductwork may not be indicated or planned for in the design. HVAC systems require a substantial amount of space, and cramping the ductwork areas only leads to awkward installations that can cause the HVAC system to be inefficient or noisy. If the addition of any bump-outs or chases for the ductwork will affect the cabinet and fixture layout, this information should be determined and reported to the dealer or designer so that modifications can be made before cabinets and fixtures are ordered. When remodeling around a hot-air system, registers can be added or relocated. When planning the bathroom, consult the manufacturer or a subcontractor before finalizing a design.

HYDRONIC (HOT-WATER) SYSTEMS

In a forced-hot-water system (found in homes built before 1940), a boiler heats water that circulates through pipes (Fig. 9.13*a*). The pipes lead to fan coil units, convectors, or radiators. These units radiate heat to the room air. The cooled water recirculates back to the furnace, where it is heated again and returns back to the radiators or registers. Convectors consist of a core of fins that are heated by hot water. The air passing over these fins is warmed. Fan coil units work on the same principle, but have small fans that push the warm air out into the room. Earlier hot-water systems operated by gravity and did not have a circulating pump. A circulating pump can be added on this type of hot-water system.

In more elaborate bathroom layouts, the walls are lined with cabinets, making it difficult to locate baseboard units. A valance unit can be used, or the radiation necessary to offset the heat loss of the bathroom can be located in an adjoining sitting area, dressing area, or other space immediately adjacent to and open to the bathroom. The HVAC subcontractor can tell you if the system can be modified or if convector or fan coil units can be relocated. The pipes for this often run through walls, so you need to trail the path to determine whether pipes inside a wall need to be removed or modified. When adding to a hydronic system, be sure that the new radiator units are made of the same metal as the old, or this will be a sure invitation to corrosion. In extreme cases where the equipment cannot be located in an adjacent

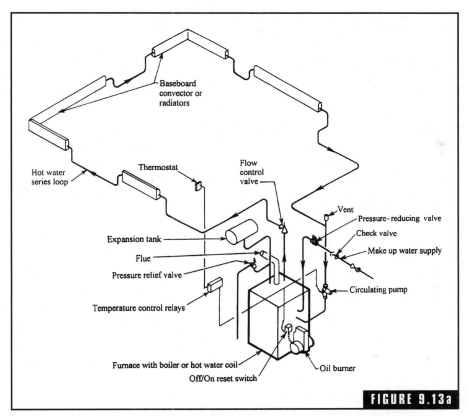

Baseboard convector or radiators

Hot water series loop

Thermostat

Flow control valve

Vent

Pressure-reducing valve

Check valve

Make up water supply

Expansion tank

Flue

Pressure relief valve

Temperature control relays

Circulating pump

Furnace with boiler or hot water coil

Off/On reset switch

Oil burner

FIGURE 9.13a

(*a*) **Hydronic or hot-water series loop heating system.** (*b*) **Increasing size of hydronic (hot-water) heating system. Through use of additional zone valves, this allows control of added heating by controlling flow of heated water by using a thermostatically regulated zone valve.** (*c*) **Hydronic system expanded using added circulator pump. Thermostat control signals circulator pump to flow heated water to new loop, while old circulator pumps only to original loop.** *(Leon E. Korejwo, Illustrations.)*

space, part of the wall space must be left free for the installation of a convector with or without an integral fan unit to help distribute the warmed air.

Hydronic systems can be modified to suit the homeowner's needs if a bathroom is part of a new addition. The addition may be heated using the existing furnace. Two methods to add on to an existing system are zone valves or an additional circulating pump and piping. Zone valves are electronically controlled units that are actuated when heat is required in the room. Heated water is pumped by a circulator through the zone valve to baseboard convectors (Fig. 9.13*b*). A circulating pump may be added to the existing system if that unit is not adequate to move the needed hot water (Fig. 9.13*c*). New piping, baseboard convectors, and a pump are installed with little disturbance to the existing heating system.

Generally, hydronic systems are not designed as combination heating-cooling systems. Chilled water pumped through the system can be used for cooling if valance units are installed throughout the house. This is not a typical installation, however. When a separate cooling system is installed, the registers may be located in the ceiling, and no difficulty will arise.

The piping and radiators of old-fashioned steam heat systems are best left alone. Because of the age of these systems, the radiators and fittings are quite worn and difficult to repair or replace should a problem occur during your installation.

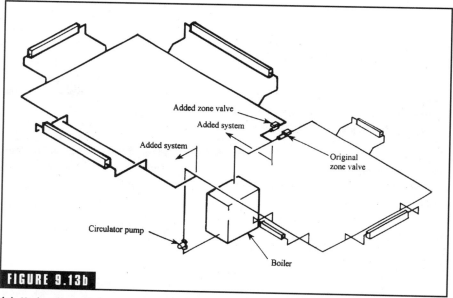

FIGURE 9.13b

(*a*) Hydronic or hot-water series loop heating system. (*b*) Increasing size of hydronic (hot-water) heating system. Through use of additional zone valves, this allows control of added heating by controlling flow of heated water by using a thermostatically regulated zone valve. (*c*) Hydronic system expanded using added circulator pump. Thermostat control signals circulator pump to flow heated water to new loop, while old circulator pumps only to original loop. (*Leon E. Korejwo, Illustrations.*)

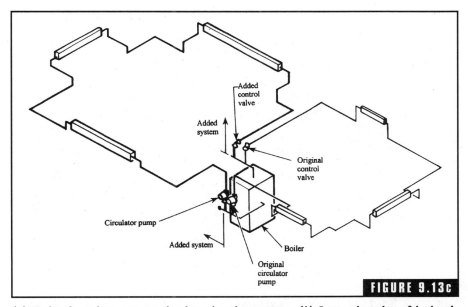

FIGURE 9.13c

(*a*) **Hydronic or hot-water series loop heating system.** (*b*) **Increasing size of hydronic (hot-water) heating system. Through use of additional zone valves, this allows control of added heating by controlling flow of heated water by using a thermostatically regulated zone valve.** (*c*) **Hydronic system expanded using added circulator pump. Thermostat control signals circulator pump to flow heated water to new loop, while old circulator pumps only to original loop.** (*Leon E. Korejwo, Illustrations.*)

AUXULIARY HEATING SYSTEMS

In addition to a primary heat source, auxiliary heating may be planned in the bathroom.

Almost every bathroom needs auxiliary heat, to raise the temperature quickly when the user steps from the bath. On a cold winter morning, after a long, hot shower or bath, nobody wants to step out into a cool bathroom; today, such discomforts are not necessary. A small auxiliary wall- or ceiling-mounted heater can fill in and keep the user warm on chilly days when the main heating plant is not running.

The two most popular types of auxiliary heaters are electric or gas space. Of course, the heater should be placed where someone getting out of the tub or shower will benefit from it. However, plan the location of the heater most carefully in a bathroom; thus, place the wall heater where there is no possibility of a person being burned on it or of towels or curtains catching fire from it.

Bathroom heaters warm rooms by two methods: convection and radiation.

Convection heaters warm the air in a room; the air, in turn, transfers the heat to surfaces and objects that it contacts. Wall- or ceiling-mounted convection heaters usually have an electrically heated resistance coil and a small fan to move the heated air.

Radiant heat is perhaps the most desirable auxiliary heating system. It emits infrared or electromagnetic waves that warm objects and surfaces; these waves hit the intervening air without warming. Radiant heaters using infrared lightbulbs (heat lamps) may be surface-mounted on the ceiling or installed in the ceiling between joists or in the wall between studs, and may require ductwork to the outside. Radiant heating panels are generally flush-mounted on a wall or ceiling.

SUBFLOOR RADIANT-HEATING SYSTEMS

If installing a new slab or subfloor, consider installing radiant-heating pipes below. They are supplementary heating sources of warmth that evenly radiate heat upward, where it does the most good. In addition, rather than having to design around radiators or typical baseboard heat units, these heating systems are built in under the floor, giving designers more options. The homeowner has more even heating and more space.

Major benefits to these systems is that, unlike forced-hot-air systems, these radiant systems cannot spread dust, pollen, or germs throughout the house and, once installed, are generally maintenance-free. These subfloor heating systems can be placed under most any flooring materials—hardwood, ceramic tile, and carpet—however, they are not recommended for under linoleum. There are systems for both resistance electric and hydronic heat for floors.

Subfloor electric heating systems. Many manufacturers have introduced electric cable floor warmers that act like heating coils, permanently placed beneath wood, tiles, and even carpet. Most of the new types on the market are mounted on top of the subfloor, have certified insulated cables, and are powered by their own 120-volt box with their own thermostat. These systems rely on electricity to provide heat (8 to 15 watts per square foot, depending on the floor material) and are designed as a secondary heat source, not the main heat source for the home.

Subfloor hydronic heating systems.   There are several distinct methods of installing hydronic radiant heat in flooring suitable for bathrooms (Fig. 9.14*a–f*). Heated water is circulated through tubing beneath the surface of the floor. The warmth is projected upward toward the entire room. Tubing is arranged in a series of interconnecting loops resembling a bunch of paper clips laid side by side. This is commonly known as *hydronic radiant heating.* The advent of flexible plastic tubing specifically designed for this purpose has made installing

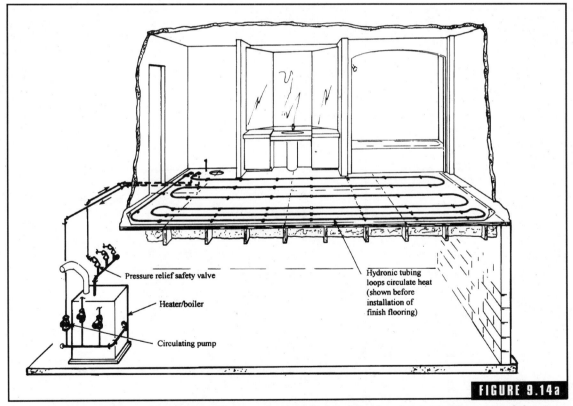

Pressure relief safety valve

Heater/boiler

Circulating pump

Hydronic tubing loops circulate heat (shown before installation of finish flooring)

FIGURE 9.14a

(*a*) A generic circuit with tubing arranged in rows about 12 inches (30.48 cm) apart in the center of the room. The runs are located closer together near the outside wall to compensate for heat loss in that area. (*b*) An above-grade design. (*c*) The gypsum-based method above floor. (*d*) Thin slab concrete installation. (*e*) Plate system above the subfloor. (*f*) Plate system where the tube runs below the subfloor. (*Leon E. Korejwo, Illustrations.*)

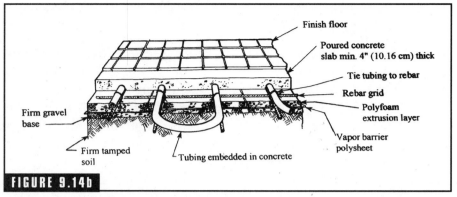

Finish floor

Poured concrete
slab min. 4" (10.16 cm) thick

Tie tubing to rebar

Rebar grid

Polyfoam
extrusion layer

Vapor barrier
polysheet

Firm gravel
base

Firm tamped
soil

Tubing embedded in concrete

FIGURE 9.14b

(*a*) A generic circuit with tubing arranged in rows about 12 inches (30.48 cm) apart in the center of the room. The runs are located closer together near the outside wall to compensate for heat loss in that area. (*b*) An above-grade design. (*c*) The gypsum-based method above floor. (*d*) Thin slab concrete installation. (*e*) Plate system above the subfloor. (*f*) Plate system where the tube runs below the subfloor. (*Leon E. Korejwo, Illustrations.*)

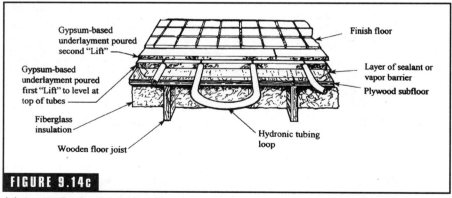

Gypsum-based
underlayment poured
second "Lift"

Gypsum-based
underlayment poured
first "Lift" to level at
top of tubes

Fiberglass
insulation

Wooden floor joist

Finish floor

Layer of sealant or
vapor barrier

Plywood subfloor

Hydronic tubing
loop

FIGURE 9.14c

(*a*) A generic circuit with tubing arranged in rows about 12 inches (30.48 cm) apart in the center of the room. The runs are located closer together near the outside wall to compensate for heat loss in that area. (*b*) An above-grade design. (*c*) The gypsum-based method above floor. (*d*) Thin slab concrete installation. (*e*) Plate system above the subfloor. (*f*) Plate system where the tube runs below the subfloor. (*Leon E. Korejwo, Illustrations.*)

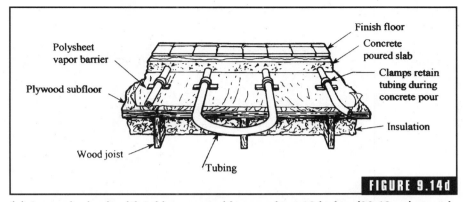

FIGURE 9.14d

Polysheet vapor barrier

Plywood subfloor

Wood joist

Tubing

Finish floor

Concrete poured slab

Clamps retain tubing during concrete pour

Insulation

(*a*) A generic circuit with tubing arranged in rows about 12 inches (30.48 cm) apart in the center of the room. The runs are located closer together near the outside wall to compensate for heat loss in that area. (*b*) An above-grade design. (*c*) The gypsum-based method above floor. (*d*) Thin slab concrete installation. (*e*) Plate system above the subfloor. (*f*) Plate system where the tube runs below the subfloor. (*Leon E. Korejwo, Illustrations.*)

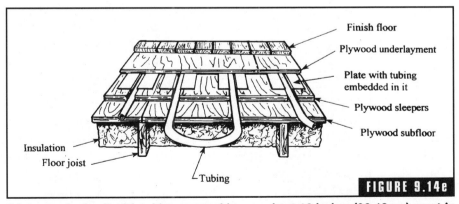

FIGURE 9.14e

Finish floor

Plywood underlayment

Plate with tubing embedded in it

Plywood sleepers

Plywood subfloor

Insulation

Floor joist

Tubing

(*a*) A generic circuit with tubing arranged in rows about 12 inches (30.48 cm) apart in the center of the room. The runs are located closer together near the outside wall to compensate for heat loss in that area. (*b*) An above-grade design. (*c*) The gypsum-based method above floor. (*d*) Thin slab concrete installation. (*e*) Plate system above the subfloor. (*f*) Plate system where the tube runs below the subfloor. (*Leon E. Korejwo, Illustrations.*)

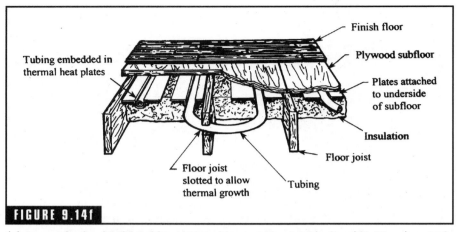

Labels in figure: Finish floor; Plywood subfloor; Plates attached to underside of subfloor; Insulation; Floor joist; Tubing; Floor joist slotted to allow thermal growth; Tubing embedded in thermal heat plates

FIGURE 9.14f

(*a*) A generic circuit with tubing arranged in rows about 12 inches (30.48 cm) apart in the center of the room. The runs are located closer together near the outside wall to compensate for heat loss in that area. (*b*) An above-grade design. (*c*) The gypsum-based method above floor. (*d*) Thin slab concrete installation. (*e*) Plate system above the subfloor. (*f*) Plate system where the tube runs below the subfloor. *(Leon E. Korejwo, Illustrations.)*

hydronic floors increasingly popular. Options involve the type of deck used either on-grade concrete slab, thin concrete slab layered on traditional wood-framed floor, or gypsum-based underlayment poured above a wood-framed floor. These use the mass of the material as a heat sink to radiate the warmth from the tubes embedded within it.

A current type system using plates installed in the tubing and placed on plywood floors without the need for poured layer is also available for use on wood framed floors. The plates act as heat sinks. This method employs strips of plywood, called *sleepers,* laid parallel to the tube runs. Heat-transfer plates that retain the heat as well as distribute the warmth in lieu of concrete mass are used. Tubing is pressed into the plates and then surrounds the tub aiding heat transfer, and locates it neatly between the plywood sleepers and another layer of plywood. The retention of heat necessitates insulating below the floor to ensure the delivery of sufficient heat to the room above as well as minimized heat loss to areas not intended to be heated.

In all cases the system requires a boiler to heat the liquid, a circulator pump, and a planned tubing circuit to efficiently deliver heat where it is most useful. The raising of the floor level because of the extra layers must be considered. Concrete adds considerable weight to the floor load and may be limiting. Partition walls will require the use of adhesive or careful placement of fasteners to ensure that the tubing is not pierced. Floorcovering should be of a type that will aid the transfer of heat; tile or wood is ideal, whereas thick rugs act to insulate and hold the heat underneath. This is a brief description of all that is involved, and a specialist should be consulted to lay out the circuit and select tube materials. In the case of the gypsum-based product, it is available only when installed by dealers. Factors such as these can determine the degree of success, but the result is worth the trouble.

ELECTRIC HEAT

Because electric heaters are easy to install and clean to operate, they are a popular choice for heating bathrooms. Besides the standard wall- and ceiling-mounted units, heaters combined with exhaust fans, lights, or both are available. Options include thermostats, timer switches, and safety cutoffs. Many units require a dedicated 120- or 240-volt circuit. It may be more practical to equip your bathroom with an electric space heater, which can be recessed in the wall or ceiling, or with an electric heat lamp.

If electric ceiling cables or panels are used in a bathroom, there is no particular problem except interference from the soffit work over the upper cabinets (if any). Other electric-resistance-type heaters are available, including panels of glass or metal that are mounted on the wall, units that have a small fan that circulates the heated air, and hot-water baseboards in which the water is heated by electrically heated elements similar to those used in a water heater. Also available are resistance units that may be inserted in the branch supply ducts of a central-air duct system. Make certain that an electric heater is properly grounded and is equipped with a thermostatic control so that it will shut off at a given temperature. In some areas these may be subject to inspection or code restrictions.

Ceiling heaters. If wall space is not available for baseboard units and a toespace installation is also not practical, electric cable can be applied to the ceiling. It is also possible to install electric-resistance panels on the ceiling to furnish radiant electric heat. They are used with plastered or plasterboard ceilings. The wires are fastened to the ceiling before installing the finished wall surfacing. These panels are rectangular in shape and resemble acoustical tile. With electric-resistance heating, a separate cooling system must be installed. In bathrooms where space is at a premium, a ceiling heater may be the answer. This handy unit combines a circulating air heater with a ventilating fan and two overhead lights. It works with lights alone, lights and fan, or heater and fan.

Toekick heaters. For bathroom installations, a small unit that resembles warm-air system registers may be installed, off to one side, in the toekick area of the vanity (rather than in the center of the vanity where it may blow heat directly onto the user's feet and legs). These units are equipped with small blowers to provide air circulation over the resistance elements, a warm welcome on a chilly morning. A toekick heater can heat the whole bathroom adequately.

Wall heaters. A wall heater should be on its own dedicated 220-volt circuit. These heaters have a 1500-watt capacity, and are adequate for heating an entire bathroom. Because it has its own thermostat, it can be turned on and off independently of the house heating system.

Light-heater combination. A light-heater combination is typically mounted in the ceiling and furnishes light as well as heat. It will increase the air temperature slightly; however, the heat produced is seldom sufficient to warm the entire bathroom. These combination devices do not need separate electrical circuits.

GAS HEATERS

Gas heaters are available in a variety of styles and sizes and for either propane or natural gas. Though most are convection heaters there is one radiant type: a catalytic heater. Regardless of how they heat, all gas models require a gas supply line and must be vented to the outside; therefore, the heater should be placed on an outside wall. Otherwise, you will have to run the vent through the attic or crawlspace and out through the roof. Most gas heaters are flush-mounted on a wall or can be recessed into a wall between two studs. There are freestanding stove units available which are an attractive feature for a spacious master suite. Options include electric ignition and wall-mounted thermostats. It is best to have a professional run gas lines; in any case, you must have the work tested and inspected before the gas is turned on.

HEATED TOWEL BARS

Besides gas and electricity, another heat source has reappeared on the bathroom scene: hot water. The original idea was to warm bath towels, but now these hydronic units—wall- or floor-mounted—are being used as "radiators" as well. Electric versions of the towel-bar heater are also available.

RADIATORS

While radiators provide a good form of heating and are often found in older homes, they are a real problem when one of them sits right where a new fixture is desired or does not suit the new decor. What can be done? Here are three basic solutions to solving the problem of a radiator in the bathroom:

1. *Cover it.* Build a cover that matches or complements the rest of the new bathroom design. But make sure that this cover allows proper circulation to heat the bathroom adequately.

2. *Move it.* Is there another location in the bathroom for the radiator? Perhaps moving it to another wall might improve the bathroom design and the heating, although this option can be costly. If a radiator is moved, it probably will still have to be covered. Remember that a radiator is located purposely to heat the room in the most efficient way. Moving it may leave a cold spot at a window.

3. *Replace it.* The old-style radiator can often be replaced with a new baseboard unit that gives more versatility in decorating the walls. These old radiators are generally of cast iron and are of column, large-tube, or small-tube design. The output of these units is expressed in British thermal units per hour (Btu/h), 1000 Btu/h (MBtu), or in square feet *equivalent direct radiators* (EDRs). Columns and large-tube radiators are no longer manufactured, but small-tube radiators are still available. When radiators are replaced by modern equipment such as convectors, finned tubes, or baseboard radiators, the replacement must be sized to supply a similar amount of heating. It is always best to consult the literature published by the manufacturer of the equipment for the exact amount of heat output of the unit.

Caution: For safety, no matter how cold the bathroom gets, portable heaters are *never* recommended as a source of heat for a bathroom. Electricity in close contact with water is a disastrous combination.

Air-Conditioning and Cooling Systems

As already mentioned, it is possible to combine heating and cooling in a central system. This is usually a good choice. It is also possible to have a separate central cooling system. In addition, window air-conditioning units or through-the-wall units may be used to cool the bathroom. This option eliminates the need for duct work, but it is not as attractive, and it might not be as efficient. With individual units, occupants can control their own comfort. If a central unit is used, some people can be chilly while others are warm. Independent units are easy to install, unlike central units, which require extensive ductwork and considerable time to install.

Window units fit into the opening of a double-hung window, and special units are available for installation in casement windows. The units vary widely in cooling capacity: from 5000 to 35,000 Btu/h. Room air is circulated through the unit, where it is cooled, dehumidified, and filtered. A condensate drain is not necessary since the moisture condensed from the air is evaporated into the outdoor air. The units are electrically operated, and many of the small ones can be plugged into existing electrical outlets. The larger units require 220 or 240 volts and use up to 200 amperes of electricity. They require a separate circuit installed specifically for the air-conditioning unit.

Through-the-wall units are simply window units that have been provided with a metal sleeve built into the wall, which makes the installation more permanent (Fig. 9.15). The chief advantage of the through-the-wall unit is that the window is not obstructed by the air-conditioning unit, and the unit may be placed high on the wall so that the distribution of the cooled air is more efficient. The chief disadvantage of the through-the-wall unit is that when the unit must be replaced after some years of service, it may be difficult to find another unit that fits the sleeve. Some manufacturers have standardized the size of the sleeves, but there are still many nonstandard units. Plan a larger opening in the wall framework and studs, with an adjustable side for the future.

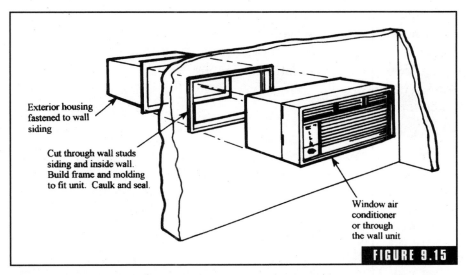

FIGURE 9.15

Exterior housing
fastened to wall
siding

Cut through wall studs
siding and inside wall.
Build frame and molding
to fit unit. Caulk and seal.

Window air
conditioner
or through
the wall unit

A portable air conditioner installed through the wall. *(Leon E. Korejwo, Illustrations.)*

HEAT PUMPS

Heat pumps have become one of the most popular, as well as flexible, forms of home heating and cooling because of their excellent energy efficiency. They provide both heating and cooling in one system, and they can be installed almost anywhere (which is extremely helpful if space is limited). While the heat pump's source of energy is electricity, it does not produce heat directly from the electric current. Heat pumps use electricity to move heat from one place to another. In the heating mode, the heat pump extracts heat from outside the house and delivers it inside. In the cooling mode, it extracts heat from the house and takes it outside. There are geothermal heat pumps that take water from wells drilled for this specific purpose. The heat from the earth is transferred via a pump and piping, to heat exchangers in the homes. This type of system would be applicable to a new-construction home or one in which the entire HVAC unit is being replaced. It would be unlikely and expensive to install as an auxiliary system for such a small addition as a bathroom.

Ventilation

Certain elements of the bathroom can be quite annoying, such as early-morning chills, steam, fogged mirrors, excess heat, and moldy wallpaper and shower curtains. To resolve these problems, every bathroom needs a good ventilation system. In fact, most building codes require that bathrooms have either natural or forced ventilation.

The two types of ventilation are natural ventilation (open windows and skylights) and mechanical ventilation (fans to draw elements out of the room).

NATURAL VENTILATION

The most common form of bathroom ventilation is with operable windows which provide natural ventilation. Skylights are another way to provide natural ventilation, while allowing natural light into the bathroom without the concerns of privacy associated with windows (for more on skylights, see Chap. 10).

MECHANICAL VENTILATION

Mechanical ventilation systems should be designed to vent the entire room to the outside. Systems which do not exhaust to the outside do not provide ventilation; they just recirculate the air in the room. Because the homeowner can't always open a window, every bathroom should have a ventilation system that expels odors, household cleaner vapors, and so on, and more importantly—because bathrooms generate large amounts of humidity—for controlling moisture.

For a bathroom without any windows, forced ventilation is required by code. In fact, some codes specify that the exhaust fan must be on the same switch as the lights. However, even if the room has good natural ventilation, consider adding forced ventilation. Recent research suggests that a vent fan should be used regardless of whether the bathroom has an operable window. An exhaust fan can exchange the air in a bathroom faster than an open window can, and in bad weather, a fan can keep the elements out and still remove stale air.

CFM Ratings: To remove moisture-laden air and odors effectively from a bathroom, it is important that the exhaust fan have adequate capacity and its needs match the room's volume; sized by the number of cubic feet of air they move each minute (cfm). The Home Ventilating Institute (HVI) suggests that the exhaust fan be capable of exchanging the entire volume of air in the bathroom at least eight times per hour. The following formulas can help determine the minimum cfm exhaust requirement for the bathroom exhaust fan:

■ For a bathroom ceiling about 8′ (243.84 cm) from the floor, the minimum size of the system can be calculated as follows:

Minimum cubic feet per minute (cfm) = room length (feet) × room width (feet) × 1.1

Using this formula, for example, a bathroom that measures 6 × 8′, the required fan capacity would be calculated as follows: 6 × 8 × 1.1 = 52.8; therefore, a fan capacity of 52.8 cfm of ventilation would be required.

■ For rooms with ceilings other than 8′ (243.84 cm), the minimum size of the system can be calculated as follows:

Minimum cubic feet per minute (cfm) = cubic space (room's L × W× H) × 8 (number of air exchanges per hour)\60 minutes (the number of minutes in an hour)

Using this formula, for example, a bathroom that measures 14′ long, 10′ wide, and has a 9′ ceiling would be calculated as follows: 14 × 10 × 9 × 8 ÷ 60 = 168 cfm.

Bathroom exhaust fans are manufactured in a variety of cfm ratings from 50 to 125 cfm and higher. In some situations, however, for example, if the house is tightly constructed, extremely energy-efficient, or has a jetted tub or indoor spa, it may be necessary to go beyond the minimum. For these special situations, exhaust fans with ratings up to 400 cfm are available.

Noise Caused by Mechanical Ventilation Systems: When comparing ventilation fans, also consider how loud it will be. Exhaust fans are constructed in several ways. They can be insulated, mounted on rubber, or have centrifugal blades instead of impeller blades. Some are constructed to resist vibration, and some are relatively flimsy. All these factors contribute to the noise the fan makes when running.

Most bathroom fans have a noise rating based on units of measurement called *sones.* The lower the sone number, the quieter the fan will run. Fans are rated on a scale of 1 to 4. A fan that is rated at 1 sone, the quietest, is about as loud as a refrigerator. It is generally recommended that a bath fan not exceed 3 sones. Fans rated at 1.5 sones will remove approximately 90 cfm, at 2.5 sones, 130 cfm; and at 3 sones, 150 cfm. The sone level will be imprinted on the fan.

TYPES OF FANS AVAILABLE

Once the fan capacity has been decided on, study the types of units available. Beyond the various cfm and sone ratings, bathroom exhaust fans are available with many additional features. A variety of exhaust fans are available to remove moisture-laden air and odors. Most bathroom fans have only one speed, although multiple-speed models are available.

There are the simple basic units which contain an exhaust fan only. Some of the more popular models are fans combined with built-in features, such as lights, heat lamps, and/or heating elements. Fans can be operated where the user turns it on and off like a light switch; however, a variety of fans are also available with automatic controls. Another type enables the light and fan to be turned on and off at the same time. There are even more sophisticated fans on the market which come equipped with motion or humidity sensors. The fan's operation senses when someone enters the room and senses the level of humidity in the room; the fan goes on when the humidity increases, and when the humidity decreases, the fan goes off. Exhaust fans can also feature timers; when the fan is turned on, the timer will keep it running for a specified period of time.

It is important, when choosing an exhaust fan, to be certain that the air will not be removed too quickly. Doing so may reduce the temperature in the bathroom too rapidly, causing the user to be chilled. The air should be removed fast enough to prevent condensation, while keeping the room at a comfortable temperature.

Finally, there are toilets that have built-in controls for eliminating odors.

EXHAUST-FAN LOCATION

The best location for an exhaust fan is in the ceiling, above a toilet, tub, or shower and as close to the shower or bathtub as possible. They can also be mounted in an outside wall or high on an exterior wall opposite the bathroom door. Some manufacturers offer a remote location fan that is mounted in the attic on a stud. This eliminates the transfer of vibration to the ceiling. It should also be as far away as possible from the source of replacement air (the door, e.g.). Most modern vents and heaters are trim, discreet, built-ins. Ceiling fans blend with white field tiles and draw heat and moisture from the steamy shower.

Fans can be mounted in the wall or ceiling. Exhaust fans are designed to be mounted in either the wall or the ceiling. It is usually easier to mount the fan in an exterior wall. Simply cut a hole, insert the fan, and that's about it. A ceiling unit requires ductwork to route the hot air into the great outdoors, and this is more difficult and expensive. To ventilate properly, the removal of moist air must be replaced, thus the technical term *replacement air.*

As with kitchen exhaust fans, check the path that the ductwork will take to the outside of the house. Another good idea for ventilation is to have adequate space under the door or to add a louver to a door bottom. If the door is flush with the threshold, moisture-laden air is blocked off. Keep the exhaust ductwork runs as short and straight as possible, and minimize the number of elbows and turns. If the fan's exhaust duct will have to twist and turn its way over a long distance or through several elbows (elbows cause friction, rendering the fan noisier and less efficient), a fan with greater capacity will be needed to overcome the increased resistance.

Most experts agree that the fan should be vented directly to the outdoors, not into the attic. The best options are to go straight through an exterior wall or straight up through a cap on the roof. Venting the fan to a downward-facing grille in a soffit under the eaves is less than ideal. Some experts say this can cause potentially serious moisture problems. Be certain to check with local building codes before making any final decisions. The local building code may specify where the fan must be placed. The use of smooth duct rather than flex duct can also reduce the noise of ventilating systems. In an unheated attic, when temperatures drop below freezing, the problem of moisture is observed by frost on the roofing nails. This promotes deterioration and must be corrected by venting to the outside. In some cases attics are not properly vented in spite of the bath fan.

In the bathroom, the real culprit is condensation. When the warm, moisture-laden air contacts a relatively cool surface, the result is condensation and the surface sweats. You will see the condensation on surfaces such as a toilet or medicine chest mirror. Ventilation is important. Without a designated means of escape, uncontrolled moisture will destroy bathroom materials. Moisture will build up and penetrate walls, ceilings, floors, and countertops, loosen wallcovering seams, rust fixtures, peel paint, rot wood, and so on.

Electrical Considerations

Adequate electrical provisions are quite important when planning a new bathroom installation or remodel. If fixtures are to be moved within the existing bathroom or a new bathroom is being installed, the electrical system will most likely need to be modified (relocating lights and power outlets, for hair dryers, etc.). In the case of a remodel, bringing the electrical system up to current standards or code will make the bathroom safer as well as more convenient. Although electrical needs for most bathrooms are quite simple, it is essential to making any bathroom functional. Electrical requirements in a typical bathroom usually include one electrical receptacle near a vanity, an overhead light or a fixture above the mirror, an exhaust fan, and possibly a wall heater. Codes dictate the location of outlets and switches, as well as upgrading to ground-fault-protected outlets.

When planning a bathroom, take a good look at the existing electrical system (when applicable). Note the location and number of electrical outlets and switches. Decide whether there are enough outlets, and whether switches and outlets are conveniently placed. Working with the electrical wiring in a part of the house is not extremely difficult if you take the time and effort to plan and understand the work and what is required, and proceed with safety first and foremost in mind.

Caution: Before beginning work, remember to always be certain that all electrical power is turned off to all areas. *Never* work on any live circuit, fixture, plug-in outlet, or switch. Your life may depend on it. Turn off the circuit breaker or remove the fuse and make sure no one can turn the electricity back on.

A trade license is usually required to handle electricity, so in most instances, you need to hire a subcontractor. However, as the builder, you must become knowledgeable about electrical requirements and codes and be confident that you understand their impact on each project. It is important to have a general understanding of electricity so that you can inspect the existing electrical service, if applicable, to recognize what may need to be modified, and intelligently discuss the project with an electrical contractor.

An electrician will typically be needed at two stages during construction. The first is during the rough-in stage (right after changes to the wall framing have been made) when the wiring is rerouted or threaded through walls. The second stage is after all surface materials have been applied, to finish the job, by installing lighting fixtures, outlets, and switches. Most electricians will also install wiring for telephones, intercom systems, and other facilities in the bathroom.

The *National Electric Code*

The *National Electric Code* (NEC) is the most complete, detailed set of guidelines, specifying correct installation methods and types of materials acceptable for various jobs. Codes may strictly dictate the placement of outlets, appliance switches, and even light fixtures in the wet bath areas. Failure to abide by specific electrical codes and installation practices could result in fire or electrocution. In some communities, local regulations sometimes supersede the NEC, so it is important to know what the local regulations are, too. Ultimately, the last word on what can and can't be done electrically comes from the local building code. Also, be sure that materials you intend to use are approved by the power company.

Most codes stipulate that the entire system be brought up to present-day standards anytime a change is made. Begin by determining what plumbing pipes, heating ducts, and other electrical wires are already concealed there. If existing wiring is on the verge of being in violation of current codes, you, along with your client, must decide whether to upgrade the wiring. Some builders may choose to do nothing, although it is usually recommended to upgrade any wiring that is questionable. Prepare your client for the possible additional expenses of bringing in more power to the home's main service panel. Whenever major construction and wall removal is planned, remember to figure in adequate costs for electrical removal as well.

Electricity Basics

Power from the utility comes in through a service entrance to a meter that keeps track of the consumption (total use measured in kilowatthours). The power then continues on to a service panel (located inside the house near the electric meter or in the basement directly below the electric meter), which breaks it down into a series of circuits. The term *circuit* means the course that electric current travels. These circuits deliver current throughout the house, and when the circuit is interrupted, so is the electricity. Circuit wires go through walls and ceilings to the receptacles or switches, where electricity is tapped off for use. In the bathroom, circuits supply power to electrical outlets, switches, light fixtures, fans, and heaters.

At the service panel, fuses or circuit breakers control individual circuits and protect against fire, which could develop if a circuit draws more current than it is designed to handle. In most newer installations, the safety-protecting devices are called circuit breakers (which turn on and off like a switch). In an older home, in which the original wiring is intact, the service panel may contain fuses (when a main fuse blows, all power to the house shuts off) rather than breakers. Even if the house has several fuses, replace the fuse box with an updated panel and circuit breakers. It is much more convenient to flip the reset switch on a breaker than to replace a fuse.

The number of new circuits needed and the voltage each must carry must be determined. Most houses today have both 120- and 240-volt capabilities. A single circuit breaker controls a 120-volt circuit. A 240-volt circuit is controlled by two circuit breakers which might be connected with a plastic cap. Any 240-volt circuit serves only one outlet, such as an electric clothes dryer. A 120-volt circuit might serve as many as a dozen outlets, as long as the total amperage of the lights and appliances does not exceed the amperage rating of that circuit breaker or fuse. If a circuit is forced to carry too much current, the fuse or circuit breaker will be overloaded or short-circuited, and the breaker will then automatically break the flow of current. Ground circuits (discussed in greater detail later in this chapter) are an important part of the wiring. Older homes with two-wire (120-volt-only) service of less than 100 amperes probably can't supply the electricity needed to operate a new electric heater, whirlpool tub, steam generator, or sauna. For equipment such as this, the electrical system will need to be upgraded to meet current standards.

Electrical current flows, under pressure, through the wiring in the house. The amount of current (measured in amperes) going through a wire at a given time is based on the number of electrons passing a certain point each second. Different circuits need different amperages. For example, lights typically use 15 amperes and large appliances need 20 to 50 amperes. The pressure that forces these electrons along their route is known as *voltage* (measured in volts). The voltages required for different appliances vary; lights and small appliances need only 120 volts, while large appliances need 240 volts to push the electricity through the wire. One hot wire and the neutral wire combine to provide 120 volts primarily for lights and plug-in outlets. Two hot wires combine to provide 240 volts, often used for electric heaters. The power, termed *wattage,* used in terms of both amperage and voltage is measured in watts. To determine watts used, multiply amperes by volts.

In the bathroom, fixtures such as whirlpools and spas may need their own dedicated circuit to power a pump and/or heater. Always check with manufacturer's instructions for any special equipment requirements. Permanently installed equipment, such as a bath ventilation fan, and combined with a resistance heater and room light, may require its own 20-ampere circuit. The restrictions on the proximity of electrical controls and switches to sources of water, such as the bathtub, are strict. Controls for a whirlpool tub or spa are often installed outside the bathroom because of the limited size of a typical bathroom. As stated repeatedly throughout this book, always thoroughly review applicable electrical codes.

Electrical current goes to the service panel on *three-wire service,* in which each of the two hot wires supplies electricity at approximately 120 volts and the third, or neutral wire, is maintained at 0 volts. These wires provide both 120- and 240-volt circuits in the house. Some small appliances may operate on low-voltage current, usually around 10 or 12 volts, but possibly ranging from 6 to 24 volts. Their voltage is cut down by a small transformer wired in anywhere between the appliance and the service panel. Figure 9.16 shows an approximation of typical bath wiring requirements.

Portable appliances and devices are readily connected to an electrical supply circuit by means of an outlet called a *receptacle.* A *duplex outlet* is one that has two receptacles. A receptacle with two slots is a *two-wire receptacle.* Newer houses have three-wire receptacles, which have two slots and a round hole. The third wire on the three-wire receptacle is used to provide a ground lead to the equipment that receives power from the receptacle. The three-wire receptacle takes the regular two-prong plugs still found on some appliances. However, it is wise to ground a receptacle and is required by electrical codes. Another feature of modern receptacles is polarization, in which one slot is larger than the other to accept modern polarized plugs. The larger slot connects to the white neutral wire, the small slot to the hot

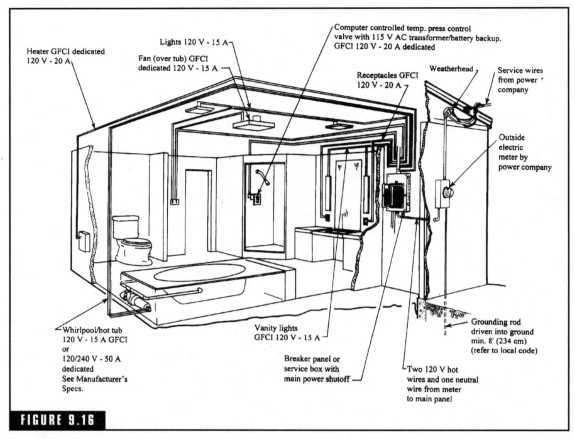

Heater GFCI dedicated
120 V - 20 A

Lights 120 V - 15 A

Fan (over tub) GFCI
dedicated 120 V - 15 A

Computer controlled temp. press control
valve with 115 V AC transformer/battery backup.
GFCI 120 V - 20 A dedicated

Receptacles GFCI
120 V - 20 A

Weatherhead

Service wires
from power
company

Outside
electric
meter by
power company

Whirlpool/hot tub
120 V - 15 A GFCI
or
120/240 V - 50 A
dedicated
See Manufacturer's
Specs.

Vanity lights
GFCI 120 V - 15 A

Breaker panel or
service box with
main power shutoff

Two 120 V hot
wires and one neutral
wire from meter
to main panel

Grounding rod
driven into ground
min. 8' (234 cm)
(refer to local code)

FIGURE 9.16

Household wiring showing bathroom circuit options. *(Leon E. Korejwo, Illustrations.)*

wire, ensuring that the switch always interrupts the flow of current so no current can flow in when the switch is off. If polarity is reversed, an exposed socket can give a shock even when the switch is off and the light or appliance isn't running.

Wherever there is an outlet or any other place where wires are joined (switch, light fixture, etc.), it must be installed in a *junction box,* a box used to contain only wiring. These metal or plastic boxes come in many sizes and shapes, with knock-out holes so that wiring can be brought in from any direction. Electrical light switches, receptacles, and light fixtures are mounted to boxes that are nailed to wall studs, joists, or floor plates, and come with various types of fasteners for different conditions of new and existing construction. The best time to install electrical boxes is while walls are opened up to the bare studs. The NEC does not permit any wire connections outside a box, and limits how many wires can be installed in any one box. Always check with the local building department as to which type of box is acceptable.

Expanding Existing Electric Service

If you open the door of the service panel (control center for electrical system), you will see all the circuit breakers or fuses. If you see blank slots with no breakers, they are places where new breakers can be installed to expand the house electrical system with more circuits. In remodeling a bathroom, you may want to add circuits. You might be able to combine some circuits that have light loads to create an open slot or two for expansion.

Older houses often were rated at only 60 amperes for the entire house. Today, houses are likely to need 150 or 200 amperes. The main breaker on the service panel should show the house rating. It is usually a double breaker in line with all the others that is larger and a different color. This rating might be the number 60 or 100 molded or pressed into the tops of the two breakers. In a remodel, consider upgrading to 150 or 200 amperes to provide circuitry for future needs. The service ampere rating is obtained by adding together the current required for general lighting, major appliances, motors, appliance circuits, and other special circuits. Circuit breakers (which, as previously stated, should be used in place of a fuse box) should be placed in an easy-to-reach location to enable the homeowner to find it in the dark.

Electric Circuits

Most residential wiring today is done using nonmetallic sheathed cable (NM cable). NM cable contains three or more individual wires, each with their own color-coded insulation. The number of the conductors grouped together in the cable is dependent on the type of circuit you are running. For example, most 110-volt circuits require three wires (including the ground wire), while some types, such as those for three-way lights, require a four-wire cable. Likewise, most 220-volt circuits will require a four-wire cable. The size of wire used in the conductors determines the available amperes in the circuit (the amount of electrical flow available). The sizes are designated by gauge number. As the numbers increase in numerical value, the amperes decrease. Be sure to check the incoming wire size. Every builder should know how to determine capacity or at least know when to call the electrician.

Bathroom Wiring Plan

Wire is composed of copper covered with insulation and then covered with a ribbed metal casing or a plastic casing. The larger the gauge number, the thinner the wire and the less current it can carry (refer to Table 9.3). The smaller the number, the thicker the wire and the more current it can carry. Large appliances need more current than the average device, such as a lamp, and therefore require heavier wire.

Modern bathrooms require an adequate supply of electricity. Of course, adequate wiring in a bathroom includes general-purpose circuits for lighting, branch circuits for small appliances, and individual major-equipment branch circuits (such as a whirlpool). The recommendations may vary from city to city, depending on standards and codes.

Using the cabinet and fixture layouts and floor plan, be sure to plot out an electrical plan to ensure that your clients receive all the wiring needed in their bathroom. Give some thought to other kinds of wire that might need to be installed in the walls. For example, in addition to general electrical requirements in the kitchens and bathrooms, clients today may also wish to have television and telephone service. For an elaborate bathroom suite, prewire phone jacks, wires for cable television, security systems, door chimes, thermostats, and

Table 9-3 Wire Size as Determined by Circuit Amperage

Wire size, AWG* no.	Circuit size, A
6	55
8	40
10	30
12	20
14	15

*American Wire Gauge.

other appliances. They should always be placed at the safest location possible.

Running future-use wires when walls are open and stripped to the studs is much easier than working with them after everything is sealed up. Rewiring can be done without tearing off wall and ceiling finishes, but not as easily as when the framing is exposed. While drawing up the plans, the designer should also provide an electrical plan (Fig. 9.17*a*), as well as a lighting plan for the electrician to work from (Fig. 9.17*b*); these plans include a table of electrical symbols (Fig. 9.17*c*). It is important to remember that no matter who provides the plan, it is best to have it verified by a local electrical inspector.

When remodeling a bathroom, it is important to replace aluminum wiring with copper wiring. Aluminum may have been used in the main service wires; however, its use in branch circuits may have been linked to a large number of electrical fires. The NEC does not permit the addition of new aluminum wiring.

Wiring Color Coding

To ensure universal wiring and safety, all electrical wiring today is color-coded. The individual wires in the cable each have a colored jacket to simplify the proper installation. The neutral wire is always white or gray. The ground wire is either bare or color-coded green. Hot wires are colored black, red, or any color other than green, white, or bare.

Grounding and Ground-Fault Circuit Interrupters (GFCIs)

The most important factor to keep in mind when working with electricity is safety; electrically speaking, the bathroom is probably the most dangerous room in the house. Bathrooms pose hazards not found in most other parts of the house because water and metal pipes are good conductors of electricity. Standard electrical outlets should be protected by GFCI devices to reduce the hazards of shock present in wet areas. On its way to the ground, the electrical current may pass through the body of any person who comes in contact with the piping system while handling appliances or switches.

The *National Electric Code* requires that all new wiring in the home be grounded (a safety measure built into every household electrical system), regardless of whether the existing wiring is grounded. In some instances, officials will make you upgrade the existing wiring

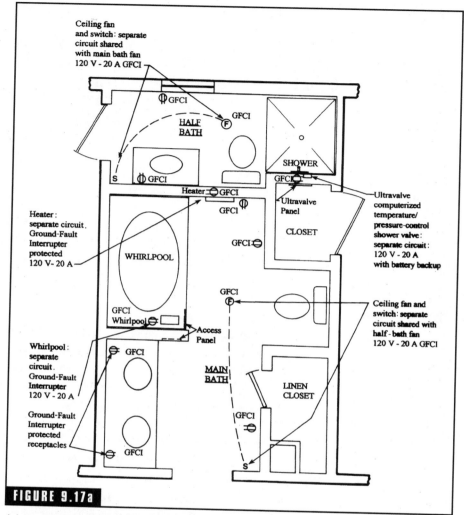

Ceiling fan
and switch: separate
circuit shared
with main bath fan
120 V - 20 A GFCI

GFCI

HALF
BATH

GFCI

GFCI

S

GFCI

Heater

GFCI

GFCI

Heater:
separate circuit.
Ground-Fault
Interrupter
protected
120 V- 20 A

GFCI

WHIRLPOOL

SHOWER

GFCI

Ultravalve
Panel

Ultravalve
computerized
temperature/
pressure-control
shower valve:
separate circuit:
120 V - 20 A
with battery backup

CLOSET

GFCI

GFCI
Whirlpool

Access
Panel

GFCI

Whirlpool:
separate
circuit.
Ground-Fault
Interrupter
120 V - 20 A

Ground-Fault
Interrupter
protected
receptacles

GFCI

GFCI

MAIN
BATH

LINEN
CLOSET

Ceiling fan and
switch: separate
circuit shared with
half-bath fan
120 V - 20 A GFCI

GFCI

S

FIGURE 9.17a

(*a*) **Bathroom electrical plan.** (*b*) **Bathroom lighting plan.** (*c*) **Electrical symbols.** (*Leon E. Korejwo, Illustrations.*)

if it is ungrounded and appears unsafe. Grounding is accomplished through the use of a third wire in the circuit (the bare copper or green-jacketed wire) and provides an alternate route for any leaking current, protecting the circuit and family members from shock. The main grounding wire connects all the metal parts within the electrical system to the service panel and from there to a ground source, usually a metal cold-water pipe, or a grounding rod buried in the earth [driven

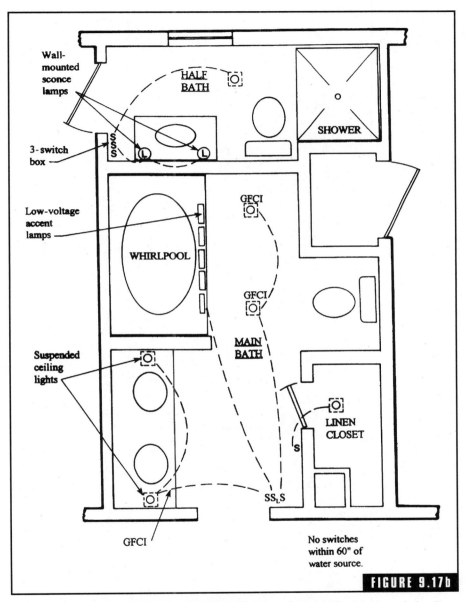

Wall-mounted sconce lamps

HALF BATH

SHOWER

3-switch box

S S S

L L

Low-voltage accent lamps

WHIRLPOOL

GFCI

GFCI

MAIN BATH

Suspended ceiling lights

LINEN CLOSET

S

GFCI

SS$_L$S

No switches within 60" of water source.

FIGURE 9.17b

(*a*) **Bathroom electrical plan.** (*b*) **Bathroom lighting plan.** (*c*) **Electrical symbols.** (*Leon E. Korejwo, Illustrations.*)

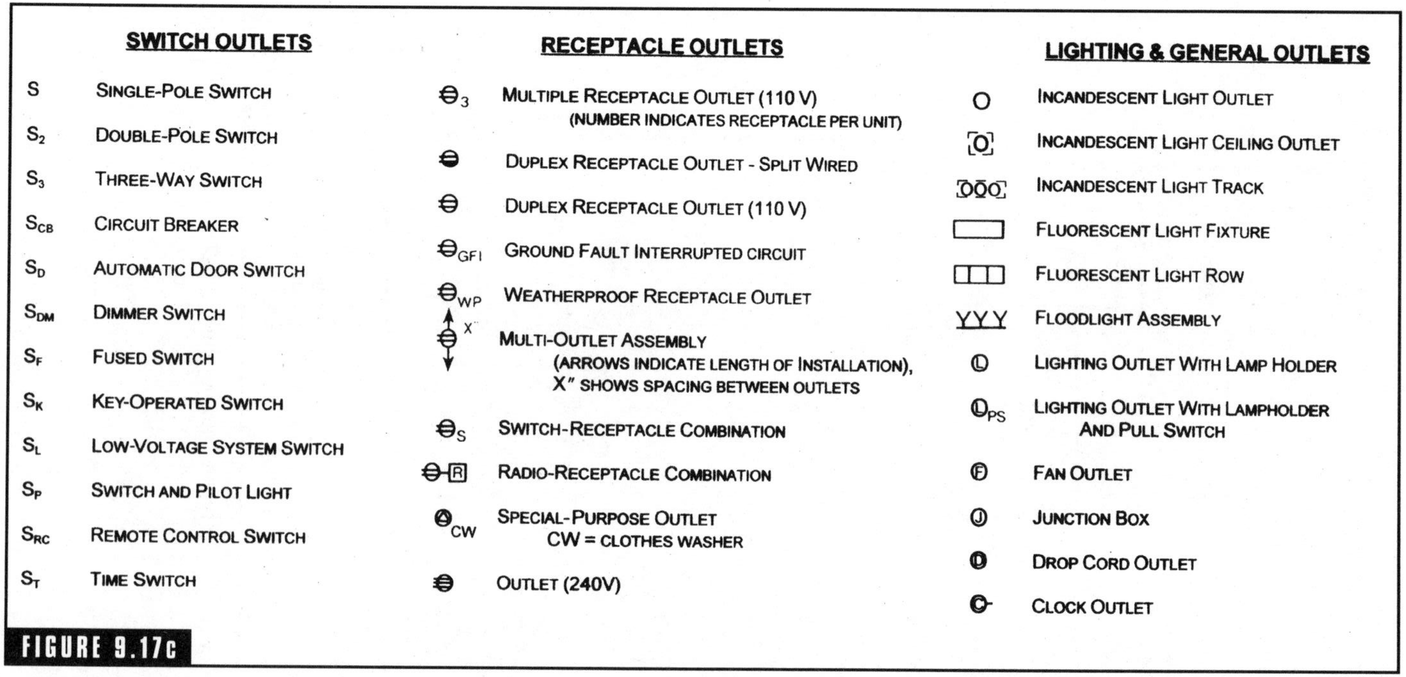

SWITCH OUTLETS

S	SINGLE-POLE SWITCH
S_2	DOUBLE-POLE SWITCH
S_3	THREE-WAY SWITCH
S_{CB}	CIRCUIT BREAKER
S_D	AUTOMATIC DOOR SWITCH
S_{DM}	DIMMER SWITCH
S_F	FUSED SWITCH
S_K	KEY-OPERATED SWITCH
S_L	LOW-VOLTAGE SYSTEM SWITCH
S_P	SWITCH AND PILOT LIGHT
S_{RC}	REMOTE CONTROL SWITCH
S_T	TIME SWITCH

RECEPTACLE OUTLETS

$\oplus_3$	MULTIPLE RECEPTACLE OUTLET (110 V) (NUMBER INDICATES RECEPTACLE PER UNIT)
$\oplus$	DUPLEX RECEPTACLE OUTLET - SPLIT WIRED
$\oplus$	DUPLEX RECEPTACLE OUTLET (110 V)
$\oplus_{GFI}$	GROUND FAULT INTERRUPTED CIRCUIT
$\oplus_{WP}$	WEATHERPROOF RECEPTACLE OUTLET
$\oplus_x$	MULTI-OUTLET ASSEMBLY (ARROWS INDICATE LENGTH OF INSTALLATION, X" SHOWS SPACING BETWEEN OUTLETS
$\oplus_S$	SWITCH-RECEPTACLE COMBINATION
$\oplus$-Ⓡ	RADIO-RECEPTACLE COMBINATION
$\oplus_{CW}$	SPECIAL-PURPOSE OUTLET CW = CLOTHES WASHER
$\oplus$	OUTLET (240V)

LIGHTING & GENERAL OUTLETS

O	INCANDESCENT LIGHT OUTLET
[O]	INCANDESCENT LIGHT CEILING OUTLET
OOO	INCANDESCENT LIGHT TRACK
☐	FLUORESCENT LIGHT FIXTURE
☐☐☐	FLUORESCENT LIGHT ROW
YYY	FLOODLIGHT ASSEMBLY
Ⓛ	LIGHTING OUTLET WITH LAMP HOLDER
Ⓛ$_{PS}$	LIGHTING OUTLET WITH LAMPHOLDER AND PULL SWITCH
Ⓕ	FAN OUTLET
Ⓙ	JUNCTION BOX
Ⓓ	DROP CORD OUTLET
Ⓒ-	CLOCK OUTLET

FIGURE 9.17c

(*a*) Bathroom electrical plan. (*b*) Bathroom lighting plan. (*c*) Electrical symbols. *(Leon E. Korejwo, Illustrations.)*

at least 8 feet (244 cm) into the ground] or in the building's foundation. Older homes may have the metal plumbing used as a ground. Code compliance is vital when remodeling this type of home. Previously installed plastic pipe that may have been inserted between sections of metal plumbing may have destroyed the grounding to sections of the house not within your contracted area. Be aware that although your project does not involve major rewiring, you may still want to consult a professional electrician during the estimating phase. When connecting appliances, fixtures, receptacles, or any other metal electrical component, always look for the green grounding screw and be certain that the ground wire in the NM cable is connected to it.

Ordinary receptacles, even when containing a grounding wire, don't completely protect you against electrical shock; ground-fault circuit interrupters (GFCIs) do. Ground-fault circuit interrupters must be installed on all receptacles, lights, and switches in the bathroom. Code requires that GFCIs be used in fans and lights above tubs or showers, in whirlpool wiring, and in bathroom receptacles. All light fixtures above the bathtub/shower units must be moistureproof, special-purpose fixtures, and no lighting fixture, including hanging fixtures, should be within reach of a person seated or standing in the tub or shower area. In most localities building codes won't give you a choice; GFCIs must be used, or at least certain items must have them and be on dedicated (serving that appliance only) circuits, including whirlpools, saunas, steam generators, heaters, and other devices where shock hazard is present.

Switches must be installed out of reach of the bathtub or shower; they should never be reachable to anyone standing in water. A GFCI breaker, which is located at the main breaker box, is so sensitive that when it detects the imbalance, it trips the breaker and shuts down the circuit when even a tiny leakage occurs. A GFCI outlet, which has its breaker and reset included right in its own wall unit, accomplishes the same effect. The shutoff action is so fast (within $1/30$ to $1/40$ second), there is not enough time to be injured. As little as 200 milliamperes (about enough to light a 25-watt bulb) can kill if you happen to be touching plumbing components or standing on wet earth. A test button and a reset button are located on either GFCI breaker or outlet. It should be tested regularly by pushing the test button, then reset by pushing the reset button.

Three ways to protect circuits with a GFCI are as follows:

1. The most inexpensive and easiest is a portable device that is plugged into the outlet of the receptacle you want to protect. It protects only that outlet.

2. Replace the receptacle with a GFCI receptacle, which offers the opportunity to protect receptacles downstream from the one you are replacing; this is a slightly more expensive method.

3. To protect all receptacles and devices connected to the bathroom, wire them to a single circuit and install a GFCI breaker in the panel box. This is the most expensive way to achieve protection.

If adding a new wall, the accepted modern standard for wiring in new houses (and in some areas may be required by code) is to put an outlet at least every 12 feet (366 cm) or one per wall, regardless of the wall's length in every wall and within 6 feet (183 cm) of every door. These outlets usually are on a 20-ampere circuit with 12-gauge wire, although the slightly smaller 14-gauge is adequate for bathroom lighting, radio, and television.

When adding one light or moving an existing light, simply adding wiring from an existing switch may be easily accomplished (Fig. 9.18a) when an additional receptacle is desired and the circuit you plan to put it on will not be overloaded. You may run new wiring from an existing receptacle as shown in Fig. 9.18b. As mentioned earlier, some appliances will require a separate, dedicated (serving that appliance only) circuit. The circuit size must be sufficient to serve the appliance's amperage rating, as listed on the appliance nameplate.

Noise Abatement

Noise in a new or remodeled bathroom can be kept at a reasonable level if the following antinoise steps are taken:

1. One of the first things to consider is the installation of sound-insulating walls. The application of an extra layer of material on a wall helps, but a staggered stud wall that allows weaving of insulation material through the studs gives a great deal of sound protection.

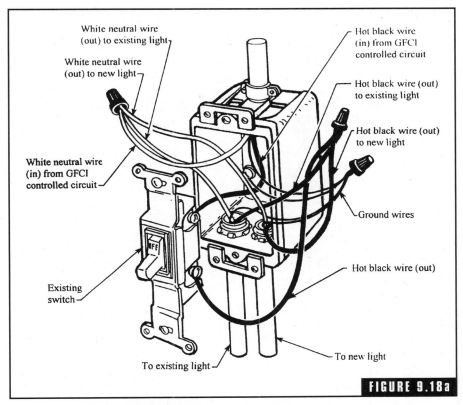

Wiring a new light from existing switch. *(Leon E. Korejwo, Illustrations.)*

2. Acoustical ceiling panels or tile, carpeting, and fabrics used for curtains absorbs most of the sound that reaches them.

3. Noise transmits to other rooms through lighting fixtures, electrical outlets, and heating ducts. Seal these with insulating material. Use insulating panels over the ceiling wallboard and beneath floor underlayment.

4. Avoid placing any switches or outlets back to back. Position junction boxes on opposite sides of the same wall to allow 36″ (91 cm) of lateral distance between them.

5. Long runs of hot-water supply creak or snap as they expand or contract. Differences of up to 100°F can exist in piping and can cause expansion up to $1/8$″ in 10′. Noise occurs when expanding

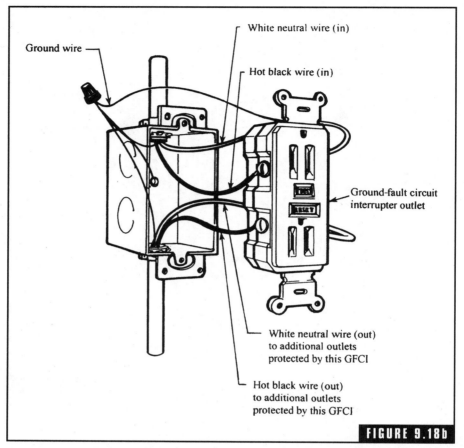

Ground wire

White neutral wire (in)

Hot black wire (in)

Ground-fault circuit interrupter outlet

White neutral wire (out) to additional outlets protected by this GFCI

Hot black wire (out) to additional outlets protected by this GFCI

FIGURE 9.18b

Wiring from an existing receptacle to a new one through the use of a GFCI receptacle. *(Leon E. Korejwo, Illustrations.)*

pipe is forced against its hangers or surrounding structural members. Allow space for growth at the end of long runs where pipes change directions.

6. Holes cut through common walls for plumbing or heating may leak noise. Seal all holes with a resilient material to isolate noise and seal against air leaks, either vertical or horizontal.

7. Make sure that room air conditioners and vent fans are properly mounted to avoid excess vibration. Ductwork should be designed without reduction in size and with a minimum of turns.

8. Install air chambers or pneumatic antihammer devices in the water lines to stop any hammering noises.

9. Attach ceiling fixtures so that fasteners are set into furring strips attached to the ceiling joists with spring clips. The clips will absorb any noise that may develop in the fixture.

Finishings: Floors, Walls, Ceiling, and Lighting

There has been a revolution in bathroom furnishings and materials, with a wider-than-ever selection, available in an amazing variety of materials, textures, patterns, and colors, and a new emphasis on easy-care materials (Fig. 10.1). Some installers may or may not be involved when the homeowners decide on the type of floor, wall, ceiling, or lighting finishings for their bathroom. However, it is very important for you to know what is available, as well as learn some basic facts about these finishings to inform your client, if and when the need arises. Whether you are subcontracting the finishing work or have excluded it from the contract altogether, the ultimate responsibility for the client's satisfaction lies with you. Therefore, being knowledgeable in the following areas is important to you. This chapter covers the most important information about the types of floor, wall, ceiling, and lighting finishings available; however, it does not cover how to completely install each particular type of finishing. For floor, wall, and ceiling installation procedures, refer to Chap. 8.

Floor Finishings

Innovations in design and manufacture have made many flooring materials easier to install. Ceramic tile, once thought to require the

FIGURE 10.1

Today's bathroom has unlimited finishing possibilities with the wide variety of materials, patterns, textures, and colors available. *(Weixler, Peterson & Luzi Interior Designers, Philadelphia.)*

skills of only a professional, can be installed today by anyone with patience and average building talent. Hardwood flooring can be purchased with durable factory-applied finishes. Vinyl tiles come with adhesive backing or can be set in easy-to-apply adhesives.

Floors, like walls, are not easy to change. Whether applying a floor material to a new home bathroom or reconditioning a floor in an existing portion of the structure, the finished flooring must be chosen carefully and wisely. The term *finished flooring* refers, of course, to the material used as the final wearing surface that is applied to a floor.

What kind of floors should be used in the bathroom? The bathroom floor should be beautiful and should complement the decor. It is an important design feature which sets the style and integrates all the bathroom components together. Aside from the kitchen floor, no other floor gets as much wear and abuse as the one in the bathroom. When choosing materials, the top priority should be how the materials will function in terms of how the family will utilize the bathroom. The following factors should be considered:

- *Durability and moisture resistance.* Determine the amount of usage the flooring must bear. For high-traffic areas, select the most durable materials. Remember that a family with small children requires a floor capable of handling the occasional tub overflow or clandestine dog bath.

- *Cost.* All standard flooring materials come in various grades, with the cost directly related to the quality.

- *Comfort.* If the homeowners object to a cold, hard surface, they may not want to use ceramic tile or masonry. Wood or resilient flooring provides a more comfortable surface; the flooring should have some resiliency.

- *Noise.* Realize that soft flooring materials, such as vinyl and carpeting, deaden sound. Wood, ceramic tile, masonry, and other hard surfaces tend to reflect sound, rather than absorb it.

- *Safety.* Safety is an important factor to consider when choosing flooring. The floor should be smooth without being slippery, and it should be level. Keep in mind that although glazed tile is common in bathrooms, it can become very slippery when wet. Textured tiles, similar to quarry tile, may be helpful here.

- *Cleanability.* New floor materials, protective finishes, and cleaning techniques make maintenance less of a consideration now than in the past. However, grout is always a maintenance consideration.

Resilient Vinyl

The development of resins and synthetics has created a family of floorcoverings called *resilient flooring.* Durable, easy to maintain, and soft underfoot, vinyl has long been a favorite in the bathroom. Resilient vinyl is one of the easiest floor surfaces to install. Almost all vinyl floors produced today are the no-wax type with a durable shine that needs minimal maintenance, is stain-resistant, and is impervious to water. There are a seemingly endless variety of color textures, patterns, and styles available, in a wide range of prices. Several quality grades are produced by any vinyl flooring manufacturer. The three common types of vinyl are:

- *Inlaid flooring.* Inlaid flooring is solid vinyl made up of tiny vinyl granules fused together so that the color and pattern go all the way through to the backing. Wear does not erase the vinyl pattern. These vinyls are the most costly, but they can last 30 years or more.

- *Rotovinyl.* Rotovinyl is produced by covering a photographic image with a layer of clear urethane. Pattern and color are only on the surface of the material. The wear layer's thickness affects price and determines how long the floor will look good. However, in areas of heavy traffic, even the most expensive rotovinyls can wear through over time.

- *Vinyl composition.* Vinyl composition coverings combine vinyl resins with filler materials. This least expensive vinyl floor type can show signs of wear in about 5 years.

The one major disadvantage to resilient vinyl flooring is that it is relatively soft, making it vulnerable to dents and tears. However, these damages can usually be repaired.

Resilient vinyl floors are manufactured in two basic types: sheet materials and tiles. Whether the homeowner chooses to have tiles or sheet vinyl installed depends, to some extent, on the use the new floor will receive.

Resilient Sheet Flooring

Most resilients are made with a solid vinyl coating called *polyurethane.* Sheet vinyls are available in widths from 6 to 12 feet (182.88 to 365.7 cm) and generally cost more than comparative grades of vinyl tiles. The principal advantage of sheet vinyl in the bathroom is seamlessness. The result is a beautiful wall-to-wall sweep of color and design (Fig. 10.2). Be aware that large rooms, usually over 12 feet (366 cm), will require seams with most types of sheet vinyl. The average bathroom floor can be laid without a seam; however, some manufacturers do produce wider rolls of vinyl.

Sheet flooring can be fully adhered (laid in adhesive over the entire floor), peripherally fastened (attached with adhesive), or laid loosely like a rug. The introduction of better materials and the manufacturer's ability to improve photographic realism has improved the ability of vinyl to mimic natural materials. The hundreds of patterns available include authentic-looking imitations of all types of flooring: brick, slate, wood, marble, terrazzo, flagstone, and ceramic tile. Resilient flooring can be laid on concrete slabs on grade (directly on the ground) or below grade (underground, as in a basement), on wood subfloors made of plywood panels or individual boards, or over an old floor, depending on its existing condition (to prepare the room for installing resilient flooring over various surfaces, refer to Table 8.1 in Chap. 8).

FIGURE 10.2

Resilient sheet flooring provides a beautiful seamlessness for any bathroom. *(Armstrong World Industries, Inc.)*

Vinyl Tiles

Vinyl (the most popular material for resilient tiles) tiles are still used, but are not nearly as popular as sheet goods. Vinyl tiles are available in 9- or 12-inch (23- or 30-cm) squares, although other sizes are available, up to as large as 36 × 36 inches (91 × 91 cm). Individual tiles either come with a self-stick backing or are laid in adhesive. Vinyl tiles are fairly easy to install, but they do take longer to install than sheet vinyl. If they are improperly installed, moisture can seep between tiles and cause damage to the underlayment and subfloor. Vinyl tiles can come loose, and the cracks between the tiles can catch dirt, making them difficult to clean.

With the tremendous variety of materials, designs, and colors available, it is possible to create just about any floor scheme that strikes one's fancy. Tiles can be mixed to form custom patterns or provide color accents. As with vinyl sheet flooring, raised surfaces give many vinyl tile products the realistic look and feel of brick, stone, slate, wood, terrazzo, marble, or ceramic tile. A new trend is with faux-wood vinyl planks which are available in 3-inch- (8-cm)-wide strips that can be installed much like the real thing—in random or herringbone patterns.

Ceramic Tile

Ceramic tile is the most popular choice for bathrooms because it is easy to maintain, tough to harm (it is fireproof and waterproof), and available in a wide variety of patterns, styles, and colors that can complement any room (Fig. 10.3). When properly installed, ceramic tile has timeless elegance and is one of the most durable floor coverings available (to prepare the room for installing ceramic tile flooring, refer to Table 8.2 in Chap. 8).

Three types of ceramic tiles are common in bathroom floor use today: glazed tiles, ceramic mosaics, and quarry tiles.

FIGURE 10.3

Ceramic tile floors provide a lifetime of durability and style for the bathroom. *(Florida Tile Industries.)*

Glazed ceramic tile can be shiny or bright-glazed, matte-glazed, or textured, and has a frostinglike layer on top that was sprayed on before firing. It is a good choice in the bathroom because liquids can't soak in. The tiles are made in various sizes and shapes and a variety of designs and colors. Some are so perfectly glazed that they form a monochromatic surface. Others have a softer, natural shade variation within each unit and from tile to tile. Sizes generally range from 1 to 12 inches square (2.54 to 30.48 cm); the most common size is $4^{1}/4 \times {}^{5}/16$ inch (10.79 × 0.79 cm) thick. Another popular option in bathrooms are the use of tiles in octagon and rectangular shapes.

Ceramic mosaics are made from clay mixed with pigment. They are available in a large assortment of colorful shapes. Mosaics are usually sold mounted in 1 × 1-foot (30.5- × 30.5-cm) squares or 1 × 2-foot (30.5- × 61-cm) octagons, $1/4$ inch (0.6 cm) thick, with or without a glaze. Smaller mosaic tiles come bonded to pieces of 1 × 1- (30.5- × 30.5-cm) or 1 × 2-foot (30.5- × 61-cm) paper or fabric mesh.

Quarry tiles are unglazed ceramic tiles that are colored through and through in natural clay colors and pastel shades. Quarry tiles are available in shapes ranging from 6- to 8-inch (15- to 20-cm) square tiles, 4 × 8-inch (10- × 20-cm) rectangles, and are normally $1/2$ inch (1.27 cm) thick. Some quarry tiles, however, must be protected with a masonry sealer after installation to prevent staining. Quarry tile is suitable for bathroom use but requires more care than other types to keep it looking great. Today's market offers decorative tile products that simulate natural materials, surfaces, and texture: rustic stone textures in colors indicative of nature's minerals. These beautiful tiles merge well with a wide array of decorative applications and color schemes.

There are, however, a few drawbacks to ceramic tile floors in bathrooms. First is its cost. Ceramic tile is very expensive when compared to vinyl floorings. Also, fragile items dropped on a tile floor will break. The tile itself is susceptible to cracking if the floor shifts or if hard objects are dropped on it. The floor can be noisy, and, if glazed, very slippery underfoot, and can therefore make getting out of the bathtub difficult. If not properly grouted, tiles can leak moisture and may come loose. Grout lines can be tough to clean and some tiles may stain or promote mildew, so a sealer may be required. Manufacturer recommendations for sealers, grouts, and installations should be consulted.

Today, many new materials are being brought out in an effort to be environmentally safe. Many of these products are so new that what was purchased 6 months ago may not be mixed with what is on the shelf today. Buy all products together, read directions, and seek the advice of reputable retailers. When in doubt, contact the manufacturer for assistance. Warranties are dependent on strict adherence to applications as directed. In addition, drying times have an effect on final durability, more so with current goods. The shelf life of some grouts may deteriorate on exposure to moisture, and those which have aged may not cure properly.

Always use tiles specifically designed for a floor installation. Tiles manufactured for walls or countertops may not be designed for use as floor tiles. Floor tiles differ from wall tiles mainly in that they are designed to stand up to foot traffic.

With built-in whirlpools and even with enclosed tubs, flooring materials such as tile will be the most desirable materials to use on the enclosing surfaces. Blending wood floors to steps and surfaces around a whirlpool as well as the walls can create an inviting atmosphere.

Wood

Even though the potential for moisture damage is high, wood floors are popular in bathrooms. New manufacturing processes have produced wood flooring that is much more durable and moisture-resistant than in the past. Prefinished hardwood flooring creates a warm, natural, and inviting look in the bathroom. Wood floors that are properly sealed (well coated with a urethane finish) resist moisture penetration, stains, scuffs, and scratches.

If the homeowner really wants to use hardwood flooring in the bathroom, it may be more functional, as well as an interesting design feature, to use wood in areas less prone to being soaked, while using a more water-tolerant surface in wet areas. Hardwood flooring is available as strips, planks, or parquet tiles.

Strip floors (the most common) are made of narrow tongue-and-groove boards laid in random lengths, typically 2¼ inches (6 cm) wide, and the widths don't vary. They are among the most economical wood floors to buy. Strip flooring actually contributes to the structural strength of a house.

Plank flooring is available in many widths, all wider than strips 3 to 8 inches (8 to 20 cm). Planks are often installed as a combination of several different random widths and random lengths (use equal-width planks, or vary the plank width to add interest). Like strip floor-ing, plank floors contribute to the structural strength of a house. Wood planks that have beveled edges form water-collecting grooves on the floor and should be avoided in the bathroom.

Parquet (*block*) *floors* are made up of small wood pieces glued together in various patterns, including herringbone and blocks. It is considered a floorcovering only and does not contribute to the struc-tural strength of a house. This type of flooring may be solid or lami-nated of several layers.

Wood flooring is available unfinished or prefinished. *Prefinished* products let the installer keep working without waiting for the stain and finish coats to dry. Prefinished hardwood flooring locks together with tongue-and-groove edges and is usually installed over a troweled-on adhesive. When fastening boards down with nails, a thin layer of building paper or thin foam (to act as a cushion) between the under-layment and finished flooring boards may be used (this minimizes future creaking). Prefinished wood flooring costs more and must be installed with extreme care.

Unfinished wood flooring must be sanded to smooth minor surface irregularities. If you have not already done so, be sure to secure loose or squeaking members by renailing or reinforcing them below the flooring. Standard strip wood flooring must be finished with a durable polyurethane to hold up to typical bathroom conditions. Be certain that the manufacturer recommends the finish for bathroom use. Fin-ishes include oil and wax (penetrating finishes) and polyurethane (a surface finish). Polyurethane is better for bathrooms because it forms a hard, clear coating that protects against stains, scratches, and wear. This flooring is best installed on sleepers when installed on a concrete slab (to prepare the room for installing wood flooring, refer to Table 8.3 in Chap. 8). There are materials manufactured for a direct glue-down of wood flooring, but wood floors installed in this manner are very prone to moisture problems. Wood flooring must be sanded and fin-ished before installing any fixtures or cabinets/vanities.

A good wood floor can last the lifetime of the house, and actually improve with age, but it needs to be refinished periodically. When the floor is worn, it can be easily refinished to look new. There are a few dis-advantages to a hardwood floor in the bathroom. This type of floor-ing may shrink in heat or swell in dampness. Inadequate floor substructure and moisture damage can present major problems. However, with proper preparation, these problems can be avoided (various applications are discussed in Chap. 8). As far as maintenance is concerned, some surfaces can simply be damp-mopped and an occasional reapplication of sealers or finishes will extend the floor's life expectancy.

Masonry Floors

Masonry materials such as slate, flagstone, terrazzo, stone, marble, and brick, have been used as flooring for centuries. They offer beautiful classic textures, are generally easy to maintain, are virtually indestructible, and provide quite a luxurious look. Today masonry floors are even more practical, due to the development of sealers and finishes.

Unfortunately, there are still a few disadvantages to masonry flooring in a bathroom. It is heavier than other types of flooring and therefore requires a very strong, well-supported subfloor. Natural stone can be very expensive, especially if it has to be shipped any distance. Many types (e.g., flagstone, slate, brick) can still be stained. Masonry floorings also have the disadvantage of being quite noisy and uncomfortable, as well as cold and slippery underfoot.

Carpeting

Should carpet be installed in the bathroom? At one time carpeting in the bathroom was very popular, but it often could not hold up to all the moisture and mildew. Today, bathrooms can benefit from the development of hard-wearing carpeting materials. If your client does want carpeting, choose types that will not retain odors, will resist mildew, and are less susceptible to water staining and absorption. Polypropylene can stand up to water fairly well and tends to be resistant to mold. However, bathrooms still tend to be better suited to a more water- and stain-resistant type of flooring. Carpets are more practical in dressing and grooming areas of the bathroom rather than in the wet areas.

Carpet can be installed directly over a well-prepared subfloor or over any type of old flooring that is clean, smooth, and free from moisture. Use a good water-resistant pad to help protect a wood subfloor. Always remove existing carpeting before installing new floorcoverings.

Ceramic tile, vinyl, and hardwood floors are all very popular flooring for the bathroom; however, they can all be very cold. Radiant-heat panels can be installed in the floor joists to resolve this problem. They can be operated when and where the homeowner chooses.

Walls

As the lead installer, turning over the finish painting and wallcovering work to a subcontractor may be an efficient and wise idea. This option can be decided on according to the size of the project. If major partition relocation occurs, hiring a carpenter, framer, or drywall professional may be more time-efficient. Offering these services expands your ability to fulfill the clients' desires. Specialists are available and better equipped to tackle the work more efficiently, allowing you more freedom to address your own specialty. Being knowledgeable about these options is still important to you.

Ease of painting and wallcovering applications varies according to the fixture and vanity cabinets involved. For example, expensive wallcoverings can be wasted if applied behind long vanities, mirrors, or wall cabinets. Installation may be easier prior to hanging cabinets. If locations and sizes of these components are marked on the wall, some time and material may be saved. Allow some average for adjustments of the vanity cabinets or fixtures. New plumbing penetrations can also be planned ahead and cuts made before finishing surfaces are installed.

One of the most important factors the installer should be aware of is that the finished appearance of the paint and wallcoverings can be only as good as the wall surface under it. The actual wall preparation is almost always the responsibility of the installer, and it is essential for attractive, long-lasting results. The walls must be clean, dry, and smooth before they can be covered. While some wallcoverings are more susceptible to showing wall imperfections (dents, cracks, popped nails, etc.), all wallcoverings do to some extent. Be sure to review all wall surfaces with any subcontractors before the work begins, and repair or touch up any areas that they might find unacceptable.

Walls in older buildings are likely to be covered with plaster. If only minor repairs are needed, it is worthwhile to retain the plaster walls. However, if major reconstruction (or demolition) is scheduled to take place, you should plan on replacing the plaster with drywall.

The walls in bathrooms can be drywalled and painted, or they can be drywalled and covered with a wallcovering such as tile, wallpaper, or paneling.

Drywall provides smooth surfaces that can be decorated with paint, wallpaper, textures, fabric, or vinyl wallcoverings. For satisfactory finishing results, care must be taken to prepare the surface properly to eliminate possible decorating problems.

To prevent many decorating problems, it is usually recommended that a high-quality latex primer or sealer be applied prior to decoration. Color or surface variations are thereby minimized, and a more uniform texture for any surface covering is provided. The sealer allows the wallcoverings to be removed more easily without marring the surface. Glue, shellac, and varnish are not suitable as sealers or primers.

Although you may decide to use a subcontractor to do drywall or final finish, you should know something about preparing the surface of drywall panels to receive the different types of final finishes.

Paint

When choosing a wallcovering for the bathroom, remember that it must stand up to heat, moisture, and frequent cleaning. Only some wallcoverings are suitable for the bathroom because of the large amount of moisture. Even wallcoverings that can stand up to moisture should not be installed unless the bathroom has a mechanical ventilation system.

By far the easiest, least expensive, and most popular of bathroom wall finishes is paint. Today it offers an almost unlimited variety of colors and hues. It can be mixed to the precise shade and color selected. Increasingly popular today are fanciful decorative paint finishes that lend a unique richness and depth to painted walls. Techniques range from the very simple, such as ragging and sponging, to the more technically difficult methods that produce the appearance of other patterns or textures, such as marbling, wood graining, and modern art.

Alkyd or latex enamel paints are among the most popular house paints sold today. Paint finishes range from flat to high-gloss. They offer moisture and stain resistance and give a smooth, easy-to-clean finish to walls. Alkyd paint (made of synthetic resins) is considered the best type of paint for the bathroom. Any painted or wallpapered surface, or bare wood, can be covered with an alkyd paint. This type of paint adheres to bare masonry or plaster, but it should not be used on bare drywall because it will raise a nap on the drywall's paper covering. Alkyd tends to be more durable than latex paint. Although it is harder to apply and may take longer to dry, it is easily sanded. For excellent durability on cabinets and woodwork, an interior/exterior, quick-drying alkyd enamel is recommended.

Latex paints are easy to work with, dry quickly (in little more than an hour), and combine the long-lasting finish with a high-gloss finish. They are not as durable as alkyds. Latex tends to tear or melt when sanded. Use of latex over unprimed wood, metal, or wallpaper is not recommended. Latex quality is identified by the type of resin used. The highest-quality and most durable latex paint is one with 100% acrylic resin. In general, high resin content is the mark of durable, abrasion-resistant, flexible paint—the kind needed in the bathroom. The higher the resin content, the higher the gloss.

Gloss and semigloss finishes work best in bathrooms because they repel water and clean easily. The glossier the finish, the more durable and washable it is. Bathrooms are typically painted with high-gloss paints which have the highest luster; they have a highly reflective finish for areas where washability is crucial and provides maximum durability. Medium or semigloss paint also has a highly washable surface, but with a slightly less reflective finish. It tends to show surface flaws, but not as obviously as high-gloss paint does.

Use an enamel undercoat on the surface and, as stated earlier, properly sand to help even the surface and reduce any visible flaws that will be more noticeable with the paint application. When remodeling, before removing or sanding any old paint, check to determine whether the paint contains lead. Lead may be harmful. Do not remove or sand paint without contacting local health officials for information on lead paint testing and safety precautions.

Remember that paint only covers the surface; it does not fill in defects. Unfortunately, wall imperfections that were not noticeable before the painting, may now show through. Refer to Table 10.1 for proper preparation of the existing surface for paint. Preparation is the key to good-looking, long-lasting results. A properly prepared surface is clean, solid, and dry, and without cracks and imperfections. Always

Table 10-1 Guidelines for Proper Preparation of an Existing Surface for Paint

Surface	Preparation for painting
New plaster	Must be clean and completely cured. Seal surface with a vinyl acrylic wall primer; dry thoroughly. Follow by 2 coats of desired paint.
New drywall*	Panels must be securely nailed or glued in place. All panel joints must be taped and filled before painting. When joint cement and/or patching materials are thoroughly dry, sand smooth, wipe away dust, then prime and paint. Seal surface with PVA [poly(vinyl acetate)] sealer; dry thoroughly. Apply 2 coats of desired paint.
Existing drywall or plaster	Treat small stains with a white-pigmented shellac, larger ones with a quick-drying alkyd primer. Spot prime patches with PVA sealer or finish paint (diluted 10%). If surface is more than 5 years old, or there is a big color change, using a vinyl acrylic wall primer over a latex finish, prime entire surface. Use an alkyd primer over an oil-base finish. Apply 2 coats of desired paint.
Bare wood†	With patching paste, fill nail holes, joints, and cracks. Sand smooth and remove sanding dust with a tack cloth. Prime all bare wood and patched areas with an alkyd wood primer; allow to dry overnight. Follow with 2 coats of desired paint. (On fir, use a latex enamel undercoater since it does not bleed.)
Previously painted surfaces†	Wash off dirt, grease, and oil buildup. Rinse thoroughly. Chip away loose, flaking paint. Patch holes and cracks with patching paste. Allow to dry and sand smooth. Prior to applying topcoat, spot-prime all bare spots with a white-pigmented shellac. Allow to dry for at least $\frac{1}{2}$ hour.
Bare wood to be stained	Fill holes with natural latex wood patch. Use a stain-controlling sealer for uniform stain absorption on soft woods. Stain in desired color; allow to dry overnight. If surface feels rough, apply a quick-drying sanding sealer and lightly sand.

Table 10-1 Guidelines for Proper Preparation of an Existing Surface for Paint (*Continued*)

Surface	Preparation for painting
Bare wood to be stained (*Continued*)	Apply varnish as applicable, thinned 10% with paint thinner; dry thoroughly; sand; apply second undiluted coat; and allow to dry for 24 hours.
Wallpaper	Completely remove existing wallpaper before painting. If necessary, use a chemical wallpaper remover. Once removed, wash off old adhesive. Rinse with water; allow wall to dry thoroughly before priming.
Metal	Remove dirt and rinse thoroughly. Sand off rust; prime. Use rust-inhibitive primer on new metal that will rust, latex metal primer on galvanized metal, conventional metal primer on aluminum. Apply 2 coats of desired paint. Do not sand between coats.
Masonry	Use acrylic or latex block filler. For a waterproof surface, follow with a hydrostatic coating. If going over a previous coating, consult dealer—all coatings are not compatible. Apply 2 coats of desired paint.

*Do not use an alkyd primer; it will raise nap in paper.
†An enamel finish is usually recommended for wood.

adhere to the manufacturer's directions as to applications, drying times, and material compatibilities. Also, a paint supplier's advice may save you time and aggravation.

As stated earlier, a good-quality, white, latex primer or sealer formulated with higher binder solids, applied undiluted, is typically specified for new drywall surfaces prior to the application of texture materials and gloss, semigloss, and flat latex wall paints. An alkali- and moisture-resistant primer and a tinted enamel undercoat might be required under enamel paints. These products are claimed to make drywall stippable, bind poor latex paint, allow hanging of wallcoverings over glossy surfaces and existing vinyls, to hide wall colors, and be water-washable.

After the painting job is complete, examine the job to verify that the specified number of coats of paint were applied to the walls. Indications of insufficient or uneven paint coverage include blotches in the finished surface or areas where the paint is not as glossy. Because the seams have been taped and spackled, the first coat of paint on the seams looks different from that on bare drywall surfaces. The difference is seldom noticeable after the second coat is applied. To easily verify whether the required number of coats of paint have been applied, ask the painter to tint the first coat of paint. When the second coat is applied, any missed spots will be noticeable. If the directions state a drying period between coats, do not rush it; shrinkage later is the cause of cracks or low spots.

Another important factor regarding paint in the bathroom is that latex and alkyd paints do not work on certain surfaces, such as acoustical panels, tile, porcelain surfaces, and glass. Special acoustical ceiling paint is needed. Ordinary paints change the sound-deadening qualities of the panels. Epoxy paint is the best paint to use on hard, impermeable surfaces such as ceramic tile, plastic, porcelain (there are many services available to resurface porcelain tubs to create color damages to suit), and glass. When using such products, follow directions, especially regarding ventilation or use of protective breathing apparatus.

Wallcoverings

Wallpaper provides an extraordinary variety in materials, styles, colors, patterns, and textures while opening up a world of decorating possibilities (Fig. 10.4a).

Wallpapers are available as prepasted, washable, and strippable—features that facilitate hanging, cleaning, and removal. Choosing the right type of wallcovering is as important as the style. Here are some factors to consider when choosing. All bathroom wallcoverings should resist moisture and hold up to frequent scrubbing. The walls should be primed with an oil-based primer before applying paste and wallcoverings.

Fabric-backed vinyl has a vinyl top layer and an undersurface of fiberglass or cheesecloth. The sturdiest kind of wallpaper, fabric-backed vinyl, is washable, often scrubbable, and usually strippable. Compared with other papers, it is more moisture-resistant and less likely to tear if a wall cracks. It usually is supplied unpasted, because

Wallpaper provides unlimited possibilities for bathroom walls. *(Anaglypta—Crown Decorative Products, Darwen, England.)*

it is often too heavy to roll if prepasted. For a bathroom that gets heavy use, only fabric-backed vinyl should be used.

Paper-backed vinyl has a vinyl top layer with a paper rather than fabric backing. The paper makes the wallcovering lighter, so paper-backed vinyl can be supplied prepasted. It is often peelable and washable.

Vinyl-coated paper can stain and tear more easily than other papers with vinyl content. The durability, strength, and stain resistance of vinyl make these papers relatively easy to install, easy to maintain, and terrific for high-traffic areas such as the bathroom. Common untreated wallcoverings are susceptible to stains and abrasions, and pattern inks may run if washed.

For unique, decorative wall treatment, choose an embossed, textured wallpaper. This type of wallcovering offers decorators a wide selection of designs and patterns. These vinyls are flat-backed for easy installation, are washable, and are peelable for easy removal. The vinyl

FIGURE 10.4b

Embossed wallcoverings and borders are ideal for areas of high moisture such as the bathroom, while providing a beautiful finish. *(Anaglypta—Crown Decorative Products, Darwen, England.)*

renders these wallcoverings ideal for areas of high moisture, such as the bathroom, and they are functional and practical. From an aesthetic point of view, the embossed pattern and traditional motifs of this wallpaper can be very ornate and representative of a more opulent bygone era. It is a white embossed wallpaper in its original form and is designed to be painted any color. This type of wallpaper can give the bathroom an entirely new personality with the imaginative use of finishes (Fig. 10.4*b,c*). Because of its raised surface, this wallpaper can hide small plaster bulges and other problem spots in old buildings. It is perfect for ceilings, and once applied and painted a metallic color, can duplicate a tin ceiling. The wallcovering is lightweight and easy to hang, and its textured surface adds an interesting new dimension to a room. No sanding or plastering is required. Surfaces can simply be covered and custom-finished. Faux finishes such as highlighting by lightly brushing the raised details, while leaving the recesses in darker tones, accents the beauty of this type of wallcovering. Sealing with a varnish will add gloss and be easier to wipe off.

These elegant designs are combined with ecosensitivity, which is a real plus because today, many homeowners are increasingly concerned about the environment. Some of these textured patterns are made from a specially formulated *acrylic plastisol,* a substance more environmentally friendly than the earlier blown vinyls.

Be sure that all special moldings have been installed before the wallcovering work begins, including any crown or chair rail molding over which the wallcovering is to be applied.

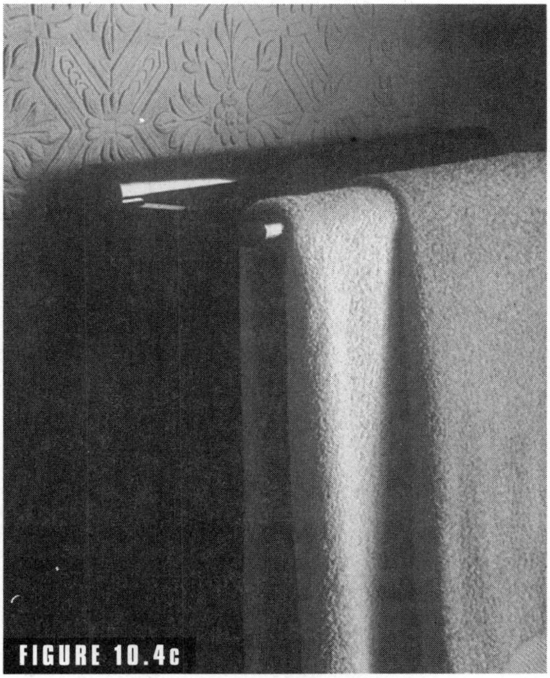

Wallcovering work should be checked carefully when complete to ensure that the wallpaper is fully adhered without air bubbles. Check around doorways and openings to make sure that all edges are well bonded. Edge guards may be advisable if the opening does not have trim to protect the edges.

FIGURE 10.4c

Embossed wallcoverings and borders are ideal for areas of high moisture such as the bathroom, while providing a beautiful finish. *(Anaglypta—Crown Decorative Products, Darwen, England.)*

Figure 10.5*a* shows the installation of a metal corner bead on drywall. Screws and nails should have been properly installed by dimpling the nail into the drywall, filling the dimple with joint compound and tape (Fig. 10.5*b,c*). This procedure ensures that the fastener won't ruin the finish by showing a circle or dent. Allow suggested drying time for joint compound before applying wallpaper. Several thin coats of compound will dry more satisfactorily and reduce shrinkage better than heavy thick coats. As with glossy paint surfaces, shiny wallpaper finishes show imperfections (especially foil papers). Seams should be tightly butted without overlapping. Pattern matching is also very important, although some patterns can be more forgiving than others.

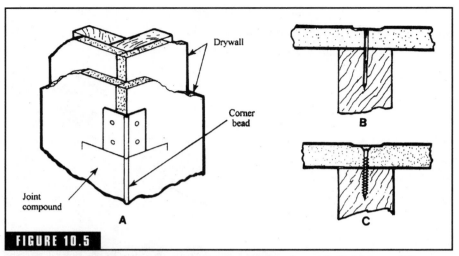

FIGURE 10.5

(*a*) Corner beads provide strong, durable protection for wall finishings; (*b*) proper depth of nail dimple in drywall; (*c*) proper depth of driven screw dimple in drywall. (*Leon E. Korejwo, Illustrations.*)

Tile

Ceramic tile makes an attractive wall surface and is especially practical in a bathroom because it is waterproof, fireproof, and durable; won't fade or stain; and is easy to clean. For walls, tile is supplied with a glaze coating that protects it against moisture; the porcelain or clay itself is hard but porous. It is almost completely scratchproof, and never needs waxing or painting. Cleaning can be done with a damp cloth, and most cleaning agents can be used. An extensive selection of colors and shapes of tiles offer infinite possibilities in pattern design on the wall (Fig. 10.6). Wall tiles range in size from small 1-inch (2.54-cm) mosaic squares to impressive 12-inch (30-cm) squares and are available in high- or low-relief designs with colorful glazes or multicolored patterns.

The most important distinction between types of tile is whether they are glazed or unglazed. Glazed tile, available in matte or shiny finish, is impervious to stains but can be scratched; it is the standard tile used around lavatories. Unglazed tile, made only in matte finish, picks up stains from oils but resists scratching; it is the best choice for floors. Basically, either type can be used on walls.

FIGURE 10.6

Ceramic tile provides a distinctive, natural look for bathroom walls and tub surrounds. *(Florida Tile Industries.)*

An infinite number of styles are available in hand-painted and fired deco tiles, which add detail and individual character to the room. The deeply detailed tiles simulate rope styles, floral patterns, and other motifs and can be mixed into the main field background, or used to carry character from floors to walls, making a unified flow of design.

Many professionals still prefer to mud-set ceramic tiles in cement-based mortar—a tricky masonry process. Fortunately, if you have decided not to hire a subcontractor to tile the walls, you can now choose from a number of masticlike adhesives especially developed with less demanding handling qualities. Grout between tile is available in colors and can be applied after the tile is set. Because of its porosity, grout must be coated with a sealer to prevent mildew from penetrating and staining. Some epoxy grouts are available, and they, too, have been found to attract mildew.

Of all the things that can be done with a wall, veneering it with ceramic tile makes the most lasting, water-resistant, and easily cleanable improvement. Unfortunately, it can also be one of the most expensive for your client.

Wood

Wood adds a natural warmth that complements many design schemes (Fig. 10.7). As a wall-surfacing material, it is supplied in the form of premilled, solid wood wainscoting (tongue-and-groove bead board 1 × 6s capped by a traditional chair rail), veneered plywood, or melamine-surfaced hardboard. Both solid-wood and plywood-backed veneers must be coated with urethane or another water-resistant coating. Hardboard panels coated with melamine (a thin layer of white plastic) are well suited for bathrooms because melamine is water-resistant and easy to clean.

The two main types of paneling, sheet and solid boards, are available in a variety of textures and finishes. What is the best? This depends on what the homeowner wants. Most paneling never needs painting, is easy to clean, and has a good resistance to dirt. The smoother the surface of the paneling, the higher the resistance. Sheet paneling is easier to apply over large, unbroken surfaces because of its dimensions. Solid boards (or strips), however, are easier to fit around openings and obstructions.

SHEET PANELING

Sheet paneling is available in large, machine-made panels, most commonly 4 × 8 feet (122 × 244 cm). The two main types of sheet paneling are hardboard and plywood.

Hardboard paneling is manufactured for use as prefinished paneling and is specifically treated for resistance to stains, scrubbing, and moisture. It is also highly resistant to dents, mars, and scuffs. Hardboard is produced by reducing waste wood chips to fibers and then bonding the fibers back together under pressure with adhesives. In

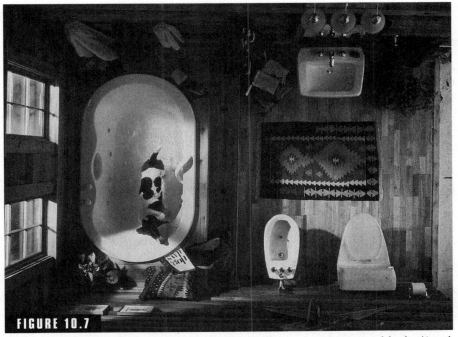

FIGURE 10.7

Wood walls, floors, and tub surrounds give this bathroom a warm, natural look. *(American Standard.)*

most cases, the material is prefinished in wood grains such as walnut, cherry, birch, oak, teak, and pecan, in a variety of shades. It may be smooth-surfaced or random-grooved. In addition, there are the decorative and labor-saving plastic-surfaced hardboards that resist water, stains, and household chemicals exceptionally well. A typical surface consists of baked-on plastic. Most hardboard is sufficiently dense and moisture-resistant for use in bathrooms. The variety of laminated plastic finishes and sizes is extensive. A tough, pliable paneling, hardboard is sold in 4 × 8-foot (122 × 244-cm) sheets in thicknesses ranging from $3/16$ to $3/8$ inch (0.48 to 1.33 cm); $1/4$ inch (0.6 cm) is usual. It is usually less expensive than plywood, but it is also less durable and more subject to warping or moisture damage. The most common surface finishes are imitation wood, generally grooved to resemble solid-board paneling. Wood imitations are available in highly polished, resawn, or coarser-brushed textures in a range of colors. Panels embossed with a pattern, such as basket weave, wicker, or louver are also available.

Plywood paneling is manufactured from thin wood layers (veneer) peeled from the log and then glued together. The grain of each veneer runs perpendicular to adjacent veneers, making plywood strong in all directions. Less expensive than most solid board strips, plywood panels are also less subject to warping or shrinkage. Any standard, unfinished plywood sheets may be used for wall paneling. In addition, there are sheets expressly intended for paneling. Just about any type of hardwood, and most of the major softwoods, laminated onto the surfaces of plywood panels can be purchased. Prefinished and vinyl-faced decorative styles are available, as well as resin-coated panels designed for painting.

Plywood face textures range from highly polished to resawn. Many types feature decorative grooves (often imitating solid-board patterns) or shiplap edges. There are two standard thicknesses: $1/4$ and $5/16$ inch (0.63 and 0.79 cm). Thinner panels are not very durable and are difficult to work with. Many are supplied prefinished and will resist staining (to a degree). Plywoods faced with genuine hard- and softwoods provide the most natural look. Some panels have a more natural surface with grains and colors that vary from panel to panel giving a more natural appearance.

SOLID-BOARD STRIP PANELING

Natural fragrance, texture, subtle variations in color and grain, and imperfections make solid-board strip paneling extremely warm and inviting. It is especially suitable around doors, windows, and other large openings—areas where extensive handling and cutting are required. Quite simply, solid-board strip paneling is any paneling made up of solid pieces of lumber positioned side by side. In some cases, standard, square-edged lumber is used, in sizes ranging from 1 $\times$ 4 to 1 $\times$ 6 inches (2.5 $\times$ 10 to 2.5 $\times$ 15 cm) and so forth. But generally, the boards have edges specially milled to overlap or interlock. The three basic millings are square edge, tongue-and-groove, and shiplap (Fig. 10.8).

When planning a wood-paneled room, one may wish to accent a wall, using boards of random widths or subdued by the use of equal-width boards. Small rooms can be given the illusion of increased size by applying the paneling horizontally. Of course, paneling can be applied vertically, horizontally, diagonally, or in combined directions. Solid-wood paneling must be finished with a good wood sealer and finished to resist staining.

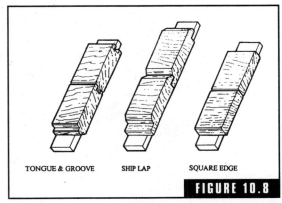

TONGUE & GROOVE   SHIP LAP   SQUARE EDGE

FIGURE 10.8

Solid-board strip paneling three basic millings: tongue-and-groove, shiplap; and square edge. *(Leon E. Korejwo, Illustrations.)*

Like sheet paneling, solid boards can be attached to new stud walls, to existing walls that are in good shape, or to a gridwork of furring strips applied over old, bumpy walls. Although solid boards are usually installed vertically or horizontally, consider a diagonal pattern. For installation details, see Chap. 8.

Prefinished paneling is probably the easiest type of wall finish. Like painting, wallpaper, and most other interior finishing approaches, a successful paneling job requires careful preparation of the surface to be covered. Be sure to complete all necessary preparations before installing any paneling.

Glass Block

Because of its ability to transmit light while maintaining privacy, glass block is very popular in bathrooms (Fig. 10.9). It can be used to make internal partition walls (shower enclosures) or as a fixed glazing material for window openings. Glass blocks are available in 3- or 4-inch- (7.62- or 10.16-cm)-thick squares with varying sizes and many different textures (smooth, wavy, rippled, etc.). Some types of glass block distort views and conserve heat more than others (an energy-efficient alternative to standard window products). It is a versatile material, waterproof, translucent, and able to be formed into straight or curved walls. Glass block provides a soft, filtered light that complements many bath designs.

Mirrored Walls

Mirrored walls can add size and richness to a small bathroom. Mirrors, along with glass block, large windows, and skylights, will open up the area, making any bathroom appear larger than it actually is. The apparent width of a narrow or cramped bathroom can be greatly

FIGURE 10.9

The use of glass block lightens the traditional elements with a touch of modern style. *(Weck Glass Block/Glashaus, Inc.)*

increased by adding a full wall with mirrored tiles. Most likely, every homeowner will want a mirror on the wall over the sink. In order to see the sides and back of the head, side mirrors that hinge toward a central mirror can be added.

Mirrored surfaces are available with marbled finishes, appliqués, etched with designs, and other embellishments which can help to carry out a room's theme and style. Mirror tiles can be laid out in different patterns for a truly unique finishing; they are commonly available in 12 × 12-inch (30.48 × 30.48-cm) squares. Light fixtures placed to bounce off a mirror help to make the bathroom even brighter.

Wall mirrors are often glued to the wall with strong epoxy, but always refer to mirror manufacturer recommendations for proper adhesives. This glue provides a strong, firm hold; however, removing mirrors often involves breaking them off in pieces. Cutting mirrors to fit is not an easy task, so you may need the skills of a glass contractor who can measure the wall before cutting the mirrors and adjust for any irregularities (such as an uneven ceiling).

Brick and Stone

Brick and stone—marble, granite, slate, and limestone—can provide a wonderful feeling of warmth and create an outstanding highlight wall in a bathroom. These natural minerals tend to be extremely expensive; however, using it as an accent can give a nice effect (along the tub pedestal, around the shower, etc.). Real brick and stone have permanence matched only by ceramic tile. But real bricks and stones do have certain disadvantages. They are porous, and dirt can sink right in. Most stone should be thoroughly sealed for use on the wall. If it is not, it can be stained by water and cleaning supplies. Mildew can also be difficult to combat when it seeps into porous surfaces. In addition, bricks and stones add enormous weight to a wall and require the support of a foundation wall. These disadvantages have led manufacturers to develop veneers and imitations. Imitation bricks and stones are made of various materials; styrene, urethane, and rigid vinyl are the most common. All false bricks and stones are highly durable and come in a wide variety of colors and styles. Some are sold in sheet form, while others are installed individually, similar to ceramic tile.

Moldings

Molding details can set the theme of the bathroom's decor and give the bathroom a whole new look, as well as help conceal the room's architectural and carpentry faults. Even in the most basic room, moldings have their place along the base of walls and around door and window frames (Fig. 10.10).

Here is a sample of the more popular types of interior trim:

1. *Baseboard* protects the bottom of the wall from wear and tear and conceals irregularities at the wall-floor joints. Quarter-round or base shoe moldings may be used to complete the trim.

2. *Casing* is used to trim doors, windows, and other openings. It may also be used for chair rails, cabinet trim, and decorative purposes.

3. *Cornices,* whether of the crown or cove type, give a rich appearance wherever two planes, such as a wall and ceiling, meet. They are also used for trimming exposed beams and, singly or in combination with other moldings, in decorative mantels and frames.

4. *Wainscot* caps are applied to the top of wainscoting. Some patterns have a wraparound lip to conceal craftsmanship defects. Others may be used to cap decorative baseboards.

5. *Chair* rail protects the wall in areas subject to chair-back damage. It is installed at a height appropriate to the furniture style.

The variety of moldings available seems endless; traditional wood moldings are available in many standard patterns and sizes. Integral molding systems include corner pieces that eliminate the need for tricky corner cuts and joints. They can be purchased prefinished (painted or stained), wrapped with printed vinyl, or natural. Lengths range from 3 to 20 feet (91 to 610 cm). While wood is still the most popular, vinyl-coated, plastic, or metal moldings, manufactured to resemble wood, are available.

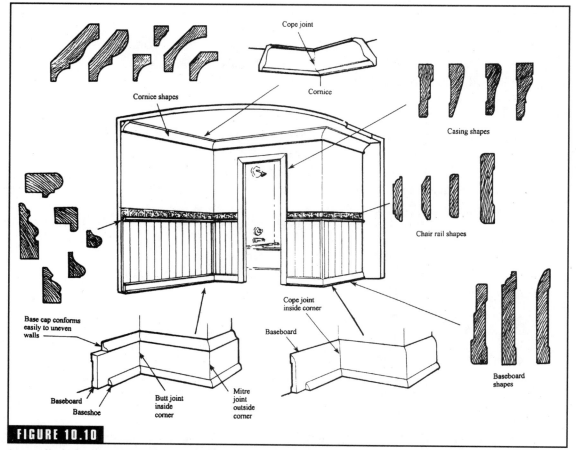

Base cap conforms easily to uneven walls

Baseboard

Baseshoe

Baseboard

Butt joint inside corner

Mitre joint outside corner

Cope joint inside corner

Baseboard

Baseboard shapes

Cornice shapes

Cope joint

Cornice

Casing shapes

Chair rail shapes

FIGURE 10.10

A sampling of some standard molding patterns and their common applications. *(Leon E. Korejwo, Illustrations.)*

In this chapter, the most important groups of wallcovering materials have been covered. However, others are available. The performance of any wall finish depends on the care with which it is installed and maintained. Always follow the manufacturer's recommendations exactly for the type of adhesive and backing material, and for the method of installation. Backing material around tubs and showers should be thoroughly sealed with waterproofing materials prior to application of the wall finish.

Ceilings

Almost everything that has been mentioned for use on walls can be applied to the bathroom's ceiling—paint, wallpaper, tile, paneling, or windows—to give the broadest possible spectrum of colors, textures, and patterns. Bathroom ceilings can be made very interesting, as well as made to fit almost any design or style of decoration, by using different angles (some drop beams and some raised ceilings), exposed beams, pitched ceilings, faux-finished ceilings, mirrors, and even hammered-tin ceilings. Skylights help brighten the bathroom ceiling, too (Fig. 10.11). It is important to remember that most experts agree that ceilings should be relatively light in color, especially in a bathroom, to maximize the reflection of light to provide more even lighting.

Combine the framing of a floor with the covering materials used for walls, and you get the anatomy of a typical home ceiling. It begins with the same joists that support the subfloor above. Next, level off the joists' bottom edges with furring strips, or—if the lumber is even to begin with—fasten drywall or plaster lath directly to the joists. There are exceptions to this construction, though. Sloping top-floor ceilings usually are attached to the roof framing and, in properly built homes, have insulation above them. You also may encounter lightweight tiles suspended below the joists of an old ceiling. Open-beam ceilings may consist of nothing more than the underside of the roof decking above.

Suspended Ceilings

A suspended ceiling can change the entire appearance of the room. Compared to installing drywall, putting up ceiling tiles or panels is a breeze. Instead of handling awkward 4 × 8-foot (122 × 244-cm) sheets, you work with lightweight materials. The most common panel size is 2 × 4 feet (61 × 122 cm), although panels are available in a variety of sizes. Many tiles on today's market won't break, stain, or chip; are easily cleaned with soap and water; and are available in a variety of colors, patterns, and natural wood-grain finishes. In addition, many manufacturers have produced ceiling tiles that are highly insulated, are water- and insectproof, have flame-retardant metal backings, and allow complete accessibility to all above-ceiling utilities. Tiles are available that provide an acoustical, soundproofing feature, as well as decorative patterns with or without the acoustical properties.

FIGURE 10.11

Ceiling skylights and a circular top window with art glass add sunlight—an important feature in the bathroom. *(Andersen Windows, Inc.)*

The use of grids, either fastened directly to the beams or suspended below them, offer many interesting ceiling treatments. Transparent and translucent panels and egg-crate grilles are made to fit the grid-work to admit light from above. Recessed lighting panels that exactly replace one panel are also available.

A dropped ceiling consisting of removable tiles allows installation work (wiring, pipes, and heating and air-conditioning components) to remain easily accessible. Ceiling tiles are available in mineral fiber (noncombustible) and fiberglass (may be fire-resistant). Mineral fiber and fiberglass are drop-in panels that work with a grid system. If the homeowner dislikes the look of drop-in tiles, or if protruding ducts or beams would require a lower ceiling than desired, box around them using a wood frame. Cover with acoustic tile and install the remaining ceiling at a more desirable height (Fig. 10.12).

Drywall

Painted drywall is the most common type of ceiling covering in use today. It is relatively easy to install, inexpensive, and provides a good-looking finished product. The same drywall panels used on walls can be used for ceilings, but reinforced ceiling panels are made to prevent

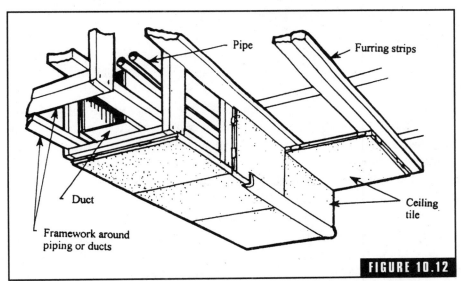

FIGURE 10.12

Drop ceiling boxed around protruding duct or beam. *(Leon E. Korejwo, Illustrations.)*

sagging between joists. However, it is harder to install on ceilings than on walls because working overhead is awkward, and the weight of the full panels can also be awkward. For ceiling installation details, refer back to Chap. 8.

There is a good chance that some of the ceiling might have to be opened up for plumbers, electricians, heating crews, or other tradespeople. Drywall is easy to cut and patch. New drywall can be blended into existing drywall very well. A coat of sealer, followed by a coat of paint, is all that is needed to camouflage any disruption of the ceiling. However, as stated previously, not all bathrooms have existing drywall in the ceiling.

Beams

Beams often add to the beauty of any bathroom (Fig. 10.13). Normal-height ceilings can be made very interesting by adding a beam arrangement—real or artificial. Certain styles incorporate patterned beams and enclosed ceiling bays (usually painted drywall). Today, ready-made, ready-to-install beams are available through most lumber dealers. They are made of solid lumber, plywood, polyurethane plastic foam, or metal. The number of beams and patterns employed depends on the size of the room and personal preference. Some room ceilings look best with the beams running in one direction only, while others look fine with crossing beams. The beams themselves can be finished or painted to match any color scheme. If you have removed a bearing wall and added a structural beam, disguise its presence by flanking it with fakes. The inside provides efficient space to hide electrical and plumbing lines or heating ducts.

Open it up. In a one-story house or a two-story house with a bathroom on the top floor, the ceiling above can be opened up to create a cathedral-type effect. Breaking out the ceiling surface, wallboard, or plaster, to reveal the joists is only the beginning. The newly annexed bathroom space will yield all sorts of decorating possibilities, such as skylights, open-beam effects, and lighting and window designs. Most importantly, the roof is dependent on the ceiling joists for rigid triangulation, so when renovating, they must not be cut without prior reinforcement such as boxing. The ceiling will now be a surface below the roof, or a new false ceiling can be made slightly below the existing roof. The walls will also be extended upward to meet the new ceiling by means of studded wall frames. New beams may be constructed around

FIGURE 10.13

Consider opening up the room with windows and the ceiling with high beams. *(American Standard.)*

the existing joists to create a more traditional beam by eliminating appropriate framing lumber such as 2 × 8s on either side of them.

If the existing roof employs prefabricated trusses, these would be very involved. Cutting such preengineered members would seriously damage the roof's integrity. In new construction, truss designers can provide designs which would allow cathedral ceilings using a false ceiling below the roof, yet still offer an angled surface.

Insulation must be considered also. If the roof is being employed, insulation between the roofing joists must allow an open space above the insulation to circulate free air. This ensures the longevity of the surface decking and shingles on top of the roof. If the insulation blocks heat the shingles, they will prematurely deteriorate or curl. Moisture buildup would destroy any timber. Vapor barriers must also be used, but do use two barriers with insulation in between. The most effective means to vent is using soffit vents at the low end and a ridge vent at the peak of the roof.

Interesting ceilings can also be created by raising the center only, achieving a very dramatic tiered appearance. These are very extensive projects which will involve extra planning and may require an architect or engineer to design safely.

Wood Paneling

Sheet paneling, plank paneling, and tongue-and-groove lumber—natural, stained, bleached, or painted—provide a charming accent. Wood paneling is not difficult to install on a ceiling and can be very attractive in the proper setting, especially on a vaulted ceiling. Installation of the sheets or planks on the ceiling is the same as application to the wall surface. Flooring strips can be nailed to the ceilings, but it is faster and easier to use hardboard panels with the desired wood facing. Take into consideration the high moisture content present in a bathroom and allow for expansion and swelling. Check the manufacturer recommended applications. Always keep ventilation in mind.

Plaster

Plaster was a common covering for ceilings at one time. It is more difficult to repair cuts, cracks, and holes in plaster than with drywall. Plaster has rises and depressions that create an uneven surface. It is not easy to match drywall to a surface such as this; however, it can be done with some skill. The wood strips and wire screen used in conjunction with plaster makes any job harder for plumbers, electricians, and others to do their installation work. If an existing bathroom has plaster, be sure to factor the extra work into the overall production schedule and budget.

Tin-stamped ceiling panels and cornice patterns drawn from the past enliven contemporary and traditional styling. Lightweight, non-combustible panels are manufactured from tin-free steel 0.010 inch (0.0254 cm) thick and properly coated for superior paint retention (for little or no maintenance and cleaning with soap and water). Conventional suspension methods are recommended for the ceiling installation of lay-in panels. Heavy-duty safety gloves should be worn when handling panels and cornices—edges can be sharp.

Bathroom Lighting

Lighting the bathroom requires careful planning, before any construction begins; remember that plug-in lamps can't be added later as in other rooms. For the homeowners to see themselves as they truly are, lighting in the bathroom must be efficient and well placed. The selection of lighting in a bathroom is very important; no bathroom is complete without adequate lighting. Poor lighting can not only make the cheeriest bathroom seem dreary but can also promote fatigue and even cause accidents. Proper lighting has long been established as being essential to safety, good health, and a general feeling of well-being. With multiprofessional households, early-morning rush hours start in the bathroom. Good lighting for shaving, applying makeup, and a variety of other tasks will make this intense time easier and safer.

The amount of light needed in a bathroom may be obtained from one source or a combination of several sources (Fig. 10.14). Factors to take into consideration are the size and use of the room. The larger the room, the greater its requirements. The lighting fixtures chosen highlight your clients' new bathroom and control the atmosphere of the room, as well as help them to perform their tasks more efficiently.

Note: A good, workable lighting plan should be established early in the bathroom project to allow for the proper placement of wiring, fixture boxes, and switches while the bathroom is being worked on.

Some of the choices you must decide on with your client are

1. Structural (built in as part of the home's finished structure; e.g., soffits, recessed) lighting or store-bought fixtures

2. Incandescent bulbs, fluorescent tubes, or halogen lights

3. Level of intensity (brightness) for both general and task lighting

4. Fixture types, including luminous ceiling, luminous panels, recessed, tracks, spots, and wall brackets

FIGURE 10.14

Natural light, recessed lighting fixtures, and hanging pendants provide for overall effective lighting here. *(Thomas Lighting.)*

Most bathrooms have four basic kinds of lighting: natural daylight resulting from windows and skylights, general lighting that gives overall illumination, local or task lighting that provides proper illumination at specific areas, and decorative lighting that emphasizes the color and decorative theme of the bathroom.

Natural Light

The current trend in lighting is large, sunny baths; everybody wants more natural light in the bathroom (Fig. 10.15). Natural light can enter a bathroom through windows, glass doors, skylights, and glass blocks—all a part of connecting the bathroom to the outdoors.

Windows furnish the natural light to brighten all areas and supplement the artificial light. Minimum property of the Housing and Urban Development/Federal Housing Administration (HUD/FHA) standards specify a window area totaling, in square feet, 10 percent of the floor area. (Well-designed bathrooms should have at least 15 percent; an area equal to 20 to 30 percent of the room's area is still better.) Whenever possible, two window areas should be planned. Glass panels in outside doors and skylights count as part of the total window area. Incidentally, skylights give a great deal of natural light without cutting down on wall cabinet space. Each square foot of skylight supplies natural lighting to 20 sq ft (1.86 m²) of floor space. A skylight can also help avoid that claustrophobic feeling in bathrooms by opening up spaces to the outdoors where there are no windows. In addition, the venting models, placed near the roof ridge, can also greatly improve natural ventilation. Narrow, horizontal windows, or clerestory windows, placed high in the wall offer a good solution to privacy concerns. However, remember that just because the user can't see out does not mean that someone else can't see in.

FIGURE 10.15

Natural light supplements artificial lighting. *(Andersen Windows, Inc.)*

Glass doors versus wood doors can double the natural lighting potential. For safety and security, be sure that the new door has tempered glass or shatterproof plastic. In addition, energy conservation is a prime consideration; double- or triple-glazed panes can help conserve energy.

Discuss with your clients the potential effects of exposure of the bathroom to sunlight. Have them consider the view from the window and the need for privacy. Also, keep in mind that natural light may illuminate the bathroom unevenly. A single window in the middle of a wall often creates a strong contrast with the surrounding area, causing a glare. For more even light, use two windows on adjacent walls, add a skylight, or compensate for the glare by illuminating the surrounding area with artificial light. Fill in shadows with built-in lighting fixtures. When natural lighting is not available, many of the same benefits can be achieved with artificial lighting.

General (Ambient) Lighting

Although natural light is extremely popular, emphasis is placed on artificial lighting as well. General lighting fills in the undefined areas of a room with a soft level of light and illuminates the room as a whole. General lighting can come from hanging fixtures, fixtures mounted on the ceiling, or recessed downlights mounted in the ceiling. It also can come from a "luminous ceiling" where light floods through an entire translucent suspended ceiling, from valance lighting, or from illuminated soffits. General lighting should be indirect, aimed to bounce off pale walls or ceiling and then into the room. Bouncing diffuses the light for even illumination over the entire area.

How much general light is needed in the bathroom? This is difficult to tell in terms of lightbulb wattages, because wattage is not an accurate measure of light intensity. However, the following system serves as a rough guide. Measure the bathroom to determine the number of square feet of floor space. Then simply apply the following minimums. If the homeowner is comfortable with more light, do not hesitate to move up from the minimums.

■ For ceiling-mounted or -suspended fixtures in the bathroom, 2 watts per square foot for incandescent and 1 watt per square foot for fluorescent fixtures are needed.

- For surface-mounted fixtures install bulbs that emit 1 watt of incandescent or 0.33 to 0.5 watt of fluorescent light per square foot.

- For nondirectional recessed lighting (fixtures mounted in the ceiling), install bulbs that emit 2.5 to 4 watts per square foot for incandescent and 0.5 watt per square foot for fluorescent fixtures.

Remember that wherever the lights are placed, they should not be too bright. Instead of improving vision, high-intensity light impairs it. The answer is low-intensity light from several sources, rather than a few dazzling pinpoints. If the plan starts with good general illumination, less light shining directly on the user will be needed to see really well.

Task Lighting

Task lighting is the local illumination needed for a particular area of the bathroom, for all mirrors (such as for shaving or applying makeup), and for the shower and tub areas. This type of lighting should be directly from the fixture to the work surface, providing brighter lighting for close work.

The lighting fixtures for task areas may be mounted on the ceiling, on the walls, or in soffits, and are often provided by pendant, track, or recessed lights (Fig. 10.16). The bathroom typically functions as a grooming area. Regardless of where the source is located, it must fall on the area in front of the user to prevent them from working in their own shadows. Light cannot illuminate the whole face evenly. The most efficient lighting for shaving or applying makeup comes from above, below, and both sides—each fixture should be capable of

FIGURE 10.16a

A three-light mirror bath bar with crystal shades can be installed above the sink. (*Thomas Lighting.*)

utilizing a 100-watt bulb. This cross-lighting technique (light from both sides of the mirror) fills in features that would otherwise be left in shadow. However, if placed closer together than 25 inches (63.6 cm), the side lights will have the disadvantage of intruding on the field of vision. The top light usually bounces off a light-colored basin below so that someone shaving can clearly see under his chin. Some mirror units come with side lights, top lights, or both. Theatrical lighting— exposed bulbs, or strip lighting—mounted around the mirror or cabinet, or soffit lighting are also possibilities for lighting the vanity area. With well-illuminated work areas, time is saved and the possibility of accidents is greatly reduced. Remember to have proper shielding for each light, so that no one ever has to look directly at a bare bulb or fluorescent tube.

If lighting the shower stall or tub area, most codes require enclosed waterproof and vaporproof downlight units with neoprene seals. Do not place light switches where they can be reached by someone in the tub or shower, or by anyone using a water faucet; all light switches should be located at least 6 feet (1.83 m) from the tub and shower. An infrared heat lamp is a good idea for instant heat when the user steps out of the tub or shower.

If the toilet is in a separate compartment, it can also have its own light fixture. Installing a centered ceiling fixture that uses one 60- or 75-watt incandescent bulb, or one 30- to 40-watt fluorescent tube are just a few suggestions.

Decorative (Accent) Lighting

While general lighting and task lighting provide required illumination for the work areas of the bathroom, decorative lighting focuses attention on an area or object, such as a whirlpool or a piece of artwork, with a concentrated beam of light. Today, fixtures

FIGURE 10.16b

A one-light bath bar can be mounted flanking the sides of the sink. *(Thomas Lighting.)*

are available from manufacturers for every possible decorating theme or budget and are used to highlight architectural features, to set a mood, or to provide drama. With whirlpools and spa developments, bathrooms are evolving into more recreational and therapeutic areas. These attractions mean longer usage taking place in the evening and after dark. Mood lighting and special effects can greatly enhance these enjoyable hours. Guests will be entertained in areas never before used for that purpose, so creative mood lighting is certainly worthwhile. Proper accent lighting should be three to five times ambient lighting levels. Control a light with a dimmer switch, and it can also serve as general lighting. Accent lighting is usually provided by recessed, track, or wall-mounted fixtures. In the bathroom, use it to wash a wall, play up interesting textures, or spotlight a unique bathroom fixture or fireplace.

Lightbulbs and Light Tubes

It is important to know the general characteristics of light sources to choose types appropriate for each bathroom application. By knowing how to work successfully with each type individually, or with a combination, it is possible to achieve lighting results that are visually comfortable, functional, and beautiful. Light sources can be grouped in categories according to the way they produce light. The key to good lighting starts with the right bulbs.

INCANDESCENT LIGHTS

Incandescent bulbs have filaments of tungsten that give off light when heated by electric current. The light from incandescent bulbs (clear, frosted, or tinted)—the oldest of our light sources—is warm in color quality and imparts a friendly, homelike feeling to interiors. Use of incandescent bulbs in the bathroom is recommended because the light they produce has natural, complexion-flattering properties. Under this light source, the warm colors (oranges, reds, brown, etc.) are enhanced, while the cool colors (blues and greens) are subdued. Generally, when the overall atmosphere of a room is on the warm side, the full values of the warm colors are acceptable when lighted with filament bulbs. Inside-frosted standard-service incandescent bulbs, ranging in wattages from 15 to 300, are the most commonly used types. Some of these wattages are available in other finishes. Because of a fine white inner coating in these bulbs, light is distributed over the entire surface, eliminating a bright spot near the center. Tinted bulbs are recommended for locations where the specific effect of a warm or cool mood or atmosphere is desired. In general, tinted light subtly accents like colors and subdues complementary colors.

Incandescent reflector (R-type) and projector bulbs (PAR-type) can be used where a very definite application of either a moderately concentrated spotlight or a more widespread floodlight beam is desired (Fig. 10.17a). Remember that for the best results and the most economical operation, all incandescent bulbs should have the same voltage rating as that of the power-supply line. Low-voltage incandescent lighting is especially useful for accent lighting; new types are constantly being developed. Operating on 12 or 24 volts, these lights require transformers to step down the voltage from standard 120-volt household circuits.

A good suggestion is to mount one wall fixture or pendant lamp on each side of the mirror, with each side light containing two 60-watt or 75-watt bulbs.

FLUORESCENT LIGHTS

Fluorescent light sources offer higher light efficiency, cooler operating temperatures, and longer life than incandescent bulbs of comparable wattage (Fig. 10.17b). The average fluorescent tube delivers three to five times as much light as an incandescent for the same wattage and lasts 20 times longer. For these reasons, they are most adaptable to and very commonly used in custom-designed, built-in installations, as well as in surface-mounted and recessed fixtures.

Fluorescent light sources commonly used in the home range in size from the 4-watt, T-5, 6-inch (15 cm) length to the 40-watt, T-12, 48-inch (122-cm) length. ("T" means tubular and the number equals the diameter in eighths of an inch.) The length of the tube given in all cases is the overall nominal length, including the required sockets.

All fluorescent light sources require a current-limiting and control device called a *ballast*. The ballast limits the amount of current used by the lamp and provides the proper starting voltage. For the operation of some fluorescent tubes, an automatic switch known as a *starter* is required, in addition to the normal wall switch. The starter is a small, replaceable metal can that is inserted into the fixture body or channel.

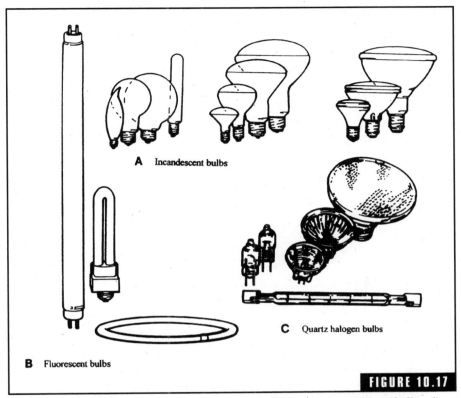

FIGURE 10.17

(*a*) **Typical incandescent bulbs;** (*b*) **fluorescent bulbs;** (*c*) **quartz halogen bulbs.** *(Leon E. Korejwo, Illustrations.)*

   The choice of fluorescent tubes is simply a matter of deciding first whether a warm or a cool atmosphere is desired for the bathroom. When the bathroom atmosphere and color rendition are of prime importance, the corresponding warm or cool tube would be chosen. Otherwise, warm-white or cool-white tubes serve if light output is the more important requirement. If planning to illuminate the mirror with fluorescent fixtures, look for tubes designed for vanity illumination or tubes that produce daylight spectrum light. Lighting from standard fluorescent tubes can be cold and harsh, and may not be acceptable for makeup application. One suggestion is to use one 24-inch (60.96-cm), 20-watt tube on each side of the mirror. Use two 24-inch (60.96-cm), 20-watt tubes on the ceiling or above the mirror.

Manufacturers have developed fluorescent lamps in many color balances, from cool white to natural, or soft white. Deluxe cool-white tubes strengthen all colors nearly equally and give the best overall color rendition. Daylight tubes strengthen green and blue. Deluxe warm-white tubes simulate incandescent light and are recommended when these two kinds of lights are used in the same room. New types of fluorescent tubes are constantly being introduced. Consult a lighting specialist to keep up with the new lighting sources.

QUARTZ HALOGEN BULBS

Bright-white quartz halogen bulbs are excellent for task lighting, pinpoint accenting, and other dramatic accents (Fig. 10.17c). Halogen is usually low-voltage, but it may be standard line current. Halogen bulbs are tiny bulbs that give out a lot of lumens on 12 to 20 volts. It is actually a form of incandescence, but the lamp is filled with halogen, and the tungsten filament is a different design. It produces as much light as an incandescent bulb 10 times its size, consumes half as much power, and lasts up to seven times longer.

The popular MR-16 (minireflector) bulb creates the tightest beam and creates drama by varying the levels of lighting intensity on objects and areas. For a longer reach and wider coverage, choose a PAR bulb. An abundance of smaller bulb shapes and sizes fit pendants and undercabinet strip lights. They are used in strings hidden in toekicks for general illumination, on top of wall cabinets, and under-wall cabinets for task lighting.

Low-voltage lighting takes a transformer that is usually quite small. The system requires a transformer to convert the normal household current to the lower voltage requirement. Low-voltage systems also require special rheostat dimming controls. Overall, the miniature size, halogen gas, and precise beam result in superior optical efficiency and long life. However, be aware that halogen does generate very high heat and has a high initial cost.

TUNGSTEN-HALOGEN LAMPS

Tungsten-halogen is a special type of incandescent lamp that has its filament in a quartz enclosure which is filled with a halogen gas. As the result of a regenerative cycle, the evaporated tungsten is removed from the bulb wall and redeposited on the filament. As a result, lamp blackening is eliminated and lamp life is roughly doubled compared to standard incandescent lamps.

Xenon Lamps

Xenon lamps are widely used for their increased brightness and lumen output over similar wedge-base incandescent lamps. An excellent alternative to halogen, xenon lamps are cooler with comparable color rendition.

Increased energy conservation is constantly creating new lighting with lower power consumption. Clients may want to know which kind uses less power, so try to keep yourself informed in this area.

Types of Lighting Fixtures

Bathroom lighting requirements depend on and vary according to the size of the space, ceiling height, ceiling color, overall bathroom color scheme, finishes used, and the general layout of the bathroom. A room designed with dark cabinets, deep-toned countertops, and a cathedral ceiling requires more light than a white-on-white bathroom. A light color on the ceiling reflects 60 to 80 percent of the light. Light colors reflect nearly twice as much light as deep, dark colors. Finding the right light is relatively easy because there are so many different light fixtures.

Ceiling and Recessed Fixtures

The easiest way to obtain good general lighting is by using one or more ceiling-mounted fixtures. Recessed housings are installed during rough-in construction and are one of the most permanent elements of the bathroom design. Therefore, a lighting plan must be considered early.

Today a wide range of well-designed ceiling fixtures of the surface-mounted or pendant type are on the market. Recessed (downlights) fixtures are a popular choice in today's bathrooms (Fig. 10.18). These fixtures can handle ambient, task, and accent needs, as long as they are fitted with the right baffle or shield. Recessed incandescent downlights should be placed 6 to 8 feet (183 to 244 cm) apart. Remind your client that the type and size of the shielding material, the position of the fixture relative to viewing angles of the occupant, and light distribution are all important. Ceiling-mounted fixtures in the bathroom can be seen within one's field of view and consequently should have only half the

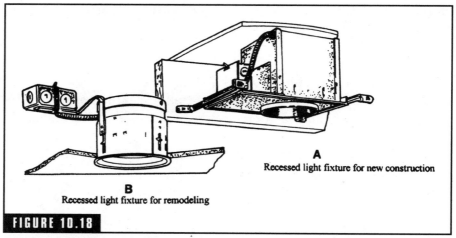

A
Recessed light fixture for new construction

B
Recessed light fixture for remodeling

FIGURE 10.18

(*a*) **Recessed light fixture for new construction; (*b*) recessed light fixture for a remodeled bathroom.** *(Leon E. Korejwo, Illustrations.)*

surface brightness of similar fixtures in utility areas. Similarly, pendant fixtures (directly in the line of sight) should have half the surface brightness of ceiling-mounted fixtures. Most luminous small-diameter pendant fixtures should use 25 watts or less, as they serve only for decorative accent. However, pendant fixtures of very dense or opaque materials may use much higher wattage without causing discomfort.

A well-shielded fixture distributing light up, down, and to the sides (by itself) creates a much more pleasing atmosphere in a room than one that produces only downward light. Fixtures suspended from the ceiling and reflecting all or nearly all of their light to the ceiling for redistribution produce very comfortable (although bland) general lighting.

Recessed fixtures provide no light on the ceiling. Because most of the light is directed downward, the wattage and the number of fixtures needed should be at least double the number of surface-mounted or pendant fixtures used to light the same area. Keep in mind that while any downlighting done in recessed fixtures holding R- or PAR-type bulbs may be most decorative in the light patterns and shadows they cast, they are not suitable for general lighting because they are not diffused enough for comfortable visibility throughout the bathroom. Typically, however, downlights follow countertops or shine on the lavatory (sink). Recessed lighting is integral to the architecture, economical, and applicable to all architectural styles and interior designs.

LUMINOUS PANELS AND CEILINGS

A ceiling can be fully illuminated, or it can have just one panel of light. In the latter case, a panel of louvered or diffusing material—usually about 4 by 6 feet (122 by 183 cm) in size—is mounted on the ceiling or suspended from it, with the light source concealed behind it. Most of the major fixture manufacturers offer kits consisting of plastic diffusers in pans, sheets, or rolls; a suspension system with a gridwork of wood, metal, or plastic; and fluorescent fixtures to mount above the suspended luminous panel.

For shadow-free general lighting throughout the bathroom, the luminous ceiling is the answer; however, for the shaving and makeup area, different provisions for lighting are necessary. But such a lighting plan is usually possible only where there is a cavity of at least 10 to 12 inches (25 to 30 cm) above the desired ceiling line. Frequently, the cavities between the ceiling joints are used as a part of or the whole space needed for the luminous ceiling fixtures. For uniform lighting, use a minimum of one 40-watt fluorescent tube for every 12 sq ft (1.11 m^2) of room area, or one 60-watt incandescent bulb for every 4 sq ft (0.37 m^2) of panel. For proper light diffusion, all surfaces of the cavity must be highly reflective and must have a matte texture. White lampholders for incandescent tubes are also needed. In addition, any other materials within the cavity, such as joists, conduits, and pipes should be painted white. The ceiling panels themselves are usually made of translucent plastic, with decorative metal gridwork providing the necessary support. Manufacturers of luminous ceilings can provide design and installation instructions for their particular products.

TRACK LIGHTING

Of all the bathroom lighting options, track lighting offers complete decorating freedom and provides endless opportunities to achieve function and accent lighting. Track lighting is a concept of accent light that can be as flexible as the imagination. It can be recessed, surface-mounted, or suspended by pendant stems. Most of these movable, adjustable track systems can be swiveled, angled, and pointed in any direction, or grouped for every functional design effect. Fixtures come in myriad styles and give the look of built-in lighting without the installation hassle. Tracks mount on ceilings or walls for task lighting at specific areas or general bathroom illumination. For task lighting, fit track fixtures with spotlight bulbs; for general illumination, install more diffuse floodlight bulbs. For best illumination, tracks or downlights should be installed at least 2 feet (61 cm) away from a wall.

COVE LIGHTING

Coves are particularly suited to rooms with two ceiling levels. In these applications they should be placed right at the line where a flat, low-ceiling area breaks away to a higher-ceiling space. The upward light emphasizes this change of level and is very effective in rooms with slant or cathedral-type ceilings. However, the lighting efficiency of coves is low in comparison with that of valances and wall brackets. Coves which are usually mounted high on the wall direct all of their light upward to the ceiling, where it is, in turn, reflected back into the room. The illumination effect produced by cove lighting is soft, uniform, and comfortable. Cove lighting should be supplemented by other lighting fixtures to give the room interest and provide lighting for seeing tasks.

VALANCE AND SOFFIT LIGHTING

A valance board installed between the cabinet tops and ceiling is an easy and effective way to obtain general bathroom light (Fig. 10.19a). The valance faceboards, which shield a continuous row of fluorescent tubes running the full length of the cabinets, can be simple and unobtrusive, or they can be as decorative and stylish as the imagination allows. A wide variety of faceboard materials are available that can be trimmed, scalloped, notched, perforated, papered, or painted. Faceboards should have a minimum width of 5 inches (13 cm) and seldom should be wider than 10 inches (25 cm). They should not interfere with the opening and closing of cabinet doors. To obtain proper upward diffusion of the light, the top of the fluorescent fixtures and the top of the faceboard should be at least 10 inches (25 cm) from the ceiling. The faceboard should also be mounted a minimum of 6 inches (15 cm) from the wall or soffit face to permit air to circulate freely around the fluorescent tubes. It is a good idea to tilt the faceboard in 15 to 20° to shield the light source from anyone sitting in the bathroom. The inside of the valance board should always be painted flat white.

Where the space above the wall cabinets is not enclosed and there is at least 12 inches (30 cm) between them and the ceiling, the bare fluorescent channels can be mounted on the top of the cabinets at the rear

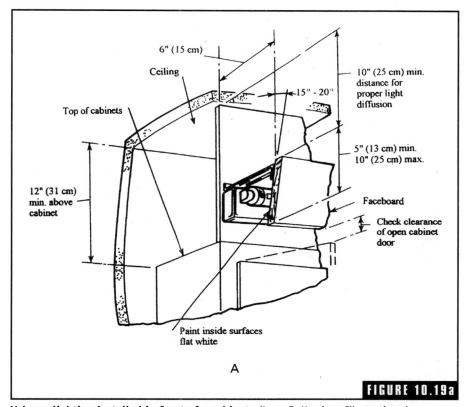

Valance lighting installed in front of a cabinet. *(Leon E. Korejwo, Illustrations.)*

(Fig. 10.19*b*). The channel should be tilted on 45° blocks for upward diffusion of light. If the fluorescent tubes can be seen from across the room, a 3- to 5-inch (8- to 13-cm) board can be fastened on top of the cabinets at the front. This faceboard can be finished to match the wall cabinets.

The underside of an architectural member is known as a *soffit.* If the soffit area above the cabinet is at least 12 inches (30 cm) high, it is possible to illuminate the perimeter of the entire bathroom. The continuous two-tube fluorescent fixtures are fastened to the wall at the back of the cavity, and the soffit is faced with either translucent plastic or glass (Fig. 10.19*c*). The inside of the cavity should be painted flat white or lined with a reflecting material. To be most effective, the ceiling itself should be white or a very light color.

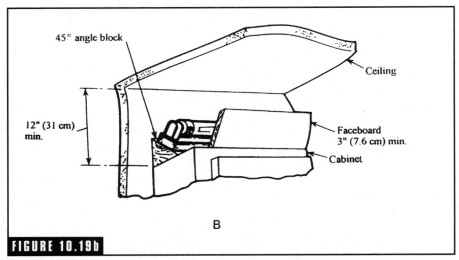

FIGURE 10.19b

Valance light above the cabinet. *(Leon E. Korejwo, Illustrations.)*

Another way to have an illuminated soffit is to extend it out from the cabinets 16 to 24 inches (41 to 61 cm) and, on the ceiling of this extension, install continuous, two-tube fluorescent fixtures (Fig. 10.19d). The bottom of the extension is then covered with either translucent plastic or glass. The result is a soft, intimate light all around the cabinet walls. This extended soffit method is very similar to the cornice lighting that is often used in other rooms of the house to dramatize wall textures and wallcoverings (Fig. 10.19e). An open soffit between wall cabinet and ceiling can also house decorative uplighting to lift the ceiling or enclose the area with wallboard or molded plaster, extending the soffits past the cabinet fronts and adding recessed downlights. Also, strips of small lights can be installed in the toekick or soffit.

UNDERCABINET LIGHTING

When overhead cabinets are present, the best method of lighting the counter surface below is to fasten fluorescent channels either to the bottom of the cabinets at the front (preferable) or directly under the cabinet on the back wall. The channels may be painted to match the wall, if desired. An opaque shield is recommended, and it may be of metal, wood, or laminated plastic to match the cabinets or countertops.

The wattage used depends on the total length of counter areas. Use the longest tube that fits, and fill at least two-thirds of the counter length. These wattages are good for up to 22 inches (56 cm) above the countertop, a height for wall cabinets that is rather uncomfortable for most householders. A two-socket incandescent bracket with 60 watts in each socket is the equivalent for each 3 feet (0.914 m) of countertop, but incandescent light is not as popular for undercabinet applications as fluorescents.

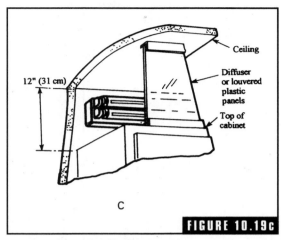

Soffit lighting above cabinets. *(Leon E. Korejwo, Illustrations.)*

In framed cabinets, the face frame helps shield the eyes from undercabinet lights. Frameless cabinets do not have a protecting shield, so a 2-inch (5-cm) bar has to be added along the front of the cabinet. Some frameless cabinets have recesses built into the cabinet

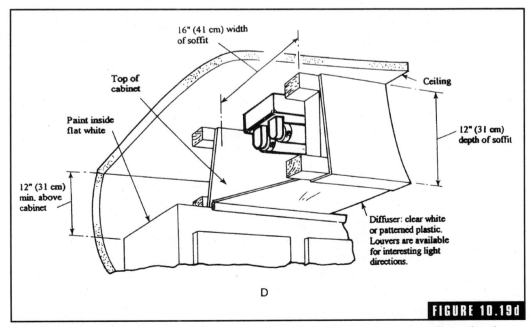

Soffit lighting extended above the cabinet or in- front of a wall. *(Leon E. Korejwo, Illustrations.)*

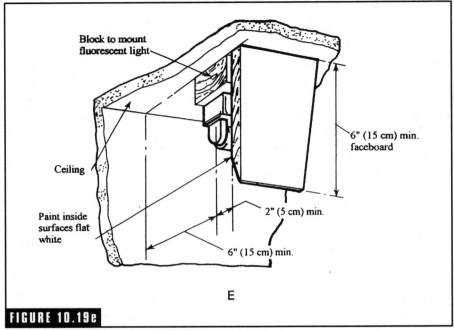

Block to mount
fluorescent light

Ceiling

Paint inside
surfaces flat
white

6" (15 cm) min.
faceboard

2" (5 cm) min.

6" (15 cm) min.

E

FIGURE 10.19e

Typical cornice lighting. *(Leon E. Korejwo, Illustrations.)*

bottoms where lights can be mounted. Some halogen undercabinet lights plug into a track attached to the cabinet bottom and that shields the eyes.

Note: To ensure safety, check with local codes regarding the placement of lighting fixtures, with respect to distances from open water, to prevent shock hazards.

The lighting levels of the bathroom can be controlled by both switching and dimming. As a bare minimum, the general illumination and the task lighting should have their own separate switches. It is always best, of course, to have each lighting arrangement on its own switch. Be sure to plan and show which switch operates which light source and indicate whether it is a single or multiple switch or a dimmer. Plan to add a three- or four-way switch if the bathroom has more than one entrance. Switches are usually placed 44 inches (112 cm) above the floor on the open (or latch) side of doorways.

For special lighting effects in the bathroom, dimmer controls can be used on both incandescent and fluorescent light sources. This type of control is especially desirable around whirlpools (or other activities), where variable lighting levels would be useful for creating different moods. Several sizes and varieties of dimmer controls are available for incandescent bulbs. The smaller-sized controls can be used in place of a standard switch, which makes installation extremely simple. For larger-sized dimmers, a double box may be needed. For uniform dimming, all tubes controlled by one dimmer should be of the same size.

With states and communities now providing energy-conserving guidelines in their building codes, the Illuminating Engineering Society (IES) developed a residential lighting power budget or limit formula, which is based on well-organized task lighting and the use of energy-efficient lighting equipment. It is important to become familiar with these codes and guidelines for developing bathroom lighting plans.

Finishing Touches and Accessories

The final bathroom finishing accessories involve many small details. At this point in the project, the following may need to be completed: level and fasten in place accessories such as grab bars; soap dishes (those not previously built into tubs and showers); shelves; towel bars, hooks, pegs, and rods; toilet-tissue holders; toothbrush holders; and mirrors (makeup, shower shaving mirrors, etc.). If not already installed, all cabinet pulls, hardware, and switchplates should be installed. There are an unlimited number of possibilities which add to each individual homeowner's needs and help give each bathroom its own personality.

Completion

With the majority of the bathroom project complete, the installer must complete all touchups, repairs, alignments, and adjustments that are inevitably needed at the end of a project. Typically, this work represents a small portion of the total project. This last portion of the installation project is the most difficult to complete and is also the most crucial in ensuring client satisfaction.

Perhaps the most effective way to complete a job quickly and neatly with a satisfied client is by using a quality-control precompletion checklist. Table 10.2 is an example form for a final inspection with the

Table 10-2 Final-Inspection-before-Punch-List-with-Customer Form
Applicable for Bathroom or Kitchen

Job name:_____

Job address:_____

Cabinetry

    Kitchen cabinets are installed properly; enough screws. They must be plumb and level.

    Doors and drawer fronts are aligned properly.

    Doors and drawer hardware are functioning properly.

    Cabinet surfaces are free of scratches and nicks.

    Glass or plastic door inserts are installed securely and are unbroken.

    Accessory items are installed as specified.

    Cabinet shelves are installed with proper number of chips.

Countertops

    Countertops are securely attached to base cabinets or means of support.

    Backsplash is installed if required.

    Backsplash is scribed to wall if irregular wall surface exists.

    Countertop is caulked as required.

    Countertop is free of surface scratches.

    Solid surface and stone countertops are correctly finished.

    Countertop joints fit tightly and are sealed.

Appliances

    Dishwasher is screwed in; air gap is installed.

    Food waste disposal is clear and operating properly.

    Water connection is made to refrigerator; ice maker is functioning properly.

    Range/cooktop is installed; all burners are functioning properly.

    Oven is securely installed in opening; oven and broiler are functioning properly.

    Microwave oven is securely mounted, if required, and operating properly.

    Hood is securely mounted, connected to ductwork, and operating properly.

Electrical

    All outlets and switches work; wall plates are straight and level.

    All outlet wall plates are installed tightly to drywall or finish surface.

    Electric panel is labeled for new circuits.

    All light fixtures have lamps installed and are working properly.

    Batteries are in smoke detector, if required.

    Final inspection is completed.

Table 10-2 Final-Inspection-before-Punch-List-with-Customer Form
Applicable for Bathroom or Kitchen (*Continued*)

Plumbing

    All fixtures are working properly.

    Fixtures are not chipped or showing signs of finish damage.

    Fixtures are secured to wall, floor, or countertop surface.

    Tub and shower are caulked, including at floor.

    Aerators and escutcheon plates are installed.

    All gas connections are working properly.

    Final inspection is completed.

HVAC

    Diffusers are installed and working; return air grille is installed.

    System is operable; thermostat is properly installed if required.

    Filters have been replaced after construction is completed.

Drywall/Paint/Wallpaper

    Drywall is finished properly and sanded.

    No loose nails or nail pops are apparent.

    There is no damage to drywall from electrical or plumbing work.

    Painting is complete; sufficient coats have been applied.

    Wallpaper has been installed, if required, and is properly adhered.

Finish Flooring

    Grout is cleaned from tile.

    Mastic is cleaned from sheet goods and vinyl tile.

    Base materials (shoe molding, vinyl base, etc.) have been installed.

    Seams in sheet flooring are sealed correctly.

    Thresholds and reducer strips have been installed.

General

    Job broom-clean or maid-clean as appropriate.

    Windows and newly installed glass have been cleaned.

    Trash has been removed.

    Countertops and cabinet surfaces, interior and exterior, have been cleaned.

    Yard and any staging or storage areas have been returned to good order.

    Owner has received all warranty and operating literature for materials and equipment installed.

Comments:

_____

_____

Signature   Date

Source: Courtesy of National Kitchen and Bath Association, 1994.

customer. When you feel the project is complete, and you have completed any lists you may have prepared for yourself, as well as any subcontractors, you should schedule a meeting between the homeowner, dealer or designer, and architect (if applicable). The focus of this meeting is to produce a list of items to be completed before final payment. Any items not on this list that need work or repairs may be done under the warranty. The final bill must be paid before any warranty work can be done to prevent the never-ending list where final payment is postponed over and over again as more items are added to the checklist.

Because of the excellent quality control during the installation, the checklist does not need to contain more than 10 items. Be aware that the client will point out most of these items. To assure your client that you are committed to the highest level of client satisfaction, you should also add a few items to the list.

As the end of the installation project approaches, you need to step back and review the installation to see if everything is up to the level of quality you have established. You, as the installer, are responsible for deciding whether work is acceptable or is defective. This step is extremely necessary.

You need to completely review all the flooring, drywall, carpentry work, cabinet installation, and fixture installation as well as the electrical, plumbing, and HVAC work done by the subcontractors. More importantly, be certain that all code inspections are satisfactorily completed. Knowing, or at least being familiar with, the codes that are in effect and double-checking before a code inspection, should help to ensure a smooth approval by the official. Check every outlet and light switch, every door, and every drawer to be certain that they operate correctly and are free from visual defects. Although you can come back to take care of any problems after a project is finished, it is much easier to have mistakes corrected while the crew is still on site. You and your client both want the job finished quickly and professionally. To make sure that all goes well, Table 10.3, prepared by Home Tech Information Systems, Inc., listing things to check before making the final payment, is presented here. Preparation for this final inspection is helpful. This list helps you review every segment of the installation job. In addition, keep a written list of items that need attention as you see or think of them. When the items on this list have been completed, you are ready for the quality-control precompletion punchlist with the client.

Table 10-3 Quality-Control Precompletion Punch List

Owner _____

Address _____

City, State, Zip _____

Telephone _____

Job Location
_____
_____

Job No. _____ Date _____ 19 ____

List of items to be completed
prior to final payment of $ _____

_____

_____

_____

_____

_____

_____

_____

_____

_____

_____

_____

Amount to be retained in escrow pending completion of above items $ _____

It is agreed that when the above list of items is completed, approval for final payment will be authorized. Any omitted or defective items noted after final payment will be covered by Builder's Warranty.

Submitted by (Inspector):	Date	Owner	Date
Contractor	Date	Owner	Date

Source: Home-Tech Form 334.

Final Repairs

Immediately take care of any items that need to be corrected. Schedule any subcontractors needed to return to the job. Since they may not be able to handle the job right away, give the subcontractors a deadline for completion of the work. Although it seems like common sense, assemble all items for the subcontractors into one list so that they can take care of all the items in one visit.

Be aware that nicks and scratches on vanities, countertops, and cabinets are unavoidable. Plan on making a few surface repairs to them on every bathroom installation project. Countertop and cabinet dealers sell stains and touchup kits to match the finish of the cabinetry, and nicks and scratches can be repaired so that they are unnoticeable. Never try to blame a subcontractor for having scratched a cabinet. It is more efficient to make the repair with the touchup kits rather than trying to place blame. Be sure to order the touchup kit from the cabinet manufacturer when the cabinets are ordered. Do not wait until it is time to make repairs to try to obtain the touchup kit.

Final adjustments to cabinet doors, drawers, and hardware may also be necessary at this stage of the project. Anything more than minor adjustments should have been done at an earlier point in the installation. Frameless cabinets with fully adjustable hinges make door alignment relatively easy, but framed cabinets are difficult to adjust once they are installed and the countertop attached, because door and drawer misalignment in framed cabinets is generally due to the twisting or racking of a cabinet unit that was not installed plumb and level.

Check to make sure that all cabinet hardware is properly aligned and securely attached to the cabinets. Although this detail may seem minor, imagine how unhappy your clients will be when they open a drawer and the handle comes off. In addition, be certain that drawers slide out smoothly, and that the safety features that keep the drawer from being pulled all the way out are working correctly. Mirrors or medicine cabinets should be firmly mounted, and level. Shower doors should operate smoothly, as well as faucets and drains. All caulking should be neatly finished.

Final Cleanup

Cleanup procedures need to be reviewed at this stage of the installation. On completion, you are responsible for leaving the bathroom spotless and ready for use. The installation estimate should include a line item for a final professional cleaning of the job. Following are several items to be taken care of before the cleaning service can begin:

1. All debris must be removed from the job site, including areas that were used for staging and assembly, both interior and exterior. If installers have their own cleanup and trash truck, the driver must allow time not only for cleaning up but also for the time spent traveling to dispose of the refuse.

2. Remove all canvas runners and polyurethane covers. If possible, these can be saved for the next job.

3. If you relocated any of the client's personal possessions during the installation project, they should now be returned to their original locations.

The professional cleaning service should clean all bath fixtures, floors, windows, light fixtures, plumbing fixtures, countertops, and cabinets (inside and out), as well as any areas adjacent to the bathroom which may have been affected by the installation; this includes dusting, wiping down woodwork, and shampooing carpets. When this work is completed, the bathroom must be ready for use.

Client Education

Once the installation is complete, you should take the time to answer any questions your client may have about the operation and use of equipment (whirlpool, luxury shower operation, etc.). It is also important to review the manual and warranty papers with the owner.

Another important factor to be covered is the routine maintenance and cleaning of fixtures and equipment. Try to answer some of the inevitable questions that every client with a new bathroom wants to know. Your experience will tell you what some of these commonly asked questions are. Always present this information in a positive way.

At this point, cabinet maintenance is an important topic to be addressed. Make sure that the client is aware of the type of finish on the cabinets and knows how best to care for it. Enamel and polyurethane finishes can be wiped clean, but they also withstand cleaning with a mild, nonabrasive cleaner. Streaks on high-gloss surfaces can be prevented when cleaning by adding a little vinegar to the cleaning water.

Woods and veneers with natural-looking, penetrating finishes can be waxed to provide added protection against stains. These finishes should be polished periodically to renew their luster, and wax should be applied once or twice a year. Nonpenetrating wood finishes, such as polyurethane, can be wiped clean with a damp cloth. Wax should not be used.

Decorative laminates and melamine cabinet finishes can be wiped with a wet cloth or a sponge. These surfaces can handle most nonabrasive cleaning products without surface damage. However, clients should understand that water should not be left on the edges of laminate cabinets or near seams where it could penetrate into the substrate and cause the laminate to lift as the core material expands. Wax or oil-based polishes are never to be used on a laminate finish.

The care and maintenance of fixtures and equipment, such as whirlpools, showers, toilets, bidets, and saunas, is another important topic to be reviewed with the client.

As a final word on the subject of customer education, it must be pointed out again that it is your responsibility, as the bathroom contractor, to establish and maintain cordial relations with your customers. If you are able to establish pleasant relationships, the associations with your customers will be not only more agreeable but also immeasurably more effective.

Postcompletion Meeting

Some installers find it beneficial to set up a postcompletion meeting with the dealer or designer to review the installation. This meeting can be held a few days after the bathroom installation project is completed. It provides an excellent opportunity to discuss areas of the work that you feel were successful or those which may have been problematic (be constructive). The communication should help strengthen your relationship with the dealer or designer, and help ensure many future installation projects.

GLOSSARY

The following terms are used in the planning and remodeling procedures necessary for the installation of a good bathroom.

ABS   See *acrylonitrile butadiene styrene.*

accessory   A handrail, toilet-paper holder, towel bar, or other item that complements the fixtures and fittings; an important part of each bathroom center.

accountability   Responsibility for one's actions or work.

acrylonitrile butadiene styrene (ABS)   Rigid plastic drainpipe.

actual dimension   The true size of a piece of lumber, after milling and drying; see also **nominal dimension.**

air gap   In a water-supply system, the distance between the faucet outlet and the flood rim of the basin it discharges into. Air gaps are used to prevent contamination of the water supply by backsiphonage.

alkyd   Synthetic resin paint base. Alkyd resin has largely replaced linseed oil.

American National Standards Institute (ANSI)   An association that sets construction and performance standards.

American Society for Testing and Materials (ASTM)   A U.S. agency universally recognized for testing methods and performance criteria of materials, including plumbing pipe, fittings, and solvent cements.

American Society of Mechanical Engineers (ASME) A U.S. agency that sets standards for machinery, tools, and their products.

ampere (A) Measurement of the rate of flow of electricity (sometimes referred to as "amp").

ANSI See **American National Standards Institute.**

antiscald control valve (pressure-balancing valve) Single control fitting that contains a piston that automatically responds to changes in line water pressure to maintain shower temperature; the valve blocks abrupt drops or rises in temperature.

apron The trim board placed immediately below the window stool.

asbestos A material comprising several minerals used as a noncombustible, nonconducting, or chemically resistant construction material.

ASME See **American Society of Mechanical Engineers.**

backflow The term used for negative water pressure.

back panel The piece of material making up the back of a cabinet.

back rail The top and bottom horizontal members on the back of a cabinet. They are used for mounting the cabinet to the wall with screws.

backsplash The tiled wall area behind a sink or countertop. A portion of the countertop often extends up the wall at the rear of a base cabinet.

balloon frame Wood frame in which studs are continuous from the sill to the top plate of the top floor.

bar graph A graph or chart schedule that lists categories of work down the left side and dates for the duration of the project across the top of the schedule. The projected start and completion of each category of work is plotted on the chart.

barrier-free, handicapped-accessible fixtures Fixtures specifically designed for wheelchair users or for those with limited mobility.

baseboard The finishing board covering a finished wall where it meets the floor.

base cabinet Those cabinets which rest on the floor and support the countertop to provide a working surface. A base cabinet commonly has a single drawer over a single door.

base corner filler A special accessory item used to turn a corner in the most economical way.

base drawer unit A base cabinet composed entirely of drawers.

base end panel An accessory item which is used to provide a finished end.

base filler An accessory used to fill spaces resulting from odd wall dimensions that cannot be filled using standard base cabinets.

base plan Transferring rough measurements of an existing room to a scale drawing; a convenient scale for planning a bathroom is to make $\frac{1}{2}$ inch (1.27 cm) equal 1 foot (30.48 cm).

batten Thin molding of rectangular section used to cover a joint.

beam A horizontal load-bearing part of the building.

bearing capacity How much weight a floor can support or bear.

bearing wall A wall carrying more than its own weight, usually supporting floor or ceiling joists.

bidet A bowl-shaped bathroom fixture designed for personal cleanliness used to wash the perineal area.

blind cabinet A cabinet that has a shelf, pull-out, or swing-out apparatus to provide access to a corner.

blind corner base A base cabinet used to turn a corner and use all available storage space.

blind corner wall A wall cabinet used to turn a corner and use all available storage space.

blocking Short member bracing, such as 2 × 4s, between two longer framing members.

blueprints A general term for a set of plans for a project.

bottom panel The material used in the bottom of a base or wall cabinet.

branch Any part of a piping system other than a riser, main, or stack.

branch circuit One of several circuits in a building, originating at the service entrance panel and protected by a separate circuit breaker or fuse.

British thermal units per hour (Btu/h) A measure of heating or cooling.

building code Rules adopted by a government for the regulation of building.

building drain The lowest house piping that receives discharge from waste and soil stack and other sanitary drainage pipe and carries it to the building sewer outside the house.

building official The person who is legally responsible for enforcing building codes.

butt joint A joint framed by butting the ends of two pieces together without overlapping.

cantilevered Two beams or trusses that project from piers toward another that when joined, directly or by a suspended connecting member, form a span.

cap Fitting with a solid end used for closing off a pipe.

casing Inside or outside molding which covers space between a window or door jamb and a wall.

cast iron A manufacturing process used to mold metal when it is so hot that it is in a liquid state.

cast polymer A fixture and surfacing material created by pouring a mixture of ground marble and polyester resin into a treated mold, where curing takes place at room temperature or in a curing oven.

CBD See **certified bathroom designer.**

center stile The vertical member that separates doors on two-door base and wall cabinets. Also used on blind corner wall and base cabinets.

center-to-center distance In mounting faucets, distance between centers of holes on a sink deck; in pipe fitting, distance between centers of two consecutive pipes.

certificate of occupancy A written certificate issued by the local building official at the completion of the project that permits owners to occupy the home or a portion thereof.

certified bathroom designer (CBD) Evidence of certification means that the designer has completed and mastered rigorous instruction, including certified training programs in room layout, storage planning, cabinet installation, plumbing, and lighting. Each association has a continuing program to inform members about the latest building materials and techniques.

certified cabinet A cabinet that, through testing, has been verified as meeting the quality and performance requirements of the standards program of the NKCA.

cfm rating See **cubic feet per minute (cfm) rating.**

change order An amendment to the original contract to perform changes or additional work.

check valve A one-way valve for water flow.

chlorinated poly(vinyl chloride) (CPVC) Rigid plastic tube for hot and cold water.

circuit breaker A safety device that keeps the electrical branch circuits and anything connected to them from overheating and catching fire.

cleanout Accessible opening in the drainage system used to provide access for removing obstructions.

clearance space A term used to describe the space necessary for the safe and convenient use of fixtures.

close grain   Small, closely spaced pores or fine texture.

closet bend   Gently curved elbow that connects toilet to drain system.

close-in   The point of time in a project when wall materials are installed and when access to plumbing and electrical lines within the walls is closed off.

compression fitting   Easy-to-use fitting for copper or plastic tube; pushed in and hand-tightened.

concrete slab   Used as a base for building when there is no basement or crawlspace.

condensation   Process of water vapor turning to liquid water.

conductor   Wire intended to carry electric current.

conduit   A hollow metal tube that contains electrical wiring.

contract installer   A self-employed installer offering installation services to retailers, dealers, and designers.

convection heat   Air heated by an element and then circulated.

coped cut   A profile cut made in the face of a piece of molding that allows for butting it against another piece at an inside corner.

corner block   The piece of wood used to square and strengthen the corners of base cabinets.

corner cabinet   A cabinet designed to fit specifically in a corner.

counter frontage   The measurement of the counter along its front edge.

countertop battens   Strips that add thickness to a countertop.

countertop fasteners   The mechanical items used to secure the countertop pieces together.

coupling   Fitting used to connect two lengths of pipe in a straight run.

coupling nut   A device that holds a supply tube to a faucet inlet or a toilet inlet valve.

CPM schedule.   See **critical path method (CPM) schedule.**

CPVC   See **chlorinated poly(vinyl chloride).**

crawlspace   A 2 × 3-foot-high space under the floor.

credentials   Evidence of training and education that establish an installer as a qualified professional.

critical distance   Maximum horizontal distance allowed between a fixture trap and a vent or soil stack.

critical path method (CPM) schedule   Type of schedule that uses a diagram or network to show the sequence and interrelation of the categories of work of a project.

cubic feet per minute (cfm) rating   Cubic feet per minute that a fan is capable of moving.

cubic footage   A measure of volume; the product of length times width times height.

customer analysis   Evaluation (or "sizing up") of a customer to determine whether that customer is likely to be difficult to work for and cause the installer to lose money on the project.

dado joint   A joint formed when the end of one member fits into a groove cut partway through the face of another.

dead load   Weight on the floor that is not moving.

diagonal wall cabinet   A wall cabinet designed to turn a corner on an angle.

diffuser   A device used to deflect air from an outlet in various directions. Also a device for distributing the light of a lamp evenly.

dimensional stock   Solid lumber pieces of specified length, width, and thickness.

dimmer control (rheostat switch)   A device used to vary the light output of an electric lamp.

door   Cabinet component used to cover an opening in the cabinet base frame. Also an entryway to the bathroom.

door frame   The outside portion of a frame-and-panel door.

door panel   The inside portion of a frame-and-panel door.

dovetail   A projecting part that fits into a corresponding indentation to form a joint.

drain   Any pipe that carries wastewater or waterborne wastes in a building drainage system.

drainage system   All the piping that carries sewage, rainwater, or other liquid wastes to the point of disposal or sewer.

drain stack   The portion of the plumbing in the bathroom that is used to remove wastewater.

drain-waste-vent (DWV) system   A system that carries water and waste out of the house, allows sewer gases to escape, and maintains atmospheric pressure in drainpipes.

drawer cabinet   A cabinet that features two, three, four, or five drawers.

drawer front   The exposed front portion of the drawer box. Same as drawer face.

drawer pull   The hardware on a drawer used to pull it open.

drawer suspension   The mechanism used to guide the drawer box when it is being opened and closed.

dry run Before applying grout, the process of placing the tiles to check the layout; usually tile spacers are used to indicate the width of the grout joints.

DWV system See **drain-waste-vent (DWV) system.**

elbow Fitting that changes the angle of two lengths of pipe; used for making turns (e.g., a 90° elbow makes a right-angle turn).

electrical system Includes the electric meter, wiring, receptacles, switches, and lights, to provide electricity.

elevations Drawings of the walls of a bathroom, made as though the observer were looking straight at the wall.

encapsulation In reference to asbestos, wrapping asbestos material in a material or paint that prevents loose fibers from floating in the air.

end panel The material that makes up the sides of a cabinet.

endsplash The portion of the countertop used to protect walls and tall cabinet sides where the countertop joins them.

equipment The plumbing fixtures, storage units, and counters used in a bathroom.

escutcheon A protective plate used to enclose a pipe or fitting at a wall- or floor-covering. Decorative trim piece that fits over a faucet body or pipe extending from a wall.

exhaust system A system in which air is captured by a ventilation unit and is exhausted outdoors.

face frame The exposed front portion of the cabinet which provides shape and strength to the cabinet.

fascia The front of a soffit area.

faucet Fixture valve that opens and closes the flow of water to the fixture.

fiber core Sheet core material made from compressed wood fibers that have been impregnated with a waterproof phenolic resin. Density of material develops great dimensional stability and resistance to warping and twisting. Core is veneered on both sides for use as doors, drawer panels, and overlays.

filler An accessory used to fill spaces resulting from odd wall dimensions that cannot be filled by using standard cabinets.

filter Device for removing sediment from water and improving taste and odor. Sometimes used in a potable-water system.

finish coat The final covering applied to cabinets to provide a tough durable surface.

finished paneling   Prefinished sheets that can be used to provide a matching surface for walls, cabinet ends, and peninsula backs.

firestop   A 2 × 4 nailed horizontally between studs to inhibit the spread of a fire between uninsulated stud cavities.

fitting   The term used for any device that controls water entering or leaving a fixture. Faucets, spouts, drain controls, water-supply lines, and diverter valves all are fittings. *Fittings* is really a technical name for faucets and are sold separately from fixtures.

fixture   A fixture provides the required means for using water. Each fixture has a purpose connected with the homeowner's use of water, and each must have certain features to serve its purpose. Fixtures—lavatory, bathtub, shower, toilet, or bidet—can be costly plumbing items and should exactly suit the homeowner's needs.

fixture supply   Water-supply pipe that connects a fixture to a branch water-supply pipe or directly to a main water-supply pipe.

flange   Flat fitting or integral edging with holes to permit bolting together (a toilet bowl is bolted to a floor flange) or fastening to another surface (a tub is fastened to a wall through an integral flange).

flat or slab doors   Doors made of flat pieces of lumber, particleboard, or plywood with a veneer surface.

flexible connector   Bendable piece of tubing that delivers water from a shutoff valve to a fixture or appliance.

floor plan   The horizontal section of a bathroom showing the size, doors, windows, and other features in the walls.

flowchart   A written, week-by-week schedule of the critical tasks to be accomplished on a job.

flue gas   A toxic gas produced during the combustion of fossil fuels.

flush-mounted installation   A method of installation in which a lavatory is installed completely even with the surrounding deck.

frame-and-panel door   A type of door constructed of several separate pieces fastened together.

frame construction   A method of construction where thin component parts form the sides, back, top, and bottom of a cabinet.

framed doors   Doors made of laminate or wood that can be of a slab configuration, with a wood, thick PVC edging, or a metal frame around the doors and drawers.

frameless construction   A method of construction where the core material sides of a cabinet are connected with either a mechanical fastening or a dowel system.

frontage   A measure equaling the horizontal dimension across the face of an appliance, base cabinet, counter, or wall cabinet. To be credited as having *accessible frontage,* a component must be directly accessible from the area located in front of the component. In accordance with this definition, cabinet space (base or wall) and counter surface located in corners are not credited in counting accessible frontage.

full bath   A full bathroom is typically equipped with three fixtures: a lavatory, toilet, and a bathtub or shower or a combination tub-shower.

full-shelf option   Base cabinets are manufactured with half-shelves standard. A full shelf can be added at an additional cost.

furring   The building out of a wall or ceiling with wood strips. The wood strips are used to level parts of a ceiling, wall, or floor before adding the finish surface; commonly used to secure panels of rigid foam insulation.

fuse   Safety devices that keep electrical branch circuits and anything connected to them from overheating and catching fire.

gallons per minute (gpm)   Flush volume in toilets.

gasket   Device (usually rubber) used to make a joint between two parts watertight. This term is sometimes used interchangeably with *washer.*

grain   Pattern arrangement of wood fibers.

granite   An igneous rock with visible coarse grains, used as a surfacing material.

ground-fault circuit interrupter (GFCI)   A device that monitors the electrical circuit at all times and, on detecting a ground fault (a leakage on the line to ground), removes power to the circuit.

ground wire   A bare copper wire or a coated green wire which does not carry current.

grout   A binder and filler applied in the joints between ceramic tiles. May come with or without sand added.

gusset   Brace installed in corners of base cabinets to provide strength and a means of attaching the countertop. Also used in peninsula wall cabinets to ensure positive installation.

half bath   A half bath, also often referred to as a *powder room* or *guest bath,* is typically a two-fixture room containing a lavatory and a toilet, along with some limited storage space.

hanging strip   A portion of the cabinet back through which screws are attached to the wall.

header   The framing component spanning a door or window opening in a wall. A header supports the weight above it and serves as a nailing surface for the door or window frame.

heat gain   Heat that is gained from the sun's rays.

hinges (self-closing)   A type of hardware used to attach doors to the face frame. They are spring-loaded and, as a result, close automatically if the door is partially closed.

hinging   A term applied to single-door cabinets to identify whether the hinges attaching the door to the face frame are on the right or left side.

hollow core   A panel construction with plywood, hardboard, or other material bonded to both sides of a frame assembly.

hydronic   Method of distributing heat by hot water.

independent contractor   A self-employed person offering services to other companies. To be classified as an independent contractor, an individual must be truly independent from the companies for which the person performs services.

installation delivery system   An established system for providing installation services that describes the roles of manufacturers, distributors, retailer-dealer-designers, and installers.

integral   A method of installation whereby a fixture is fabricated from the same piece of material as the countertop material.

island   A cabinet or group of cabinets which are freestanding (not attached to a wall).

jamb   The inside vertical finished face of a door or window frame.

joist span   The distance a joist is allowed to stretch between walls.

joists   The framing members that are the direct support of a floor.

junction boxes   Rectangular, octagonal, or circular boxes made of plastic or metal, which house connections between wires.

kiln-dry   To remove excessive moisture from green lumber by means of a kiln or chamber, usually to a moisture content of 6 to 12 percent.

laminate   A surfacing material used on wall areas, countertops, cabinet interiors, and cabinet doors.

lamp   An artificial light source, such as an incandescent or halogen bulb or a fluorescent tube.

lap joint   Two pieces of dimensional stock overlapping each other and bonded together.

lavatory   Sinks, called *lavatories* by the fixture industry, with standard fittings, accommodate washing, shaving, tooth brushing, and so on.

layout   A drawing showing how cabinets and appliances will be arranged within a bathroom.

lazy Susan corner base cabinet   A base cabinet, installed in a corner, that contains revolving shelves.

lead installer   An installer who has been trained to handle most installation projects as a one-person crew and given responsibility for the job from start to finish.

ledger   A horizontal strip (quite often wood) used to provide support for the ends or edges of other members.

level   Exactly flat in the horizontal plane, or the instrument used to determine horizontal flatness.

liability insurance   Insurance covering the insured against losses arising from injury or damage to another person or property.

lineal footage   A measurement of distance of lengths, such as the distance around the perimeter of a room.

lintel   The horizontal structural member supporting the wall over an opening.

live load   Temporary load imposed on a building by occupancy and the environment.

load-bearing walls   Walls on the exterior or interior of the home that carry the load of the roof down to the foundation.

locknut   Nut used to secure a part, such as a toilet water inlet valve, in place.

main   Principal pipe to which branches are connected.

marble   Recrystallized limestone. A brittle stone used for countertops and flooring.

mastic   Thick-bodied adhesive or sealant.

mechanical systems   Includes heating and cooling equipment, any fans that provide ventilation, and the water heater.

meter   Measurement device to measure utility usage such as electric, gas, and water service.

millwork   Finished woodwork, machined, and partly assembled at the mill.

model code   A standard building code published by one of several model code organizations.

moisture barrier   Material or surface with the purpose of blocking the diffusion of water vapor; the same as a vapor barrier.

molding   Prefinished pieces of various shapes which are used to improve the visual appearance of areas where cabinets meet walls, ceilings, and other structures.

monorail Metal center guide or rail for supporting and guiding a drawer roller.

mortise A notch or hole cut into a piece of wood to receive a projecting part (tenon) shaped to fit.

mounting rail Top and bottom horizontal members on back of cabinet, used for mounting cabinet to the wall with screws.

mullion A vertical piece that separates and supports windows, doors, or panels.

muntins The small members that divide the glass in a window.

National Kitchen and Bath Association (NKBA) An association that sets standards for kitchen and bathroom installation and serves as an information clearinghouse for specialists in this field.

nailer A structural support.

NKBA See **National Kitchen and Bath Association.**

nipple Short piece of pipe with male threads used to join two fittings.

nominal dimension The stated size of a piece of lumber, such as a 2 × 4 or a 1 × 12. The *actual dimension* is somewhat smaller.

nonbearing wall Wall or partition that does not carry a load from above.

O-ring Narrow rubber ring; used in some faucets as packing to prevent leakage around stem and in swivel-spout faucets to prevent leakage at base of spout.

obstructions A term applying to exposed obstacles, such as pipes, in a bathroom area.

on-center (OC) distance A phrase used to designate the distance from the center of one regularly spaced framing member to the center of the next.

one-wall (or one "wet wall") layout A bathroom with all the plumbing located in a row, arranged along a single wall, is the simplest bathroom design for a limited space.

open grain Large pores or coarse texture.

out-to-out measurements Measured from one outside edge of a window, opening, or space to the other outside edge.

overflow An outlet positioned in a tub or lavatory to allow water to escape in case a faucet is left on.

overlay Decorative panel fixed to a door or drawer panel surface rather than inlaid.

overload Excessive electric current in a conductor. The danger is from overheating. Circuit breakers interrupt circuit on detecting overloads.

panel doors Doors that have a frame composed of two horizontal rails and two vertical stiles, with a thinner panel floating in between.

particleboard   Reconstituted wood particles that are bonded with resin under heat and pressure and made into panels. Particleboard has a tendency to swell when exposed to moisture.

partition walls   Walls that divide spaces within the home but are not load-bearing.

PB   See **polybutylene**.

PE   See **polyethylene**.

pie-cut cabinet   A type of corner cabinet that abuts two walls, with both sides usually, but not necessarily, equal.

pipe, fixture supply   The pipe bringing water from behind a wall to a fixture.

pipe-joint compound   Sealing compound used on threaded fittings (applied to external threads).

pipe, vent   The pipe installed to provide airflow to or from a drainage system or to provide air circulation within the system.

pipe, waste   The line that carries away the discharge from any fixture except toilets, conveying it to the building drain.

plate   Horizontal member at the top or bottom of a wall. The top plate supports the rafter ends. The bottom or sill plate supports studs and posts.

plumb   A term applying to a perfectly vertical measurement: straight up and down. The vertical equivalent of *level.*

plumbing appliance   Special class of plumbing fixtures, such as water heaters, water softeners, and filters.

plumbing code   A set of rules that govern the installation of plumbing.

plumbing fixture   A receptacle or device, which demands a supply of water, either temporary or permanently connected to the water-supply system. It discharges used water or wastes directly or indirectly into the drainage system.

plumbing system   Includes potable-water supply and distribution pipe; plumbing fixtures and traps; drain, waste, and vent pipe; and building drains, including their respective joints and connections, devices, receptacles, and appurtenances within the property lines of the premises. It also includes water-treating equipment, gas piping, and water heaters and their vents.

plywood   A panel made of layers (plies) of veneer bonded by an adhesive. The grain of adjoining piles is usually laid at right angles, and an odd number of piles are bonded to obtain balance.

Polybutylene (PB)   Flexible plastic tubing for hot or cold water.

Polyethylene (PE) Flexible plastic tubing for cold water outdoors.

Polypropylene (PP) Rigid plastic pipe used for traps.

Poly(vinyl chloride) (PVC) Rigid plastic pipe for cold water outdoors. Also, off-white piping used for DWV systems.

PP See **polypropylene.**

preconstruction conference A meeting attended by the retailer, dealer, or designer; installer; and customer, among others, prior to the start of construction, for the purpose of informing the customer what is to occur during construction.

preliminary preparation Steps to be taken in advance of cabinet installation.

pressure regulator Device installed in a water-supply line to reduce water pressure.

pressure-treated wood Lumber and sheet goods impregnated with one of several solutions to render the wood virtually impervious to moisture and weather.

productivity The level of efficiency in project production; increased productivity can create increased profit.

pull Knob or handle on doors and drawers.

PVC See **poly(vinyl chloride).**

quality control The process of working to ensure that projects are completed in a quality manner in keeping with established industry standards and customer requirements.

R value A rating system given to insulating material that rates heat-retention capability.

racking Twisting or warping out of square, due to uneven floors, walls, or pressure being applied as a result of forcing into position.

radiant heat Heat transferred through invisible electromagnetic waves from an infrared energy source. Much of the heat transfer is accomplished by radiation through space from warm building surfaces such as floors, walls, or ceilings.

radon An invisible pollutant that comes from trace amounts of uranium in the soil.

rail The horizontal members of a cabinet face frame.

receptacle Electrical device into which a plug may be connected.

reveal The offset or exposure of the jamb edge that is not covered by the trim.

right of recision   A customer's right under federal law to cancel a transaction within 3 business days of contract signing.

rimmed   A mounting method in which a lavatory sits slightly above the countertop with the joint between the lavatory and the countertop concealed by a metal trim.

riser   Vertical run of pipe.

riser pipe   A supply pipe that extends vertically, carrying water, steam, or gas.

roll-out shelf cabinet   A base cabinet unit with interior shelves installed on drawer glides.

rough-in   The installation of parts of the plumbing system that must be done before installing the fixtures, including drainage, water supply, vent piping, and installation of the necessary in-the-wall fixture supports; usually done before the walls are closed in. The term is also applied to the dimensions used for roughing in.

roughing in   The framing stage of a carpentry project. This framework later is concealed in the finishing stages.

rough opening   The rough-framed opening into which window and door frames are installed.

run   Horizontal or vertical series of pipes.

sanitary fitting   Fitting with smooth bends and no inside shoulders to block flow of waste; used to join DWV pipe.

sash   The framework which holds glass in the window.

sash size   The overall measurement of a window sash.

sauna   A dry-heat bath taken in a well-insulated room lined with untreated, kiln-dried, softwood (walls, ceiling, and slatted benches inside the sauna are generally constructed of a water-resistant softwood such as redwood or cedar) and heated by igneous rocks. The heat causes the body to perspire extensively, cleansing the skin and its pores.

scribe allowance   Small extension of sides beyond the back and frame stiles beyond sides for trimming to ensure proper fit.

scribing   A technique used to adjust for wall irregularities. Scribing is used in fitting countertops, molding, and fillers.

sealer   A protective coating applied to the cabinet during the finishing process.

self-closing   A term applied to hinges which assist in closing a door.

self-rimming   A mounting method in which a lavatory is designed to sit on top of the countertop.

service box   The control center for the home's electrical service.

shelf clip   An item used to support the adjustable shelves in wall cabinets.

shim   A small angular piece of wood used to compensate for unevenness in wall and floor surfaces.

shimming   A technique using small wood pieces to compensate for unevenness in wall and floor surfaces.

sink cutout   The opening cut into the countertop so that a sink unit fits below and rests on the countertop.

sink front   A cabinet front, with no sides, back, or bottom, used as a low-cost substitute for a sink-base cabinet.

sink-front bottom   A piece of material used to cover the floor area behind a sink front.

slab-on-grade   A foundation or floor created by pouring concrete directly on prepared ground.

sleepers   A series of 2 × 4s laid flat on a slab, used under a finished floor made of wood strips.

slip nut   A device used on a drain (such as a sink trap). Threads onto one pipe and compresses a washer around the other to form a slip joint.

soaking tub   Unlike a whirlpool, a soaking tub does not have jets (although they can be added). These tubs do not require an integral heater and are available in platform, recessed, and corner models, with rectangular or round interiors of fiberglass or acrylic.

soffit (bulkhead and fascia)   The area between the cabinet top and the ceiling. When this area is closed off, it appears to be part of the ceiling.

softwood lumber   Lumber produced from coniferous or evergreen trees that have needles or scalelike leaves and remain green throughout the year.

soil stack   A large DWV pipe that connects the toilet and other drains to the house drain and also extends up and out the house roof; the upper portion serves as a vent.

spa   A bathlike unit, usually with a high, rounded shape that is deeper than a whirlpool. Unlike a whirlpool bath, spas are rarely drained after each use. Because they cannot double as bathtubs, spas are better adapted for outside installation.

spacer   Short piece of unthreaded plastic or copper pipe cut to size; used when repairing or extending pipe. Sometimes referred to as a "nipple."

span Distance between supports.

specifications Descriptions, in words, of the materials to be used on a project, as well as how to install them.

spud washer On a toilet that has a separate tank, the spud washer is the large rubber ring placed over the drain hole. The tank is placed over the spud washer.

square At a right angle or perpendicular to an adjacent surface.

square footage A measure of area equal to the product of length times width.

stack General term for the main vertical pipe of soil, waste, or vent pipe systems.

stack, vent Vertical pipe providing circulation of air to and from any part of the drainage system.

staging area A space that is reserved for the receiving, unpacking, and initial assembly of materials for a project.

steam bath A steam bath is good for sinus conditions, allergies, and asthma; helps loosen tight muscles; and also increases the flow of blood and supply of oxygen to the body's tissues.

stile The vertical members of a cabinet face frame.

stops Strips of wood nailed to the head and side jambs to prevent a door from swinging too far when it closes. Stops also keep window sash in line.

storage A general term used to denote any space that is used for storing linens, supplies, or other items in the bathroom. Most storage space is provided in cabinets and vanities, but other special storage devices such as closets, medicine cabinets, and freestanding furniture may be employed.

structural system The shell of the house: the foundation, walls, and roof.

studs Wall framing members, generally 2 × 4s to which cabinets are to be attached.

style A term referring to the design and decorator effect of the cabinet door.

subcontractor A person or business that agrees to render services and/or provide materials necessary for the performance of a project under contract to another contractor, retailer, dealer, designer, or installer.

subfloor The floor surface below a finished floor. In newer homes the subfloor is usually made of sheet material such as plywood; in older houses it is likely to consist of diagonally attached boards.

subrail Horizontal interior framing member, not a part of the front frame assembly.

substrate A material that lies below a finish material and provides support for the finish material.

subtraction method A technique used to check for and ensure layout accuracy.

supply branches The two sets of pipes that run horizontally through the floor joists or concrete slab and deliver water from the supply main.

supply risers Water-supply branches that run vertically in the wall to an upper story.

suspended ceiling A ceiling system supported by hanging it from the overhead structural framing.

tailpiece The short pipe leading from a faucet or lavatory drain.

tall cabinets Large cabinets which are 84 inches (213.36 cm) high. These cabinets are designed to supply a large quantity of storage space.

T-fitting A T-shaped fitting (also called "tee") with three openings. It joins a branch pipe into a run of pipe.

tenon A projecting part cut on the end of a piece of wood for insertion into a mortise to form a joint.

three-quarter bath A three-quarter bath contains a toilet, lavatory, and a shower stall instead of a tub.

three-wall layout A bathroom with all the plumbing located along three walls. It offers the greatest design flexibility and provides the largest wall and counter spaces of all the three basic bathroom plans.

toespace The open area at the lower portion of the base cabinet. This space allows a person to stand close to the cabinet without kicking it.

top panel A piece of material making up the top of a wall cabinet.

trap Bent pipe section or device that holds a water deposit and forms a seal against the passage of sewer gases from a waste pipe into the room.

trim The finishing frame around an opening such as doors and windows; also decorative building elements often used to conceal joints.

trusses An assembly of members, such as beams, which frame a rigid framework.

tube A supply pipe that is sized nominally by copper water tube sizes.

turnkey installation services Installation services provided as an integrated part of the sale of a bathroom project.

twin-track hardware The item which guides and directs the drawer when it is being opened and closed.

two-wall layout   A bathroom with all the plumbing located within two adjoining walls.

U value   Opposite of R value.

underlayment   Nonstructural subflooring that lies under the sheet flooring. Also, a form of particleboard that has a low density and low resin content.

undermounted   Installed from below the counter surfaces.

union   A fitting that joins pipes with a method for future disassembly without cutting or taking the entire section apart.

unit dimension   The overall outside dimensions of a manufactured window.

utility cabinet   A tall cabinet providing large amounts of storage space.

utility filler   An accessory used next to tall cabinets to fill spaces resulting from odd wall dimensions that cannot be filled by using standard cabinets.

vacuum breaker   A device used to prevent wastewater backflow into a water-supply line.

valance   An accessory which is generally used to fill the area between wall cabinets next to a lavatory.

valve   Fitting for opening and closing the passage for water; controls the flow of water.

vapor retarder   A plastic sheet, 4 mils thick, that is unrolled to cover soil, primarily for crawlspace systems where there is no basement. A vapor retarder is also used to provide a barrier over unfaced wall insulation.

veneer   A thinly cut slice of decoratively marked wood. Produced by sawing, slicing, or rotary process.

vitreous china   A form of ceramic or porcelain that is glasslike.

volt   The unit for measurement of electrical pressure.

wall cabinets   Those cabinets which attach to the walls and provide storage space above the countertop work area.

wall filler   An accessory which is used to fill the space resulting from odd wall dimensions that cannot be filled with standard wall cabinets.

wall units   Cabinets fixed to walls with screws.

warp   Any of several lumber defects caused by uneven shrinkage of wood cells.

warranty   A written guarantee offered to the purchaser of a product or service that the product or service will be free from defects for a specified period.

washer   A flat, thin ring of metal or rubber used to ensure a tight fit and prevent friction in joints and assemblies. This term is sometimes used interchangeably with *gasket.*

water heater   A plumbing appliance used to heat water.

water meter   A device used to measure the amount of water that flows through it.

water softener   A plumbing appliance used to reduce the hardness of water, usually through the ion-exchange process.

water-supply system   A water service entry pipe; water distribution pipes; and the necessary connecting pipes and fittings, control valves, and appurtenances in or adjacent to the building or premises.

wattage   Measurement (in watts) of the amount of energy consumed by a light source.

wax ring   A wax seal used to seal the base of a toilet to prevent leakage.

well   A driven, bored, or dug hole in the ground from which water is pumped.

whirlpool   A bathtub operated with a motor, pump, and air jets. Jet designs vary, but generally have high volume and low pressure (a few strong jets) or low pressure and high volume (lots of softer jets). Can be adjusted for water volume, air-water mixture, and direction.

wide-bottom rail   A rail used to replace the toespace on base cabinets.

window rough opening   The opening left in a stud wall for the window.

window sill   The exterior slanting ledge of a window frame.

window stool   The interior horizontal ledge that seals a window at the bottom.

wood floor system   Used when a home has a basement or crawlspace.

workers' compensation insurance   A program that provides funds to employees who are injured during the course of performing work for the company by which they are employed. The funds for this program are derived from premiums that are paid by employers.

zoned heat   A division of the house into two or more parts with a separate heat source for each part.

Metric Conversion Charts

1. Actual metric conversion to centimeters is 1 inch = 2.54 cm.

2. Actual metric conversion to millimeters is 1 inch = 25.4 mm. To facilitate conversions between imperial and metric dimensioning for calculations under 1 inch, 24 mm is used.

3. To facilitate conversions between imperial and metric for calculations over 1 inch, 25 mm is typically used.

Length Conversion Chart

Inches	Centimeters	Inches	Centimeters
1/8	0.32	69	175.26
1/4	0.64	72	182.88
1/2	1.27	75	190.5
3/4	1.91	78	198.12
1	2.54	81	205.74
3	7.62	84	213.36
6	15.24	87	220.98
9	22.86	90	228.6
12	30.48	93	236.22
15	38.1	96	243.84
18	45.72	99	251.46
21	53.34	102	259.08
24	60.96	105	266.7
27	68.58	108	274.32
30	76.2	111	281.94
33	83.82	114	289.56
36	91.44	117	297.18
39	99.06	120	304.8
42	106.68	123	312.42
45	114.3	126	320.04
48	121.92	129	327.66
51	129.54	132	335.28
54	137.16	135	342.9
57	144.78	138	350.52
60	152.4	141	358.14
63	160.02	144	365.76
66	167.64		

Area:

   100 square millimeters = 1 square centimeter

   100 square centimeters = 1 square decimeter
   100 square decimeters = 1 square meter
   100 square meters = 1 are
   10,000 square meters = 1 hectare
   100 hectares = 1 square kilometer

Square measure:

   1 square inch = 6.4516 square centimeters
   1 square foot = 9.29034 square decimeters
   1 square yard = 0.836131 square meter
   1 acre = 0.40469 hectare
   1 square mile = 2.59 square kilometers

Long measure:

   1 inch = 25.4 millimeters
   1 foot = 0.3 meter
   1 yard = 0.914401 meter
   1 mile = 1.609347 kilometers

Length:

   10 millimeters = 1 centimeter
   10 centimeters = 1 decimeter
   10 decimeters = 1 meter
   10 meters = 1 decameter
   100 meters = 1 hectometer
   1000 meters = 1 kilometer

Liquid measure:

   1 pint = 0.473167 liter
   1 quart = 0.946332 liter
   1 gallon = 3.785329 liters

Linear drawing measurements:

1 millimeter (mm) = 0.03937 inch	1 inch = 25.4 mm	12 inches = 304.8 mm
1 centimeter (cm) = 0.3937 inch	1 inch = 2.54 cm	12 inches = 30.48 cm
1 meter (m) = 39.37 inches	1 inch = 0.0254 m	12 inches = 0.3048 m

Conversion Chart for Various Parameters Factored into Bathroom Installation

Quantity	Metric (SI) unit	Metric (SI) symbol	U.S. equivalent (nominal)
Length	millimeter	mm	0.039 inch (in)
	meter	m	3.281 foot (ft)
			1.094 yard (yd)
Area	meter	m^2	10.763 sq ft (ft^2)
			1.195 sq yd (yd^2)
Volume	meter	m^3	35.314 cu ft (ft^3)
			1.307 cu yd (yd^3)
Volume (fluid)	liter	L	33.815 ounces (oz)
			0.264 gallon (gal)
Mass (weight)	gram	g	0.035 ounces (oz)
	kilogram	kg	2.205 pounds (lb)
	ton	t	2,204.600 pounds (lb)
			1.102 tons
Force	newton	N	0.225 pound-force (lbf)
Temperature (interval)	kelvin	K	1.8°F (degrees Fahrenheit)
	degree Celsius	°C	1.8°F
Temperature	Celsius	°C	(°F-32)5/9
Thermal resistance		K·m^2/W	5.679 ft^2·h·°F/Btu
Heat transfer	watt	W	3.412 Btu/h
Pressure	kilopascal	kPa	0.145 lb/in^2 (psi)
	pascal	Pa	20.890 lb/ft^2 (psf)

Decimal Equivalents of Inch Fractions

Fraction	Decimal	Fraction	Decimal
$1/64$	0.015625	$33/64$	0.515625
$1/32$	0.03125	$17/32$	0.53125
$3/64$	0.046875	$35/64$	0.546875
$1/16$	0.0625	$9/16$	0.5625
$5/64$	0.078125	$37/64$	0.578125
$3/32$	0.09375	$19/32$	0.59375
$7/64$	0.109375	$39/64$	0.609375
$1/8$	0.1250	$5/8$	0.6250
$9/64$	0.140625	$41/64$	0.640625
$5/32$	0.15625	$21/32$	0.65625
$11/64$	0.171875	$43/64$	0.671875
$3/16$	0.1875	$11/16$	0.6875
$13/64$	0.203125	$45/64$	0.703125
$7/32$	0.21875	$23/32$	0.71875
$15/64$	0.234375	$47/64$	0.734375
$1/4$	0.2500	$3/4$	0.7500
$17/64$	0.265625	$49/64$	0.765625
$9/32$	0.28125	$25/32$	0.78125
$19/64$	0.296875	$51/64$	0.796875
$5/16$	0.3125	$13/16$	0.8125
$21/64$	0.328125	$53/64$	0.828125
$11/32$	0.34375	$27/32$	0.84375
$23/64$	0.359375	$55/64$	0.859375
$3/8$	0.3750	$7/8$	0.8750
$25/64$	0.390625	$57/64$	0.890625
$13/32$	0.40625	$29/32$	0.90625
$27/64$	0.421875	$59/64$	0.921875
$7/16$	0.4375	$15/16$	0.9375
$29/64$	0.453125	$61/64$	0.953125
$15/32$	0.46875	$31/32$	0.96875
$31/64$	0.484375	$63/64$	0.984375
$1/2$	0.5000	1	1.0000

BIBLIOGRAPHY

American Standard, Inc. 1997. *Product Library* (Compact Disc). Piscataway, NJ.

Better Homes and Gardens. 1996. *Baths—Your Guide to Planning and Remodeling.* Des Moines, IA: Meredith Corp.

Better Homes and Gardens. 1980. *Complete Guide to Home Repair, Maintenance and Improvement.* Des Moines, IA: Meredith Corp.

Better Homes and Gardens. 1983. *Your Baths.* Des Moines, IA: Meredith Corp.

Better Homes and Gardens Special Interest Publications—Kitchen and Bath Ideas. Summer, 1995. Des Moines, IA: Magazine Group of Meredith Corp.

Better Homes and Gardens Special Interest Publications—Remodeling Ideas for Your Home. Summer, 1995. Des Moines, IA: Magazine Group of Meredith Corp.

Better Homes and Gardens Special Interest Publications—Kitchen and Bath Products Guide. Spring/Summer, 1995. Des Moines, IA: Magazine Group of Meredith Corp.

Black & Decker Home Plumbing Projects & Repairs. 1990. Minnetonka, Minnesota: Cy DeCosse, Inc.

Day, Richard. *The Practical Handbook of Plumbing & Heating.* New York: ARCO Publishing Company, Inc.

Germer, Jerry. 1995. *Bathrooms—Design, Remodel, Build.* Upper Saddle River, NJ: Creative Homeowner Press.

Hemp, Peter. 1994. *Installing & Repairing Plumbing Fixtures.* Newton, CT: The Taunton Press, Inc.

Hilts, Len. 1981. *The Dremel Guide to Compact Power Tools.* Dremel, Division of Emerson Electric Co.

House Beautiful—Kitchens/Baths. vol. 18, no.1, Spring 1997. New York: The Hearst Corporation.

Hughes, Herb. 1980. *Adding Space Without Adding On.* Upper Saddle River, NJ: Creative Homeowner Press.

Jacobs, David H., Jr. 1995. *Bathrooms Remodeling Projects.* Blue Ridge Summit, PA: TAB Books, Inc.

Kitchen & Bath Design News. May 1995, October 1996, November 1996, December 1996, January 1997. Melville, NY: PTN Publishing Co.

Kitchen & Bathroom Plumbing. 1987. Alexandria, VA: Time-Life Books.

Kitchen & Source Book, 1995. New York: Sweet's Group/McGraw-Hill, Inc.

Korejwo, Pamela L. 1998. *Kitchen Design, Installation, & Remodeling.* New York: McGraw-Hill, Inc.

Lewis, Darrel L. and Walter W. Stoeppelwerth. 1995. *Kitchen & Bathroom Installation Manual, Volume 2.* Hackettstown, N.J.: National Kitchen & Bath Association.

Love, T. W. 1976. *Construction Manual: Rough Carpentry.* Carlsbad, CA: Craftsman Book Co.

Philbin, Tom. 1992. *Costwise Bathroom Remodeling.* Toronto: John Wiley & Sons, Inc.

Rowan, Bob, and Melvin Fenn. 1988. *Tradesmen in Business.* White Hall, VA: Betterway Publications, Inc.

Scharff, Robert, and the editors of *Walls & Ceilings Magazine*. 1995. *Drywall Construction Handbook*. New York: McGraw-Hill, Inc.

Scharff, Robert. 1975. *The Complete Book of Home Remodeling*. New York: McGraw-Hill, Inc.

Scharff, Robert, and Kenneth M. Swezey. 1979. *Popular Science, Formulas, Methods, Tips and Data for Home and Workshop*. New York: Harper & Row.

Stoeppelwerth, Walter W. 1994. *Kitchen & Bathroom Installation Manual, Volume 1*. Hackettstown, NJ: National Kitchen & Bath Association.

Stoeppelwerth, Walter W. 1997. *How to Implement the Lead Installer Concept*. Bethesda, MD: Home Tech Information Systems, Inc.

Sunset Books, Editors. 1991. *Decorating with Paint & Wall Coverings*. Menlo Park, CA: Sunset Publishing Corporation.

———. 1992. *Ideas for Great Bathrooms*. Menlo Park, CA: Sunset Publishing Corporation.

———. 1995. *Basic Plumbing*. Menlo Park, CA: Sunset Publishing Corporation.

———. 1996. *Bathrooms—Planning & Remodeling*. Menlo Park, CA: Sunset Publishing Corporation.

———. 1996. *Creating Beautiful Floors*. Menlo Park, CA: Sunset Publishing Corporation.

Sunset Books and *Sunset* Magazine, Editors. 1992. *Flooring—How to Plan, Install, & Repair*. Menlo Park, CA: Sunset Publishing Corporation.

Thomas, Steve, and Philip Langdon. 1993. *This Old House Bathrooms: A Guide to Design and Renovation*. Little, Brown & Company, Ltd.

Time-Life Books, Editors. 1985. *Bathrooms*. Alexandria, VA: Time-Life Books.

Time-Life Books, Editors. 1987. *Kitchen & Bathroom Plumbing*. Alexandria, VA: Time-Life Books.

Time-Life Books, Editors. 1989. *Kitchens and Bathrooms*. Alexandria, VA: Time-Life Books.

Wing, Charlie. 1990. *The Visual Handbook of Building and Remodeling*. Emmaus, PA: Rodale Press.

Woman's Day Innovation Series—Kitchens & Baths. 1996. Volume VI, Number 4. New York: Hachette Filipacchi Magazines, Inc.

Woodson, R. Dodge. 1993. *Home Plumbing Illustrated*. Blue Ridge Summit, PA: TAB Books.

The following is a complete list of all of the manufacturers, corporations, etc., that have contributed photographs, illustrations, research, literature, etc., to this book:

American Standard, Inc.
One Centennial Avenue
P.O. Box 6820
Piscataway, NJ 08855-6820

Belvedere Communications
130 East 59th Street
13th Floor
New York, NY 10022

Andersen Windows, Inc.
100 Fourth Avenue North
Bayport, MN 55003-1096

Bentley Brothers
2709 South Park Road
Louisville, KY 40219

Armstrong World Industries
P.O. Box 3001
Lancaster, PA 17604

Crown Corp., NA
30-12 Hoton St., Suite 101
Denver, CO 80202

Crown Decorative Products
Darwen, England

Brandywine Tile & Flooring
The Clock Tower at the Market
Place
Rt. 23
Morgantown, PA 19543

Fantec
1712 Northgate Boulevard
Sarasota, FL 34234

Finlandia Sauna
14010-B S.W. 72nd Avenue
Portland, OR 97224

Florida Tile Industries, Inc.
P.O. Box 447
Lakeland, FL 33802

Home Tech Information Systems, Inc.
5161 River Road
Bethesda, MD 20816

Juno Lighting, Inc.
2001 S. Mount Prospect Road
Des Plaines, IL 60017

Kohler Company
444 Highland Drive
Kohler, WI 53044

Leon E. Korejwo, Illustrator
Box 5800, R.R.#5
Blimline Hill Road
Mohnton, PA 19540

KraftMaid Cabinetry, Inc.
P.O. Box 1055
15535 South State Avenue
Middlefield, OH 44062

Merillat Industries, Inc.
P.O. Box 1946
Adrian, MI 49221

National Kitchen & Bath Association
687 Willow Grove Street
Hackettstown, NJ 07840

Phillips Communications
233 South 6th Street—#1701
Philadelphia, PA 19106

Planit–Autograph
699 Perimeter Drive
Suite 300
Lexington, KY 40417

QuakerMaid Kitchens of Reading, Inc.
4203A Pottsville Pike
Reading, PA 19605

Saunatec, Inc.
575 East Cokato Street
Cokato, MN 55321

Weck Glass Block/Glashaus, Inc.
415 West Golf Road
Suite 13
Arlington Heights, IL 60005

Wellborn Cabinet, Inc.
P.O. Box 1210
Ashland, AL 36251

INDEX

Note: Boldface numbers indicate illustrations.

ABOUT THE AUTHOR

Pamela Korejwo has written for and about the construction industry for many years. She is the author of *Kitchen Design, Installation, and Remodeling*, and has contributed to a number of popular McGraw-Hill books, including *Drywall Construction Handbook, Roofing*, and *Residential Steel Framing Handbook.* The daughter of a former home contractor, she recently became a principal associate of her father's consulting company, L.E.K. Illustration, which does technical illustration and design.

ABOUT THE ILLUSTRATOR

Leon Korejwo has more than 30 years' experience as a mechanical designer and has won numerous national and international awards. He has illustrated a number of books, among them *Kitchen Design, Installation, and Remodeling; Diesel Engines, Heavy Duty Trucks, Motorcycle Maintenance Handbook;* and *Residential Steel Framing Handbook.* For many years he operated his own home construction business. He is president and owner of L.E.K. Illustration.